Islam and the Rule of Justice

Islam and the Rule of Justice

Image and Reality in Muslim Law and Culture

LAWRENCE ROSEN

THE UNIVERSITY OF CHICAGO PRESS CHICAGO AND LONDON

The University of Chicago Press, Chicago 60637
The University of Chicago Press, Ltd., London

Published 2018
Printed in the United States of America

27 26 25 24 23 22 21 20 19 18 1 2 3 4 5

ISBN-13: 978-0-226-51157-3 (cloth)
ISBN-13: 978-0-226-51160-3 (paper)
ISBN-13: 978-0-226-51174-0 (e-book)
DOI: 10.7208/chicago/9780226511740.001.0001

Library of Congress Cataloging-in-Publication Data

Names: Rosen, Lawrence, 1941– author.
Title: Islam and the rule of justice : image and reality in Muslim law and culture / Lawrence Rosen.
Description: Chicago ; London : The University of Chicago Press, 2018. | Includes bibliographical references and index.
Identifiers: LCCN 2017037408 | ISBN 9780226511573 (cloth : alk. paper) | ISBN 9780226511603 (pbk. : alk. paper) | ISBN 9780226511740 (e-book)
Subjects: LCSH: Islamic law—Interpretation and construction. | Islam and justice. | Islamic law—Social aspects. | Law—Social aspects—Middle East.
Classification: LCC KBP440.32 .R67 2018 | DDC 340.5/901—dc23
LC record available at https://lccn.loc.gov/2017037408

∞ This paper meets the requirements of ANSI/NISO Z39.48-1992 (Permanence of Paper).

FOR MARY AND TITA

Contents

Illustrations

FIGURES

Acknowledgments

Portions of this book were written while I was a fellow of the Stanford University Center for Advanced Study in the Behavioral Sciences, and I am most grateful to its director, Iris Litt, and staff. Particular chapters in this book have profited from the helpful suggestions of scholars in the field and I am pleased to be able to thank them in the notes, without, of course, holding them in any way responsible for the final product. Lectures based on various chapters have also benefited from comments by participants at Cardozo Law School, University of California at Los Angeles, University of Victoria, University of British Columbia, Simon Fraser University, the U.S. Naval Academy, and the Central Illinois Mosque and Islamic Center of Champaign-Urbana, Illinois. To all I am most indebted. Edmund Burke, III, and Abdellah Hammoudi, as always, have listened critically to my arguments and are as blameless for the results as they are blameworthy for stimulating my thinking.

Parts of several chapters appeared in earlier forms and are reprinted here by agreement: "Studying the Muslim Courts of Morocco," in *Islam in Practice*, ed. Gabriele Marranci (London: Routledge, 2014): 21–33; "Understanding Corruption," *American Interest* 5, no. 4 (March/April 2010): 78–82; "A Guide to the 'Arab Street,'" *Anthropology Now* 3, no. 2 (September 2011): 41–47; "Will the Middle Class Save the Middle East?," *Contemporary Islam* 5, no. 2 (2011): 185–90; "Power vs. the People," a review of Elizabeth F. Thompson, *Justice Interrupted: The Struggle for Constitutional Government in the Middle East*, *Literary Review* (London), October 2013, pp. 23–24.

This book is dedicated to Mary Schmidt and Teresita Tiansay Voelkner, dearest of friends.

INTRODUCTION

Approaching Islamic Law

Some years ago I co-chaired a meeting of French and American scholars of North Africa. To stimulate discussion I suggested that at our first, informal session we share stereotypes about one another's different approaches to the region. The advantage, I suggested, was that we would all know that they are just stereotypes—but (I quietly assumed) we would all, to some extent, really believe that they are true. Through stereotypes we could, however, express ourselves unreservedly and then hide behind the excuse that what we were saying was, we knew, just an exaggerated likeness.

The exercise worked wonderfully well: the French told us that Americans come into the area for a few years and then rush off to the next part of the world, while they devoted their entire careers to one place; and my American colleagues told the French that they were too wrapped up in structural schemes to see the ambiguities in which we colonials delight. No one took offense, we all felt better afterward, and we all appreciated that although stereotypes can be unfair, and even if they contain a grain of truth, they may do far more harm than good.

It is somewhat in this spirit that I begin by addressing a set of misperceptions of Islamic law. Although the central focus of this book is to analyze rather than debunk, it is desirable, at a time when the actions of the Taliban and ISIS would seem to validate Western fears and misunderstanding, to address some of the oversimplified views commonly held about Islamic law. A few precautionary notes are, however, worth highlighting.

The predominant focus of this book is on the Arab world, even though it represents only a fraction of the world's Muslim population. Moreover, when I speak of "the Arabs" it is necessarily in rather general terms, the phrase having to encompass a very wide range of local and historical instances. But if one approaches this diversity in the sense of embracing a

FIGURE I.1. Anti-shari'a protest sign, Idaho (conservativeinfidel.com).

range of variations on shared themes, rather than as seeking some definitive essence, readers may wish to ask themselves two interrelated questions: In what sense does what is being described correspond to what has been learned about other parts of the Muslim world, such that one is stimulated to think more carefully about each of those situations? And in what ways do these variations affect one another and the non-Muslim world, since none of the countries or situations described exists in isolation? Taken in this spirit the specific situations to be presented here may help in formulating more precise questions raised by the practice of Islamic law.

That stereotypes of Islam, the Middle East, and Muslim law—favorable and unfavorable—are widespread is evident from even the most causal reading of the Western press. When the Archbishop of Canterbury (2008) suggested that Islamic law forums might be appropriate for handling certain family law matters of Muslims living in the United Kingdom he was roundly excoriated by those who acted as if he had proposed stoning adulterers or hacking off the hands of thieves, notwithstanding the frequent recourse to similar religious courts by Britons of other faiths. In March 2014, the Law Society of Great Britain offered instructions for drawing up a will in conformity with Muslim inheritance practices that grant one-half portions to women as opposed to men and no inheritance to children born out of wedlock, but the outcry was so great that eight months later the Society withdrew its practice note.[1] In the United States 70% of Oklahoma voters favored passage of a referendum barring any use of Islamic law (characterized by the promoters as "a totalitarian socio-political doctrine"), only for a federal court to save them from utter embarrassment by ruling the law unconstitutional.[2] Similarly, former Speaker of the House of Representatives Newt Gingrich has said that shari'a is "a mortal threat to the survival of freedom; the heart of the enemy movement from which the terrorists spring forth" and therefore "we should frankly test every person here who is of a Muslim background, and if they believe in sharia, they should be deported."[3] One town in Canada initially barred the use of Islamic law within its precincts even though there was not a single Muslim living there, while the province of Ontario forbade any religious court involvement in family law disputes, to the considerable consternation of Jews, Catholics, Jehovah's Witnesses, and indigenous peoples who use such forums regularly.[4] In short, one only has to keep up with the nightly news and op-ed commentary to witness images of Islamic law as brutality against women and punishments of Biblical intensity in order to realize how deeply these stereotypes influence the popular imagination.

Even scholarly literature is not entirely immune from misplaced emphases, especially as concerns a tendency to assume that Islamic law lives in the scholars' texts much more than in the daily lives of the courts and ordinary citizens' understanding of the law and its implementation. By contrast, the orientation throughout this book—as might be expected from one who is both an anthropologist and a common law lawyer—is toward Islamic law as a living system, one that is found as much in the marketplace and the home as in the textbooks, a law that is deeply subject to local custom, factual context, permissible interpretation, client choice, and judicial discretion. Just as Islam is what Muslims believe and do, Islamic law is where it is practiced and documented, influencing the decisions of daily life, underscoring the broad assumptions about human nature and human relationships, and supporting the sense of a world whose orderliness is highly contingent on and contextually embedded in those moral and commonsense propositions that suffuse the social lives of the community.

Some of the more prevalent misconceptions Westerners hold about Islamic law would, therefore, include the following:

ISLAMIC LAW INVARIABLY DISADVANTAGES WOMEN AND MINORITIES. Would it come as a surprise to learn that, based on the studies available, Muslim women win at least a significant part of their family law cases—anywhere between 65% and 95% of the time? The image of Islamic law as invariably antagonistic to women's interests is both wrong as an absolute claim and far more complicated in its actuality. As we will see in chapter 4, women are certainly not treated the same as men in Muslim family law codes or traditional legal propositions, but the handling of their court cases is not simply one of gross gender discrimination. In such venues they commonly receive more nuanced attention for a wide range of reasons, not the least being that Muslim courts are, in their procedures and presumptions if not in all of the classical texts, significantly more accommodating than might seem to be the case.[5] For many Muslims justice concerns equivalence rather than identical treatment, and it is against this background that some of the anomalies we will encounter may be comprehensible.

What is true for the results women achieve in court is also broadly applicable to other groups that have resided in predominantly Muslim countries. True, the testimony of a Jew or Christian was traditionally not counted equally to that of a Muslim, and contracts recognizable to the one confessional group might not be honored by the courts of the other. At the same time, contractual relations—including commercial partnerships and joint ownership of property—were not infrequent. Indeed, in a surprising number of instances Muslim courts did, in fact, recognize the documents drawn up by non-Muslim tribunals. Chapter 3 will, therefore, afford an opportunity to consider some of these relationships in detail and to speculate as to their utility in the current situation involving Israelis and Palestinians.

JIHAD IS AN INTEGRAL PART OF THE SHARI'A. Jihad means "struggle," which for some Muslims continues to designate armed encounter with those who oppose Islam in whatever way. But its deeper meaning is that of struggling with the moral virtues that reason, if properly developed, can nurture against the temptations of passion and the many forms of ignorance that confront humans in a world of premonitory chaos. Indeed, jihad can also mean a kind of trust, even in the more technical sense of the trust a government exercises over common property, especially property that has been obtained in the course of solidifying the state. Thus in one sense Islamic law is not simply a justification for violent action against unbelievers but an informing sensibility, consonant with and integral to a range of other moral propositions, that challenges the law to live up to its role as a check on power and a vehicle that services the common good.

In this regard, it is true that, on its surface, Islamic law and custom hold that one may not displace a tyrant if further chaos ensues. Instances do, however, exist of legal officials forcing the replacement of a tyrant, so the question arises as to whether there is a principled basis in Islamic law for balancing power and if so through what mechanisms. The answer lies less in institutions than in the personal responsibility of individuals and the allies they muster for support. Unlike many European countries, who used law as a vehicle for the centralization of the state, power was commonly more divisible in the Arab world, and, as we will see throughout this book, that fractionation of power has deep roots in the cultures of the region.

When, finally, we ask whether there is a comparable basis to the American Founders' emphasis on "virtue" that could help revivify constitutionalism in the Arab world it will be with the recognition that there are indeed cultural precepts, and not only political structures, upon which such reconstruction might be built. And since jihad also concerns the holding of property for the common good, as we shall see in chapter 4, it is a concept that could play a positive role in so fraught a conflict as that over the land of Israel-Palestine. Thus even jihad, a concept that for Westerners conjures up only a portion of its overall meaning, may be one of those cultural artifacts reminding us that when it comes to law and justice the whole story is not embodied in the formal structure of intensely politicized institutions alone.[6]

THE DISCRETION OF ISLAMIC LAW JUDGES IS VIRTUALLY UNBOUNDED. It was Max Weber who spoke of *kadijustiz* as a type of thinking in which judges have recourse to few if any generalizing precepts and standards. Although Weber himself realized that this model did not apply to actual Islamic law or the decision making of actual Muslim judges (in singular form, *qadi*) the image has stuck, and with it the idea that, as Justice Felix Frankfurter once said, the qadi sitting under a tree dispensing justice off the top of his head is hardly the model for rational adjudication.[7]

That every system of law incorporates judicial discretion is hardly an original insight. The question is not whether it exists everywhere but how it is constrained and articulated with other aspects of a society's overall legal, political, and moral system. In the case of Islamic law, as this book will suggest, Muslim judges are by no means simply left at large to decide as they please. On the contrary, legal procedures, cultural assumptions, analogic categorizing, development of new codes and constitutions, and the ethos of judges who endeavor to apply the law with a clear sense of social consequence all play a role in the distinctive styles of implementing discretion. More akin to common law than civil law, Islamic law stresses procedure, with many forms of substantive law, as Sir Henry Maine said of the common law, being "secreted in the interstices."[8] Sometimes contrast is thrown into relief when a Muslim encounters the procedural differences of a foreign legal system, as I discuss in chapter 8 on the American trial of Zacarias Moussaoui, or when extra-legal customs are envisioned as part of the shari'a, as will be seen in chapter 3. In each of these examples we have the opportunity to get beyond both ideal type and less than ideal stereotype to grasp more fully the structure and implications of judicial discretion as actually practiced by Muslim judges.

ISLAMIC LAW IS PREDOMINANTLY CHARACTERIZED BY BRUTAL PUNISHMENTS. The more extreme examples of Islamic criminal law gain much Western attention, even when they seem as ludicrous as they may be mean-spirited. Examples of the absurd can be found as recently as 2002 when the Egyptian jurist al-Qaradawi mused as to whether a condemned woman may be sent to her execution without a male chaperone. In other instances mullahs have suggested that allowing fornication to go unpunished is the cause of earthquakes, and have punished grocers for mixing tomatoes (feminine) and cucumbers (masculine) on the same vegetable stand.[9] Most Muslim countries have established criminal codes that do not simply track the forms of Islamic law reputedly applied in the past. Extreme fundamentalists may seek to apply ancient rules, but even those states that profess to have embraced full Islamic law rarely apply its potential penalties. Thus the stoning of an adulterer was recorded only once in Ottoman history, and the Pakistani state did not formally apply its own rules during the restoration of strict Islamic law under the regime of Zia ul-Haq.[10]

In other instances, blaming a spirit (*jinn*) of the netherworld for a person's misdeeds has sometimes been employed as a fiction for not holding an accused to the prescribed punishment.[11] In still other cases matters that in the West are regarded as within the purview of the state are regarded as private. Saudi Arabia permits hospital-based destruction of an eye-for-an-eye. Yet such a practice is very rare and the system of blood money as a substitute for draconian punishment may actually constitute a check on the power of the state by private action. A compensatory payment (*diya*) thus involves the decision of the victim's kin as to whether a punishment should be applied, while the role of the state in pressing for forgiveness to the financial disadvantage of victims seeking blood money becomes an important part of the overall adjudicative process.[12] Conceptualizing an appropriate punishment is actually an inextricable part of fact determination, and as we shall see the facts in Islamic law courts are deeply entwined with cultural assumptions that need to be carefully unpacked.

THE SHARI'A EMPHASIZES RELIGIOUS DUTIES AND COLLECTIVE INTERESTS, NOT INDIVIDUAL RIGHTS. The shari'a is more than a set of legal propositions: It concerns ritual duties, moral obligations, and social relationships. In the sense that it seeks to maintain the community of believers (*umma*) it is indeed oriented toward the collectivity. But the fact that it does not cast itself in terms of individual "rights"—in the sense in which, say, Western constitutions are cast—does not mean it is unconcerned with individuals. On the contrary, if, for example, the emphasis on contract is to place litigants back into a situation in which they may be able to continue their relationship and negotiate their own differences, then concern with the individual is by no means buried in the collective. Indeed, as my opening chapter's discussion of a typical Muslim court will suggest, assessing the whole person is a vital aspect of the cultural style found throughout Arab cultures.

Moreover, the shari'a is deeply entwined with local circumstance and as such with whatever shape the concept of the individual has acquired in a particular locale. So, for example, in the places of high Arab tradition the law may categorize the rights of individual women quite differently than is true for localized groups operating under traditional precepts or nations influenced by Western concepts of human rights. And individuals who have wider networks of alliance may be held to higher standards than those whose effects in the world of relationships are assessed as more limited. Whatever the range, the idea that the law completely subsumes the person within the group is as misleading as assuming that all cultures and religions conceive of the individual in precisely the same terms. As we shall see, to most Arabs the unity of the self—the idea of a person as a congeries of traits and ties all of which are present at any given time and cannot simply be divided into different and possibly incompatible roles—finds support in both the letter and the practice of the law.

ISLAMIC LAW IS CONCERNED WITH ENFORCEABLE RULES NOT PROCEDURAL JUSTICE. When we think of Islamic law we may be tempted to consider it as a set of rules, whether applied to behavior and decorum or the distribution of an estate to various categories of kin. But at least of equal importance—and arguably of even greater significance—are the procedures and criteria applied in the assessment of cases and controversies. Courts, for example, make great use of local experts and those who qualify as "reliable witnesses." Judges may assign priority for ending a dispute through an oath on the basis of who they assume is most likely to know the truth of a situation, and they commonly assess the extent and intensity with which parties are attached to their viewpoints as they consider the consequences for the social relationships that may flow from one or another judicial decision. Even written statements are commonly read as if the writer were being quizzed orally, so that questions may go less to the proper form of the document than to asking who this person is—to whom is he connected, to what implications must his attachments draw our attention. If we think of Islamic law as substantive rules alone we will miss out on understanding why the legal process is so integral to the law's legitimacy and such a crucial vehicle for the articulation of social values at large. In the final section of the book we will also see that the rule of law is not simply about the rules of law, and that an authentic sense of orderliness and natural justice may need to be grounded on propositions that are not reducible to strict regulations.

ISLAMIC LAW IS STUCK IN THE PAST AND LACKS CREATIVITY. The static nature of Islamic law is often said to be proven by the classical proposition, current in the years after the Prophet's death, that "the gates of independent reasoning" have been closed, that innovation and admixture of any sort are to be frowned upon, and that the orderliness of the community can only be retained if everyone adheres to the approaches codified by stories of the Prophet's utterances and deeds and the redactions of the four main schools of Islamic law that developed in the years after his death. We now know, however, that if the gates were closed the key, as someone once said, was left rather conveniently under the mat. Independent reasoning not only continued through the ages but has always been entangled with the wisdom and attachments of its spokesmen, the needs of its adherents, and the changing economic and political necessities of the day.

We will see, for example, that some contemporary Muslim judges have independently developed a concept of the best interests of the child, even violating at times the codified requirement that custody go to a relative of established category. We will encounter judges who are prepared to accept illegal squatters' agreements in order to bring them within the scope of the law, or courts that accept the testimony of someone from a minority religion despite formal rules to the contrary. And we will uncover the use of new scientific evidence justified by citation to a Quranic story or acceptance of the judgment of one whose opinion is clearly in the minority. In each instance it will be evident that Islamic law has always been a living and changing law, that it is not an entity that remains rigidly attached to an age long since passed. It is, therefore, as true in the law as in life that, as the Arab saying goes, three things are certain—life, death, and change.

THOSE WHO APPLY ISLAMIC LAW ARE FULLY UNDER THE CONTROL OF THE STATE AND LACK ANY JUDICIAL INDEPENDENCE. An independent judiciary is the capstone of Western constitutionalism. By contrast, legal personnel in contemporary Arab regimes may seem to lack autonomy both structurally and operationally. Historically, though, Islamic judges often exercised significant independence from the regime in power.[13] Structurally, virtually all contemporary Muslim countries have a ministry of justice that oversees the appointment and activities of the nation's courts, and judges are well aware that placement and advancement depend on how the ministry views them. But this is true for most European countries as well. The centralization of the judicial machinery is not necessarily coincident with its control by the regime, however much that might be the case in certain instances. Rather, if one looks at the full range of the courts' activities those of the Arab countries are not always and inevitably under the thumb of the regime. Lawyers have taken to the streets of Cairo to protest corruption, local communities have rejected centrally appointed personnel, and courts have employed equitable concepts to assuage the perceived unfairness of a given policy or written rule. Legal personnel often express a desire to practice their profession without having to be beholden to anyone or anything other than the canons of their own design. No one can doubt that the law courts are frequently misused by central governments in the Arab world.[14] But it would be shortsighted, as we will see when I discuss the "Arab Spring" (chapters 5 and 6) and the nature of corruption, to imagine that judges and lawyers are invariably complicit in these acts and that they are not without their own ways of trying to assert their pride, independence, and commitment to their profession.

"THE CHAIR IS NOT ONLY MORE COMFORTABLE BUT MORE INFLUENTIAL THAN THE BENCH." This formulation by Noel Coulson (1964) is indicative of many textualists' approach to Islamic law. Undoubtedly the solicited opinions (sing. *fatwa*) and treatises of scholars and jurisconsults have been—and in many instances continue to be—of great importance. They have set the tone as well as given direction and legitimacy to the entire system. But these jurisconsults do not decide the cases that actually come to court. Indeed, they are usually recruited by parties on opposite sides of a case and are not necessarily the central figures involved in what has been called "bargaining in the shadow of the law." Islamic law is not like the civil law systems of Europe that fill gaps in the codes by relying primarily on the writings of scholars. Instead, Islamic law works case by case, using the advice and consultation of non-court personnel but not simply depending on their treatises or their recommendations. However, unlike Anglo-American common law, historically the Islamic law judges did not produce case reports, did not look to appellate opinions for strict guidance, and (unlike civil law systems) did not use codes to find the right category under which to place a given case. But that does not make their system any less similar to common law approaches, for they partake of the two key ingredients of the type, namely they elicit facts primarily from the litigants and the court-affiliated experts (rather than their own investigation and interrogation), and they allow local circumstance to bubble up from below by attending carefully to the broader relationships among the parties and the practices of the local area.[15] In the process, the state appears less central to the entire process than is the case in civil law systems.

Even the jurisconsults—like judges, religious figures, and big men of whatever ambition—have had to build up personal followings in order to establish, by virtue of the repercussions of their own social networks, that they were men of consequence whose opinions others should adopt. The result has been a system not unlike that which characterizes other domains of social and political life—where, for example, leadership is not inherited but must be established and maintained personally—a form of legitimization that, because of its use of concepts and procedures that resonate in many other contexts of life, could largely garner popular legitimacy. The law, therefore, is not in the texts alone but in the culturally embedded style of judgment and the ways in which the law is drawn from and into everyday life.

CUSTOM IS NOT A SOURCE OF LAW IN ISLAM. The standard view of Islamic law, at least in most of the scholarly literature of the West, is that the sources of the law are the Quran, the Traditions of the Prophet, and the four main schools of law that developed in the early years of Islam. What is often not regarded as a source, however, is custom. For those Western scholars who approach Islamic law from the perspective of European civil law systems this makes a certain sense, for that approach has classically regarded the two domains as completely separate, the inclusion of custom into a code rendering it no longer custom. But, as social scientist Matthew Erie summarizes the findings of more recent scholarship: "Actual practice, however, has shown that custom has had a much more expansive role than classical theory admitted."[16]

Indeed, in Muslim countries, as in common law systems, custom is not segregated from law but is drawn upon in a wide variety of ways in fashioning legal approaches.[17] In the United States that may happen, to take just one example, through the acceptance by courts of "custom and usage in the trade," which may be decisive in certain commercial cases. In Islam local custom is the unmarked category, the source that does not need to be specified separately precisely because it is integral to the application of law in a great many cases. Custom may, therefore, serve as substantive guidance (as in accepting how contracts are formed differently by local groupings), as procedural supplement (as in the presumption as to what objects belong to husbands versus wives), or as factual assistance (as in the determination of who is most likely to know the truth of a matter and thus have the right to take a decisory oath first). Moreover, through all areas and periods one encounters some version of the saying that, short of it violating one of the few specifically law-like propositions in the Quran, custom and contractual provisions take precedence even over the shari'a. Thus Muslims in Malaysia (who are descended from matrilineal peoples of Sumatra) will say that their inheritance rules, which do not always track those in the Quran, *are* Islamic, just as Berbers in North Africa resent being told that their customs are not Islamic when, from their viewpoint, those customs are not separate from Islam but are indeed their form of Islam.[18] Seeing the role of custom from this perspective, then, both the legitimacy of Islamic law and its capacity for inclusiveness of widely diverse groups can be more readily appreciated.

* * *

Each of the forgoing images of Islamic law will be probed in the chapters that follow. When, for example, we consider the way in which squatters mimic the formal law in Morocco, we will see how alternative and pluralistic choices of law are incorporated into a constantly developing and creative approach to legal problems. When we look at Muslim-Jewish partnerships and how they might be adapted to the current Palestinian-Israeli dispute, we will see how practicality has long ruled relationships mistakenly seen as completely segregated. And when we consider whether it is the middle class that will be responsible for the formation of a legal and constitutional structure that will end domestic chaos, we will analyze the connections linking economic roles and legal development. Similarly, we will see the implications for views of Islamic law when we consider what the concept of corruption entails, why the Arab Spring was only tangentially about implementing the shari'a but centrally about establishing a rule of justice, and how, in conclusion, new constitutions might be grounded not only in structural constraints but in shared cultural orientations. Indeed, in what may seem an odd sort of way, looking carefully at the trial of accused terrorist Zacarias Moussaoui can cast light on how different the cultural styles of eliciting evidence and articulating one's story in a legal context can be and how that difference can highlight the assumptions and misunderstandings about both law and justice made by both legal systems.

It was Samuel Butler who said that "there is a science of the aspect of things as well as of their nature," and from the perspective of an anthropologist who is concerned with the often unforeseen connections among the multiple domains of life it is precisely an exploration of aspects rather than a taxonomy of essences that often has the greatest heuristic value. Turning a given feature of a culture to see its facets and linkages or assessing how the items arrayed add up to more than the sum of their parts is to avail oneself of the benefits of a synoptic view—an overview, a view of instances and manifestations—no less than an analytic one. This means seeing Islamic law as part of culture and not simply as a refined attribute of faith. Perceiving Islamic law through the lens of culture is to take seriously the connections its adherents suggest and demonstrate in their everyday lives, and hence to rejoin, at one extreme, the most recondite of legal precepts and, at the other, the most vital sources of the law's legitimacy. Throughout, the common theme we see is that Islamic law is integral to that broader set of categories by which people grasp their world and create their own experience of it. And if it is true that nothing is so sad as the failure to understand another's culture, then hopefully this narrative of Islamic law may, in its own way, encourage us to bridge that doleful gap.

PART ONE

Following the Law

CHAPTER ONE

Going to Court

Everyday Life in a Muslim Court

For Westerners Islamic law (shari'a) may seem a subject of arcane knowledge or potential threat. Neither properly reflects the truth. Islamic family law, for example, is deeply entwined with the cultures in which it is embedded, whether it is in the Arabic-speaking world, the Muslim portions of South and Southeast Asia, or the countries to which many Muslims have migrated. When seen up close, in the proceedings of the courts and in the assumptions about people and relationships that Islamic judges draw upon, one has the opportunity to understand much of Muslim life and society. In examining such courts in North Africa and the writings of scholars who have spent innumerable hours observing actual disputes, one can see the rich array of factors that informs a legal system that affects nearly a quarter of all humankind. For our purposes, the microcosm through which we gain entry to this world is that of the qadi's court of a medium-sized city in Morocco.

* * *

Seated at a café one morning in the city of Sefrou, Morocco, I glanced across the street and was struck by a thought. For months I had been working on various aspects of social organization among the people of the city and several tribal groups living in the Middle Atlas Mountains just beyond the town's southern limit. I had tried following various aspects of family life, including marriage and divorce, through life histories, genealogical renditions, and documentary sources. But as I looked at the small crowd gathered across the street I realized I had been missing an additional opportunity, for the people across from me were awaiting entrance to the biweekly sitting of one of the local courts, and it became immediately apparent that here was a domain in which people were not only seeking legal recourse to their various disputes but that it constituted a venue through which I could see a host of cultural assumptions and relationships at work.

I already knew a bit about the courts. I knew, for example, that the one across from the café addressed civil and criminal matters, whereas the court adjacent to the mayor's office handled cases involving matters of personal status (marriage, divorce, filiation, inheritance) as well as those property cases based on documents drawn up by the notaries of that court. I knew, too, that the Code of Personal Status adopted just after independence in 1956—a code that was to be amended several times over the course of the many years I have continued working in the courts—had embraced much of the traditional Maliki school of Islamic law that had governed decisions before and during the French Protectorate (1912–56), but that there was a good deal of discretion, custom, and procedure that also went into any judicial mix. What I needed now was to gain access to the records and proceedings of that court.

Research permission is the bane of most anthropologists' field experience, but the Ministry of Justice graciously supplied me with a letter authorizing my access to the court records and proceedings. When I presented the letter to the chief judge of the region, he personally introduced me to the judge (*qadi*) who specialized in personal status cases, and (in what was to develop into a decades-long friendship) encouraged me to feel free to talk with him at any time.

From the outset I realized that I would have to pursue my study on three fronts simultaneously. Because I needed help deciphering the handwritten court records, I hired a local schoolteacher, a holder of the equivalent of a bachelor's (and later a master's) degree in Islamic law from the ancient mosque university in Fez, the Qarawiyyin.[1] Together, we set ourselves up in the clerks' office to sample and read cases. This had the advantage that we could not only get the clerks' help with documents that ranged in clarity from prized examples of high calligraphy to the nearly indecipherable but that we could also see how the clerks shaped the issues and counseled those who, in the majority of instances, were representing themselves.[2]

The second leg of my work involved attending court sessions. The qadi, a small man with a bright red fez permanently affixed to his head and a soft gravelly voice, was not always easy to understand. Nor were the participants who shouted, gesticulated, cried, or mumbled, always with one or another regional accent. A uniformed aide was also present, and as in any Moroccan office his role was that of conceptual translator to the official in charge, keeper of order among those petitioning for help, and shameless devil's advocate for any proposition he thought the judge ought to consider. The qadi kindly placed me on a bench perpendicular to his desk where I could face everyone addressing the court and where he could lean over occasionally to explain what was happening as well as allow me to listen in to the sideboard conversations with his aide and the occasional lawyer.

The final leg of my work involved following litigants out of court. Having by then lived in the area for some time and being able to converse in colloquial North African Arabic, I was in touch with a wide range of people in the countryside as well as in the city. Thus when I encountered cases involving individuals or families I knew in other contexts I was able to go to people related to or living close by the litigants—and sometimes to the parties themselves—and find out a lot more about the disputes than could be gleaned from the record or the proceedings alone. Ultimately, it was the combination of all three facets that helped me understand the cases I came across.

One of the first cases I observed was exemplary of many others. A man I will call Hussein brought suit against his wife, referred to here as Fatma, claiming that she had left their home in violation of an earlier court order. He had even sent intermediaries to get her to return, but she refused. Fatma, however, claimed that it was her husband who threw her out and that she had returned previously only for him to beat her. She also filed a countersuit requesting that the couple move to a new place of residence, that she be paid prior support, and that some of the household furnishings be returned to her. Initially, the judge let the couple argue among themselves, as he later explained, to see what their relationship was really like. He then asked if the home had enough furnishings to be livable and if her relation with her husband had been consistently bad. She answered no to the first question and yes to the second. The qadi also noted that the couple's marriage certificate showed they were married three years before the case began, that the husband had paid a bridewealth sum of about seventy dollars, and that the court experts had determined what, in the event of a divorce, the proper level of support should be for a rural woman like Fatma.

In court Hussein said he would not move to a new residence because his wife was always trying to cause trouble, that the furnishings she was claiming were not very valuable, and that while it was her duty to do so it was he who actually supplied the bedding for the marriage. He cannot pay the support, he said, because he is poor, and asked why in any event he should have to pay the support since it is she who is at fault for deserting him. Fatma, however, said her husband is not poor and demanded that he take an oath in support of that claim. She even produced a notarized document in which witnesses testified that she had indeed previously returned to her husband but left three days later after the beating, a claim to which she told the court she was also prepared to swear a holy oath. Finally, the judge asked if Hussein had any proof to support his assertion that his wife had not returned to him, to which the husband answered no.

The qadi then made the following findings: that a wife has the right to request a new residence among people who could serve as witnesses to her treatment; that the husband admitted to having her things and not having paid support; and that the wife had provided proof of having once returned to their home. Therefore, a new dwelling must be found and Hussein must pay the back support and return the possessions that belong to his wife, but Fatma must return to live with her husband. Hussein later appealed the qadi's decision, but the higher court upheld the judgment without further comment.

The case thus contains a host of revealing features. In Islam it is the payment of a sum of money or goods from the husband or his family to the wife or her marital guardian (traditionally her father) that makes the marriage, rather than some religious ceremony. Indeed, it is by garnering such a bridewealth payment that a man demonstrates that he is someone who has a network of supporters, this being the key feature (and hence the functional equivalent of a rite of passage) by which manhood itself is defined. Each man must form relations of debt as proof of his capacity to negotiate the world of kinship and allies, and that by being deeply enmeshed in ties to others his own actions have become reasonably predictable and reliable. Forging such bonds with others shows that a man is conforming to the expectations of Islam and common sense by becoming a person whose knowledgeable actions have real-world social consequences.

Because marriage is essentially a contract various conditions are read into it by the law while other provisions may be added by agreement between the parties. Thus support and provision of a proper home are legally required of the husband, though recent changes in the law provide that wives—who may now be better educated and regularly employed than their husbands—may be equally responsible for these costs. While a husband could, in the past, divorce his wife arbitrarily—even without her knowing about it until it was an accomplished fact—recent changes in the law require that a husband register a divorce at the court, where the judge may impose certain costs on him. Moreover, the law reads in, often as a matter of local custom, certain rights for the wife. Thus Fatma's demand for a new place of residence 'among righteous people' (*bin qaumen saliḥin*) is really a protection for her: In case of difficulties with her husband she will need reliable witnesses, who are not related to either party, to support her claims.

Moreover, at least in Morocco, a legal fiction also works in the wife's favor, for the marriage contract invariably lists the bridewealth payment but is typically silent about the goods (called "the furnishings of the household," *attat l-bayt*) that should be purchased for the wife to bring into the union. When I first began work in the region the usual practice was for the groom's bridewealth payment to go to the bride's marital guardian (*wali*) who, by local custom, would add to it and purchase the household furnishings. As a result of the 2004 reforms in the code, however, a woman is no longer required to be represented by a marital guardian, though many women continue to see the use of such a person as a protection in the marital negotiations and the consequences of marriage.[3] But the earlier presumption about the items supplied by the woman or her family continues to operate. Thus in the event of divorce virtually all "furnishings" are thought to belong to the wife, even if they were acquired later in the marriage. As a result, one tactic commonly employed by the wife (often with the help of her mother) is to keep getting the husband to buy household items as a deterrent to the exercise of his power of divorce or as insurance should such a divorce ever occur. That all divorces must now come from the court has, by all accounts, had little effect on this pattern.

Other clauses could have been added to the marriage contract by the parties. Fatma, for example, could have bargained for a provision that requires her husband to issue a divorce either on her demand or under certain conditions. She could also have demanded that he not move her very far from her own relatives or that he not take another wife without divorcing her first, clauses that are, however, rather more frequent among the urban and reasonably well-off than among rural people like Hussein and Fatma. More common nowadays for urbanites is a clause that assures the wife that she may continue to work outside of the home. Additionally, the wife and/or her family may have accepted only part of the bridewealth initially, the remainder being due upon the death of the husband, divorce, or on the wife's demand, a condition that may have been included particularly if the man is marrying up socially, if the bride's family suspects his motives and reputation, or as an instance of the general cultural recognition that debt secures relationships.

The case of Hussein and Fatma also showed how Moroccan judges tend to conduct their hearings. Usually they begin by determining exactly who is connected to whom in a case and the range of their communal relationships. In addition, they often let the parties start challenging each other in order to see just how strongly they feel about the matter at hand. Whereas courts in Britain and the United States tend to restrict the issue before them to some narrow legal question, Muslim judges commonly try to figure out what sorts of ties people have within their community. Judges tell me that they want to know what people have done in the past as a way of helping to decide what the impact of the court's decision will be on the array of individuals to whom the parties are attached. Moreover, judges indicate that they think of each case as virtually unique. Since no two people are the same and their situations constantly alter, the idea that similar cases should be decided similarly—so central to much of Western ideas of justice—seems to them an oxymoron. And whereas Western court officials often think of themselves as extremely effective at determining facts (as, for example, through forensic and scientific assessment), the Moroccan judges, like their Arab compatriots elsewhere, imagine that they are particularly adept at assessing persons.

That is why, in Hussein and Fatma's case, the use of witnesses was so important. For what litigants like Fatma try to do is to bring at least three, and preferably twelve, witnesses before one or two pairs of court notaries who quiz the witnesses individually and document their testimony, as, for example in this case, that Fatma had indeed previously returned to her husband. In the past, individuals had to be certified as "reliable witnesses," that is, as persons whose networks of ties would tend to lead them not to lie lest they lose their credibility as partners in various enterprises and relationships. The document that Fatma received from the notaries was highly persuasive to the court. Had Hussein produced a similar document, as happens in a number of cases, the court would have tried to resolve the issue not through further factual inquiry but by deciding which group was most likely to know the truth or to have sufficient distance from the litigant as to appear more believable.

In ways both formal and subtle, then, I was beginning to see that women were not utterly without countervailing powers in this society. Indeed, watching the women in court, far from it being an exercise in observing male domination or utter deference to the judge, was (as some of the films noted below exhibit so graphically) to watch strong-willed women who often knew their legal rights and were prepared to argue strenuously for their recognition.

Several other features also began to command my attention as a result of learning about cases like those of Hussein and Fatma. Students of

Islamic law usually emphasize the classical texts, particularly those from one of the four main schools of law that, having developed in the early centuries of Islam, are predominant in different Muslim countries. And while judges may indeed refer to passages in these texts on occasion, particularly in colonial and postcolonial times they have been mainly bound by codified laws. In the Moroccan case, the Code of Personal Status (*Mudawwana*) adopted in 1956 was somewhat liberalized a generation later and still further in 2004, a few years after the enthronement of the present King Muhammad VI. The present revised code significantly enhanced the ability of women to obtain divorces and some portion of the marital property. But key to Islamic legal practice is not simply what is in the texts or the codes but the procedures and the broader cultural assumptions that both enable and cabin judicial discretion. So, if the court felt that it was truly at an impasse in determining crucial facts—such as whether Fatma did or did not own certain furnishings—a decisive oath, taken at the mosque or a saint's shrine on a Friday, could be offered to whichever party the court felt was most likely to know the truth. Alternatively, in a question like that of Hussein's claimed poverty or the proper level of support for Fatma, the court could turn to experts attached to it for guidance.

Moreover, the court employs certain assumptions about people that are widely shared in the culture. For example, most people believe that men and women are fundamentally different, but that anyone who develops his or her reasoning powers and thus has exercised greater control over one's natural passions may transcend the disposition of their gender. Justice is thought to lie in treating people in a manner that is appropriate to their category, without denying the possibility of having personal characteristics that do not simply fit into an unalterable mold. Thus, one sees cases in which, notwithstanding the code requirement that custody of a child go in certain instances to the father, the court awards custody to the mother because she is more educated or has a more stable income. Indeed, in recent years the courts in Morocco and other Arab countries have quite independently developed a concept of the best interests of the child, just as they have also begun to rely more on notions of probability given that people move around so much that it is less easy than it once was to know a person's background, connections, and reliability.[4]

Scholars sometimes distinguish between "formal" and "informal" mechanisms of social control—proceedings that involve an institution that specializes in such matters versus the multiplicity of ways in which parties and the surrounding community may offer alternative dispute resolution mechanisms or bring pressures to bear on a wide range of people who have an interest in the dispute at hand. So, for example, it was common, as in the case of Hussein and Fatma, for the husband to make use of intermediaries (sing. *wāsiṭa*) in an attempt to get his wife to return to him.[5] One recent survey of Moroccan litigants shows that 84% had first tried to use go-betweens—usually family members, but occasionally neighbors—to help settle their dispute. In other instances one may go to the descendant of a local saint, to a respected elder, or even to a judge or notary outside of the court in an attempt to have the problem mediated. Gossip and potential scandal—particularly if it may affect others' relationships—may also prove effective in resolving a dispute.

Working in the court also made it quite apparent that the judge's willingness to consider a very wide range of factors was consistent with the belief that a case is often about something more than the issue with which the judge has been presented. In a number of cases I was able to see, for example, that a marital dispute was connected to a fight involving other family members over property or inheritance, or that a claim to marital support was, say, as much a dispute among the descendants of a saint over the income from gifts brought to the ancestor's shrine. This was just one of many places, then, in which the discretion of the judge to consider these other issues is crucial. And since most people told me that the decision in any legal case is not necessarily the end of the dispute I was not surprised to learn that many subsequent suits and nonlegal encounters continued well after what might seem to have been a final judicial decision. Indeed, as many judges have told me, the court's goal is not so much to definitively resolve the dispute as to put people back into working relationships where they might then be subject to various social constraints. Few judges or litigants expect that the court's judgment in all instances invariably settles the issues once and for all.

Not everything that happens in court, then, can be fully grasped from what one sees during the public sessions or reads in the records. That is why it proved so valuable to follow a number of cases out of court in order to see the law in its fullest life. When, therefore, I encountered a case for the first time involving someone from a small rural settlement where I was doing more detailed studies, I made a point of trying to determine what else besides the facts mentioned in court might have been involved.

In this case Lahsen, sixty, claimed to have married Kanza, forty-five, with a proper bridewealth payment. However, he said, she had consistently refused to have the marriage contract signed even though they had been living together as man and wife for some months before she ran away. Kanza's lawyer told the court that she does not even know who this man is. Lahsen, however, presented a document in which twelve witnesses, all close neighbors, went separately before two different sets of notaries to swear that the couple had indeed been married for seven months before she left. The judge accepted Lahsen's claim, recognized the witnessed document as equivalent to a marriage contract, and ordered Kanza to return to her husband. When I mentioned the case to friends from their settlement, however, matters appeared more complex than were visible from the court proceedings alone.

The plaintiff, I was told, was a rather shady character who used to be well-off but had wasted his money and was now unemployed. He had married one woman after another for short periods of time, and soon after their marriage Kanza realized her mistake and left him. She tried, through relatives and even the local prosecutor, to get Lahsen to divorce her, but he would not. When the court ordered her to return to him she refused to do so and even allowed herself to be sent to jail for failure to obey the court's order. After that, people from their settlement went to Lahsen, told him this was all very shameful, that she was bringing disgrace on him by allowing herself to be incarcerated, and that he should divorce her. He finally agreed, provided that Kanza forgave him any support payments. Unlike another man from their village, who engaged in frequent marriages and then made his wives so miserable that they were willing to pay him to get out of the union, in this case it was a combination of social pressure and shame that finally resulted in the divorce.

Cases like these were not, however, the only ones that might come before the qadi. While matters of marriage, divorce, and inheritance predominate in those chambers of the unified legal system that are usually known as the qadis' courts, jurisdiction over certain types of property matters may actually lie simultaneously with the qadi's court and with the civil/criminal court.[6] An elderly man named Hamed thus told me about the time he added a room on top of his house, one wall of which could have been used by his neighbor. When the neighbor refused to pay his share of the common wall, Hamed should have gone to the qadi's court, preferably with witnesses, and obtained a document certifying the neighbor's nonpayment. But Hamed did not do so. Now, years later, when the neighbor started to add a room to his house that made use of the party wall, Hamed had a choice. In the qadi's court the presumption is that the person who starts to use an existing wall must have paid his share unless a notarized document to the contrary is presented. But in the civil court, which at that time had overlapping jurisdiction on various property matters, the presumption was exactly reversed. There, the burden was on the person now trying to use the shared wall to prove that he had contributed to its construction. After so many years, however, the neighbor could produce no witnesses. So, by carefully choosing his court Hamed was able to prevail.

While Hamed's party wall case was no doubt an unusual situation, analogous tactics are constantly being employed, whether within or beyond the formal courts. One might, for example, seek an advisory opinion from an Islamic law scholar to present as guidance to the qadi. I have seen records in which numerous brief opinions were presented by each side, always written on a scrolled-up document. (People joke that if you offer the scholar enough money he will write it as long as a grown man's arm and if you pay him even more he will write it on both sides of the document—which is actually never done.) What this also demonstrates is that, particularly in the past but not without continuing implications, it is the reputation of a judge that is crucial, sometimes for his being susceptible to the influence of a noted scholar, sometimes for knowing that he is less likely to be overturned now that the modern legal system allows for cases to be appealed. To this day one hears stories of judges who are wise or clever in ferreting out the truth from contentious and not always truthful litigants—even by disguising themselves, going out into the marketplace, and encountering one of the parties in a transaction like that being contested—and whose judicial opinions may later be cited as a minority but preferred view.

In the past, the Berbers—who had a highly developed system of their own customary law that they regarded as fully consistent with Islam—had yet another practice. One party could require a group of co-swearers drawn from the defendant's kin group or his nearby settlements to take an oath in the latter's support. But because the plaintiff could choose the lead swearer (*noqran*)—and would always choose someone who they hoped would be unwilling to risk his reputation to support a false defense—the plaintiff was able to pressure the defendant's own group of associates to make him settle the matter. Another device was to challenge an opposition group to a public sing-off (what anthropologists call a song duel) at the conclusion of which the people gathered around would express their opinion as to who should prevail, a pressure that often resulted in a quick settlement.

If studying Islamic law as it is actually practiced troubled some of my original assumptions, other observations surprised me even further. I was astonished, for example, to learn that not infrequently Moroccan Jews would bring their cases against one another to the Muslim court even though they had legally recognized courts of their own. Historically this was not uncommon throughout the Middle East. As we will see in chapter 4, studies of the Ottoman records, for example, are rich in such cases, as are the records of Morocco itself. By the time I began fieldwork in Morocco the Jewish community had largely departed, but I did see a couple of instances—and found records of many more—in which a Jew would bring suit in the court of the qadi rather than go to his own Jewish law court. These cases usually involved business relationships, rather than marital situations, but the fact that these cases might be brought before the Muslim courts was a clear indication of the complex relations that had made Morocco a place where Jews and Muslims had workable and interlocking ties of both a personal and financial nature over the course of many centuries.

Learning about the formal and informal mechanisms available to women to deal with their marital situations also attuned me to look more widely at a number of other relationships and cultural concepts. Further readings in the history of Islamic law and conversations with colleagues working in other parts of the Muslim world, for example, indicated that local practice was crucial to both legal and religious issues. Indeed, it is a mistake to think of Islam as a single, invariant thing emanating in pure form from seventh-century Arabia and becoming increasingly adulterated the farther out it has reached in the world. To the contrary, there is neither one pristine form (notwithstanding the claims of certain denominational adherents) nor—more crucially—is the amalgamation with local custom seen as a dilution by those who combine it with the "high" sources of Islamic law. Indeed, one of the reasons Islam could spread (and continues to spread) with such success is that there is very little required to be a Muslim—basically, just the profession of faith in one God and Muhammad as the last of His prophets. Local custom, then, is seen *as* Islamic not as some falling away from Islam's original form. Almost everywhere one encounters such sayings as "custom governs law" or "a contractual stipulation may take precedence even over the shari'a." Whether it is those Muslims in Sumatra and Malaysia who trace descent through the woman's line and thus practice inheritance that does not conform with the rules in the Quran, or North Africans who (to the chagrin of the Wahhabis of

Saudi Arabia) believe in the intercession of saints, the capacity of Islam to incorporate local beliefs without people losing any sense of their being Muslim is a crucial factor in understanding why Islam is what people do and think, not just what is in some scholarly text. This amalgamation of religious precept and localized practice is no less visible in the courts than in any other domain of Moroccan life.

As we have seen, judges make a number of their decisions about the facts of a case based on their perception of those who appear before them. To inquire, as they often do at the outset, about a person's "origins" (sing. *asel*) is not only to ask about where one was raised but about those sources of one's social nurturance, the customs by which one engages others, the extent to which one has used study or attachment to knowledgeable others to develop one's reasoning abilities, and the ways in which a person of such background characteristically goes about understanding the actions of another. In the past there were even experts in physiognomy attached to some Moroccan courts. But they were not there to assess a person's "character" based on some physical feature: They were there to determine if someone was really from the place he said he was from. So, if a man said he had a contract with another based on a handshake but the experts said that the place he says he is from does not accord with the shape of his nose or the cast of his eyes, and that the people from whom his features indicate he really stems make contracts with certain verbal statements and never with handshakes, then he is not telling the truth and should not win the case. This may seem "irrational" to a Westerner until one thinks about all the factors that go into a jury's appraisal of a person's credibility, from "body language" or sweating to other forms of demeanor on the witness stand. And throughout much of the Arab world such assumptions send a clear signal that one must remain embedded in one's alliances if one is to carry credibility in the world. In other words, just as one can be a Muslim and practice an amalgam of local customs not all of which match some others' concept of "pure" Quranic doctrine, so, too, legal decision making may incorporate any number of highly distinctive local ways of thinking about people, truth, and property—all of which are still thought of as Islamic.

And therein lies an important question that can easily be put the wrong way. For one can ask: How Islamic are these contemporary courts, with their codes and their use of some modern science?[7] But that puts the matter incorrectly if, as in other domains of life, what might seem a contradiction to those of one culture is not viewed as such by members of another.

It would be a mistake, then, notwithstanding all the influences of European codes or appellate structures, to think that the participants regard their process as less Islamic due to the inclusion of these other elements any more than they regard wearing Western-style clothes, shopping in a mall, or using a watch to determine the time to break the fast as inherently illogical or antithetical to their religion. For Islam, whatever else is true about it, is very much a religion of worldly engagement. It lives in the marketplace and in the negotiation of one's web of obligations, not because people are constantly asking if their bargains strictly accord with Islam or whether their profession of honest dealing will threaten supernatural sanction, but because Islam teaches that God endowed humankind with reason so people might better their situation and those of their dependents. By demonstrating one's reliability in the world of human affairs one shows conformity to this divine plan. Worldly involvement is thus a moral and a religious act. It lives not as abstract propositions but in the concatenation of features one discerns in another. A court is not a mosque, but it is a place for the enactment of those assumptions about human nature and human relations that are at the center of Islam, and the application of law is, therefore, no less a form of Islamic practice than are prayer or fasting or pilgrimage.

Spending time in Muslim courts underscores that, by and large, they are places that feel familiar to those who make use of them. The language is not the technical talk of lawyers; the assumptions about people and relationships are rarely those of arcane legal fiction or professional appraisal. As one looks at the use of these courts in the contexts that I discuss in this book, one sees that this familiarity, which underpins the very legitimacy of the legal process, has become a vital aspect in the interaction of law and culture in Muslim societies.

CHAPTER TWO

Why Do Women Usually Win in Muslim Family Law Courts?

Women win their cases in Muslim courts anywhere from 65% to 95% of the time. In an era when headlines are filled with the atrocities committed against women by Nigeria's Boko Haram, Afghanistan's Taliban, and Syria/Iraq's Islamic State (ISIS), that fact might not seem to accord with the assumptions of most Westerners who imagine women to be consistently disadvantaged by Islamic law. Admittedly the number of studies of court proceedings on which these figures are based is limited. Moreover, matters may not be as they seem: Women could be winning only because they are fronting for male kinsmen or are winning only a small part of their claims, sometimes at the price of relinquishing other, quite valid claims. However, they may also succeed because court procedures and presumptions actually favor women. Building on the work of Middle Eastern historians and field studies in contemporary courts, my research indicates that women who pursue their cases to decision do, it fact, win with considerable frequency, and that the ability of courts to respond to changing social circumstances reveals a more subtle and varied picture of Islamic legal practice than is commonly maintained in the Western imagination. Given these findings the relation of statutory change to actual adjudication requires a more nuanced approach than has heretofore been accorded.[1]

* * *

If the fact that women commonly "win" their lawsuits in Muslim family courts roughly 65% to 95% of the time comes as a surprise, then something clearly cries out for explanation—whether in terms of Western assumptions or in terms of the state of scholarship on the subject. That women do succeed to a considerable extent in their suits in no way negates the deep concern owed to women in the region who are often the subject of male violence and domination, or who must battle against discriminatory statutes and biased decision makers. To the contrary, the simultaneous existence of women's frequent mistreatment and their relative success in the family law cases they see through to a judicial decision only render both subjects worthy of the most serious consideration, even though I will focus exclusively on the latter issue.[2] To understand, then, what might be going on in a wide range of Muslim courts, we need to look first at the limitations on the available data, then at the data themselves, and finally at a series of possible explanations about the position of women and the nature of Islamic legal proceedings.

Limitations on the Data

Considering that Muslims currently account for nearly a quarter of all the people in the world and that the position of women in Islamic law is an issue of frequent attention, remarkably few studies have been done on the actual operations of Muslim courts.[3] Many factors have contributed to this situation, but two stand out. First, in recent decades relatively few social scientists have chosen to concentrate on the study of courtroom proceedings outside of the West, and fewer still have worked in the courts of the Muslim world. Indeed, as theories in the social sciences have not arisen mainly from such legal studies and as law faculties have seen little need to employ such comparativists, incentives for work in the field have been limited.[4]

In addition, text-based scholars have dominated the field of Islamic law studies and have not shown predominant interest in modern courts, continuing to focus instead on historical situations and the high literary tradition of the Islamic legal text writers.[5] Elsewhere, survey data on attitudes toward legal reform are frequently offered in isolation from people's actual experiences in the courts.[6] Similarly, the heroic work performed by a number of women's and human rights organizations in the Muslim world tends to focus on changes in the formal laws rather than on the collection of detailed data about actual court proceedings.[7] The few deeply ethnographic studies we possess are largely from outside the Arab countries, though also lacking are studies from many parts of South Asia, the Gulf region, and Central Asia. As we will see, the picture is notably better for the field of Ottoman historical studies, where a number of scholars have used court records to construct a refined view of the status of women and minorities appearing before Muslim judges in the areas under the control of the Sublime Porte.

Moreover, interpretation of the available material poses a variety of problems. For example, in most parts of the Muslim world cases are not commonly published, nor have documents been systematically collected or organized.[8] Many Muslims have a scrolled legal document kept in some reasonably safe place, and copies of cases can usually be found in the offices of urban and rural courts—sometimes fairly well kept and orderly, too often dependent on the knowledge and care of a clerk who may no longer be in residence. Cases are rarely if ever collated to indicate the gender of the winning party, so one must go through the records by hand to retrieve the relevant information. In many family law courts women bring cases more frequently than men, but it can be difficult to tell if their rate of winning is affected by their gender or is due to their having been the one who initiated the case.[9] Nowadays, more of the records are either typed or entered on a computer, but the researcher is often still confronted not only with a language to be learned but handwriting that ranges from that of which a skilled calligrapher would be proud to documents that would cross the eyes of a trained epigrapher. Even where we do have statistics the criteria of definition are not always so clear as to be unquestionably comparable.

In my own work in Morocco, for example, the process of obtaining data relating gender to outcome has been extremely time-consuming. Case records range from the cryptic to the reasonably comprehensive, though transcriptions of actual testimony are almost always absent. In those locales or periods where typewriters are absent, I have always had to have someone assist me in deciphering handwritten documents. Sitting in their offices, however, one could not only watch the clerks' interaction with potential claimants but see the ways in which they were fashioning records so as to include or omit information—particularly personal information about the women—that a scholar might regard as vital.[10] In addition to data that could be reduced to quantification much of my approach to the broader, non-statistical question of women's success in the courts, like that of other ethnographically oriented scholars, has depended, first, on these documents and courtroom attendance, but secondly, on following many of the litigants out of court and interviewing innumerable people over many years about their legal cases.[11] Notwithstanding these limitations the available data are quite intriguing.

The Data

The impetus for this study stems from the data I have collected over many years in Morocco. Working intensively in the qadi's court of Sefrou starting in the mid-1960s (with frequent research visits through to recent years), it became evident that women were "winning" a substantial majority of their legal claims.[12] Taking as a baseline a random sample of 135 personal status cases handled by the court in 1965, I had found that of cases that went to decision women won the entirety of their claims in 23 cases (45%) and won most of what they sued for in another 10 cases (20%), while husbands won entirely in 18 cases (35%).[13] The court thus ruled in favor of women almost two-thirds of the time. Conversations with court personnel suggest that the rates of women's success have held up, if not increased, in the years since.

As a result of this initiation into the courts, I was led to wonder how common findings of this sort might be in other times and parts of the Muslim world. An extensive search of the literature has turned up many studies that support the general proposition that women win their cases with noteworthy frequency. Indeed, no study has been found in which women disproportionately lose all or part of the cases they bring. In the following pages every study I have encountered will be cited regardless of how the figures turn out. These studies are sometimes quantitative, sometimes impressionistic, yet the results remain essentially similar.

Ziba Mir-Hosseini, for example, reports that in Rabat, Morocco in 1987, of 67 cases that were initiated by women the court (in the author's phrase) "accepted the complaint" 77% of the time, and even 52% of the time when lawyers were involved on both sides.[14] In the same year in Casablanca, of the 547 cases initiated by women that went to decision 95.6% were "accepted" by the courts, while 85.9% of the cases (73 of the 85 suits) initiated by men were "accepted." Plaintiffs of either gender thus displayed high rates of success for at least a portion of their suits, it being true for Morocco—as for most of the other countries studied—that an opposing party often files a counterclaim, hence the high rates of success when all of the related suits are considered may actually involve partial victories for each. Thus of 54 requests in Casablanca that year by husbands demanding that their wives return to them, the court accepted the request in 49 cases (90.7%), many of those cases no doubt being coupled with countersuits (e.g., for support) that wives very commonly win after first returning to the marital home. It is also very important to note that 82.9% of all such cases (N=316) were withdrawn, abandoned, or dismissed, a factor that is common throughout the Muslim world. Mir-Hosseini's Moroccan data therefore suggest that plaintiffs of either gender win with great frequency if they see their cases through to a decision, and that (as appeared in my own studies) women certainly do no worse than men—and characteristically succeed at very high rates—particularly if they are the ones who initiate the suit. While Mir-Hosseini's data do not speak exactly to the frequency of women "winning" their cases in whole or in part, the author is undoubtedly correct in viewing the court as an arena where the negotiation of a contentious relationship does not simply reduce to the powerlessness of women.[15]

Other studies in Morocco show that, following the liberalization of the Code of Personal Status in 2004, women were highly successful in obtaining divorces if they pursued their cases to judgment. Sources indicate that women obtain divorces in virtually all cases when pleading the newly permitted grounds of marital discord (*shiqāq*), though frequently at some financial cost.[16] Perceptions seem to match results: In a study of 102 litigants in various Moroccan cities, it was found that 26% of the respondents to a questionnaire thought the judgment in their case favored only the woman, 25% that it favored the children, 23% that it favored the family as a whole, 14% that it favored the man, and 8% that it favored just the woman and the children.[17]

One of the more extensive statistical analyses is that of Amina Chemais, who studied the records and interviewed participants in the proceedings of a special court for personal status cases in Cairo in the 1970s and early 1980s. Although her statistics are not couched in terms of wins and losses the inferences are clear. In a sample of 100 cases for each of the ten years 1972–82, the author states that divorces were granted 95.5% of the time in those cases (469 out of 1,000) based on a wife's claim of the husband's absence. Many of the claims also contain witness evidence of the husband's ill-treatment of his wife (29 cases), his taking of another wife without the complainant's agreement (four cases), and claims for non-payment of the bridewealth (three cases).[18] In 45 cases the wife said she was still a virgin and the marriage had not been consummated. Of the 14.9% of all divorce actions based on the husband's desertion (N=149), only 15.4% of the women's claims were denied; of the 20.4% (N=204) based on a claim of "harm," 74% of the claims were granted, the majority of the denials being grounded on the husband's absence from the proceedings or the judge not finding the witnesses believable. Only 0.5% of the divorces claimed that the husband was at fault because of insanity or impotence. In short, women would appear to win the vast majority of their cases, though many have a mix of causal grounds.[19]

Studies conducted by Al-Sharmani and others in Egypt yield similar results. Referring to cases that occurred after the 2000 reforms permitted a form of *khul'* divorce—in which the woman can effectively demand a divorce in exchange for giving up certain financial claims on her spouse—Al-Sharmani shows that for the women who bring these cases: "Of the 69 *khul* informants, 67 won the lawsuit and obtained a judicial divorce."[20] She further notes, apropos the 38 cases filed by a wife claiming "harm," that "all complete cases were decided in favour of the wife . . . 16 of the informants filed for divorce on the grounds of absence. All of the informants won these lawsuits."[21] In those cases where the issue is whether a husband has provided adequate protection and guardianship over his wife (*qiwāma*), the author states that "the obedience cases won by wives consistently outnumber those won by the husbands."[22] These cases may arise either by a husband's claim that the wife refuses to live in the matrimonial home (*nushūz*: often translated as "recalcitrance") or by her claim that the husband has failed in his duty of protection/guardianship insofar as he has not, for example, paid her dower or has appropriated her property, abuses her physically or verbally, or has acted according to reasons sanctioned by custom (*'urf*) though not enumerated in the code (e.g., refusing to let her visit her family, continue her education, or seek medical assistance). Overall, Al-Sharmani's data indicate that in roughly the first decade of this century women who claimed valid reasons for not being "obedient" won 17.8% (N=289) of the 1628 cases filed while men won 3.1% (N=50), the remainder not reaching decision. In the 309 cases initiated by men for nushuz, men did win 19.7% of the time (N=61) and women 6.8% (N=21), though the rates for these small numbers were reversed in some of the courts surveyed.[23]

Other studies support these findings. Writing about the court she studied in Yemen between 1983 and 1995, Anna Würth states: "The majority of suits are won by the parties who bring them: 69 percent of plaintiffs who see their cases through to a conclusion emerge victorious."[24] She then offers the following data: "Women win a total of 79.5 percent of the suits they bring, men about 40 percent. In divorce cases women are successful nearly 90 percent of the time, and decisions are made in their favor in the majority of cases dealing with post-divorce issues. Only about 50 percent are successful, however—the same percentage as for men—in suits over support payments and marital obedience. In nearly half of these verdicts both parties are granted their demands in part." In a statement that, as we shall see, resonates for studies of many other Muslim courts, the author concludes: "The South Sanaa family court and probably most other family courts in Yemen function fundamentally as institutions run entirely by upper-class men for poor women wronged by other (poor) men, mostly by their spouses and sometimes their male relatives."[25]

Working from a sample of court records in the subdistrict of Deir Abu Said, Jordan—mostly dating from 1959–60, with some records dating from 1965 and 1966—Richard Antoun reports that 63 cases involved a wife's demand for maintenance (35% of which were approved, 5% rejected, and 60% dropped), 25 concerned a husband's demand for conjugal obedience (of which 12% were approved, 32% rejected, 40% dropped, and the remainder not accounted for), 11 sought the termination of maintenance payments, and a small scattering involved other claims.[26] While such figures do not permit conversion to simple characterization as "wins" and "losses" by gender, Antoun does assert that "within the court setting and in the context of the traditional framework of Islamic law, a number of options exist by which women not only can solidify their position in a conjugal family but also can claim their individual rights against male members of their consanguine and conjugal families. In forwarding such claims, they invoke both Islamic and customary procedures, principles, and norms."[27]

Ido Shahar's study of the Israeli shari'a court in West Jerusalem in 2002 shows that, in a sample of 305 cases, women "won" 207, or 68% of the time. However, Shahar cautions that what "win" means is not easy to determine since, as we shall see in many other instances, suits mix a variety of claims, may represent only partial victories for one or both parties, or may (as, for example, in some custody cases) actually pit the child's mother against the husband's mother.[28] Without overemphasizing their precision, Shahar's findings nevertheless accord with those of many other investigators in showing that, whatever else, women do achieve notable response to their claims in the court.

Susan Hirsch's study of several Kenyan Muslim courts in the mid-1980s shows that in one court that heard a total of 125 cases, men (N=17) won 23.5% of the cases that went to decision and lost 29.4% (the remainder reaching no resolution or being settled), while women won 42.5% of their cases (N=108) and lost 1.9% (the rest of their cases being settled or unresolved).[29] Of those cases that were settled, women attained what they were claiming 81.4% of the time (N=43) while male claimants (N=6) succeeded half of the time, the results being categorized as "mixed" in 14% of the cases (N=6) initiated by women and 33% of the time (N=2) where men were the claimants.[30] The author concludes:

> Most women who file cases are successful. Even if men fail to comply with case decisions or settlement agreements, the decisions themselves and the authority

> they represent are important tools that women use to change their positions within troubled domestic circumstances. . . . But why do women win in Kadhi's Court? First, most women tend to bring good claims to court. . . . Perhaps more importantly, kadhis take women's claims seriously. By recognizing women's perseverance, kadhis minimize the power that men assert through pronouncements, even about Islamic law. . . . In short, women win cases in part because kadhis are in conflict with other men [including elders] for authority.[31]

Historically, too, the pattern is clear. Haim Gerber, from his work in the Ottoman records, reports that "in all but a few cases, it was the social underdog who initiated the case—women versus men, non-Muslims versus Muslims, commoners versus members of the elite. The court is seen mainly as a tool of the common people to defend a modicum of legal rights. . . . Women won seventeen of twenty-two cases against men; non-Muslims won seven of eight cases against Muslims; commoners won six of eight suits against *askeris* [members of the official elite]."[32] Citing Gerber, Wael Hallaq seconds this point: "That those who initiated litigation in the court were the social underdogs is now certainly beyond debate. . . . That they won the majority of cases and that they found in the court a defender of their rights is equally a foregone conclusion." He also cites Abraham Marcus when saying: "The social underdogs thus knew what their rights were before approaching the court, a fact that explains why they won the great majority of cases when they happened to be plaintiffs."[33] Judith Tucker, after citing this same passage from Gerber's work, goes on to say:

> Here the emphasis is placed on how ordinary members of a society understand the rights they enjoy by way of legal doctrine, and how they act on their own behalf to secure these rights which are always under pressure in a stratified society. As Gerber and all other researchers who have looked at the Ottoman court records will testify, people went to the courts in droves, for notarial purposes but also for claims and disputes of various kinds. In the case of Gerber's study, the ways in which they resorted to the legal system had significant implications for society: they were leveling the hierarchical playing field. Islamic law provided the doctrines and institutions that made this possible—this is a remarkable fact that surely belongs in any history of the law.[34]

Additional historical studies from diverse Muslim regions demonstrate that the findings of more recent Muslim court studies undoubtedly find resonance in other times and places. Richard Roberts reports that in the period 1905–12 women won 62% of the time (99 cases out of 160, and anywhere from 80–100% of the time in some years) in the Muslim courts of the Bamako, Mali region of the former French Soudan.[35] Similarly, in the Ndar, Senegal region, Ghislaine Lydon reports: "Muslim judges *tended* to rule in favor of women's requests for justice, especially in the case of [*khul'a*] divorce. . . . Only rarely were women turned down or 'returned to their husbands'. . . . [A] woman had to be prepared . . . to purchase her freedom, as it were. . . . [W]omen frequented the court with great ease, presenting their cases and claims, demanding that the ruling qadi investigate their deserting husbands, and bringing their monies to pay their legal dues."[36] Elsewhere Lydon writes:

> Overall, the *qadis* of Ndar tended to rule in favour of women's divorces, but they did not curb the excessive demands of husbands when negotiating compensation or deliberating bridewealth payments. . . . In the nineteenth century women frequented the court with great ease, presenting their cases and claims, demanding that *qadis* investigate their deserting husbands, and negotiating costly divorces. At the same time, the *qadis* of Ndar invariably granted circumstantial divorces to men for reasons of spousal abandonment, or for more litigious matters such as neglect or physical abuse.[37]

Returning to contemporary courts, Erin Stiles's work in Zanzibar shows that in 1999–2000 in the community she studied women "won" the cases they opened 44% of the time (N=25 out of 57 cases) and lost 14% of the time (N=8), the remainder having been settled or the litigants stopped coming to court. Put differently, women won 76% of the cases they saw through to a decision (25 out of 33 cases), while the men "won" about 53% of the cases they initiated (N=7 out of a total of 13 cases) and lost far more than the women at 31% (N=4), the remaining cases having been dropped. But, as with all of the other reported findings, Stiles has to qualify her observations:

> Women do lose fewer cases than men as plaintiffs . . . and many of the cases that were settled ended in divorce. However, often the ruling would please neither party, and it was often difficult to determine who was more favored in the ruling. Even if a woman "won" a case by getting a ruling in her favor, it did not mean that she went home happy or got the outcome that she wished for. The same was certainly true for men. Also . . . many cases did not end simply with

> a ruling from the *khadi*, and the eventual outcome might have been very different. In the official court register, victors in cases were not marked. . . . For the sake of preparing the table [of case outcomes], however, I determined that a woman or man was successful if the ruling rectified at least part of her or his initial claim [although] I am not fully comfortable with representing case outcomes in this way, and I would ask readers to consider cases individually since the outcomes were more complex than what is indicated in the table.[38]

In a study of West Bank Palestinian courts for 1965, 1975, and 1985, Lynn Welchman reports that "the majority of maintenance claims [*nafaqa*] are won [by wives]; if the husband acknowledges that the wife is not living in the house and that he is not paying her maintenance, the only *shar'i* [Islamic legal] defence he can offer to her maintenance action is to establish that she is *nashiz* [disobedient] and has therefore lost her right to maintenance."[39] In cases where a husband seeks to have his wife placed under judicially ordered oversight or returned to his home (*ta'a*), "in claims followed through, a husband had only a one-in-three chance of winning. . . . In 1985, only 20% of all *ta'a* actions raised in the three courts ended with the husband being awarded *ta'a*."[40]

Drawing on 26 cases reported to her by Algerian lawyers and another 82 unpublished cases analyzed from the records of the First Appeal Court of Algiers for 1986, Ruth Mitchell states that

> by far the largest number of cases in the sample examined involved divorce and its effects. Most of these divorces were requested by the husband. The 1404/1984 Family Code gives the husband an absolute right to divorce, but the judge may grant damages to the wife for any harm (*ḍarar*) she has suffered. The notion of "fault" currently plays a large part in Algerian court decisions, mainly to determine whether the wife is entitled to damages. Even though many husbands tried to prove that the divorce was their wife's fault, in practice the courts mostly decided that divorce was the husband's fault. Out of the 27 cases where the husband requested divorce, or appealed a decision attributing the divorce as his fault, 26 [i.e., 96%] were pronounced as the husband's fault. . . . Several lawyers said that it was rare for the wife to ask for divorce, and that if she did so, she would be deprived of damages and custody of the child. It was surprising, therefore, to find 17 cases where the wife requested a divorce under Article 53. Divorce was granted in 13 cases [i.e., 76%], refused in two cases [i.e., 11.7%], and in the other two cases a commissioner was appointed to investigate the wife's complaints. All 13 divorces were pronounced as the husband's fault. In

> six cases, the wife was awarded damages, in 10 cases she was given an *'idda* payment [separation support until divorce becomes final] and in six cases she was awarded custody of the children.[41]

In a number of instances we lack exactly comparable statistics but the conclusions of the investigators are clear.[42] In her study of the Muslim courts of Singapore from the mid-1950s until the early 1960s, Judith Djamour writes: "In 1961 there were 61 divorces registered by order of the Shariah Court; 50 of the 61 were at the request of the wife. . . . In 1962, the Shariah Court ordered the registration of 99 divorces; 78 were at the request of the wife. . . . [T]he records of the Shariah Court *seem* to show that more women are eager to rid themselves of their husbands than vice versa. What the figures do not automatically reveal is that most of the women who obtained [divorce] decrees had been neglected or abandoned for months or years."[43] Speaking of his work in Indonesia in the 1960s, Daniel Lev writes:

> Confronted so frequently by women who have suffered from unhappy marriages, religious judges tend to be sympathetic and quick to justify divorce, even at times when the plaintiff wife is clearly dissembling or at fault. This characteristic stands out in contested cases as well as those in which husbands do not appear—usually indeed because they have deserted. Popular impressions have it that Islamic courts favor husbands, undoubtedly because Islamic legal rules do so, but in general the opposite bias is more common. The essential reason for this bias is that the clientele and social function of Islamic courts elicit judicial attitudes favorable to wives. It may be that the generally stronger social position of women in much of Indonesia, particularly Java, compared with other Islamic countries, has pushed Indonesian Islamic courts further in this direction than is the case elsewhere in the Islamic world.[44]

Updating the Indonesian situation, other investigators have concluded:

> Contrary to common assumptions about Islamic courts, nearly two-thirds of applicants in the Religious Courts in Indonesia are women. Even more counterintuitively, the vast majority of women win their cases, most of which are decided procedurally on the basis of codified state versions of sharia. These confer on women and men alike similar rights to what is virtually "divorce on demand." One ground available to both parties is simply "absence of harmony" in the marriage.[45]

Similarly, Sarah Vincent-Grosso's study of a court of first instance in a lower middle-class district of Tunis in 2007–8 offers a wealth of qualitative information, although the basis for her quantitative references is unclear. She refers to 51 cases of divorce where the woman claimed harm (*darar*): 36 of the cases went to decision, 16 (44%) of which were "accepted" by the court while 20 (56%) were rejected, apparently for insufficient proof. Of the remaining cases, six resulted in a divorce by mutual consent (*bi-ttaradi*) between the parties, six were changed to a claim by the woman for a divorce without grounds (*insha'an*), and three couples were reconciled.[46] In a separate passage, Vincent-Grosso notes that there were 13 successful cases (62%) out of a "sample" of 21 brought by wives seeking a divorce for harm, and eight (38%) in which the claim was unsuccessful—though all of the latter had yet to receive "final judgment" (i.e., could still be appealed). Where women did not win a divorce for harm they could still obtain a divorce with virtual certainty if they were prepared to risk a less favorable financial result by seeking the divorce "without grounds."[47]

Other writers support the general thrust of these findings for the following diverse regions and periods:

Andalusia and North Africa, 1100–1500: David Powers's study of records of this early period leads him to conclude:

> According to popular stereotype, Muslim women are passive agents who have little or no freedom and whose lives are controlled by their husbands and/or agnatic relatives. It is therefore noteworthy that in all four of the cases examined here, women are active agents who used their wits, savvy and knowledge of the law in an attempt to overcome the powerful asymmetries of the rules of marriage and divorce. . . . It appears that these women were familiar with the law and capable of manipulating it in an effort to advance their own interests. . . . [T]hese cases are not isolated examples.[48]

Lower Egypt during the Ottoman period: Abdal-Rehim writes:

> A usual cause for a wife's demand of divorce was the husband's non-fulfillment of the marriage contract. If the wife proved this to be so, normally through "acceptable" witnesses, the *qadi* found for her and granted her the divorce without compromising her financial rights. . . . The picture of family life and women's role presented by archival records is clearly a much different one than is usually assumed for women during the Ottoman period. Far from being the "slaves" of men by whom they were ruled, the picture is one of shared responsibilities

in which the wife is given custody of her children and becomes the preferred guardian for her minor orphan children and their inheritances.[49]

Palestine in the early 1900s: Iris Agmon writes: "It appears that women were far from helpless or inept but managed quite well to find their way within the system of rights and obligations imposed by *shari'a*, customary law, and the changing circumstances—rights and obligations that differed greatly from those of their husbands. . . . [I]t would appear that the courts or, more precisely, the judges, contributed a great deal to women's ability to realize their rights."[50]

Egypt in the first half of the twentieth century: While noting that his is a qualitative study and "any quantitative conclusions that I offer should be viewed as preliminary and tentative," Ron Shaham writes:

> To conclude, about 50% of the applications for divorce were granted by Egyptian *qadis*, who applied the statute relating to judicial divorce without inhibition, undeterred by its deviation from Hanafi doctrine. The most impressive finding is that the *qadis* fulfilled the expectations of the legislators by interpreting the term "injury" broadly. . . . Thus injury became an effective instrument that enabled women to complain of a wide range of physical and mental harms.[51]

The author ends his analysis by stating:

> The image of women appearing before the courts does not correspond to the image of the Islamic submissive woman created by old Western scholarship. The social inferiority of women is indeed revealed in the court records, yet at the same time the courts were the battleground for those women who overcame social obstacles and had the courage to demand their *shar'i* [Islamic law] rights. The appearance of women in the courts demanding their legal rights is not a novel phenomenon in Islamic societies, yet it seems that modern change and the legal backing offered to women by the statutory legislation have strengthened their confidence in applying legal strategies for improving their status.[52]

Bodrum, Turkey, 1950–1967: June Starr and Jonathan Pool report:

> There were one hundred thirty-eight divorce and twenty-seven adultery cases heard by the Bodrum [district] courts out of the 3,350 cases [including many criminal cases] in our records. . . . Women file twice as many "routine" suits

> in the Bodrum courts as do men. While only 4 percent of the women filing such suits failed to appear when their cases were scheduled, 8 percent of the men filing routine cases failed to appear. Women not only filed more, but they won more. Of "routine" suits which reached decisions, 98 percent of the ones brought by women were won, as opposed to 93 percent of those brought by men. [Authors' note 22: Non-routine case decisions were classified in such a differentiated and ambiguous way that we could not confidently assign them to "plaintiff won" and "plaintiff lost" categories.] Of 138 divorce cases heard from 1965 through 1967, almost half were brought by wives. With the exception of adultery, the types of cases brought by women against men did not differ greatly from those brought by men against women or between members of the same sex, except that women sued men more often for child support. . . . Women, possibly the most traditionally deprived group of all, are increasingly turning to the court to redress at least some of their grievances—in some ways they already use the courts even more efficaciously than men. At least in its treatment of women and debtors we find evidence that the court is not merely serving to reinforce the traditional power structure.[53]

In her related study of divorce actions in the same region Starr reports:

> If we compare the percentage of divorces granted to men and women who initiated divorce proceedings, we find a substantial increase for women, from less than 33 percent in 1950 to an average of 68 percent in the 1965 through 1967 period. (The comparable figures for men were 42 percent and 57 percent.) As a result, divorces granted to women rose in number from less than half of those granted to men in 1950 (6 versus 14), to the same number or more than the same as those granted to men in 1965 through 1967 (15 versus 11; 16 versus 15; 14 versus 14, respectively). . . . These results indicate that women were increasingly using the courts to obtain divorces that had been unheard of before Ataturk's reforms and that the courts themselves were growing more responsive to women as plaintiffs.[54]

Muslim courts in the countries of the West: Hard data from Muslim courts in Britain, Europe, and North America are sparse, but the general thrust of the studies we possess also suggests that women commonly find relief in these tribunals. Of course, the situation is complicated by the fact that the Muslim proceedings may not be recognized by the state and people frequently obtain a decision from both systems. A qualitative study based on 212 interviews carried out during 2006–10 in the U.S.

and Canada among Muslim men and women who had been involved in divorce proceedings nevertheless showed that 36% of the cases were initiated by women, that imams were reluctant to recognize unilateral divorces by men, and that if women persisted they commonly succeeded in obtaining an Islamic divorce.[55] Several media reports in Britain suggested that women were being pressured by the Muslim court officials to remain in unfavorable, even abusive, marriages. In a number of situations, as in the Muslim countries proper, women seeking a divorce have been more or less compelled to give up some of their bridewealth payment (*mahr*) or the marriage gifts that effectively serve as a dowry.[56] However, a careful review of those proceedings that have been filmed not only shows that the cases represented actually resulted in the woman obtaining a divorce but that the comments of the presiding judge are neither markedly different from those obtaining in secular courts nor clearly biased against women.[57]

Possible Explanations

How, then, might we account for the success that women appear to have in the family law cases in which they are involved? There are at least half a dozen ways in which we might explain these findings:

1. WOMEN ARE NOT ACTUALLY WINNING. The possibility exists, of course, that it is not the women who are actually winning these cases but the men in their families. That is, cases that concern women—whether they involve support or residence or potential inheritance—actually affect the financial and social situations of their male kinsmen and it is they, rather than the women, who are prompting the suits and gaining from their successful outcomes.

It is certainly true that men stand to gain (or lose) in many of the cases that are brought: They may be called upon to support women whose husbands leave them or their children uncared for, claim a stake in the return of a bridewealth payment, have an interest in the portion of the dowry still owed their kinswoman, or be called upon to contribute to the payment necessary to get the husband to issue a divorce.[58] Historians of the Mamluk and Ottoman periods (thirteenth to sixteenth centuries, but especially the late fourteenth to fifteenth) do suggest, for example, that many court cases resulted from a family's interest in the payment of the remainder of the bridewealth.[59] But they also note that even in this era women's property rights were more extensive than once thought. Yossef Rapoport notes that marriage was highly monetized, with men often in debt to wives who had loaned them money; that the sums given the bride by her family were substantially larger than the bridewealth payment, thus forming a kind of "pre-mortem inheritance"; that marriage often involved only a partial payment of the bridewealth, the remainder of which could be demanded at any time by the wife; that women frequently engaged in paid work, often living unmarried; and that complicated stratagems used to get around legal rules undermined patriarchal authority.[60] Similar patterns can be found in a number of contemporary Muslim communities.[61] And undoubtedly tangled networks of debt and social expectation imply that multiple interests may be involved in any legal dispute. But for all the involvement of other family members it is difficult to see a large number of the actual law cases we know about as simply vehicles through which men are contesting with one another.

Moreover, observers of Muslim court proceedings note that women commonly argue their cases with great vigor.[62] Already in the mid-nineteenth century outsiders were indicating that women spoke up strongly in such instances. One observer of the period, quoting yet another, writes:

> European visitors to the mahkamas [law courts] of Algiers bear witness to the spiritedness of women litigants, and suggest what it was that [the qadi] meant by 'disorders.' Again, it is a visitor from England who offers the most graphic description. The Reverend J. W. Blakeley reported in 1859: ". . . those women I heard were very voluble and far more vehement than most male witnesses, and in one or two instances were obviously snubbed by the qadi for wandering from the point at issue, but with as little effect as is generally produced by a similar proceeding upon an Irish woman at Bow Street."[63]

As for the present, no one can watch films like Ziba Mir-Hosseini's *Divorce Iranian Style* (1998), *Bastards* (a documentary by Deborah Perkin), *Divorce Shari'a Style* (2007; a film that follows cases heard by Britain's Islamic Shari'a Council), *Justice at Agadez* (2006; which follows an Islamic law judge in Niger), the fictional (but very accurate) Iranian movie *A Separation* (2012), or sit through numerous sessions of a local Muslim court and not be impressed with the intelligence and ardor with which women commonly present their claims.[64] As Mir-Hosseini says for postrevolutionary Iran: "It appears that there is little match between the legal status of women within marriage and their actual position, as inferred by marital dispute cases. Women, as seen in these cases, challenge the standard image of powerless Muslim women who have little say in their marriage and are at the mercy of their husbands. These women, aware of their rights and their limitations, are able to manipulate the legal system to acquire a degree of autonomy. They have a voice in determining the terms of their marital life."[65] Sometimes this maneuvering is in terms of legal propositions; at other times it is a matter of relying on various social, economic, and psychological powers. Writing about medieval Egypt—but perhaps in ways that still have great currency—Huda Lutfi says:

> Egyptian women participated actively in public life and devised strategies that enabled them to do so. Two classic female strategies that appear to have been commonly used were the denial of sexual pleasure to and the threat of separation from a husband who tried to exercise control over a strong-willed wife. . . . Women wielded power in their immediate surroundings; they shaped their daily habits and religious rituals according to their own needs in the Cairene urban context. . . . Unlike the stereotypical submissive and obedient wife, the Cairene women . . . were strong willed and defiant of male and shar'i authority. They often used classical female strategies to obtain what they desired from recalcitrant husbands. . . . These strategies were complemented by two institutional practices, which may have given the woman greater leverage in her relationship with her man: her frequent use of the judge's court to ensure her legal rights and her demand of a 'bed fee' for her sexual services.[66]

Thus, while it is true that male relatives may serve as spokesmen in some instances and are frequently present and interested in the outcome, the women themselves play a very significant role in pursuing a case to a favorable result. Increasingly, too, in many countries monetary payments go directly to the woman, although admittedly we have no solid information to state with certainty the frequency with which they may be compelled to pass payments along to their male kinfolk—or find it politic to do so—whether unilaterally or in exchange for a long-term promise of protection and support. Thus we are left with the distinct possibility that women are not mere surrogates for male litigiousness even though we are also left with the possibility that such is the case in an indeterminate number of instances.

Women must maneuver, within the range of resources they have available, to position themselves as well as they can, particularly when the formal rules frequently favor males.[67] Increasingly, many women understand their legal rights and insist upon them. Writing of the skyrocketing divorce rate in Iran and the "increasing willingness of Iranian women to manipulate the Iranian legal system to escape unwanted marriages," a *New York Times* reporter indicated that women use the deferred *mahr* (*mahrieh*)—the unpaid sum owed as a kind of marriage insurance that can be demanded by the woman at any time—as a bargaining chip to be forgiven if the husband will agree to a divorce.[68] Here, too, as Arzoo Osanloo indicates, women in Iran are not only employing a language of rights but commonly know the law better than do the men because they must understand the complexities while men can simply invoke a demand for divorce.[69] Often, however, pressures from within the family constrain women from being able to pursue a legitimate claim for abuse or failure of support.[70] Nevertheless, in Iran, where the divorce rate has tripled in a decade, as one woman told a reporter, "the period in which people were prejudiced against divorce is over."[71]

In other instances women are even willing to place themselves in jeopardy of criminal proceedings—or actually allow themselves to be jailed—in order to get a familial issue properly raised before the court or to demonstrate their intense need to be free of the relationship.[72] Moreover, if the goal or orientation of the courts is often to place litigants back in a position of negotiating their own differences, the pressure on a woman to compromise her claim, even if it results in a partial victory for her, may be at the cost of foregoing a legal right she might have obtained had she the ability to see the case through to a formal decision.[73] Notwithstanding changes in the laws of some Muslim countries that make it easier for women to assert their rights, the fact of negotiated settlements and the complexities of counterclaims may, therefore, not only lead women to settle for less than the law allows but maintain the law's focus on individual cases rather than the development of more generalized legal precepts.

Here, too, though, the realities of the outcomes do not entirely vitiate the women's success in court. Winning a significant part of one's lawsuit is hardly tantamount to defeat, however much one may have been entitled to more. And if courts were merely antithetical to the interests of women in the generality one would hardly expect to see even these partial victories. The frequency with which women win some substantial part of their cases is clear from the records of a great many of these Muslim courts and thus any simple assertion that women are categorically failing to win in some significant sense of that word—and that when they do win the victory is really that of their male kinsmen—would seem to be insupportable.

2. WOMEN WIN BECAUSE THE CASES THEY PURSUE ARE THE "EASIER" ONES TO DECIDE IN THEIR FAVOR. It is also possible that it is mainly the more egregious cases or those where the facts are indisputable that account for many of the women's victories. These may be instances, as is quite often the case, in which the wife's claim is based on the husband's absence, such that the failure of the court to locate him—or his failure, for whatever reason, to appear in court—renders the women's cases more straightforward. Or the cases women win may be those involving the clear mistreatment of wives, cases that are validated by reliable witnesses none of whom supports the husband. Where the circumstances are not in dispute, then, the court may have little need to go into great detail. In other instances the outcome may be deeply connected to the willingness of the judge to open up all the issues connected to the dispute or seek a fuller understanding of the woman's situation. As deputy qadi Mahmud Salama told a researcher in Gaza in 2003 about potential judges, "I want to know whether the applicant is able to give a speech, whether he is familiar with the people's daily problems, and whether he is concerned about participating in solving these problems. *Qudāh* [judges, plural of *qadi*] are not expected to sit behind the bench and only follow the book; that qualification is tested in the written exam. They are expected to be active in people's daily life and deliver the message of Islam. Islam means that we are one body; when one organ suffers from an illness, the whole body feels the pain and fever."[74] Given that family law cases are often very fact-dependent, that they involve considerable judicial discretion, that one of the parties may not be susceptible to the court's prodding to settle, or that the husband may have a reputation for bad behavior or pointless litigation the court may be more favorably disposed to the woman's side of the matter.[75]

Undoubtedly, the "easier" the case the more likely and the more feasible it may be for a woman to pursue it to judgment. She may still have to overcome the difficulties of procedural delays, the cost or inconvenience of attending multiple proceedings, and the male bias of the institutions encountered. "Nevertheless," as Laila Abed Rabho says of the women who take their cases to court in West Jerusalem, "some Muslim women have been prompted by their dire straits to penetrate this male bastion. By learning about their legal rights according to the *shari'a* and revealing their marital problems in public, they have pushed past the boundaries of what is expected of a 'proper' Arab Muslim woman. Moreover, they force the male Muslim establishment to treat them according to the ethical as well as the social rules of Islam."[76]

It is also true, as we have seen, that whoever brings the case has a greater chance of winning all or part of the claim, perhaps, again, because neither would bring the matter to court if he or she did not indeed have a strong case.[77] But since cases may be brought for any of a host of reasons—because the real issue is about something other than the subject of the suit (e.g., a long-standing interfamilial property dispute, rather than a claim for marital support), because suits are sometimes brought simply to harass another party, or because the initiator is trying to extract a payment by the opponent—any simple correlation of plaintiff and ease of decision would probably be insupportable.[78] The records we have also indicate that, whatever proportion of the cases appear as facially favorable to women, a large number are contested and thus subject to greater scrutiny by the court for the relative merits of each side's arguments. Given this data it is difficult to claim that women win simply because the courts are skimming the most favorable cases off the top. Such a reading would contradict the presence in so many of the records of situations in which more than summary judgment is involved.

3. WOMEN ARE WINNING ONLY PART OF THEIR LEGITIMATE CLAIMS. Women often sue on multiple claims but only win part of what they seek. Rather than actually compromising a legitimate claim—and thus, as we have seen, actually losing their case—they may be winning, but only on one or several of the issues contested. Alternatively, they may win on the claim they have litigated but lose on a counterclaim by the husband or be saddled with an undesired requirement applied by the court. For example, a woman may request both support and the return of certain of her possessions but gain on only one of her claims. Or, she may claim arrears of maintenance but the husband may prevail on his claim, which the wife resists, that she first return to his bed and board. She may, in many Muslim countries, retain financial interests if she can convince the court to divorce her but lose such benefits if her husband can show cause for having repudiated her.

Furthermore, the amounts that women receive in compensation may be highly specific to their gender—and almost certainly to their socioeconomic stature—in ways that disadvantage them as compared to men.[79] Women may also be particularly reluctant to reveal intimate details of their marriage in a court proceeding.[80] Even when women do win, enforcing judgments can be very difficult. Thus as Anna Würth is careful to note in the case of Yemen: "'Winning' a divorce petition or a suit for support has its limits: winning an action for divorce entails losing all financial rights from marriage but gaining the freedom to try again; winning an action for child support or support during marriage boils down to an entitlement too low to survive on and hard to enforce." [81]

It may also be inappropriate to think of women as the real victors in cases decided favorably for them if, in fact, they are forced to give up legitimate claims in order to gain a partial victory. An example from the family law courts of many Western countries may help to clarify this point. Not infrequently, in a divorce proceeding a man will claim custody of the couple's children not because he truly wishes to have custody but as a bargaining chip in financial negotiations with the wife. A mother, then, may do almost anything not to lose her child and in the process forego an otherwise valid claim for support or other property considerations in order to get her estranged husband to relinquish his claim for custody. Similarly, as Aharon Layish found in the Israeli Muslim courts, "in many dozens of cases, the wife at the time of the divorce renounced the custody money or maintenance for the children, provided that they remained in her custody," and that "[m]ore than two-thirds of all divorces by agreement involved renunciation by the wife of certain rights, or compensation to the husband."[82]

Thus, in the Muslim world a benefit to which a woman is often entitled may have to be given up if she wishes to prevail in some other regard. This is institutionalized in some instances in that form of divorce (*k͟hul'a*) where, for example, a woman relinquishes a claim to the remainder of a bridewealth payment or some level of support if the husband (who may alone have the power to do so) will issue her a divorce. In Iran, for example, "over 50 per cent of all divorces for any given year [1980–86] registered in Tehran are *khul'*, in which by definition the wife forfeited her *mahr* [dower, bridewealth]."[83] In 2000, Egypt essentially institutionalized divorce on demand for women under the name of *khul'a*, though such a course requires the loss of at least some of the financial claim a woman might otherwise be able to assert.[84] Many Egyptian women nevertheless prefer to give up the possibility of some, often very uncertain, support from their divorced husband in order to receive welfare payments that require a single mother to be legally divorced.[85] The changes in the law of personal status instituted in Morocco in 2004 allow both men and women to seek a court-pronounced divorce based on marital discord (*s͟hiqāq*), a process which, though it requires both compulsory conciliation and a finding by the court of some basis for the claimed discord, has sharply increased the incidence of divorce and the relative ease with which women can obtain a divorce. The introduction of this new basis for divorce does not, however, appear to have eradicated the potential for a wife having to make financial concessions in order to prevail.[86] To say, then, that women "win" in such situations may be misleading: It may be better to say that, given the limited choices with which many women are faced, a compromised agreement may be preferable, from the wife's perspective, to the available and realistic alternatives.[87]

Additionally, judges frequently pressure women to modify or even drop their claims. However, this process is highly ambiguous. On the one hand, a woman may be told that she should be more circumspect, that she should recognize the adverse consequences for the family of her suit, or that she ought to appreciate that decisions and power properly lie with the husband. At the same time, these comments may be a sop thrown to the husband whose pride or overall standing gets some support even though the court is going to rule against him. Indeed, as I note below, this may be part of the concern that men may become a problem for the state if they do not seem to get some respect in the courts.

Women may also react to court pressure with a variety of countermeasures. They may plead and cry, they may threaten and curse. The latter suggests to the court that women can create a good deal of chaos if not attended to; the former that they are impoverished, benighted, or otherwise downtrodden and the Muslim state needs to attend to their plight.[88] Some women even try to compel judges to attend to their needs by seeking to create a supernaturally sanctioned obligation (*'ar*) in them, in much the same way one might to a saint or a patron. In all such instances, the woman may need to persist through the stage of the proceedings where she is pressured to act like a proper wife, a proper woman, a proper litigant before the judge will rule in her favor. And since we know from many other studies that often what people seek is not just to win a case but to have their felt sense of injury attended to, the court's ritual of pressuring the woman may be importantly satisfying to the man and to a society that sees its courts as a primary agency for upholding idealized roles for wives and husbands. Indeed, given that the court has to constantly construct its legitimacy by securing a following, the process is part of the whole style of amassing that legitimacy which inheres not in the institution proper but in the judge as a whole person.[89]

Notwithstanding these caveats, if women were simply losing their cases because the Muslim courts are prejudiced against women or because Islamic law as a whole is uniformly skewed to their disfavor we would not expect to see so many instances in which women do, in fact, win at least a significant portion of their claims. Again, whether one wishes to see this as a glass that is half empty or half full, or as a form of discrimination and hence a violation of foundational human rights, one must at least entertain the possibility that, as both interviews and court records suggest, this is not just a story of women losing out in a system that is invariably stacked against them.

4. THE COURTS ARE PLACES THAT HELP POORER WOMEN. The studies we possess also suggest that it is often relatively poor women, rather than those who are well-off, who bring their cases to court. People from higher status families often regard proceedings in open court as shameful—as washing one's dirty linen in public—and prefer alternative dispute resolution mechanisms.[90] This may involve the use of a go-between (*wāsiṭa*), asking a judge to hear the case informally, or filing papers through lawyers to start negotiations but not actually appearing in court. Particularly where the case involves a woman leaving her marital home, a man seeking his wife's forcible return, or disputes over details of personal finances, the more wealthy or positioned often prefer to treat these matters outside of the public eye.[91]

A number of scholars have suggested, then, that Islamic courts have long been primarily oriented toward poorer women's concerns. Drawing on her studies of the Ottoman records, Judith Tucker writes: "In general, the muftis and courts chose the approach that led away from confrontation and conflict and toward harmony in the community, as well as the protection of its weaker members."[92] Donald P. Little writes of an earlier period: "That women of apparently humble status in late fourteenth-century Jerusalem had ready and sympathetic recourse to its judges and courts is no longer earthshaking in light of recent scholarship on the status of medieval Muslim women but is interesting nonetheless."[93] Najwa Al-Qattan's study of Ottoman records from Damascus in the years 1785–1860 shows that Jews as well as women commonly found favor: "The court often provided weaker individuals with legal protection against those who were tempted to use religion, gender, or ignorance of the law to reap undue advantage."[94] Tucker does acknowledge that officials favored the social status quo and male prerogatives: "Still, their ability to respond with flexibility, creativity, and even compassion to concrete legal problems in their communities remains a hallmark of their approach to the practice of law."[95]

Protection of the weaker party is not merely some high-toned ideal, but an emphasis, as Haim Gerber has put it, on "compassion for [the] weak and needy" that has long characterized Islamic law.[96] Similarly, Nahda Shehada says of the Gaza courts: "Concern for protecting the rights of the weak, while maintaining social harmony, is a principle pervading the system."[97] Indeed, Iris Agmon claims that the notion of social justice constitutes an organizing principle in shari'a courts. That is to say, within the patriarchal framework of Islamic family law, the courts (i.e., the qadis) make an effort to protect and defend the needy and the weak. The patriarchal gender hierarchy is not challenged by this policy, but the weaker parties usually improve their situation following the litigation in court (hence the appropriateness of the term "bargaining with patriarchy"). Agmon further relates this tendency to the "user friendliness" of the shari'a court (an attribute which allows even an uneducated litigant to present her or his case in court).[98] As deputy qadi Mahmud Salama of Gaza told a researcher about choosing candidates for the bench: "Another important issue is the fact that the *sharī'a* court is mostly used by poor people, particularly women. *Qadāh* [judges] should be sensitive and empathetic and able to convey the ethical message of Islam when communicating with them."[99]

This compassion may also be strategically placed, for the overriding concern in Muslim cultures is often the fear of *fiṭna*, chaos, that unraveling of the associations people have negotiated among themselves which binds them together—however contentiously, however variably—into a community of believers. And since the primary goal of the qadis' courts, it may be argued, is often to place people back into workable relationships—in which they continue to negotiate their own ties—the quest for an at least momentarily peaceful resolution is consonant with coming to the assistance of the relatively powerless party to the dispute, usually the woman.[100] The result may indeed be to command her to return to her husband as a condition of receiving support owed her, or it may be to give official sanction to her having (in effect) to purchase her husband's divorce by forgiving a debt. But the result is still for her to receive *some* remedy she sought from the court rather than be entirely disadvantaged.[101] If, then, the courts serve, in whatever part, as a counterbalance to the powers of men this may account for the high degree of frequency with which women win at least a substantial portion of the cases they have brought.

5. LEGAL PROCEDURES AND PRESUMPTIONS WORK IN FAVOR OF WOMEN. Islamic law, whatever its emphasis on substantive legal propositions, focuses a good deal of attention on the modes by which evidence is adduced, the assumptions about persons and events deployed, and the presumptions by

which courts approach factual uncertainties. Presumptions that can work in women's favor include recognizing the legitimacy of a marriage wherever possible or permitting a woman to take a decisory oath that cuts off a man's claim.[102] Ziba Mir-Hosseini, writing about postrevolutionary Iran, describes the time when she addressed a question to the presiding judge on behalf of a woman who did not understand precisely what it meant for her to be "obedient" to her husband while bringing a suit for support: "'I know the court's presumption is that a wife is in tamkin [in fulfillment of her wifely duties] as long as she stays in the marital home. But what happens, for instance, if a wife says she is in tamkin but her husband says she is not? Whose word does the court accept?' The judge replies, 'The wife's, of course.'"[103] Maaike Voorhoeve writes of Tunisia: "One of the family judges indicated that if the wife files for divorce without grounds or if she abandons the marital home, the court gives the wife the benefit of the doubt, leaving it to the husband to prove that he is not violent with her, and indeed, this is done on the grounds of *sharia*."[104] Similarly, in a case from Egypt in 1954 a judge ruled in favor of a wife who worked outside of the home because such labor may be presumed to be in the public interest and the husband had not explicitly insisted on his priority right to control such activity.[105]

Judges may also shift the burden of proof away from women when the court, in its discretion, denominates one or another party as the "plaintiff" who bears that burden, for whoever is designated the one most likely to know the facts in the case may also be the one entitled to take a decisory oath and thus summarily win the case.[106] Additionally, many Muslim countries now place the burden on the husband who wishes to take an additional wife to prove his need for one. Malaysian national law, for example, states: "Before permission can be granted for [a husband] to engage in polygamy he has to prove that the intended polygamous marriage is 'just and necessary,' that he has the financial means to support all his wives and dependents, that he would be able to accord equal treatment to all his wives, that the proposed marriage would not cause harm to any existing wife in respect of her religion, life, body, mind, morals or property, and there would be no reduction in the standard of living of the exiting wife and dependents."[107] Evidence may also favor women in that it is often assumed that all household items were part of the woman's trousseau even if acquired after marriage, and thus remain with her in the event of divorce or widowhood.

Other procedures may also work to women's benefit. Though it can result in considerable delay women may have a greater chance to prevail when men fail to show up for hearings or cannot be served with a court notice. Judith Tucker shows, too, that the Ottoman courts of Syria and Palestine commonly allowed women not only to retain custody of a child despite rules favoring the husband's kin but even to oversee the finances relating to that child.[108] Similarly, most countries allow provisions to be inserted in the marriage contract that, for example, grant the woman the power to effect a divorce.[109] Procedures like these are by no means uniform or always to the woman's advantage: They may also incorporate requirements imposed on women that are not equivalent to those affecting men.[110] But women who are disfavored by the substantive law (e.g., in that they cannot arbitrarily divorce their husbands) may prevail, at least in part, because of procedural elements that may or may not have received textual elaboration or codification.

Indeed, Muslim judges, in their discretion, frequently open the bounds of relevance quite widely, and in the process hear more fully about the woman's situation and its context.[111] They may seek a basis for reconciling the parties, in accord with Quranic injunctions, or seek the underlying basis of a dispute that may only tangentially be about the marital relations as such.[112] June Starr reports of Bodrum, Turkey, that in those cases where the judges feel that "social relationship factors are overwhelmingly convincing . . . the violation of a legal norm is considered less important than the social relationship aspects of the case. . . . In cases of this type, the judge attempts to create structure and introduce values into relationships where social norms have dissolved, are ambiguous, weakly developed, or never occurred."[113] This broadened search for information may render the judges more favorably disposed toward female litigants, both for having heard their personal stories and for having learned about the broader societal repercussions of the decision to be made. In one study of the issuance of advisory opinions in Egypt, for example, Hussein Agrama reports: "When a person came with a question, the mufti [of the Fatwa Council of al-Azhar] would very often ask more general questions about the person's situation before he formulated an answer. Many times, I would see the mufti listening carefully, and allowing the questioner to talk at length. There was a sense that he was fashioning his answer to the specific situation of the questioner. This may have partly explained why sometimes different answers were given to similar questions."[114] Cases drawn from the use of binding arbitration in Syria also indicate that, whether in an attempt to determine the facts and the sentiments of the parties or as a way of trying to mediate their dispute, the court-appointed arbitrators seek a wide array of information in the course of their inquiries.[115]

A corollary to opening the bounds of relevance concerns the style of person perception that is quite common in regions of North Africa and the Middle East.[116] For while people may initially be assessed in terms of a category into which they fit, the quest for information commonly extends to a wide range of a person's knowledge and social relationships. Thus a woman who might not be entitled under the law to custody of a child, if she is better educated or employed than the spouse, may be awarded custody in furtherance of the belief that to do so is in the best interests of the child. By thus partaking of a broader cultural scheme for appraising persons women may, in an appreciable number of instances, also come out as the beneficiaries.[117]

Other countries employ compulsory conciliation, in which the parties must go before intermediaries. But, however much they may be pressured to accede to the intermediaries' approach, the disputants are not bound by their recommendations.[118] Compulsory conciliation—as in Egypt, Iran, Syria, and Tunisia—may also expand a woman's ability to state her claim, and the possibility exists (for example, in the Egyptian case) that since one of the conciliators must be a woman and both must be trained professionals the complaining woman may have a better opportunity to be heard.[119] Arguably, the greater the search for information and the more particularized the approach of judge or advisory opinion writer the more a woman's situation and personal difficulties will come to the attention of the listener, and quite possibly contribute to an opinion that is favorable to the woman. Agrama, however, expresses some concern: "Do women now have the protection of the law? Or on the contrary, do women and their rights continue to be *abandoned to* the law, its endless proliferation, its incessant suspicion, the uncertainties of its ever-present exception, and its continual entanglement in the question of religion and politics?"[120] Similarly, in Malaysia, where the Islamic figure (*kadi*) acts more as an arbitrator while a separate figure denominated as the judge enters formal decisions, researchers note:

> As for the task of fact-finding, the *kadi*, having to listen to candid confessions, arguments and statements of the disputing parties, often is able to reconstruct those events that lead to a conflict much more realistically than can the judge. The latter is quite unable to do this because he can only probe into those relationships between the parties involved which the *Syariah* [Islamic law] has predetermined as capable of causing conflict. Therefore, not only is the judge incapable of finding out the range of events that lead to the case at hand but

> more often than not he ends up collecting information about events which may not have occurred at all. Although both the *kadi* and the judge take Islamic law as their point of reference, the decisions produced by the former represent a more realistic and pragmatic attempt at finding solutions to the problem at hand than those issued by the judge. The latter's concern, we argue, is not so much with understanding the real problem, and those aspects of social relationships within and outside the family from which trouble arises, as in applying the appropriate *Syariah* laws.[121]

Indeed, since most Muslims regard their customary practices not as separate from Islamic law but *as* Islamic, the positions of the classical schools and their personnel may get inextricably entwined with local custom. For example, in Libya, John Davis points out "how improbable it is that at any time in this period [1932–79] people who went to law saw themselves as engaged in a struggle between custom and proper law. . . . They did not see themselves as giving up a coherent body of Customary Law that covered all aspects of human and divine relations in favour of a different and alternative *sharī'a* Law. Nor did they see themselves as partisans of one law, losing a struggle against another sort of law."[122] It would, therefore, be a mistake to ignore the vital role played by custom, which in many cases not only takes precedence over all but the most central of shari'a precepts but affords additional tools that judges can use to ameliorate or exacerbate the situation of local women.[123]

6. IT IS NOT WOMEN WHO ARE BEING "FAVORED," BUT MEN WHO ARE BEING CONTROLLED. There are those who would argue that both "traditional" Islamic legal systems and their contemporary state-dominated manifestations are not so much attending to the needs of women as they are attempting to control the acts of men, particularly as they may threaten the state. Frances Hasso notes: "I view state-initiated marriage and family projects as largely functioning to manage life, resources, and behavior for purposes of efficient rule. Codification and other rationalizing mechanisms have increased the centrality of these undemocratic states and their opportunities for intervention in the most intimate aspects of daily life."[124] Hasso continues: "While MENA [Middle East and North African] states are often recognized by feminists to support a patriarchal agenda, they only do so to the degree that such a system reinforces state interests. Indeed, it is men and not women who state authorities and religious elites are more likely to consider threatening to family and social stability. Allowing men

patriarchal authority within their families is a useful means to assuage and manage them, given that these states are generally minimally accountable to their citizens."[125] Such an approach may be grounded on the belief that men are creatures of reason whereas women are seen as subject to their passions, a notion that may be enshrined in law, as exemplified by the memorandum on Article 56 of the United Arab Emirates' Personal Status Law which explicitly states that a man's domestic authority arises out of his ability to "reason" and "control his emotions," qualities lacking in women.[126]

That Muslim courts may, however, alter their substantive approaches in terms of these categories is not without interest. Instances could be cited, therefore, of Muslim judges who favor child custody for a woman over that prescribed by law for the man when it is the wife who is more educated and hence more capable of expressing reason than her unlettered or unemployed husband. In other situations men may have to pay more in compensation to their wives because of surrounding circumstances. However, that fact alone may actually carry the dual implication of state control over men's conduct and reinforcement of women's dependent status.[127] Whether courts are actually balancing women's abilities against deference to men as a way of diverting potential challenges by the latter to state and religious authorities may, therefore, depend more on one's interpretations than on any set of determinable facts. In a number of instances, however, it is quite clear that when states have been perceived as interfering too much in a man's sense of his domestic control sharp reactions have indeed occurred.[128] In other instances—Iran, for example—the state may attempt to be no more than the umpire in private contestations, thus seeking to avoid any blame for undesired rulings and hence any risk to its own legitimacy. Proving that such interpretations are true from the record of judicial proceedings in family law courts is probably impossible. But to the extent that both the state and religious authorities do have a vested interest in the distribution of powers, within and beyond the family, the possibility that the balance of deference may indeed be affected by the assumptions of human nature in the service of those in power is an interpretation that cannot be dismissed out of hand.

7. THE CONCERN IS MORE WITH JUSTICE THAN WITH LAW. It could be argued that what the courts are doing is pursuing a very distinctive concept of justice, one that is based not on equality in the sense of treating all parties identically, but on treating people *equivalently*—that is, according to what

is appropriate to persons of their category. Indeed, the word in Arabic (*musāwāh*) that means "equivalence" (and which comes from a root meaning "to smooth over," "to put in order," "to reconcile two persons") is also the term for "equality before the law." Most of the cases that come to court involve people who must first be placed in category, whether that is by gender, education, or other social and personal factors. Since most family law cases involve men versus women, and since the division of labor by gender often plays a role in their expected behavior, judges may start from a baseline of gender. But they then frequently modify their placement of the person and situation as additional background information is adduced. While often not acknowledging identical powers for men and women, judges frequently indicate that in order to effect what is true for the category of women it is indeed necessary and correct to weigh matters in a manner that, notwithstanding their inherently subsidiary status, may redound to women's benefit either because they are weak and dependent or because they have added to their gender-based status by education, work, or some other factor. In other instances, Muslim judges work with local concepts of what is fair or just. Noting that women won in all three of the inheritance cases described in his study, John Bowen writes: "The judges themselves did not justify their stance in legal terms . . . but [by] a set of everyday principles . . . [a] kind of equality [like] the fingers of a hand. . . . That village men and women work together in the fields, equally sharing the burdens and fruits of their manual labor, offers concrete proof that equality and fairness are appropriate bases for choosing among alternative interpretations of the law. . . . [Judges strive] to make the law fit with the norms of social life, and social life with the norms of the law."[129]

Thus the judgments that do favor women are part of the larger process and goal of weighing entities that in many, though not all, respects may be regarded as incommensurable in an attempt to achieve that concept of justice which is to be found by assessing equivalence. The evidentiary quest, then, is to match people to categories of personhood and circumstance, not to apply the same measures to all; the need is to approximate the felt sense of justice that, by refusing to reduce all persons to static categories, furthers the general sense of how society and Islam are meant to work. What we would need in order to understand this larger context, of course, would be a greater range of cases—those, for instance, in which a knowledgeable man is held to a higher standard than a poorly educated one (in much the way our mothers may have held us to a different standard because "you should know better") as well as cases involving a variety of different backgrounds and contexts. Just as women may hold the good opinion of men and their sense of "honor," so, too, they may test the sense of justice as a process of weighing equivalencies and succeed, in part, when that process takes precedence over a more generalized aversion to socially restricting stereotypes.

* * *

It is always difficult for scholars addressing the situation of women in Islamic law to appear, on the one hand, properly sensitive to the inequalities women encounter in the legal systems of the countries under consideration and, on the other, to stand back long enough to see precisely what these systems look like when observed in their everyday operation. Writing a generation ago, Andrea Rugh stated:

> Seen over time and cumulatively, the reforms in personal status laws reflect a gradual shift in the gravity of family life from a preponderance of the legal weight in favor of the husband's position to an increasing consolidation of the woman's position as central in the family. If we take this shift to represent where the valued social arenas lie—ones considered worthy of sustaining the battle until a strong foothold is gained—then Egyptian women's choice of family is in some ways comparable to American women's choice of public life as the place where consolidation of interests is worth the price.[130]

Such "progress" is, however, under-reported and uneven at best. For example, although Mohamed Morsi of Egypt, when he first took office as president, resigned from the Muslim Brotherhood (though not its political party), he reaffirmed that his government would not support the United Nations declaration against violence to women and never demurred from such statements as those by Osama Yehia Abu Salama, a Brotherhood family law expert, who said: "A woman needs to be confined within a framework that is controlled by the man of the house [and if her husband beats her] show her how she had a role in what happened. If he is to blame she shares 30 percent or 40 percent of the fault."[131] Moreover, "the law's delay," the costs and impediments to actual implementation of statutory changes, and the difficulties women often encounter in gaining enforcement of a court order can seriously undermine any formal victory in court.[132] Where, as in Malaysia, the secular courts are required to defer entirely to Muslim courts on matters of personal status a woman may also be denied remedies she might possess were she of another faith or able to bring an appeal.[133] In addition, it cannot be stressed too often that even if a woman 'wins' all or part of her case she may, enforcement issues aside, find herself (and her children) in greatly reduced circumstances for which no further remedies are available.

Yet it is also clear that reduction to simple stereotypes may seriously misrepresent the present and the past of women's legal situation both within and beyond the domain of family law. Thus, in addition to their work on matters of personal status many historians have questioned whether women's property rights may also have been more extensively protected by Muslim courts than previously thought: "Popular belief, if not serious scholarship, maintains that the position of women in pre-twentieth century Islamic society was an extremely depressed one," a belief, Gerber continues, that has been stubbornly adhered to by many Western scholars.[134] Noting that "it is difficult to overestimate the importance of the Islamic court and its archives to the history of family life in the urban centers of the Ottoman Empire," Beshara Doumani, using materials from Nablus and Tripoli in the 1720s and a century later, says that "a considerable number of legal disputes between kin are over properties that pass through the female, not male line. . . . One should not jump to the conclusion, however, that the vulnerability of property to conflicting claims is due solely or even predominantly to gender. The preponderance of such cases in the court records may be explained by the fact that the Islamic court could be counted on to uphold the right of women and their descendants to property in the face of opposing local customs and cultural ideals."[135] In his sampling of 47 civil court cases and 49 religious court cases involving family property from Aceh, Indonesia, in the 1940s to the 1990s, John R. Bowen, too, finds that women win in the former courts 72% of the time, men 28%, and in the latter courts women win 60% of their cases, men 40%. While noting that earlier and later courts may not be so conducive to women's property claims and that success, as we have seen elsewhere, depends greatly on who initiates the case, Bowen nevertheless concludes that "the overall data indicate that the Islamic court has worked in the interest of women."[136]

Similar suggestions have been made for the situation of women in the Maghreb and Andalusia. Maya Shatzmiller, for example, writes: "My finding that women's property rights in the Mālikī West were generally upheld despite the existence of certain legal constraints corroborates the findings of scholars who have studied women in the Ottoman Empire during later periods."[137] And while the situation remains unknown or far less favorable in certain countries, the data clearly indicate that courts are not immune to the continual changes that affect women's financial and occupational, to say nothing of familial, concerns.

The broader changes in women's economic and marital circumstances do not, then, exist in isolation from legal responses. Take just one example. The age of marriage has increased dramatically in numerous Muslim countries in recent years, with many women not marrying until their late twenties and many men until their thirties.[138] As the age of marriage for both men and women has increased and as more women have entered the public sphere, some countries (e.g., Morocco, Tunisia) have liberalized their laws while others (e.g., Jordan, Algeria, Iraq, Gaza, Turkey, Yemen) appear to have backtracked.[139] As more women enter the workplace the discrepancy between what the statutes and texts assume about marriage and the realities of actual married life may be substantial.[140] The proliferation of female lawyers in some countries, coupled with the use of female judges, conciliators, and instructors in women's legal rights—to say nothing of the work of various NGOs, online advice, and increasing female literacy—may also make many women feel more comfortable bringing their cases to court. At present 70% of the judges in Algeria are women and 60% of the lawyers, while 25% of judges in Morocco are women with well over a thousand women practicing law. Bahrain has announced its intention to replace Egyptian judges as part of an effort to achieve 50% women judges, the first woman lawyer was appointed in 2013 in Saudi Arabia, and women judges have been appointed even in Iran, Malaysia, and under the Palestinian Authority on the West Bank.[141]

As the formal legal context has varied so, too, the context for "bargaining in the shadow of the law" has undoubtedly varied. Data concerning attitudes toward change are nevertheless susceptible to more than one interpretation. Thus, a survey in March 2000 of some 1,200 randomly selected respondents in Gaza and the West Bank showed that when asked if they would like to see a law, like that in Egypt, that allows women to file for divorce if they waive their financial rights, 68% of the men said no but 63% of the women also said no. Moreover, "seventy-one per cent of women support women's rights to divorce as such, but the majority of them (44 per cent) think that women should not lose their property rights in order to do so. Among males, a lesser 61% support women's right to divorce as such, but only 28 per cent of those oppose women losing their property rights in order to do so."[142] This may, of course, be an example, in the words of one analyst, in which "the uncertainty of the unknown is more frightening than the unfairness of the known and therefore people are willing to sacrifice hopeful possibilities for practical realities."[143] As the rates of divorce in Muslim countries (and among Muslim immigrants to the West) have risen sharply in recent years the ability of Muslim courts and legislatures to respond is also being seriously tested.[144]

Notwithstanding these limitations it is vital that—without appearing either apologetic or insensitive—we face the situation of women in the Muslim courts as directly as possible, and set aside the stereotypes encountered in the West long enough to see what is actually occurring. Seen in this light the studies we possess indicate that the powers of the judges are not simply applied to the detriment of women. Shaham's assertion applies well beyond the confines of his particular example when he says: "Generally speaking, it seems that most Egyptian *qadis* were not a social avant-garde who initiated social reforms through their decision making. They were, however, attentive to social change and used the personal discretion afforded them by the *shari'a* to introduce to their courts a humanistic approach with respect to women and children."[145]

To speak of women "winning" may, as we have seen, draw too sharp a line. For while we can say that in a very large proportion of the cases women do achieve at least part of the claims they have taken to court, it might be just as appropriate to say that the available data only suggest that women are better off after having litigated their claims than they were before doing so. Both ways of conceptualizing the issue remain imprecise in the current state of our knowledge. No less importantly, neither a bare statistic—that is, women "win" a specified percent of the time—nor the assumption that Islamic law always disfavors women is enough, and only further unbiased research and thoughtful inquiry among the participants themselves will aid in a more realistic understanding of the actual role of Islamic law in the family lives of Muslim men and women.[146]

Nor should anyone imagine for a moment that even to the extent that women do prevail that they do so easily or without overcoming considerable obstacles. To the contrary, the fact that so many cases are not pursued to judgment, that many women are dissuaded from asserting their rights in the first place, and that when cases are brought there are often substantial pressures to avoid direct confrontation can only be read to suggest that women must have considerable courage, resources, and finesse to see matters through to a formal decision.[147] Nor is the full extent of forced marriage (often of rape victims or the underaged)—much less the true range of domestic violence, suicide, or those hounded into the demi-monde of prostitution and drug addiction—adequately considered even within the reported cases.[148] The Moroccan Ministry of Justice, for example, reports that each year judges grant some 30,000–40,000 exceptions for underage marriage, often as a result of the rape of the young girl.[149] So-called honor killings, which number in the thousands in countries like Pakistan, may be extrajudicial and completely unsupported by any passage in the Quran, yet it would be naive to suggest that they do not, in those instances, interact significantly with the formal elements of the law.[150] Not infrequently, too, changes in the legal code do not necessarily carry over into practice, where the recalcitrance of conservative judges or local custom may all but preclude the implementation of formal protections for women.[151]

In an age when women living under the Taliban, the Islamic State, or Boko Haram are subject to vicious attacks in the name of an Islam most believers regard as gravely distorted, one cannot be cavalier about the prospects for women's legal rights in a number of venues. Nevertheless, the evidence is compelling that women do indeed prevail in a striking number of instances in the courts of the Muslim world. If we in the West are to transcend our own stereotypes—and to limit their impact on policies affecting the Muslim world and the Muslims in our midst—it is imperative that studies of the actual state of matters be extended and their implications squarely addressed.

CHAPTER THREE

Parallel Worlds

Shadow Law and Political Culture in Morocco

Scholars have frequently noted the pluralistic nature of law, including in the Muslim world—the existence of alternative forums or personnel through which a dispute may be addressed.[1] *In many instances people have set up their own "courts" which may bear similarities to but are not staffed by state officials; in others respected elders or intermediaries provide alternatives to the formal courts. Both of these phenomena have received significant scholarly attention.*[2] *But little notice has been given to the occasional existence of a particular kind of parallel world of law, one in which the formal institutions of the state are avoided but parties nevertheless mimic the documentation and potential implications of the formal system, often through recourse to persons who are knowledgeable about or even involved in the official system.*

In the example to be explored, squatters in Morocco have often approached individuals who work with the state-run system to have them draw up purchase, construction, rental, and partnership contracts in the same form in which they could have been obtained from court notaries if the squatters' activities had been legal. Indeed, illicit settlers sometimes build their clandestine homes according to local building codes, even though these dwellings have no legal status. Similarly, they may approach any person they deem conversant with state-enforced law to prepare such documents—a local man working in a ministry in the capital, a respected businessman, or the stray anthropologist studying the courts.[3] *This shadow system may thus imitate state law or seek to fulfill professed state aims. The practice may also stem from distrust of the state or the perceived corruption of the legal system and governmental agents. Whatever the motivation and despite the lack of formal legal validity, parties are aware that some municipalities and courts do, on occasion, attend to these extralegal arrangements. Indeed, one reason for obtaining such documents is the hope that, like the construction itself, the arrangements will eventually be "regularized"—that is, brought within the ambit of state law because they accord with state-supported forms. In other instances, individuals track the formal legal system because documents they obtain carry meaning within their own circle even though they lack state-recognized legitimacy.*

Thus one is confronted with an intriguing world that is partially hidden from view, a world in which the law is mimicked yet not directly applied, a world in which the rules of law may be active but lack any formal enforcement, a world that shadows the "real world" of law and forms a context for the lives of many people of different levels of education and income. It is this world to which I want to turn our attention in some detail.

* * *

Youssef Halim runs a store on the main street of the Ville Nouvelle in the city of Sefrou, Morocco—a city currently numbering some eighty thousand people located about fifteen miles south of Fez. For many years the store was an *épicerie*, and though he now sells books and school supplies it still contains a tiny room at the back with barely enough space for Youssef's small desk and a couple of chairs. There, in the mid-1960s, when Youssef was one of my first language teachers and general informants, I would cram myself into the corner and watch as people came to him to arrange their property issues. For Youssef was not only a shopkeeper but the expert on land matters for the local court. In that capacity he drew on his experience working as a contractor with his father during the late colonial and early independence period, and was often commissioned by the court to measure and assess properties, certify boundaries, and advise on the terms of agreements. Many of the people who squeezed into his office were there to complete work related to court cases and the formalities of legal transfers. But Youssef was also concerned to have me observe another group of clients, people who had no legally cognizable claim to the land or houses where they lived but who nevertheless came to him to prepare documents concerning those properties.

Beginning primarily in the early 1960s people from the poorer sections of the old walled city, as well as immigrants from the countryside, had begun establishing squatter settlements around the periphery of the municipality. Such settlements were hardly new to Morocco and many other cities of the Middle East: The well-known *bidonvilles*—the squatter settlements with their corrugated roofs and bric-a-brac construction that still surround cities like Casablanca and Rabat—had existed for many years.[4] In Sefrou, too, several clandestine building sites also existed.[5] The pattern of development was one that was replicated in many places. On abandoned or unused land settlers would put up what appeared to be an animal enclosure of thorny branches. Then at night, hidden by the darkness and the corral, they would begin to construct dwellings. Sometimes they would start by building a small mosque—which might in turn be cleverly named for one of the king's sisters or children—and even attach some of the dwellings to one of its walls, reasoning that government bulldozers would be less likely to tear down a mosque and might thus leave the quarter itself intact.

The main settlement of this sort in Sefrou was referred to in those days as Cher Ben Seffar, the Berber term *cher* (pronounced with a hard *ch*, as in *cherry*, and meaning a small rural "settlement" or "hamlet") suggesting much about the look of the place and the imputed origins of many of its inhabitants. The land had been part of a French farm until a few years after Morocco gained independence in 1956, and though the more accessible parts of the land remained under cultivation the portion that slopes down toward the northeastern edge of the city had been gradually populated by squatters. The area was formally under the rural administrator (*qaid*) in charge of the zone stretching well back of the city into the Middle Atlas Mountains, the territory mainly of the Ait Youssi tribe. In fact, however, the settlement wound up as a sort of administrative no-man's land. The government-appointed mayor of the city (or *pasha*, as he was then called) wanted nothing to do with the settlement—in terms of either supplying it with water and other utilities or of overseeing its affairs—and the *qaid*, too, wanted no responsibility for it. So, the settlement grew apace, formally ignored by all of officialdom.

Unlike the more temporary-looking *bidonvilles*, however, Cher Ben Seffar was gradually being constructed of solid materials—concrete blocks, more permanent roofs, and even second stories. More intriguingly, even though the settlements were illegal and unrecognized, many of the residents found their way to Youssef in the process of establishing their dwellings. There, hunkered in the back office, they would have Youssef draw up documents concerning their land or houses just like those used in the regular courts. The paperwork might refer to boundary lines, proportions of ownership, or any other provision common to legally viable contracts about land or buildings. Moreover, the parties would consult with Youssef about the existing building codes and would commonly build their residences in conformity with those codes. They knew perfectly well that there was no formally enforceable basis to any of these actions. Nevertheless, the reasons they gave for this practice made sense in a certain way.

First, they said, they hoped that by following the formal rules the city would be more likely to recognize their property holdings as lawful and would supply them with electricity, sewerage, and (most particularly) water, which otherwise had to be carted in from distant municipal sources. Such strategies are hardly unique to Morocco. In Cairo, where two-thirds of the population live in squatter settlements, residents not only tap into utilities illegally and are then charged for them but in one area they even built their own on-ramp to the main circle route and later had it made official through the appropriate government agency. Secondly, the residents of Cher ben Seffar argued that custom is not separate from law but is an integral aspect of it. They would refer to various maxims to support the notion that practice *is* law as well as citing propositions deeply embedded in Islamic law. People would say, for example, that "when you are away your right (*ḥaqq*) is away," which suggests that an unattended claim is not automatically entitled to enforceability and hence that land whose putative owner does not assiduously and continually assert his claims may be appropriated by those who make beneficial use of it. Another Moroccan saying they employed is that "a contractual stipulation takes precedence over the shari'a (*shert kat-ḥakem 'al shra'*),"[6] a proposition whose equivalent can be found in virtually all Muslim countries and periods of time Indeed, it is a proposition that underscores both the consistency of sacred law with the Quran's emphasis on contractual relations and, in the Moroccan case, the Maliki version of the shari'a with its emphasis on that which is socially beneficial (*istiṣlāḥ, istiḥsān*).[7] Additionally, local custom may—as in the case of local inheritance practices—trump even Quranic propositions. Thus Moroccans, like many other Muslims, will assert that "our custom *is* our form of shari'a," a claim that carried special force when, in the early 1930s, the French colonial regime attempted to divide Berbers from Arabs by placing the former under Berber customary law and the latter under the shari'a, only for many of the Berbers to join in revolt asserting that their custom *is* shari'a.[8]

The fact, too, that the squatters obtained written documents, even though many of the people were not literate, added to the feeling that what they were doing had some predictability and legitimacy if only in terms of their own informal standards. On occasion, then, these documents could be produced before mediators or others to support their claims. In each instance the squatters saw in their actions a way to express the belief that local practices that do not contradict some indisputably clear divine ordinance (e.g., that there is only one God and Muhammad is the last of His prophets) are not only consonant with shari'a but *are* shari'a. By combining the existing codes with the principle that practice is law, they envisioned their relationships as "legal" and potentially susceptible to administrative recognition.

But there is another cultural element at work in this connection. For Moroccans it is the person who makes propositions credible, not the other way around. Whether it is a witness in court or an expert to whom one attends, it is by constructing a web of worldly consequential associations that a man comes to be believed. Being an officeholder may certainly add to one's store of credibility, but it is not to the office that people address themselves but to the whole person for whom that attachment is only one of the many features that define him. The idea, therefore, that one might act only in a given role rather than amalgamate one's position with all the other attachments one possesses is almost unimaginable. By using Youssef, who is both a quasi-official and a locally admired and scrupulously honest expert, the squatters could thus support their claims by adding that personal element—the involvement of a man of consequence—which is so crucial to legitimizing almost any kind of action in Moroccan culture.[9]

Although the squatters' hopes for official recognition encountered frustrating delay at the administrative level, they were, given the cultural features outlined, exposed to less hostility from some of the judges in the state-run courts. For example, I once mentioned this tendency to seek documents through Youssef to the chief judge of the district, a man who later served as a high court justice. I suggested that the efforts of the squatters were a feckless practice since the documents had no legal validity. The judge's exact words were very striking: "We cannot leave these people outside of the law (*ma-imken-l-nash n-khali-hum ʻal b-rʻa shrʻa*)." In fact, he said, he would be willing to recognize their paperwork in various kinds of land disputes or inheritance situations. By his assertion—and particularly his use of the (colloquially pronounced) word for *shariʻa*, rather than mere "custom" (*qāʻida*, *ʻurf*) or state-generated rules (*qānūn*)—he was, in a sense, ratifying both the squatters' strategy and the propositions to which they had reference, not because he (any more than other judges) believed that law and custom are utterly separable entities but precisely because he shared the overarching emphasis on local practice as essential to preserving orderly relations, a goal he said was at the heart of the shariʻa itself.[10]

Although I have not been able to identify in the court records any cases that clearly turn on a squatter agreement as such, it is my understanding from clerks and from Youssef that such cases do arise under general contract terms and are dealt with by court officials informally, as when they act as mediators who employ their official position to conduce an out of court settlement (*ṣulḥ*) between the parties.[11] It may also be relevant to note that the courts are highly dependent on experts like Youssef for all sorts of matters—for example, level of support for a wife of a given social standing, the appropriate bridewealth when a judge oversees a dependent's marriage, the physical condition of a woman claiming abuse—and hence their concern with local practice is integral to the application of Moroccan law generally. The chief judge's willingness to enforce such agreements no doubt gained further support by virtue of the fact that the use of such parallel approaches to authority are also to be found in other domains of Moroccan life. Since culture and law always have reciprocal effects it is, therefore, important to appreciate just how these parallel approaches play out in the broader context of Moroccan political culture.[12]

The parallel system of law gains further support from the fact that it is a political style that is not restricted to the realm of the courts. It is thus quite common, for example, for Moroccans to go to an official from their home region who has been placed in another location in order to have their disputes resolved, a practice Clifford Geertz once called the "shadow qaid" system.[13] The practice, as I have suggested, is related to the fact that in Morocco the office one holds is generally regarded less as a depersonalized institution than as an aspect of the personhood of the individual who momentarily occupies it. Any such "shadow qaid" pattern is, then, not a simple locational issue. Rather, it demonstrates that anyone who has become a "big man" may find that people come to him regardless of location to help with their problems. An example may help.

In the late 1960s, a man named Qaid Said (from the Ait Zaikum fraction of the Ait Youssi tribe, but formally *qaid* in the separate Ain Dalia region of the Middle Atlas Mountains) would often be sought out by people from his home area who were involved, in most instances, in a property dispute. The *qaid* would sometimes address the issue himself, though on other occasions he would arrange for descendants of a local saint (pl. *shurfā*) to meet with the parties. While other officials used their displaced position to firm up support in their home region, in truth, people said, Qaid Said was unusual in that he was careful not to intrude too much on the prerogatives of the *qaid* in whose jurisdiction the property was located. Because Said was also regarded by many as the unofficial head of the Ait Youssi tribe, and because he was an important figure in the Movement Populaire political party (the so-called Berber Party) who had been imprisoned by the French during the struggle for independence and was a close ally of King Hassan II, it would be a mistake to think of him solely in terms of his position as *qaid*. Rather, his is an example of someone who cumulated many attachments such that, whatever else, people might go to him regardless of where his official power lay to address disputes in his home region.[14] The pattern was hardly limited to the 1960s: Informants insist that it is common up to the present.

Thus, in Morocco it is not roles that define persons but the concatenation of their webs of indebtedness.[15] To seek a person who has no formal power in one locale but has fashioned his ties to acquire power elsewhere gives to such an individual that air of being a big man—a person of "word," to use the Moroccan idiom—whose credibility may carry over into multiple domains. And when one adds to this the Moroccan penchant to travel to whatever location may prove most effective to one's purpose it is not uncommon to seek such an intermediary wherever he may be found. Notwithstanding the government's attempt to move officials from their home territories lest they favor those to whom they are attached by local ties of kinship or alliance, the fact is that such officeholders may act informally as conduits for dispute settlement among people who seek them out in the territories far from the home area they share. Whether it is best to refer to what is at issue here as a "system," a "practice," an "occasion," or a "pattern" of displaced political authority, it is clear that seeking multiple yet interrelated sources for managing one's affairs is further supported by its manifestation in the parallel world of law.

The use of an intermediary whose formal power lies in a different location may, of course, further legitimize the state system. The use of a respected intermediary (*wasīṭa*) is a common practice throughout the Arab world and the sanctions they can be brought to bear by such an individual add markedly to whatever powers of personal persuasion a go-between may possess. Thus, such a person may be connected to the litigants by ties of kinship, residence, economic involvement, or political alliance, and all of these crosscutting attachments may be utilized to get one or both parties to accept the suggested resolution. But an intermediary who also occupies some official position is in a different position from other kinds of intermediaries because he might be able to use his official attachments to enforce his recommendation in ways non-officials cannot. The air of officialdom is an add-on that makes it possible to imagine that some recognizably official form of enforcement may attend this person's approach. The result may, however, only increase the ambiguity of the situation, since involving the state is not always desirable—either for the disputants or the official. As we saw with Qaid Said, balancing the formal and informal systems is a delicate game, but the displaced use of a formal official, though sharing many features with the informal use of an intermediary, opens the possibility for yet another variant of the parallel system of law that affords disputants a range of mechanisms for addressing their differences.

Squatters and users of alternative personnel and procedures are not the only examples of a parallel world of law. Migrants working in Europe, for example, frequently obtain documents from Morocco even though by meeting the host country's formalities they have conformed to the only legal requirements that would render their arrangements enforceable under various bilateral treaties.[16] Indeed, such migrants commonly obtain not just documents notarized by the court back in Morocco but some piece of paper drawn up by a noteworthy figure that asserts a claim of status or property holding. Again, such papers may or may not be honored by Moroccan courts, but they do serve to regularize relationships and to attach people to the credibility of those issuing these documents and to their potential enforceability by state-backed institutions. Women migrants in particular, seem eager to obtain such documents, reasoning that any claim they may subsequently put forth will have greater credibility the more they are able to obtain proof of support from respected figures back home.[17]

Other examples show the range of variation along these same parameters. In Israel there is an organization that, even though the state does not allow same-sex civil unions, issues a document with the pictures of both parties. Also on it is an affidavit simply stating that they are a committed couple. The document has no legal value, but people will show it when, for example, visiting a partner at a hospital. This is another example in which the lines between state and informal realms are blurred. As in illegal settlements, those who seek such documentation for their personal relationships may think of these informal regimes as ones they want the state to eventually recognize (and thus, for now, they mimic state forms) or because they simply want some sort of orderliness to their relationships whose style may be superficially similar to that of the state but of such different meaning as to be a counter to the state.[18]

Parallel worlds of law may, then, exist in many forms—as the antithesis of the state, as supplementary models of the state, or as alternatives that co-exist alongside the state. The implications of their existence are as varied as their forms, but it is worth considering, in general terms, what some of these may be.

PARALLEL SYSTEMS MAY SUPPORT THE LEGITIMACY OF STATE-BASED INSTITUTIONS. If imitation is the sincerest form of flattery then any type of alternative legal setting that tracks the official system's rules and forms may be seen as a compliment paid to it. Thus even though it may constitute a way of avoiding the cost, delay, corruption, or publicity of the state-run system, the use of the state's forms by an informal system adds legitimacy to those employed by the state. Of course, in the case of the Moroccan squatters the mimicked form may leap over the state to what is conceived (or at least rationalized) as the shari'a itself, but to the extent that state-run courts are the predominant enforcers of the shari'a support for a common set of documents may actually add to the state's claim to legitimacy.[19]

This may be particularly so if parties are (to borrow a popular concept from the law and society literature) "bargaining in the shadow of the law."[20] That is, if they are forging their ties with an eye to what the law would make of their situation—each, perhaps, using the threat, fear, or expectation of the formal law's approach as a tool to gain advantage or security—this act alone would appear to strengthen the reach of the law, however indirectly. The desire for judicial validation may be present in the squatters' agreements or attention to existing codes, although in the Moroccan case the evidence suggests that the emphasis is less on how a court to which a dispute may later be taken would handle the case than how such arrangements may contribute to administrative regularization.

PARALLEL SYSTEMS MAY UNDERMINE THE LEGITIMACY OF STATE-BASED INSTITUTIONS. The very fact that people avoid state institutions may suggest a lack of confidence in them, an unwillingness to consign one's fate to these institutions alone. If someone avoids the official who has jurisdiction over a given person or issue, if one constructs agreements through respected persons who lack any state-backed enforcement power, and if one does so because the procedures or rules of the law feel unfair or unfamiliar, its personnel corrupt or its employment costly, the result can only be to call into question, and thus weaken, the claim of the state to be operating for the well-being or with the consent of the governed. The challenge to the state may not be direct, but in time alternative forums may take on such an important role in a people's institutional life as to displace state-run institutions altogether.

In its most extreme form a completely separate set of courts from those of the state may develop. Various jihadist groups—whether in Afghanistan, Somalia, or Syria/Iraq—have fabricated such courts and used them as a direct challenge to state power.[21] In other instances the sheer existence of an alternative forum may be seen as an implicit attack on the state. So, for example, the disputes over the creation of Islamic courts in North America, Britain, and Europe have occasioned pointed criticism and proposed legislation by those who feel that the concept of a unified national legal system is being undermined. In such circumstances, alternative forums may operate within the existing system as mediational panels whose decisions may or may not be recognized by state courts, or as religious panels that can only concern themselves with issues internal to the religion as a voluntary association. Obviously, form alone does not determine the extent to which those who avail themselves of these alternatives regard their choice as consistent with religious or cultural attachment, opposition to the overarching state, or features of both.

THE USE OF PARALLEL SYSTEMS SIMULTANEOUSLY STRENGTHENS AND WEAKENS STATE POWER. It may seem odd to suggest that parallel structures simultaneously strengthen and weaken belief in the formal law and its statist claims. But since such a possibility is neither logically nor sociologically impossible, it may in fact be precisely the result when certain cultural features are taken into consideration. Here I have recourse to the argument I have formulated elsewhere, that there is a deep-seated ambivalence to power in Arab cultures, that a kind of "tribal ethos" lends credence to the belief that power should not remain too long in too few hands, and that there are numerous practices—from humor and bargaining stratagems to conceptions of time and mechanisms for keeping all options available—that contribute to such a cultural emphasis.[22] We may even be seeing a manifestation of this dispersal of power in the belief in the parallel world of the *jnun* (sing. *jinn*, the creatures of the netherworld elaborated in the Quran) since their emphasis by women and the poor often work as a threat and limitation on those who wield power over them.[23] The dispersal of power across parallel domains is also seen in the not uncommon practice of placing one son in one political party or religious brotherhood (*zāwiya*) and another in a rival organization, both as a hedge against lack of affiliation with the powerful and as a check on such powers. Informants in Casablanca thus recently explained their inconstant voting behavior by telling an inquiring anthropologist that they did not want to be coopted by any one political party, preferring instead to insure that power was divided. Since context, personal disposition, and perceived implications affect parties differently, their shared sense that power must always be approached while keeping alternatives alive contributes to the retention of parallel structures as a hedge against the limitations of powerful individuals and as a vital aspect of that repertoire of relational possibilities a free man needs if he is to move to effect in a highly changeable world of relationships.

Consistent with this cultural emphasis is the recognition that parallel tracks may also have occasional crossover points. For example, litigants may bring a case involving divorce in the state court at the same time that an associated property dispute is being pursued through the parallel process, and the strategy and outcome of the one may significantly affect the other. In a sense, then, simultaneous opportunities and institutions may be employed, each of which may reinforce or undermine the other. Using multiple avenues simultaneously or sequentially may also be another manifestation of the general ambivalence to power insofar as it may limit the state monopolization of all avenues of redress.

In the realm of parallel structures, then, this very ambivalence to power finds great cultural support. Parallel practices reinforce the basic norms of law while simultaneously diversifying the bases of power so that relationships can remain open-ended, subject to maneuver, and free from totally centralized control.[24] The further implication follows that this is a dynamic aspect of political culture, one that can no more be pinned down to singular institutions or their momentary personnel than can the moves in a game of chess. Though rules do exist they stand in service of maneuverability, and in the case of Moroccan culture the image of a free man as one who can seek advantage in whatever forum or relationship best suits the moment has enormous cultural currency.

NEITHER THE STATE NOR GROUPS — WHETHER RELIGIOUS OR POLITICAL — CAN FULLY CONTAIN THE PENCHANT FOR PARALLEL ALTERNATIVES. Non-state institutions—whether political parties, NGOs, or religious movements—may, of course, seek to incorporate this pattern of parallel law into their own programs. Indeed, they may use such mechanisms to assert even greater legitimacy than the state itself is accorded. Here one could point to those fundamentalist groups that have put together a range of non-state services, including medical facilities and disaster aid. Whether as organized parties or informal organizations, fundamentalists play on the corruption of the state system to attract adherents. Such corruption has increased exponentially in recent years in Morocco, as throughout the Arab world, where any court case may now require the payment of bribes simply to get a convenient place on the docket or to have paperwork completed in a timely fashion. By contrast, the fundamentalists not only offer a certain degree of legitimacy to their law-like activities but hope to appear much freer of corruption than the state system.[25]

It is, frankly, unclear to what extent people are resorting to leaders within the fundamentalist movements to attend to their property arrangements and disputes, though they do appear in a number of instances to consult with members of such groups about family matters. All we know is that in various parts of the Muslim world recourse to fundamentalist organizations rather than state institutions for matters of personal status does not appear to be uncommon.[26] Bear in mind, however, that even where states are relatively strong and stable, government-funded social support systems are minimal and state institutions are often perceived as corrupt. Parallel worlds of law and administration no doubt exist in such places and would reward closer study. Whatever these studies may show to be the case, it would be wise, however, to assume that there will be countervailing currents to the momentary claims of legitimacy, and that leveling devices, alternative centers of power, and intensely person-centered practices will prevail over—or at least stand in the wings as a counter to—the claim of any depersonalized institutions.

* * *

Cher Ben Seffar has changed a great deal over the decades. Wandering through it now one certainly would not think of it as a squatter settlement: The houses are of durable materials, and the streets and shops lend it the appearance of a quarter of the city like any other. By the late 1990s the popular name of the settlement had changed to *L'Mexique*, perhaps reflecting its poorer rural immigrant population or as an ironic counter to *Californie,* the name given to one of the fanciest quarters in Casablanca. Whatever may be the etymology of its new name, a number of factors have contributed to the overall change in the status of the settlement. Within the last couple of years the head of the municipality—now, for the first time, elected by popular ballot and called "head of the municipal council" (*ra'īs l-baladīya*) rather than *pasha*—actively brought the settlement within the ambit of the city boundaries and supplied it with municipal services. A member of the successor to the communist party and eager for transparency in all of the city's actions, he rendered the area administratively no different from other parts of Sefrou.[27] However, new squatter settlements have grown up in still less desirable areas, mainly on the steep hillsides above the Fez road, where, as in Cher Ben Seffar previously, water and electricity are unavailable.[28] How much the use of a parallel set of documents and mimicry of the urban regulations contributed to the regularization of Cher Ben Seffar itself is impossible to specify precisely, but everyone—from the mayor to the residents—attributes at least a portion of the result to this parallel practice.

The existence of such parallel worlds of law thus raises intriguing issues of comparison, including the relation of such mechanisms to the reinforcement of ties of kin and community, the relation of such practices to the changing sources of legitimate authority, the use of procedures and propositions drawn from Islamic law and applied within this parallel world, and the use of innovative vehicles for enforcement in the absence of state sanctions. As in the famous nineteenth-century satirical novel *Flatland: A Romance of Many Dimensions*, in which those who are able to see multiple dimensions deride the monarch for his inability to see but one, the squatters may have appreciated that in a multifaceted view of their situation lies their greatest security. But the state may also have tolerated parallel tracks for their mutual benefits and because, in a world in which socio-logic is not the same as mathematical or philosophical logic, parallel worlds may not have to wait until infinity to intersect. For those engaged in nation building the existence of such parallel structures may, then, serve as an additional source for development, a way of attending to one's own track by watching the other's carefully, or as an unnoticed end-run by each on the state or its uncertain institutions.

Youssef died in the summer of 2015. But to the last he sat in his back office and people from the newer squatter areas came to him at times for documents that look real, feel real, and undoubtedly have real repercussions. To them this is no less the world of law and political culture than are the mayor's office or the courts. It is in this parallel world that a not insignificant part of the law may continue to reside in a number of Muslim countries: To ignore it is to risk having a truncated view of the life of the law in these cultures.

CHAPTER FOUR

Back to the Future?

Muslim-Jewish Partnerships

When I began working in the land registry office in Fez, I was surprised to encounter a number of properties that were jointly owned by Muslims and Jews. Then when I began to read the records of the qadis' courts I was further surprised to discover cases in which two Jews came to Muslim courts rather than those of their own faith. And when I began reading about Muslim-Jewish commercial and legal relationships over the course of the centuries I was confirmed in my amazement at the frequency with which members of the two confessional communities engaged in commercial transactions that included the use of one another's legal concepts, personnel, and proceedings.

This astonishment says as much about my own initial naïveté about the history of communal relations in North Africa and the Middle East as it does about the stereotypes commonly possessed by Westerners about these relationships. Hence I was prompted to look more closely at the specific economic and juridical ties among members of these two groups. Understandably, given the near total departure of Jews from these lands in recent times, the issues would seem to be only of historical interest. But as one listens to older Muslims and émigré Jews tell of the close and workable ties they often had with one another, and as one appreciates the reasons why this should have been so, the question arises whether there is not some overlooked base upon which current Israeli-Palestinian relationships might yet be ameliorated. In what follows, then, I want to indicate, partly through my own research but rather more extensively through the archival work done by a number of other scholars, just how these connections among Muslims and Jews operated in the past and then to suggest how they might be drawn upon in the context of current Israeli-Palestinian tensions.

* * *

The stereotype is wrong. It says that to the extent Muslims and Jews got along at all in the countries of North Africa and the Middle East they did so because of their separation. Notwithstanding a fair degree of autonomy in family matters, non-Muslims were in this view almost entirely subject to the laws, taxes, and powers of the Muslim rulers such that commercial and legal relations were limited and largely conducted at the sufferance of the dominant population. The occasional romanticization of Muslim Spain aside, "tolerance" was at best more a matter of religious minorities being ignored than treated with relative equality, and, in the conventional metaphor, the whole pattern looked more like a mosaic of discrete parts than a web of interconnecting strands. From this perspective, comparisons to the historic treatment of minorities in Europe may have made the Middle Eastern situation look reasonably good, but only in a highly relative sense. As scholarship on the actual relations of Muslims and Jews has progressed we have learned that, contrary to a simply negative image, the pattern of communal relations has long been far more subtle and complex.

Consider first the information gleaned from the records and interviews I have encountered in my own fieldwork in the city and region of Sefrou, Morocco. Land records clearly show that numerous properties in the past were owned jointly by Muslims and Jews and that neither was simply fronting for the other.[1] These land records were particularly accessible because all of the materials they contained had been translated into French during the Protectorate and are exceptionally rich because people put in all sorts of documents—wills, contracts, notarized statements—as they went about establishing their property titles. In the notebooks kept by court notaries dating from as early as the turn of the twentieth century I also found various contracts, including, for example, ones in which a Muslim rented an apartment in a quarter of the old city from a Jew.[2] Informants confirmed that a wide variety of such contracts and partnerships were common in Sefrou—indeed all over Morocco and North Africa—and ranged from agricultural loans and joint ownership of all or part of a common dwelling to the purchase of future crops and agreements for payment in a distant location. Similarly, court records contained cases in which Jews would seek notarized documents from the pre-Protectorate Muslim court or records of a lawsuit brought against a Muslim for failure to repay a debt or for breach of contract.

Suits continued into the period of French domination and the post-independence era as well. For example, one quite lengthy and complex case in the records concerns a Jew who sold a parcel of land to a Muslim and then sued him over the proper measurement of the property and the amount due.[3] Jews even represented Muslims in their cases before Muslim officials, Jewish lawyers later being favored by many Muslims for their honesty and discretion, as well as the fact that, as outsiders, they would not later seek the kind of cloying obligations fellow Muslims might try to negotiate (e.g., help with arranging a relative's marriage or assistance in a political matter). That the Jews should have sought documentation from the Muslim courts and had recourse to them for disputes is more striking for the frequency with which they engaged in these intercommunal relationships than that Jews should have made occasional use of the Muslim/state legal system. That each should have made use of the other's laws and personnel—and sometimes both simultaneously—is especially striking.[4]

Here, the historic record for Morocco is revealing. In the magnificent multivolume collection of cases and commentary initiated by Louis Milliot in the early colonial period, for example, a case can be found in which a Jew sues a Muslim for a debt, which in turn precipitates a complex question about the nature of a Muslim father's responsibility for the debts of his son and the credibility of rural witnesses attesting to the relations of urbanites with whom they are not wholly familiar.[5] In another instance, faced with the question whether a portion of the debt owed a Jew by a Muslim involved an impermissible charge of interest, the appellate court recognized as customary the practice of Jews to charge interest. As a result, the court accepted the oath of the Muslim based on that presumption and ruled that only the principle of the debt was owed.[6] In many other instances, however, Muslim judges, not unused to the many ways Muslims got around the prohibition on charging interest, were willing to recognize (or at least turn a blind eye to) similar agreements worked out between Muslims and Jews. More strikingly, Milliot offers a case in which two Jewish brothers came to the Muslim court to resolve a dispute over the exercise of a right to the use of a small store whose ultimate title was held by the Islamic charitable trust (*ḥabus*). Milliot speculates that in this instance the Jews did not go to their own confessional court because of problems that court might have had enforcing its decisions, though it may have been because the usufructory right in question (*guelsa*) was itself quite different from the use rights that Jewish courts authorized.[7]

Jessica Marglin recovers and elucidates a broad range of Arabic and Hebrew sources from nineteenth-century Morocco involving Muslim-Jewish legal relationships that deepen our understanding of the legal relations of these two communities.[8] The cases show that it was quite common for Jews to go to the notaries (*'udūl*) of the Muslim courts to obtain documentation of their relation with a Muslim. Documents from such notaries were, of course, always recognized in the Muslim courts; acceptance of those obtained elsewhere depended on the judge's discretion and local practice. In some Muslim countries the testimony of a Jew as well as documents and other forms of evidence were not formally supposed to be recognized if the matter ever resulted in a law suit before a Muslim judge. On occasion Muslims sought documentation from the Jewish authorities, and parties of each religion not infrequently obtained documents from *both* the Muslim and the Jewish officials.

Courts and scholars in various parts of the Muslim world have taken divergent approaches to the question whether the oath of a Jew could be accepted, the predominant view in Arab countries being negative, though proponents do cite a Tradition of the Prophet that allowed a Jew to take an oath denying liability.[9] In Morocco, however, Islamic courts always accepted the oaths of non-Muslims. In at least one case, as Marglin shows, a Muslim notary went to a synagogue to take the oath of a Jew on a Torah, probably in the belief that the Jew would be more fearful of divine punishment or public opprobrium for lying if the oath was taken in this fashion.[10] Similarly, like the local Muslims Jews might seek advisory opinions from Muslim scholars. And while rabbis commonly forbade Jews on threat of excommunication from taking a case to a Muslim court, instances of such suits are nevertheless clear from the records. Indeed, sometimes a party—including a woman with a marital dispute—might threaten to go to the Muslim court as a way of pressuring the Jewish authorities to attend to his or her problem, while at other times the Jewish authorities simply ignored one of their co-religionists going to Muslim courts.

Actually, in using the Muslim courts to obtain a speedier result or enforcement not available from the Jewish courts we may, as Marglin says, have an instance of "how Jews and non-Jewish courts reinforce the authority of the Jewish courts."[11] We can see this process at work when Muslim courts, though formally barred from doing so, occasionally even accepted a settlement reached in a Jewish court in a case involving two Jews contesting a matter of inheritance or where the Muslim court, clearly aware of Jewish law on a matter, took such law into account in making its decision.[12] While the Jews of Marrakech and Fez did have their own prisons for recalcitrant debtors and other offenders, the Jews were frequently dependent on the Muslims to incarcerate a fellow Jew and, being reluctant to send any Jew to such a prison, preferred to encourage the parties to reach a settlement.[13] Marglin has found no cases in which two Muslims came to a Jewish court for adjudication. However, Goulven does claim to have heard of such instances, though he gives no details.[14] In my own work I have been told not of Muslims coming to Jewish courts to have their claims decided but of them coming to respected Jewish scholars to mediate their disputes. In addition, older Jewish and Muslim informants both cite instances of two Muslims going to the site of a Jewish saint—many of whom were shared by Muslims and Jews—where they would swear an oath to resolve their differences.[15]

The archives Marglin has consulted thus support a series of conclusions: that "although the blurring of jurisdictional lines was by no means rare, it was nonetheless the norm for Jews to bring most intra-Jewish cases to rabbinic courts and most inter-religious cases to sharīʿa courts,"[16] that "Jews were a regular presence in sharīʿa courts,"[17] that "Jews' experience in sharīʿa courts was not radically different from that of Muslims,"[18] that while instances of Muslims coming to Jewish religious courts for documents was "somewhat exceptional, they were neither rare nor insignificant,"[19] and—perhaps most significantly—that there was a good deal of mutual knowledge and borrowing of one another's legal approaches such that, forum shopping notwithstanding, there was a certain convergence as the two communities and systems interacted with one another.[20]

These findings are by no means restricted to Morocco in the nineteenth to twentieth centuries: Many other historians of the Muslim world have found similar relationships. This is particularly true for the period of the Ottoman Empire where we now know that "there was very considerable use of Muslim courts" by Jews.[21] Still earlier, the Geniza records—in which documents bearing the name of God that had to be buried rather than destroyed were found in the basement of a Cairo synagogue and date from roughly the eleventh to thirteenth centuries—confirm that the interplay between Muslim and Jewish legal systems has been of long duration.[22] The studies by Uriel Simonsohn, for example, show that while rabbis heartily disapproved of Jews using the Muslim courts, particularly for such "internal" matters as inheritance disputes, the Jews not only had to make arrangements that were consistent with their overall life among the Muslims but that there were certain advantages to their using Muslim courts as a sort of public records office. While some Jewish officials refused to accept documents drawn up by the Muslim notaries others were willing to do so if they believed the officials to be honest.[23] Even Jewish divorce cases were sometimes taken to the Muslim officials, and some Jewish authorities allowed Jews who would not honor their own courts' rulings to be sued in the Muslim forum. In short, while, as Simonsohn asserts, the frequency of recourse to Muslim courts cannot be determined with any precision, the record supports the proposition that such recourse was "far from sporadic and marginal."[24]

Simonsohn's conclusions find further validation in the work of the preeminent scholar of the Geniza documents, S. D. Goitein. Relying on the voluminous correspondence found in the archive, Goitein argues that in this period the Muslim regimes lacked any clear policy about whether non-Muslims should have to go to Muslim courts to resolve their disputes.[25] One letter from the late 1110s indicates that Muslim officials thought many matters should be left to the Jews' own courts, while overall the impression the archive creates is one of local variation, with some communities pressing for a degree of legal autonomy while others willingly engaged in the same sort of pluralistic approach found in later periods and places.[26] The Geniza documents thus demonstrate a wide range of ways in which the legal systems of the two communities interacted. We read of a Muslim court in 1175 recognizing the finding of a Jewish court that a Jewish merchant was bankrupt,[27] of documents having been made out by both Muslim and Jewish courts,[28] of a Muslim judge upholding a Jewish judge's decision,[29] of a Jew attesting to facts before a Muslim notary whose documentation was then accepted by a Jewish court,[30] of a woman threatened with excommunication for suing her brother in a Muslim court,[31] of Jewish courts sending debtors to be judged by the Muslim court,[32] of Muslim courts that wanted to handle Jewish inheritance cases because part of the estate might otherwise devolve to the state,[33] of Jews being accepted as witnesses in a Muslim court where the parties were all Jewish,[34] of a non-Jew making a settlement with a Jew in a Jewish court,[35] and of women taking their property or marital cases to Muslim courts despite pressures to do otherwise.[36]

The data from other times and parts of the Arab world also speak to similar approaches. In his study of Jerusalem under the Ottomans in the sixteenth century, Amnon Cohen states that "Jews and Christians voluntarily came to the kadi for rulings in matters that touched on members of other religions and also in matters concerning the people of their own community."[37] In her study of the Damascus courts between 1775 and 1860, Najwa Al-Qattan shows that non-Muslims came to Muslim courts not just for financial documents but that numerous intra-community cases were also brought there, "the vast majority of which involved marriage, divorce, child custody, and inheritance." Such findings seriously question whether in Ottoman times the legal status of non-Muslims was indeed characterized "by the twin principles of separation (judicial autonomy) and inequality (legally sanctioned discrimination)."[38] Exactly why Jewish judges allowed matters to go to the Muslim qadi is uncertain, but scholars are increasingly convinced that the view of Ottoman judicial organization as one that encouraged legal separation of faith communities is more a refashioning by later scholars of Turkish history than an accurate portrayal of Ottoman legal organization at the time. Certainly the inability of the Jewish authorities to punish people may have played into this pattern, though the use of fines and social ostracism was quite effective in places outside of Ottoman control, such as Morocco. Al-Qattan finds that non-Muslims explicitly sought the application of shari'a even in cases involving members of their own families when, for example, they found Islamic inheritance laws more favorable or that the documents they obtained from Muslim notaries would be more efficacious in any later dispute.

Moreover, as Al-Qattan notes, the Muslim courts "often provided weaker individuals with legal protection against those who were tempted to use religion, gender, or ignorance of the law to reap undue advantage."[39] Rarely would the testimony of a non-Muslim outweigh that of a believer and, as elsewhere, non-Muslims, notwithstanding those instances in which their testimony was accepted, understandably preferred to offer testimony from Muslims on their behalf. However, when they did testify, non-Muslims' oaths, "which were invariably accepted, were deemed sufficient to override the unsubstantiated allegations of Muslim plaintiffs."[40] Al-Qattan also notes: "Not only did the Hanafi school of [Islamic] law require qadis to comply with *dhimmi* [protected non-Muslims] intra-communal solicitation [to hear their cases but], they were also obligated to apply the law as if the individuals were Muslims."[41] As elsewhere, non-Muslims had some choice among judicial forums, thus leading Al-Qattan to conclude "that legal, cultural, and institutional causes contributed to the creation of a complex and relatively fluid and just legal arena . . . where the Muslims of Damascus . . . came face to face with their Jewish and Christian neighbors in a public and open sphere that catered to their needs in a fair and orderly manner."[42]

More contemporary examples may also be cited in which Jews have made use of Muslim courts for their own internal disputes. Based on his studies of Egyptian records from the 1930s, Ron Shaham finds a continuation of the pattern of Jewish use of the Muslim courts from Ottoman times and earlier. Islamic law gave more favorable treatment than did Jewish law for certain aspects of child custody, and Muslim courts were better able to enforce support orders. A wife seeking relief from an unbearable marriage might even convert to Islam and obtain a divorce from the Muslim court. Although Jewish authorities opposed recourse to the Muslim courts, Shaham writes:

> These injunctions and measures did not prevent Jews from going to Muslim courts, because the rabbis could do little if the Muslim court's decision gained the consent of both Jewish parties or if the qāḍi ordered the parties to go to the Jewish court for its approval of his decision. The Muslim authorities, on their part, forbade the religious leaders of the Jewish community from preventing their co-religionists from taking to the qāḍi a case against another member. Moreover, Muslim authorities imposed severe punishments on Jewish judges who ordered their co-religionists not to apply to a Muslim court or who punished Jews who had taken their case to a qāḍi.[43]

In a particularly intriguing example Mark S. Wagner discusses a case from Yemen in 1914 in which, in what might be taken as the quintessentially internal religious issue, two Jewish factions were at odds over whether a mystical text, the kabbalistic *Zohar*, might legally be studied by members of the Jewish community. The case was submitted to the Muslim authorities. Clearly drawing analogies from their own conservative approach to innovations in Islam, the Muslim jurists consulted were of the opinion that the *Zohar* should not be studied. Wagner notes: "Each side would later accuse the other of having brought the case to a non-Jewish court, something which Yemenite Jews seldom admitted but routinely did."[44]

In Morocco, Omar Boum, returning to his native Berber village in the Anti-Atlas Mountains south of Marrakech, found that it was quite common for Jews and Muslims to borrow features of one another's legal systems. Jews were able to tap into multiple legal regimes in order to modulate their actual relationships with the Muslims. They made use of local customary law, Islamic law, Jewish law, and state law as situational possibilities presented themselves, manipulating their subservient status and personal networks "to shape different legal jurisdictions to their own benefit."[45] Moreover, Boum implicitly grasps a key fact missed by many Western scholars, namely that local practice is regarded *as* Islamic, not something set apart from it.[46] In addition to relatively full autonomy within their own quarter the Jews were, therefore, able to engage in what Boum calls "legal syncretism" to construct a range of alternatives in their dealings in the marketplace. In a sense this should not come as a surprise since there is a good deal of sharing and borrowing in a wide variety of rituals, philosophy, and organizational aspects of the two communities. Indeed, anthropologists noted early on that generally speaking even tribal communities are not sharply separated from one another, borrowing concepts and practices regularly as they experiment with one another's styles of life.[47]

A rough pattern thus seems to be discernible across a considerable expanse of time and space, one that challenges those stereotypes holding either that Muslim tolerance of religious difference was manifest by hermetically sealing off distinct legal domains or that the non-Muslims who sought or were forced into Muslim courts were treated altogether differently than Muslims availing themselves of the same proceedings. Issues of enforcement, blame, bribery, and individual advantage obviously played into the choice of courts to which a Jew might take his or her need for documentation or adjudication, and clearly the range of variation cannot be ignored. But the common question arises whether the image of an overarching politico-legal system operating in many Muslim countries for many years might itself be founded on a set of assumptions that need to be subjected to greater scrutiny.

If we look at the broader nature of Muslim-Jewish relations—and with full awareness that we are doing so in a very generalized manner that cannot be said to fit each instance exactly—we may be able to understand a bit better how this kind of legal pluralism fit with the social and economic ties that characterize so many moments and venues of Muslim-Jewish interaction. Jews, it may be argued, were resident strangers in the Arab world, with all the advantages and disadvantages that situation entailed. Like any stranger, they occupied a position, ironically, of some intimacy. In a society in which one must constantly negotiate a network of people one hopes to be able to call upon for assistance, the interchangeable nature of the forms in which reciprocity may be sought become crucial. Thus a "favor" done in the marketplace may be reciprocated by help in arranging marriage to a client's offspring or aid in a political venture. But because many of the forms of reciprocation—like marriage and political help—were almost always excluded from the full array of possibilities expectable from a Jew, one could have relations with a Jew that were not subject to the same expectations and demands involving a fellow Muslim. As *resident* strangers the Jew could then see and hear things that Muslims might be reluctant to mention to anyone else, knowing that it might affect an obligation they do not wish to undertake or the use of information they prefer to hoard against unwelcome demand. Indeed, one could have the kind of intimacy one may have with someone who does not quite "count"—even engaging in what Hesse called "the intimate disclosure to the stranger," something we may experience when we tell a person briefly seated next to us on a plane things we might never tell our closest friend. Relations with Jews thus had the psychological benefit for Muslims of being able to reveal a private detail with relative certainty that others will not be able to make unwarranted use of it.[48]

Seen from this perspective a Muslim could invest a Jew with a degree—or at least an alternative form—of trust that might be less readily achieved in the ever-demanding, entangling web of indebtedness one had to form and service among fellow Muslims. Moreover, trust among fellow Muslims implied a kind of mutual limitation, each person holding himself somewhat apart even as some commitment had to be forthcoming. This feature is writ deeply into Arabic cultural terms and concepts. It has been said that in Arabic every word means something and its opposite, and in the sense that many terms seem to be like the two sides of a single coin this is clearly evident in the terminology of trust. Thus the word that means "to depend upon" (*wat͟hiqa*) means, in a related form, "to bind, fetter, or captivate," while a word that translates as "to entrust" (*wakala*) means, in a related verbal form, to be "indifferent or non-committal." The deep-seated ambivalence with which all negotiated relationships are approached thus manifests itself as a curious blend of opposites—being involved and being withholding, being secured and being tied up, being related and being ensnared. How and with whom one can establish relationships that render such ambivalent ties workable becomes a crucial aspect of personal maneuvering and institutional construction.

Contractual relations are especially relevant in this context. We tend to think of contracts in terms of their forms and stipulations, and usually as involving individuated transactions. But many contracts, as a number of legal scholars have argued, are better seen as predominantly relational: They are envisioned not simply as formal, one-off agreements but as encounters—often repeated many times over by the same parties—that have consequences for an expansive array of social relationships. Such consequences figure significantly both in their engagement and, when disputes occur, in assessing their implications for the networks of affiliation that hold people together. Defects in a contract are therefore often not measured against the terms and form they incorporate but the cultural conventions through which relationships are entered and pursued. That contracts in the Muslim world were commonly stated in the past tense was a demonstration of an association that was being ratified rather than created by the writing alone.[49] Indeed, written instruments were usually regarded as the reduction to writing of verbal statements which, in any dispute, were then inspected in terms of *who* these people are more than the correctness of the form of contract they had signed.

Contracts, therefore, were, as in so many other domains of Arab cultural life, an extension of that personalism through which one engages others in multiple contexts, a way of being known by those with whom one associates, a manifestation of one's encounters in the marketplace and social life at large. As such, the interpersonal nature of the arrangements and their appraisal could contribute significantly to the willingness of both confessional communities to look at relationships through a shared set of cultural norms more than an array of seemingly disparate institutions and legal regimes.

Against this background the willingness of Muslims and Jews to borrow cultural features from one another in a wide variety of ways is not altogether surprising. We know that in many instances both communities have long partaken of shared saints, rituals, and customs, so it is expected that they might borrow one another's legal approaches as well. If we add the fact that in both communities the doctrine is well recognized that local custom frequently takes precedence over stated law and that such customs are either broadly shared or not seen as incompatible with the shari'a, another's legal approach may be adopted, or at least acknowledged, under the heading of a local practice. Jewish law also at times adopted local customs of the majority population consistent with the idea that one must follow the laws of the kingdom in which one resides.[50] Thus Jews could go into Muslim courts not only for reasons of enforcement or the lack of adequate organization of their own courts but because the range of permissible approaches was not altogether different from that encountered in other interactions with the dominant population. And as intimate strangers the Jews were not a threat to the Muslim system of law any more than were their engagements in parallel rain prayers or gift-giving during one another's religious festivals. Similarly, the fact that, on occasion, Muslims would seek documentation of their commercial relationships with Jews from the Jewish courts or even go to a Jewish scholar or saint to mediate their disputes meant that they could do so without all of the overtones of obligation that might be entailed by the use of a fellow Muslim.

A closer look at a few of the specific types of contracts employed by both Muslim and Jewish merchants in their dealings with and across confessional boundaries suggests how some of these principles might still have currency. Briefly, several types of partnership arrangements were well known in medieval times and have come down to us in various permutations.[51] All of these contractual types share certain underlying principles: that partners are equivalent to one another as contracting agents whatever the distribution of their profits, that parties are expected to use their God-given reason to pursue knowledge about their bargain and that access to such knowledge should be maximized while responsibility for its acquisition remains with each individual, and that risk is not about economic hazard as such but about not obscuring any of the key elements of the transaction. Clarity as to the terms and (depending on the school of Islamic thought) the expression of intent were vital to contractual relations, but since the ultimate goal to be achieved is orderly relationships and the avoidance of social chaos (*fiṭna*), "social utility" (*istiḥsan*, *istislaḥ*) was not infrequently taken into consideration.[52] And while, for Muslims, interest was forbidden it may be better, notwithstanding the many ways of selling and repurchasing that could accomplish the same end, to think of the prohibition not simply as a bar to usury alone but as a vehicle for avoiding unjust enrichment more broadly.

Specific contractual forms included the *mufāwaḍa*, in which each partner was fully liable for the actions and obligations of others who might be engaged in the venture. Here, any change in the equality of investment, even as the result of inheritance of another's share, would vitiate the arrangement. This type of contract would appear to have special force for Muslims. The Prophet, who was a successful businessman and whose own words and actions mirror the Quran's emphasis on creating and maintaining one's contractual ties, reputedly said that one should "enter into partnerships by means of reciprocity, for it is most conducive to prosperity."[53] Such contracts further reveal their relational nature in that they were often maintained for a lifetime.

By comparison the *'inan* is a more limited partnership, one in which partners invest only a portion of their assets and in which they act only as agents for one another rather than, as in the *mufāwaḍa*, mutual guarantors. Traditionally, this type of contract was permitted by Islamic law with a non-Muslim so long as the Muslim partner had sufficient control to insure that no illicit purpose (e.g., trading in pork or wine) was involved. In each arrangement credit could be extended so long as it did not take on the appearance of impermissible interest.

A third type of contract was the commenda (or *qirāḍ*), in which one or more investors conveys money or goods to another to act as agent, a share for each having been agreed upon and any loss being born by the investors, not the agent. Control of the enterprise thus lay in the hands of the agent, often working at a vast distance, and hence a high degree of trust was necessary if risk was to be reduced.[54]

Note that in each of these arrangements wages as such did not figure. To work for wages was seen as lacking in the equivalence of parties necessary for proper commercial relations and was thus tantamount to being a slave. Moreover, except for the commenda, these contractual arrangements were traditionally limited to Muslims and, absent religious conversion, were not permitted for a non-Muslim for fear of engagement in the trade of forbidden substances. However, there are many examples, certainly in more recent times, of Muslims and non-Muslims engaging in a wide variety of contracts, often backed by the legal regime of a colonial power or a code adopted by a newly independent nation. And in a number of instances, both historic and contemporary, hidden investors acted as fronts for partnerships that were either frowned upon or through which the participants sought the protection of anonymity from rapacious officials or intrusive relatives.

Contracts thus have a long and honorable history in Islam and Judaism alike. Indeed, concern for such arrangements often explicitly transcended religious boundaries. The respect shown to contractual agreements was of a piece with the respect accorded private property. Building on the Prophet's own statement that private property is sacred, the story is often told of the Sultan Mustapha who, when his legal expert pointed to the Prophet's utterance, ruled that even a sultan could not simply take the property of a Jew but must pay him for it.[55] The question then arises whether the history of Muslim-Jewish commercial and legal interaction might offer some basis for reconstructing a degree of trust among Palestinians and Israelis, and whether a specific proposal in that regard might not be worthy of consideration.

* * *

One of the concepts frequently sounded in international relations when addressing the problems of contending parties—one that has been mentioned repeatedly in the context of the Palestine-Israeli dispute in particular—is that of "confidence-building measures." Examples of such measures include everything from the ping pong diplomacy of China and the U.S. at the time of President Richard Nixon's opening to that country, the establishment of summer camps for teenagers of adversarial nations, and the visit to each other's country by musicians or circus performers. In a few instances joint ventures for economic development have been tried. This may include the establishment of a free trade zone or a production space such as that worked out between the two Koreas at Kaesong.[56] Private parties and NGOs may also get into the act.[57] But one possibility that has not really been tried would draw on the contractual relations and concepts of property that we have been exploring in the history of Muslim-Jewish relations. Here, in addition to the contractual tools available, two concepts may prove of supplementary value: the idea of surplus property and the bases of a nation's ultimate claim to its lands.

Israel and Palestine, each drawing in part on religiously tinged concepts, lay claim to the same land on the basis of divergent sources, ranging from Biblical edict, historical residence, and forced dispersal, to prophetic promise and assertions of moral superiority. Usually these claims are thought to be completely incommensurable, hence the foundation for any common approach beyond reach. If we look more closely, however, these are not the only foundations each has in its conceptual repertoire.[58] On the Muslim side three claims to any land title are in play. Jihad is usually thought of as a struggle for moral rectitude or conquest of a non-Muslim adversary, but it can also serve as a basis for title to land. In theory, land acquired by jihad is supposed to become *waqf* (or *ḥabus*) property, that is, land held by the Islamic charitable foundation. Such land can be traded, rented, or exchanged in quite variable ways depending on the Muslim nation and time period, and most newly independent Arab nations have converted such holdings into state-owned property controlled directly by the ruler or administered through a special ministry. Similarly, much of the land of Israel has been held by the Jewish National Fund and dispensed through that organization to individuals or such collective entities as a kibbutz or moshav.

Whether as foundational title or title gained by conquest—notions quite familiar in the United States when applied to Native American lands—the holdings are at least partly conceived in terms of a trust rather than inherently private property, thus leaving open the question of how such a trust should be categorized and administered. Sovereignty is a separable basis for title, one that, for Jews and Muslims, has distinctly religious overtones. Thus the right of any Jew to return as a citizen to the State of Israel or the claim by any Palestinian to a "right of return" to his or her ancestral lands flows from the sovereignty claimed through the underlying title of the land in question. From this theory, then, one might derive an entitlement that is short of outright privatization but which might nevertheless include a basis for working out some kind of usufructory right stemming from citizenship alone.

A third claim of title goes to a quality of land control that is still more culturally distinctive to the region. This has to do with the notion, inseparable from the very meaning of ownership in the Arab world, that a man's identity is deeply suffused by the sources of his nurturance (*asel*) and the property over which he exercises dominion. In Arabic the word *mul* becomes crucial here. The term translates correctly as "owner" but more importantly implies the control and responsibility that identify a person as someone of consequence in the world. Thus the owner of a plot of land is its *mul*, but so too a wife may be referred to as the *mul* of the house and God as "my *mul*," each usage conveying a sense of interrelationship, mutuality, and control. On the Jewish side, as Robert Cover suggests, the equivalent concept is actually that of *mitzvah* (pl. *mitzvoth*), often thought of as the enactment of a "good deed" but perhaps better translated as an "incumbent obligation."[59] Unlike rights, which have been formulated in the West against the backdrop of a theory of the social contract entered into (or at least not opted out of) by each individual, mitzvah, as Cover says, is about "collective—indeed corporate—experience."[60] Particularly where central power is absent it is the reciprocal obligation that holds society together. Indeed, says Cover, "the jurisprudence of rights has proved singularly weak in providing for the material guarantees of life and dignity flowing from the community to the individual."[61] He concludes that "in a jurisprudence of mitzvoth one must first create an argument for equality of obligation and only as a result of that come to equality of participation."[62] Here, then, in both confessional/national cases the possibility arises for thinking creatively about ways to build on the notion of property as relational and obligational—as a tie between persons rather than as the connection one has to a thing—and hence as a way of fashioning a basis for trust and cooperation. And it is here, too, that we bump into a wall.

The wall in question, of course, is the one the Israelis have built to separate large portions of Israel and the occupied territories from Palestinian-controlled lands. When it is completed the wall will stretch some 430 miles, portions of which are an elaborate fence surrounded by a two-hundred-foot exclusion zone, while the remainder is comprised of twenty-six foot high concrete slabs.[63]

The wall places 8.5% of the West Bank on the Israeli side of the barrier, commonly breaking up the Palestinians' ability to move between points in their territory. As it has developed, the wall divides villages and families and often excludes an individual farmer from a portion of his own fields. Over the course of its construction the wall has become festooned with numerous

FIGURE 4.1. Israeli-Palestine separation wall graffiti by Banksy (CCBY-SA2.0).

oppositional graffiti and paintings, notably those by the anonymous artist known as Banksy.[64] Whatever its professed merits as a safety barrier and its undoubted status as a symbol of mutual hostility, the wall is surely a barrier that partitions the land and separates the people on either side.

But if one wall is bad could two walls be good? After all, one wall may separate but two might enfold. Given the broader history of Muslim-Jewish contractual ties, how might such an arrangement build confidence in the current political environment?

What if a second wall were built, or portions of the existing wall ballooned out, to enclose rather than seal off a zone of special significance, a zone within which the forms of partnership that characterized another time might be given free reign for enterprises that could nurture mutual trust?[65] This is not quite the same as the situation that has applied to some enterprises on the West Bank. There, in fifteen industrial zones, Israelis have at times worked alongside about fifteen thousand Palestinians. These zones have contributed about $300 million a year to the Palestinian economy.[66] Rather than a government-controlled enterprise zone, however, the rules for the space suggested here would be significantly different. The walls would enclose a space between the two nations, a space in which any exploitation would have to be accomplished by a partnership between a Palestinian and a Jew. The parties would be free to negotiate their own terms and choice of laws. Whether the parties would utilize one of the historic forms of contract developed by Muslim and Jewish law or fashion something quite new, neither the State of Israel nor the Palestinian authorities would have commercial jurisdiction over the enclosed space: The parties would be free to borrow or develop their own customs and usages as well as their own forms of arbitration.[67] Grants for technological assistance—of the sort that the late Israeli President Shimon Peres sought to promote—would be available without claims of exclusive jurisdiction. As commercial practices develop over time—as the "peace of the market" may prove valuable to all—perhaps the model might be extended to other parts of the zone, and additional procedures and spaces would protect against unwarranted intrusion as the partners work out the terms of their own endeavors.

Because the principle of equivalence would operate in all such contracts, Muslim parties would be able to find in such agreements resonance with the idea that partnership entails retention of a familiar sense of personhood. Since partnership is not a form of corporation that erases individual identity for the Muslim or for the Jew, nor does it substitute interpersonal obligation with impersonal limited liability, both might be able to retain a culturally comprehensible sense of self within the partnership form—as had their predecessors for generations. Until very recently many Palestinians worked regularly in Israel and had good relations with their employers. The partners will now have to engage in similar hiring arrangements across their national frontiers.[68]

The partnership contracts would not be governed by state laws. Indeed, since for many Muslims the state is often regarded as incapable of genuine reciprocity and for many Jews relations with the state should not replace the performance of mitzvoth as incumbent obligation, within the two-walled zone the law of the contracts rather than national policies would couple with dispute resolution mechanisms appropriate to the context. Specifically, a board could be formed, comprised of an Islamic law expert, a Jewish law expert, and two merchants (one Muslim and one Jewish) who would operate initially as a conciliation or mediation board but who, in the absence of agreement between or among the parties, would have the power to make definitive judgments, all parties having agreed to such binding arbitration powers upon entrance into the enterprise zone. Hopefully, by being equally balanced between Muslims and Jews the panel would have to make occasional compromises if both are to prosper. Because, as Muslims and Jews may both be quick to recognize, ambiguity and popular perception may be more central to their arrangements than strict formulaic law, it would be expected that the law may develop more as a matter of cases than of rigid adherence to a code-like set of precepts. That mode of thought is also perfectly consistent with the style of both Islamic and Jewish legal reasoning. Borrowing and convergence having been a hallmark of the past, such a process may provide the necessary legitimacy for the future.

In some cases the arrangements would have to include willingness to recognize that the history of such contracts was itself fraught with equitable approaches more than legal rigidities, and thus the role of witnesses or clauses assuring that neither interest nor impure goods might be involved could be addressed by the parties and the community drawing on the very sorts of experiences that scholars have shown characterized such relations in the past. Indeed, still other concepts might be revitalized. Meir Bravmann reminds us that in early Islam the notion was well developed of "the surplus of property." As he explains it, a group or individual was expected to give to the poor and needy whatever exceeded one's own reasonable needs. This was not at all the same as charity; instead it was seen, particularly when the source was the result of jihad, as an entitlement on the part of the recipients. Indeed, the recipients had an obligation to accept the surplus, a proposition supported by Prophetic tradition (*sunna*). It is also supported by the story told of the wolf, dying of thirst at a filthy waterhole and "howling like a man expelled from his tribe," who would only accept the unusual offer by a man of clean water if assured that it was "surplus," thus placing him under an obligation to accept rather than constitute a "favor" for which he may be unable to reciprocate.[69] If, however, no surplus existed in a given period one could not be thought of as stingy or lacking in virtue. Similarly, in Jewish law and custom the Biblical injunction holds that, charity and tithes aside, one should leave in the fields those sheaves of grain one initially overlooked as well as those at the edge of the field, all such grain being for "the poor and the foreigner residing among you."[70]

Now if one thinks of jihad not as conquest but as moral struggle and mitzvah as obligation combined with the entitlement to the leavings and edges of the field, one might work out a method of computing some portion of the "surplus" that would be reinvested regularly in aiding those in need on both sides of the enclosed zone. And since, at least in Islam, the notion of surplus also embraced the idea of a surplus of taxes—in which any taxes beyond what was needed for the prescribed purposes were turned back to the needs of the community and the poor—some method of calculating such additional excess might also be considered.

We tend to think of all walls as being much the same. But, as Wendy Pullan suggests in her study of Jerusalem, walls may be thought of as coming in two types, thin and thick. Thin walls are more easily eliminated because they involve almost no contacts across them: They do not have entangled relationships attached to them so that when the single dimension on which they have been constructed deteriorates the reason for the wall itself disappears, the Berlin wall being one such example. "Thick" walls, by contrast, are thick not because of their physical composition but because they entail rich and interlocking relationships. Such structures are highly differentiated, rich metaphorically, and they do not so much wall off as they enclose, even facilitating interaction, as may be the case when neighbors share a garden wall allowing climbing plants to bloom or create the need for invitations that span moments of privacy. Pullan suggests that the Israeli wall is, in this paradigm, relatively thin, but just what it would take to make it come down is unclear.[71] Indeed, "thickening" the wall (in Pullan's sense) may ironically make it more compatible with peace.

I am not so naive as to think that all parties in the region will immediate jump to implement my suggestion of a second wall. When I raised the suggestion at a meeting of entrepreneurs, philanthropists, scholars, diplomats, and artists my idea was politely ignored. Nor do I expect supporters of Hamas to suddenly give up their attachment to an absolute "right of return" to all of Israel or for the most ardent Israeli settlers to forego all Biblical claims to Judea and Samaria. But that does not mean one should either approve of the status quo, with its singularly ugly wall, or that one should cease looking for ways to work with the tools at hand.

As President Obama said during his visit to Israel in May 2013: "The only way to truly protect the Israeli people is through the absence of war—because no wall is high enough, and no Iron Dome is strong enough, to stop every enemy from inflicting harm."

If the wall Israelis have built between themselves and the Palestinians does not provide permanent security it could, ironically, provide a real opportunity. Stranger things have been imagined. One is reminded of the story told about Juha, the Middle Eastern figure who combines elements of the trickster and the wise fool. One day a friend noticed Juha standing beside a huge lake tossing bits of yoghurt into the waters. "What are you doing?" he asked. "Can't you see," replied Juha, "I am throwing yoghurt into the lake." "But why?" asked his friend. "Well," said Juha, "everyone knows you have to use a bit of yoghurt to make more yoghurt and that is what I am trying to do." "But," said his friend, "you can't expect a little bit of yoghurt like that to convert an entire lake." "Ah", said Juha wistfully, "perhaps not. But wouldn't it be wonderful if it could?"

A wall can exclude. But it can also enclose—a garden, a sanctuary, a place where invitation displaces prohibition.

"Something there is that doesn't love a wall," said the poet.

Maybe, in this case, that something is the absence of a second wall.

PART TWO

Justice in an Imperfect World

CHAPTER FIVE

The Culture of Corruption in the Arab World

First, let me tell you an Arab joke, then a couple of personal stories.

The joke goes like this:

There was once a policeman and he was very corrupt. He always stopped people and asked them for bribes. It happened once that he worked all day and didn't stop anyone. He realized as the sun was going down that he didn't have anything in his pocket, so he said to himself: "I'm going to stop the next person I see." Shortly thereafter, there came a man riding a new moped. The moped appeared to be working fine and the man was wearing his helmet, but the policeman stopped him anyway. The man's papers were all in order and the corrupt policeman couldn't find a reason to ask for a bribe. "But," he said to the man, "aren't you scared to be riding out here all by yourself?" The man answered, "I'm not by myself, I have God and the Prophet with me." Smiling broadly, the corrupt policeman responded, "Three of you on that little moped? You'll have to pay a fine!"[1]

Now for the personal stories:

Gathered in the guest room of a Berber friend in the Middle Atlas Mountains of Morocco after the Friday prayers, Hussein turned from the assembled village men and asked me: Is there corruption in America? Yes, I answered. Give us an example, he said. So, as the room quieted, I gave an example of a kickback arrangement. Ah, no, said Hussein, as the others' heads shook in unison, that is just buying and selling. So I mentioned the Watergate scandal. No, no, Hussein replied to common assent, that is just politics. So I gave an example of nepotism. No, no, no, all voices cried out, that is just family solidarity. So, as I struggled to think of an example that would save the honor of my country for being every bit as corrupt as anyone else's, Hussein turned to the others and said, with genuine admiration: You see why America is so strong—they have no corruption!

A few years later I attended a meeting with workers from Grounds and Buildings to discuss the nepotism rules a committee of our university had proposed. One after another the workers expressed concern. What do you mean I can't hire a fishing buddy's

A version of this essay was originally published as Rosen 2010b. I am grateful to Adam Garfinkle for his editorial advice and for the comments of David Brooks, who awarded it one of his Sidney Awards for best articles of the year.

kid or my nephew, said one: Often guys don't show up on time or at all, but if the kid is my nephew and he doesn't get here or pull his weight I'll go to my brother who will see to it the kid shapes up. If I don't have that kind of hook in a guy how am I ever going to be sure he will do his work? To the bafflement of my colleagues on the committee, all of the workers present heartily agreed.

* * *

The dictionaries define corruption as "morally degraded," "debased in character," or "the perversion of an original state of purity." Scholars speak of corruption as "the misuse of public power for private gain."[2] But you do not have to be a total relativist to suspect that these characterizations beg many questions: Indeed, the very criteria applied often incorporate a distinctly Western concept of corruption.[3] When, for example, I asked the men in Hussein's settlement, as I have so many in the Arab world, what they mean by corruption I always receive the same answer: Corruption is the failure to share with those with whom you have formed ties of dependence whatever largesse comes your way. Theirs is a world in which the defining feature of a man is that he has formed a web of indebtedness, a network of obligations that prove his capacity to maneuver in a world of relentless uncertainty. Failure to service such attachments is thus regarded as not only unmanly and stupid but corrupt.

This is, of course, rather different from an American view of corruption as influencing the enactment of a public duty meant to be performed gratuitously. Corruption for us may also apply to a private act that tips "the level playing field." Whether in the U.S. or the Middle East there may, of course, be subtle commonalities affecting corruption. This may be true for both parties. Debt may entail fear, as one may later have to accept less than was bargained for, or one may become obliged in ways that cannot be fulfilled. Both situations may lead to cutting some corners. So, too, the cost of favoritism may simply be passed along—"a supplementary tax in disguise"—whether it is in the mafia control of waste management and construction or the more genteel pricing of pharmaceuticals and military hardware. But it is invariably the local pattern of corruption—its connections among a wide range of distinctive social, religious, economic, and political factors—that accounts for its meaning and implications. And nowhere are the cultural features of corruption more important to understand than in our encounters with the people of the Middle East.

Reciprocity is important to an understanding of the meaning of corruption in the region but it is not the only factor raised as one listens to discussions on the topic. There is an Arab saying: "God loves those who hide their sins." It sounds hypocritical to Western ears but for the Arabs it implies that it is only when a private act adversely affects others' nested sets of relationships that it becomes a matter of public concern.[4] Traditionally, therefore, unlawful sex was regarded as socially disruptive only if it could be verified by four eye witnesses, while a man carrying a bottle of liquor under his cloak could not be faulted since no relationships are affected as long as the forbidden substance remains unseen. The Afghans have a similar saying: "A shame that nobody talks about is no shame." The role publicity plays in the concept of corruption underscores its capacity to disrupt. In Arabic the word *fasād*, which means "to dirty or prostitute," may originally have implied something so eaten away from within that it can no longer act as a support, while a common term for a bribe, *reshwa*, originally meant water drawn from a well with a bucket, in contrast to the more natural flow of a stream.

Most important, however, is the concept of *fiṭna*, a term that properly translates as "chaos," and through its added meanings—"temptation," "fascination," and "disbelief"—implies not only risky allure and political disaffection but the dissolution of all those ties that hold society together. Society is thus like an electrical grid in which it is the running imbalance of pluses and minuses, the differential charge of obligations and indebtedness, that holds the system together. To render everything identical or equal is like pulling the electrical plug, while failing to engage in the process of ingratiation and recompense is to be left socially isolated. As an Egyptian woman once told anthropologist Unni Wikan, "an unreciprocated obligation is a terrible burden to have to bear." Indeed, the Prophet Muhammad is said to have warned that Islam might fail if the bonds of indebtedness that held his community together began to fray. Even the Quran (29:64) refers to this life as a sport and a game, in which it is the constant fluctuation of ties, regularized by keeping to one's contracts and sustained by sharing with one's momentary allies, that alone preserves the community of believers (*umma*) from premonitory chaos.

This fear of social chaos, highlighted both in sacred texts and common perception, is reflected in various usages. Ask Americans what they think is the opposite of tyranny and most will likely say "freedom" or "liberty." Ask the same question of Arabs and they will most likely reply, "chaos." Many proverbs support this contrast: "tyranny is preferable to chaos," "an unjust government is better than corruption," "to make a person live in chaos is worse than killing him." Corruption, as the failure to share with one's dependents, is the fearful solvent that renders social ties vulnerable to dissociation and death. And yet, it is, as Ernest Gellner suggested, that very fear of chaos that gives rise to the patterns of relationship that closet its manifestations or inform those rituals that seek to both license and contain it.[5] The rage for order is thus balanced against the rage for chaos, both of which are simultaneously generative and threatening.

Seen from this perspective, forms of interdependence that Westerners would regard as corrupt are commonly regarded in the Arab world as constitutive of a workable preservation of the political order. Like his inquiry about corruption in America, it was Hussein who, in his characteristically ironical attitude toward politics, once surprised me by saying: "You know, bribery is our form of democracy." "Really," I said, "how does that work?" "Well," he replied, "if the big man says 'do such-and-such' but someone below him is bribed to do otherwise isn't that a check on the power of the big man, and isn't the point of democracy that it be a system of limited powers?" Or, as the Middle East historian Patricia Crone (2003, 33) put it: "There was nothing shameful about patronage as such: it benefitted employer and employee alike. Wherever trust mattered as much as or more than skills, nepotism was a virtue, not a sign of corruption." Indeed, to some, bribery and favoritism are essential to the working of the state. In the Moroccan novelist Tahar Ben Jelloun's *Corruption* a bureaucrat tries to convince a reluctant colleague to accept gratuities:

> Everyone knows that most salaries are symbolic. The state knows it. It closes its eyes. It has to; otherwise there would be a revolution. Citizens participate in whatever ways are available to them to fill the gaps. It's normal. It's a national consensus, a balancing mechanism. The whole trick is to do it discreetly, even elegantly if possible. What you are placing in the realm of morality and what you call corruption I choose to call a parallel economy—it isn't even underground, it's a necessity.[6]

As an aspect of the political, then, corruption highlights the inherent weakness of the state. For it is only in relations of negotiated reciprocity—relations that partake of the face-to-face contact by which people assess one's another's reliability and obligational bonds—that a relation of trust can be forged. By contrast, the state is the very embodiment of *un*reciprocity: You cannot have a personalized relationship with so faceless an entity. "Injustice can be committed only by persons who have power and authority," said Ibn Khaldun in the fourteenth century, because only such

FIGURE 5.1. Payment of a bribe (pixabay.com).

figures can bar one from access to the multiple bases on which mutual indebtedness can be constructed. Figures of authority, then, must build up their constellations of indebtedness in order for people to begin to attribute to them the qualities of someone who will share benefits with his dependents and not (in the Arabic idiom) "eat" everything himself. It is the formation and maintenance of such a network that renders the exercise of power legitimate; it is the implicit understanding that only someone who services his network wisely will not find himself alone in his need.

The result is not a system of "amoral familism," where one justifies acts outside some bounded domain that would be immoral within: The need to form beneficial ties of reciprocity wherever possible undercuts such discreet boundaries of moral behavior. Indeed, as one seeks favorable connections or raises money to grease the system those bonds of indebtedness that grant predictability to others' behavior are further reinforced. To use another as a go-between (*wasiṭa*) to obtain a job or benefit is not generally regarded as corrupt, even though others, lacking such connections, are put at a competitive disadvantage.[7] To the contrary, such ties are constitutive of an orderly society as they hold people together by requiring them constantly to negotiate the reciprocal obligations that are the very structure of the social fabric. That such "favoritism" is seen as vital to the social order rather than a requirement of emotion or sentiment is neatly embraced in the results of a survey taken among Saudi students who said that "exchanging benefits" is perfectly acceptable but acting as a facilitator of benefits out of "sympathy" is not.[8]

Corruption, as bribery or favoritism, may just be incidental to the formation of these embedded associations and actually contribute to that sense of equal opportunity through which, as one saying has it, you could be a beggar in the morning, a vizier of the king in the afternoon, and hanged in the public marketplace the next day. Thus a survey designed in 2010 by the United Nations Office on Drugs and Crime found that in Afghanistan "the bribe system seems to be of mutual benefit for public officials and citizens: for example, citizens indicate that they pay bribes to avoid fines or receive better treatment."[9] Ironically, too, such favoritism contributes to transparency, since discerning or displaying connections are vital to one's own reliability.[10] Similarly, the whole process brings new players into the game, constrains players whose questionable conduct is known or rumored, and fits with those other mechanisms—from gossip and scandal to the deep-seated ambivalence toward power—that inform so much of Arab social organization and ritual.

But there is also a strong countercurrent to this ethos. For the whole basis of mutual dependence that renders many practices permissible has now been so overwhelmed by the disruption of "the game" that one has no way to preserve the constraints that used to accompany its organization. Now, you may have to give a "gift" to a clerk to produce a document, to a hospital attendant to visit a relative, or to a utility employee to commence service—and all without having a chance to form an interpersonal relationship on the basis of which you may seek some later return. Moroccans say that where once society operated through kin (*nasab*), and later through friends (*ḥsab*), now it works only through money (*flus*), and the more one relies on money the less one needs to service a varied array of people whose dependency is based on nonmaterial sources. Indeed, what bites deeply for many Arabs is not just that money has become the overriding medium of relationship but the sense of discourtesy that accompanies it. Where once another may have offered you tea and engaged you in an extended discussion, now people feel they are treated curtly, with no consideration for establishing an ongoing tie that may prove useful in other ways at a later time.

This loss of personalized interaction has no doubt been exacerbated by the massive movement of people from the countryside to heterogeneous cities and the state's domination of information and resources. Sadly, corruption may also accompany increased levels of education, with poorly paid government jobs and the decline of informal mechanisms of social leveling contributing to one-off relationships rather than multi-stranded, longer-term alliances. In all of this, however, one cannot underestimate how uncomfortable people feel in so depersonalized an atmosphere, how hurt they are by the incivility, how at sea they feel when a debt incurred, say, in arranging a marriage or a loan, cannot be carried over into a different form of reciprocal "favor" at a later time. As the repertoire of relational possibilities is displaced by monetized connections frustration boils over, whether in personal anxiety or in taking to the streets in protest.

In certain respects Islamic law and social practice have developed mechanisms to address official corruption. The ambivalence to power, together with the recognition that someone who builds a superior network of allies can be regarded as the legitimate holder of power are counterweights to the failure to service one's dependents and the temptation to "eat" the benefits of one's position alone. Similarly, in the past, the death of a ruler might lead to a period of social strife which served to redistribute assets and afford others the opportunity to rise to power, an odd sort of check on corruption only if one fails to see corruption in terms of reserving everything for oneself. Indeed, one could point to the emphasis on procedure in Islamic legal proceedings as a kind of anti-corruption device: To require multiple witnesses appearing before several pairs of notaries and to read documents for who is speaking in them (and hence one's general reputation) rather than whether they were drawn properly (perhaps as a result of a bribe) could all be seen as ways to limit potential corrupt practices. Yet few of these devices were so institutionalized or envisioned as mechanisms that would form part of an anti-corruption structure as to amount to a full-scale, formal system for containing the worst aspects of corruption. The question then arises whether the experience of other nations may be of some use in thinking about new ways to limit corruption.

An American army captain who served in Iraq and Afghanistan has written that to eliminate corruption in those two countries—and, one assumes, in others within the Middle East and North Africa—one must promulgate clear rules, institute a reporting mechanism to which ordinary citizens can have ready access, and constantly attend to the forms of action that the local people themselves regard as corrupt.[11] Such reforms sound admirable and may even be tailored to different local cultures. But they are not self-evident or self-executing. After all, is a lobbyist who puts one in touch with a decision maker necessarily corrupt? Is help given a client to gain entry to an exclusive club an act redolent of immorality? Can one really dissociate arguably corrupt practices from the whole web of religious, social, and economic concepts in which they are necessarily embedded?[12]

The history of anti-corruption efforts may nevertheless be instructive. If we set aside such mechanisms as executing corrupt officials or only appointing as overseers one's closest kin—hardly always effective in any event—the reduction of corruption usually entails an element that may be decisive. The reference here is not to the development of a civil service alone: Increased salaries may allay some rationalizations for accepting gifts, while job security and advancement in the service may hold off illicit entanglements in some cases. Nor can one rely on threats of supernatural sanction. Rather, it may be that in an increasingly bureaucratized society professional pride is indispensable to reform. Just as many of the lawyers and accountants, businessmen and educators in the Arab world would love to be able to practice their crafts without having to engage in petty bribery and favoritism, so, too, they need an independent forum in which those desires can receive expression and reinforcement.[13] The rise of professional associations in the United States, for example, coincided with the civil service reforms of the early twentieth century, but they did not develop simply as agencies of the state or as NGOs that mimicked, even as they avoided, government control. Rather, professional associations were to a not inconsiderable degree built on the self-respect and pride their participants craved. They were also semi-autonomous, in the formation of their codes of ethics and the vehicles for enforcing them. When one sees lawyers or teachers taking to the streets of Cairo or Casablanca to protest a corrupt legal decision or educational policy, therefore, a good deal more than political partisanship is often at work: One is seeing this yearning to express professional pride at its moment of confirmation.

Nor is pride limited to the technical professions or the craftsmen's associations. It is the base on which so many in the Arab world would hope to construct a civil society. Of the many attractions of fundamentalist organizations not the least is that they often have a reputation for being uncorrupt. Where government personnel may show up at the scene of a disaster granting more favorable treatment to some than others, socialists and fundamentalists frequently arrive first and distribute aid evenhandedly; where government agents may offer food parcels in exchange for votes, the Islamists may offer medical aid and food supplements as a generalized "gift" knowing that delayed reciprocity is often more effective and long-lasting. People will even choose to buy from a merchant with a long beard, assuming he may be more honest than one not dressed as an ardent believer. Purification has always been tried as the antidote to corruption, but it too may carry its own corrupting forms. Archibald MacLeish was right when he said there are two kinds of people in the world—the pure and the responsible. Pride can go either way in that equation, but being indispensable to both it cannot be ignored in either.

Hussein, too, was right to think that reducing corruption lies at the heart of a nation's strength. But there is no simple correlation of political form or cultural construct to its reduction. Edward Gibbon, after all, called "corruption, the most infallible symptom of constitutional liberty," and those who define it as the absence of an opportunity to be treated equally would have to indicate, for example, why in some traditions not allowing a woman to be a priest or rabbi or imam should be called corrupt. To grasp that for most Arabs equivalence is of greater relevance to justice than equality, that for them it is only realistic to believe that society is better served by webs of obligation than impersonal roles, and that institutions are always defined by their occupants and not by depersonalized powers is to enter a world of enormous decency and order, even if it is not our own.[14] Perhaps if we in the West attend to the longing for integrity that accompanies this complex web of relations and crosscutting constraints, we may still have a chance to form with the Arabs incorruptible ties of mutual indebtedness and moral worth.

CHAPTER SIX

Justice and the "Arab Spring"

A Guide to the Arab Street

At the time it seemed to many as if the earth itself had shifted. In late 2010 and early 2011, when first Tunisia and then Egypt underwent what came to be called the Arab Spring, the days of the dictators seemed to be ending, and with it the long period described by Syrian playwright Saadallah Wannous as only a "revolution of hope" was being replaced by a genuinely transformative political upheaval.[1] *The result may yet prove to be a true revolution in Tunisia but something far less elsewhere. Egypt went from military dictatorship through a brief Islamicist season and back to military dictatorship, while Bahrain (like all the other kingdoms of the region) remained essentially unchanged and the uprising in Syria turned into a civil war involving, among others, Russia and Iran. Along the way the optimism of many in the region and abroad was, perhaps, blighted by a poor understanding of some of the key cultural components of the events, components that were not entirely unique to this particular moment in Arab history and which may manifest themselves again in the future. Whatever the rule of law may come to mean in these nations, an understanding of such seemingly unrelated cultural components as the meaning of space and the role of those who only stand by is crucial to comprehending, if not predicting, the systemic implications of these events. Frequently referred to, at least in the West, as "the Arab Street," the characteristics of popular political expression in the countries that did undergo significant challenge during this period therefore need to be considered in some detail if we are not to be caught up in a new set of myths and fail to recognize the future when it arrives.*

* * *

The Arab Spring brought large numbers of people out onto the streets. The connection between popular sentiment and its overt expression, however, had to partake of a series of cultural orientations that gave the circumstances of political, economic, and social life sufficient comprehension such that, when a world seen in those terms no longer appeared to be responding to reasonable control, individuals were prepared to express themselves through open protest. Among the factors contributing to this turn of events one would have to include the following:

CORRUPTION WAS A KEY GENERATOR OF THE ARAB SPRING. Imagine being repeatedly stopped by policemen who humiliate you in front of your family by demanding a bribe; a post office where you are told to return another day, until a small "gift" suddenly produces the needed forms; a hospital where you have to pay someone to visit a relative or get an inoculation for the pilgrimage to Mecca; a school where your child's teacher (who frequently does not even show up for classes) recommends "additional work"—until another "favor" yields a passing grade. The result is, in part, a society whose surface elements seem utterly disconnected from the realities of daily life. As a young Arab doctor once told a correspondent: "We have become an 'as if' society. We pretend to work, and they pretend to pay us. We pretend to praise our leaders, and they pretend to represent us."[2] Or, as the Egyptian playwright Ali Salem put it: "Everyone has to pay for their children to take private lessons after school because the schools are so bad. Can you imagine? You prevent yourself from eating to pay for private lessons?"[3] The result is not only that students may graduate illiterate in several languages but they see their parents ground down by the corruption endured on their behalf.

Corruption, as we saw in the preceding chapter, is commonly regarded as the failure to share with one's associates, rather than simply the misuse of public office. It is a rupture in the scheme of reciprocity, the need to engage in relationships that are freely bargained throughout the web of kinship, economic, political, or marital alliances—a process whose very malleability and convertibility is thought to hold social chaos at bay. Reciprocity with the state, rather than with a particular person, is deemed impossible, and where money displaces all other resources for creating ties, where the officeholder lacks any incentive to establish with those he or she services an obligation that may be called up in another time and form, and where the sheer movement of people disrupts the expectations of mutual indebtedness, one's capacity to influence and hence predict another's behavior suffers from an increasing sense of entropy. Reciprocity can serve as a check on corruption, but only if there is considerable freedom to maneuver among the forms of exchange that keep "the game" of creating a defining network of personal allies alive. When only money makes involvement possible—when the opportunity to use rhetorical skills to capture the terms of the situation is undermined, when assistance as a go-between that can be called up in other obligations is displaced by financial wherewithal, when the claims of descent or a reputation for knowledge lose their place to a monetized common denominator—then all sense of predictability and advancement are severely affected.

Faced at every turn with the need to give without generalized reciprocation, unable to build ties in a worldly consequent fashion, people in the region were not merely humiliated but made to feel complicit. Sullied and debased in front of family members and self-regard, their sense of being tarnished finally boiled over. Then, the apprehension of insignificance trumped indolence, and the agony of incoherence surmounted fear.

FOR A TIME PEOPLE OVERCAME THE FEAR OF CHAOS. The key term here is *fiṭna*, which means "chaos, discord, and social disruption." But it comes from an Arabic root that also means "to tempt, entice, enthrall, or seduce." The Quran (Sura 64:15) can even say that "your wealth and your children are a *fiṭna* for you" because they can tempt you away from both God and the larger community of believers. In Egypt each side used the fear of *fitna* in its own way, Mubarak by sending his thugs into the square—an event made notorious by the sight of a woman in a blue bra being dragged along the ground—and frightening people with the prospect of a complete breakdown of order: "Our revolt was called chaos," says a rebel in a novel by Naguib Mahfouz.[4] The protesters, too, saw matters in terms of chaos by arguing that the moment was ripe for reconstructing relationships. Both erred in two key respects: the regime by not realizing that, at least for the moment, the categories had shifted such that chaos was not the alternative to tyranny; and the protesters by momentarily imagining that a relationship of reciprocity could be possible with an impersonal state.

If corruption was now shifted from the category of failure to share with allies to an aspect of tyranny, and if tyranny for a moment was shifted to the category of chaos rather than its antithesis, it looked as if other categories might also be reconfigured. In the event, however, the fear of chaos

FIGURE 6.1. "Woman in the Blue Bra" and related graffiti, Tahrir Square, Cairo, December 2011 (flickr, EWWE WordPress).

came back to haunt Egyptians, and in the absence of ideological leadership capable of offering a truly different classification of everyday experience the protesters slipped back into the old categories. Western models had no legitimacy. As a Moroccan judge said, "What we call chaos is what you call civil society." Absent a genuine reconfiguration of the concept of chaos, its antonyms and alternatives, *fitna*—perhaps never far from the surface of people's minds—crept back into the Arab Spring and with it the possibility of new categories of imagining a relationship to the state melted away.

WITHOUT WORLDLY CONSEQUENCE THERE IS NO MANHOOD. Arab Islam, lacking rites of passage to manhood, places great emphasis on collecting the bridewealth that makes a marriage, and thus proving one is connected in a network of obligations that alone defines manhood.[5] An old Moorish proverb says that the Christians spend their money on lawsuits, the Jews on religious festivals, and the Muslims on weddings. By 2008 in Egypt the average cost of getting married was about $10,000 in a country where the average yearly income was $3,700. There and elsewhere in the region the cost of a marriage has been rising steadily and can be anywhere from three to fifteen times annual income.[6] As a result the average age of marriage for men is now in the late twenties (with a third of all men in many Middle Eastern countries still unmarried in their thirties) and the average age of marriage for women is also now in the late twenties. The last census in Egypt showed that three-quarters of the people in the country lived in apartments, but since one has to show a place to live in order to get married the situation of overcrowding has made prospects for young couples all the more difficult.[7] Pinned between recognizable roles—a social limbo referred to as "waithood"—frustrations mount. The failure of the Arab Spring did nothing to ameliorate the problems. "A 24-year-old political activist working ten-hour shifts at an accounting firm in Assiut, one of the poorest areas of Egypt, says he can explain why his country has not had a true revolution: 'It's not a new Egypt until I have enough money to get married. It's a country of boys waiting to be men.' "[8]

The problems take different forms in different countries. In Iran the regime is so concerned that many couples are living together without getting married that they have set up an online matchmaking service.[9] The proportion of female-headed households rose in Morocco from 11.2% to 19.3% in the period 1960–91 and now stands over 22%; in Egypt the figure was also 17.9% by 2014, and it is probably comparable in many

FIGURE 6.2. Sign held by young man in Tahrir Square: "Leave [Mubarak]—I Want to Get Married" (5Areb.com).

other Arab states.[10] With jobs scarce and money having become a dominant means of establishing relationships, the youth who came out to the street represented the need to establish a worldly consequent set of associations, to show that they make a difference. According to one reporter, "many of those I interviewed said that getting married and having a family were things they dreamed of most in a post-Mubarak Egypt."[11] As an expression of the changes they hoped the demonstrations would facilitate, several couples actually celebrated their marriages in the square. More poignant, yet telling, of the many banners and signs carried by protestors in Tahrir Square was that held up by a young man, a bit of bread in his right hand, the Arabic on his pink cut-out heart addressed to Hosni Mubarak reading: "Leave—I want to get married!"[12]

In this regard the young male demonstrators seeking reform ironically share something in common with the suicide bombers of the same age. Both are seeking to alter their status, to become men of consequence in a world that values a man's effect on obligational networks above all else.[13] For many of the young male protesters in the Arab street, unable to maneuver within the existing rules, life has been reduced to groping for a way to attain genuine manhood. One shortcut to proof of manhood through network formation does exist: For the suicide bomber the proof of worldly consequence comes in a flash, when embeddedness in a network of fellow terrorists is fixed for all time and one no longer has to endure the risks that come with constantly having to service an uncertain set of interpersonal connections. This need to show one's social connectedness underscores how much common causes may yield divergent ends when the means of achieving identity are frustrated.

BYSTANDERS VALIDATE THE PROTESTS: THE ARAB SPRING WAS NOT SIMPLY A FACEBOOK REVOLUTION. Individuals and groups who come onto the street must also have the sense that there is broad support from those who merely seem to be standing by. Word-of-mouth is particularly important in gaining a sense that if one takes to the streets there is still very significant backing from those who are not actually out there with you. Through such face-to-face communication people believe they can assess truth and support. Internet and cell phone contacts have built on this prerequisite, but their power has come from the need to sense broad if silent endorsement rather than from the inherent qualities of new technology alone. Thus a number of commenters have been misled into thinking the technology made all the difference: The *New York Times* called the Arab Spring "a revolution galvanized by social networking," while Thomas L. Friedman was doubly wrong when he said "the world is now hyperconnected, and there is no such thing as 'local' anymore."[14] Not only is the local very much with us but the evidence is overwhelmingly against the view that social networking was the predominant vehicle for assessing support or marshaling protesters on the Arab street.[15] Similarly, Westerners overemphasized the role of hip hop rappers like the Tunisian El Général (Hamada Ben Amor) several of whose songs, including *Rais Le-Bled* ("Leader of the Country"), were popular among those who took to the streets in the wake of the self-immolation of frustrated and harassed fruit vendor Muhammad Bouazizi in January 2011.[16]

To speak of recent events, then, as a "Facebook Revolution" is misleading in two senses. While the arrested Egyptian Google executive and website administrator, Wael Ghonim, argued that the social media were central to events, Jeffrey Ghannem (2011), reporting for the *Washington Post*, was probably more accurate in stating at the time that "this is not a Facebook revolution." He wrote: "Facebook is a platform not particularly friendly to protest because its messages and updates are largely disseminated only to those who belong to certain groups or who know where to look."[17] The technology should not be confused with the underlying causes of the revolts, he argued, a point underscored by Sami Ben Gharbia, cofounder of a Tunisian blog collective, when he referred to Facebook as "the echo chamber of the struggle on the street."[18]

THIS WAS NOT SOLELY A MIDDLE-CLASS STUDENT REVOLT BUT WAS, IN SIGNIFICANT PART, A REVOLT OF PARENTS AND LOWER-CLASS YOUTH. Arab parents will do anything to further the education of their children. Rural parents will move to town so their children can go to school; poorer parents will forsake their own needs to purchase textbooks and school uniforms. Look closely at the pictures of those who first participated in the protests—there was a lot of grey hair in the streets.[19] In Tunisia and Egypt it was the parents who came onto the street, frustrated by a system they could neither contravene nor circumvent. As the Cambridge University YouGov poll concluded: "Indeed, in contrast to those who have portrayed the participants in the Arab Spring as predominantly young, educated and unemployed—the 'youth bulge' explanation for the uprisings—the results we've seen indicate that in most (though not all) countries, those over 35 years old are slightly more likely to take part in protests than those under 35."[20] It was the children who made the parents' involvement possible, but it was the parents who made the revolts unstoppable.

Moreover, there is substantial evidence that it was lower income youth who began the demonstrations that led to the occupation of Tahrir Square. In particular, a group called the Ultras, who had faced the government in a number of incidents at soccer games, confronted soldiers outside of Cairo and in some of the neighborhoods beyond Tahrir Square.[21] Other young opposition organizers, having previously distributed leaflets and assessed the locations of police, massed in the western Cairo slums of Bulaq al-Dakrour and by outwitting government troops were able to get to Tahrir Square. Others gathered at mosques and then moved to the Square. In each case organizers did announce some of the demonstration sites on the internet but purposely hid the key gathering points. In the words of the *Wall Street Journal*'s on-site reporters: "The plotters say they knew that the demonstrations' success would depend on the participation of ordinary Egyptians in working-class districts like this one [Bulaq al-Dakrour], where the Internet and Facebook aren't as widely used."[22]

FIGURE 6.3. Older men in Tahrir Square (LentaChel.ru).

THE ARAB SPRING WAS NOT PRIMARILY ABOUT RELIGION OR SHARI'A. The demonstrations that took place in such disparate places as Tunisia and Bahrain, though immersed in a certain mutual contagion, cannot be lumped together any more than the participants in any one place or moment shared exactly the same motivations or goals. Certainly some, like supporters of the Muslim Brotherhood in Egypt, were propelled in part by a desire to have the state informed, both in its law and its morals, by Islamic precepts. But for the most part the evidence suggests that neither religion nor the implementation of Islamic law was central to the concerns of the vast majority of those who took to the streets. As one Egyptian told the late foreign correspondent for the *New York Times* Anthony Shadid (2011): "The last thing youth are thinking about is religion. It's the last thing that comes up."[23]

It is also not necessarily a contradiction that some polls show that younger cohorts agree more than do older ones with the assertion that government should make laws based on religion. Otherwise, they fear, laws may just be one more vehicle through which the powerful, having failed to gain them the jobs and possibilities for marriage that younger people value most, may continue to let them down.[24] And certainly the disillusion with the Muslim Brotherhood after a year of Mohamed Morsi's presidency indicated an unwillingness to allow religion to be the governing factor in many of the Egyptians' view of the state.

Similarly, in Tunisia compromises have had to be negotiated about the place of religion in the new constitution, while in Syria those who first revolted against Assad's government were clearly not driven by religious motivation as such. In this regard, the contrast to militant actions in Iraq, Afghanistan, Sudan, and Somalia are striking, as none of those countries was involved in the Arab Spring, their discord having been based to a limited degree on claims of religious purity and legitimacy. It is, therefore, unlikely that, sectarian divisions notwithstanding, what brought people to the streets in early 2011 in a number of Arab countries was based on specific religious attachments. However much the Egyptians were willing to afford the Brotherhood an opportunity to govern it was, as events were to prove, not because the majority was primarily moved by religious commitment.

THE SPARK MUST TAKE A CREDIBLE NARRATIVE FORM. The way key revolutionary events are told must be believable, even if they are not true. The Tunisian story is one of a poor fruit vendor, Muhammad Bouazizi, who, as on a number of other occasions, is said to have been harassed and solicited for a seven-dollar bribe by a Tunisian official.[25] "For a man who supported his mother, five younger siblings, and an ailing uncle, seven dollars was a full day's income—on a good day."[26] Thus on December 17, 2010, following another confiscation of his goods after he refused to pay the bribe, Bouazizi was allegedly slapped by Faida Hamdi, a forty-five year old female inspector in the provincial town of Sidi Bouzid. He then set himself on fire, dying eighteen days later.

Just as Americans resist the idea that assassins ever act out of political motivation rather than personal insanity, so, too, the Arab street responded to the credible story of corruption and degradation by an officer of the state who was, adding insult to injury, a woman. Although a Tunisian court subsequently allowed Bouazizi's mother to drop the complaint against Hamdi and found that the officer had not slapped the fruit seller, the story of a poor vendor harassed by a corrupt official—and a woman at that—had already had its effect. To touch so deeply the felt sense of humiliation experienced by many Tunisians it is very likely that if the particular details of Bouazizi's story did not exist they would have had to be created. The story that sparks a revolution in other Middle Eastern countries may be particular to local circumstance; yet as one understands what

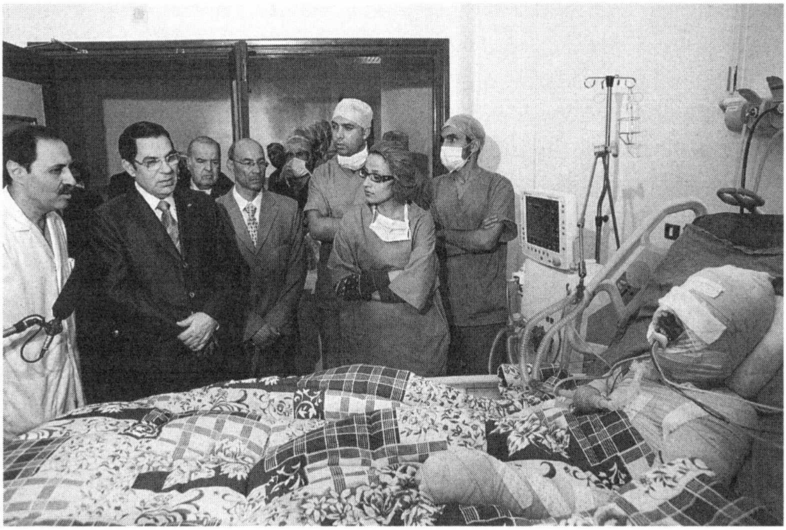

FIGURE 6.4. Bouazizi visited in hospital by President Ben Ali (Tunisian government handout).

makes each believable one can comprehend, if not predict, why inchoate sensibility may turn to overt action.[27]

THE PROTESTERS IN EGYPT'S TAHRIR SQUARE DID NOT TAKE OVER PUBLIC SPACE. In fact, the opposite is closer to the truth, for there is no concept of public space in Arab culture, only private space and state-controlled space. From the moment one steps outside one's home there is no sense of responsibility for the space one enters: No one in the Arab world would dream of cleaning up the ever-present garbage and plastic bags, much less clear room for a bed of flowers, in space that is not their own property. Places are either government-controlled space or land identified with some individual, with mosques, like prayer itself, occupying precisely that interstitial space that makes it both sacred and spiritually perilous.

Private space can, however, be extended into what Westerners might mistakenly categorize as public space. Thus on the pilgrimage to Mecca men mix with unveiled women as they would in a home, while in many Arab countries on the occasion of the Prophet's birthday shopkeepers bring carpets and tea sets from home, converting an entire bazaar into a virtual guestroom. This also goes a long way toward explaining what for many commenters was seen as a fatal flaw in the whole of the Egyptian

Arab Spring, namely the absence of leadership. Juan Cole relates a telling anecdote: "Sociologist Saad Eddin Ibrahim told me that in February 2011, when he flew back to Egypt and went to Tahrir Square, he asked the demonstrators, 'Take me to your leader.' He laughed as he told the story. 'They looked at me funny.'"[28] But their response should not have been so surprising since in these situations, where the expectations of private space are operative, people know perfectly well how to conduct themselves, thus obviating the need for additional leadership. Such ritual reversals give a different meaning, then, to spaces and reinforce the ethos of the private by the very nature of the inversion. Even partisanship was, as in a home, set aside: "it was an article of faith on the square that no parties should display their own banners."[29]

Reports from Cairo therefore consistently showed that protesters cleaned the Square (something no one does voluntarily in "public space"), spoke to the police as they would to fellow guests in one's home, and offered one another hospitality as they entered the area. Speaking of her experience, American University of Cairo Professor Barbara Ibrahim said, "before I had taken nine or ten steps into the square, I was offered biscuits and tea."[30] The Square was made to feel like home, even like a wedding party: "Gather the tea, the belly dancers, and my heart will stop bullets," chanted many of those as they marched into the Square. As in a home, women at this stage in events found the Square had the feel of private space. A reporter wrote: "Egyptian women who were in the square say they were treated with a tolerance they hardly expected. Woman after woman marveled at that. 'One of the things that gave an incredible sense of wonder was how safe I felt, [political activist Marwa] Faraok said,' I spent the night there, with all kinds of different people, and Tahrir Square became safer than anywhere else for a woman to be.'"[31] And Sherine Hafez (2012, 40) reported: "Whereas rates of street harassment of women are close to 90 percent in Egypt, not a single known case of harassment was reported from Tahrir Square during the days of the uprising."

The emphasis on treating the streets as private space was evident in various places. In Syria, men and women danced together, as they might in a household wedding.[32] In Tahrir Square it was reported that "volunteers swept streets and manned clinics, while Muslims and Christians guarding the barricades took turns to pray."[33] As they entered the Square people were searched by members of their own gender. However, "beyond the checkpoint," as the *Washington Post* reported, "distinctions vanished and they [men and women] stood side by side, defying the police, challenging

FIGURE 6.5. Ordinary citizens sweeping Tahrir Square.

the government, . . . steadfast for freedom and democracy."[34] "Dignity" (*karāma*), the watchword of the revolution, was felt and not just voiced when, at Tahrir Square, the world was, quite literally, turned outside in. Since, as suggested, everyone knows how to act in private space, the criticism that the revolt lacked leadership misses the more striking fact that those who came into the Square created a space where the values and relationships that they find in the home could be so glaringly shown to be lacking in the state.

The people in Tahrir thus turned the Square into recognizable private space, where (as in a home or on the pilgrimage to Mecca) men and women could mingle in an area of peace and cleanliness. Though inadequately reported, similar practices appear to have applied in a number of neighborhoods, where the very concept of the quarter (*ḥuma*), so central to Arab urban history, was, at least briefly, revitalized.[35] By taking control of neighborhoods and government squares, the protesters invoked their personal sense of ownership and inviolability, thus maintaining a crucial connection between their private domains and their newfound collective voice. Indeed, as in the home, they recreated a space without corruption, a place where one shared unsparingly with those characterized by ties of interdependency. Notwithstanding their heartfelt extension of the private, however, the protesters ultimately failed to create a new concept of space and with it a new concept of the relation of the people to the state.

DEMONSTRATIONS ARE OFTEN DISPLACED. Public protests are often about something other than what they seem to be about. At the time of the first Gulf War, for example, protesters in several Arab countries that joined the coalition against Saddam Hussein showed up without government knowledge or approval. They told those who inquired that, notwithstanding their ostensible opposition to their country's offer of troops to the allied effort, they were really there to demonstrate that the government could not control if and when they might choose to express their complaints. In other situations, a protest about, say, food prices may actually be a protest about the government having suddenly changed the proportion of students allowed to receive the baccalaureate degree that year. Thus it is quite possible that, for example, the protests by attorneys in Tunisia in early 2009 were less about solidarity with the people of Gaza than against the corruption of the regime of President Zine El Abidine Ben Ali, just as Egyptian strikes ostensibly protesting the failure of the Mubarak regime to criticize the Bush administration for the U.S. navy's killing of a civilian in the Suez Canal in March 2008 were largely about the workers' own poor salaries and working conditions.[36] Only careful, qualitative interviews can get at the word that is passing among demonstrators, and only careful attention to the history of such protests can help place the events of the Arab Spring in the alternative meaning structures of those who engaged in them.

A REBELLION IS NOT A REVOLUTION. In a revolution people seek to change the existing system; in a rebellion they want *into* the system. Events that seem to call for a complete alteration in political structure may actually be a claim for greater inclusion in the existing system. In Morocco, in the years after Independence, for example, when the demands of protesters in the Rif Mountains were finally addressed, what they wanted was not a regime change but a minister in the government from their area. In much the same way the legendary seventeenth-century Moroccan saint Sidi Lahcen Lyussi brought the most powerful sultan in his country's history literally to his knees only to demand the monarch's ratification that the saint shared in the king's noble descent.[37]

Protests may also be a function of highly localized issues or patronage systems, something reporters who do not know the countries or languages usually miss. Thus, according to Ernest Gellner—whose essay on rural rebellions may also have some resonance, say, in the context of Libya and Yemen—patrons must be ready to activate their networks at short notice, such that a big man may even "strike a match to see if it will work when the day comes, or he may wish to show his opponents what good matches he has."[38] Since, in the wake of the initial overthrow of some of the region's governments, the shape of many protests remained subject to alteration, inclusion rather than complete change (particularly in monarchies like those of Morocco, Jordan, and the Gulf) proved to be the acceptable end result for many of those who came out onto the streets.

As is always the case in the Arab world capturing the terms of discussion is a crucial element of social and political power. People in Egypt did not concentrate on the Arabic word for revolution (*ṭawwrat*); they spoke instead of having had "enough" (*kifāya*) and of their actions being an "awakening," the latter term having great resonance because a person who is truly adult, mature is said to be "awake" (*naḍi*). Even the word for "state" in Arabic (*daula*)—from a root meaning "to change or revolve periodically," "to have a change of fortune"—resonates with the idea of the state as a shifting set of characters rather than a depersonalized and enduring institutional structure. While the motives and desired ends of such a diverse group of participants, supporters, and national backgrounds are too easily subsumed under the broad heading of an "Arab Spring," whether most sought revolution or a more inclusive "revolving" cannot be unquestioningly presumed.

POLITICAL LEGITIMACY GROWS OUT OF NETWORKS OF OBLIGATION. The fallen regimes may have been despised but they were not (as *New York Times* columnist Thomas L. Friedman asserts) viewed as illegitimate. Legitimacy in the Arab world is not based on popularity but on the construction of a personal system of patronage. It is actually one of the limitations on those in power that anyone who can form an effective network and take power is ipso facto legitimate, whether they are also liked or despised. Such a big-man pattern, characteristic of societies infused with a tribal ethos, depends entirely on a process of justification by effective social networking.[39] The state is too impersonal to be a reliable ally. It cannot be emphasized too often that reciprocity and negotiated webs of indebtedness are not possible with such an entity: The state is *un*reciprocity incarnate. Only personal bonds of obligation can supply momentary safety, and since (as the Arabic saying goes) "your neighbors who are close are more important than your kin who are far away" it is unsurprising that many neighborhoods in Egypt immediately rallied to a form of collective security. When the reciprocity that such a system implies breaks down people seek new associations wherever they may prove most efficacious, which is why everything from kinship ties to political helpmates and religious brotherhood associations were suddenly revitalized and renegotiated. Democratic institution building as understood in the West would, then, have as its greatest challenge the shift from a cultural system of legitimacy based on personalism to one based on impersonal institutions.

THE OPERATIVE WORD ON THE STREET IS "JUSTICE." Where Americans may protest about their "rights," Arabs gravitate more toward phrasing matters in terms of "justice" (*'adl*).[40] It is true that other words were stressed on the streets of Cairo and Tunis, "dignity" (*karāma*) foremost among them. But the resonance of "justice" has deep roots in Arab cultures, and thus, like any powerful concept or symbol, condenses and renders almost tangible a set of assumptions and aspirations distinctive to a particular view of the world. In Arab culture and jurisprudence justice does not, however, mean equality. Rather, as I have earlier suggested, it implies that multiple ways of building attachments to others, in large part through the development of one's own knowledge and skills, should remain available at all times. Justice is a personal attribute, not an external circumstance; it is the fabrication of a distinctive set of relationships that are not limited by one's birth or gender, however much those features conduce to a likely result. It is not freedom in the sense of the ability to do whatever one wishes with the least possible governmental constraint that is valued but rather the capacity to employ one's God-given reason to better the situation of oneself and one's dependents. It is the limitation on opportunities to build personal bonds that yields a felt sense of injustice, and it is this subversion of justice that, in the lead-up to the Arab Spring, truly hurt.

* * *

The Russians have a saying: "It is not the future that is hard to predict, but the past." As the Arab Spring stands between past and present, prediction in both directions becomes highly problematic. When things lack a place in the past, chaos seems to have governed and the future (absent the criteria by which to understand whether there was an order to the past) becomes equally inchoate. Categories may shift for a moment—chaos may not seem the only alternative to tyranny, hospitality may not seem to envision reciprocity—but if Hannah Arendt was right in saying that a true revolution requires both a change in thinking *and* a change in relating it is hard to find grounds for calling any of the results of the Arab Spring revolutionary. Persons are still not separated from institutions, actions are not segregated from expectations of reciprocity, and the self is still not fractionated into a series of discrete roles. Without such category shifts it is difficult, then, to agree with Juan Cole that the younger generation has irrevocably altered its predecessors' approach to the state.[41] Indeed, without such category shifts it is not surprising that "the politics of hope" should have been superseded by "the politics of disappointment." Thus even in Tunisia the World Bank reports that graft has actually intensified in the years since the onset of the Arab Spring.[42]

Tahrir Square has seen many protests over the years, including mass demonstrations in 2003–4 and labor strikes in 2007–8. But by 2013, following the protests that ousted Muhammad Morsi and the Muslim Brotherhood from power, the Square was largely empty: "The smell of rotting garbage hung in the air; the crumpled banners, empty soda cans, and old corn cobs of last night's victory party smashed and strewn across the pavement. . . . [M]ost of the protesters who filled this square for six straight days, calling for Morsi's ouster, had gone home, packing up their tents, their job finally done."[43] One is therefore reminded of what Jules Michelet said of the French Revolution, which "has for her monument empty space. . . . this sandy place [the Champs de Mars], flat as Arabia."[44]

The private space is gone, the very idea of public space has yet to be created, and Tahrir Square has reverted to government space. But what happened there is not insignificant. The people in the Arab Street sank to the depths of cultural discomfort and then extricated themselves through practices that felt both familiar and authentic. They did not reconfigure the categories of their experience but they also did not abandon those concepts that bespeak their own sense of decency and authenticity, and therein may lay the greatest hope for their reimagining both past and future—as well as the greatest reason for outsiders not to meddle.

CHAPTER SEVEN

Will the Middle Class Save the Middle East?

The theory seems perfectly straightforward: At some point those who are doing reasonably well economically begin to want greater control over the governing order and press for a stronger voice in this domain—indeed, greater "democratic" involvement in the overall political system. Immediately, though, a host of questions arises. If it is an economic stake that triggers the drive toward democratic inclusion, is it control over private property that creates the democratic impulse or is it freedom of contract, access to public goods, or a quest for social security? If we call this grouping the "middle" class is it some interstitial position or role that is crucial—even some fear of slipping down to the bottom, some resentment of those farther up the scale—or is the primary motivation to solidify existing gains or perceived entitlement through political power? Indeed, what does "middle class" really mean? Is it literally being situated between other entities or does it have distinctive characteristics—even universal characteristics—that transcend relative placement? And if there is sufficient specificity as to its definition, at least for a given country and time, what is its shape and political prospects in the Arab nations of North Africa and the Middle East at present?

At a time when a number of the countries in the region are teetering on the edge of chaos, returning to military dictatorships, or mired in pseudo-democratic structures, asking whether the middle class will be their political salvation may seem misplaced or naive. Yet many outsiders continue to base their hopes for the region on the middle class and to back their belief with aid programs and seminars that connect this hope with the allied concept of the rule of law. They are even prepared to tell themselves that some intermediate autocratic step may be necessary to address security concerns while the middle class develops to the point where it can seek democratic inclusion. Since the policies of America in particular seem to favor such a combination of sociological predictability and free market inevitability, it is important to question the premises and historical validity of this assumption, particularly inasmuch as it remains a vital part of the ideology—indeed the mythology—of Western approaches to the peoples and polities of the region.

* * *

Western historians, philosophers, and politicians who assume that the middle class is indeed vital to the development of democracy often begin with Aristotle's assertion that "surely the ideal of the state is to consist as much as possible of persons that are equal and alike, and this similarity is most found in the middle classes; therefore the middle-class state will necessarily be best constituted in respect of those elements of which we say that the state is by nature composed."[1] Not everyone agrees. Karl Marx, building on Malthus's discussion of "the middle regions of society," was hardly a proponent of middle-class democratization, although he did grudgingly admit, in *The Communist Manifesto*, that, "historically, it has played a most revolutionary part. The bourgeoisie, wherever it has got the upper hand, has put an end to all feudal, patriarchal, idyllic relations. . . . The bourgeoisie, by the rapid improvement of all instruments of production, by the immensely fabricated means of communication, draws all, even the most barbarian, nations into civilization." Of course Marx thought the bourgeoisie would disappear when class conflicts lead to the fulfillment of the masses' best interest. Max Weber was also one who argued that a bureaucratic order based on the rational calculation of means to ends was no guarantee of participatory rule by the fullest array of candidates. But most Westerners continue to assume that democracy comes not from the margins but from the very middle of society.[2]

Support is usually drawn from further reference to ancient history. In the archetypal example, as Josiah Ober has argued, classical Greece, far from being impoverished, was characterized by a density of population, urban concentration, and relatively equitable wealth distribution such that upwards of 20% of each polis achieved "a level high enough above subsistence to qualify as at least minimally decent." This "middling" class (as Ober calls it) came about through heavy investment in human capital, the reduction of time spent searching for information and connections, and the sharing of new institutions across competing political entities. Equal access to these institutions—coupled with the separation of personality from political role, security against arbitrary seizure of property, and incentives to learn practical and public skills (including service as jurors, magistrates, etc.)—led to a veritable "market in institutions."[3]

Tracing a causal link between the rise of such a middle class and the development of democratic institutions, however, poses problems for both theory and practice. Is it imperative that one achieve a "take-off" level of economic well-being before developing institutional constraints? Is separating personality from institutions indispensable to participatory governance or the formation of a government of limited powers (if these are indeed the defining features of a democracy)? Must one subscribe to a belief system that balances individual achievement with collective leveling (whether by taxation or social pressure) if one is to avoid Aristotle's assumption that, as between the very rich and the very poor, "the former turn more to insolence and grand wickedness, and the latter overmuch to malice and petty wickedness"? And if we in the West wish to encourage democratic development worldwide how can we be sure that we are not simply extending our own mythic experience—whether it embraces the notion that democracies never make war against one another or that, as President Barack Obama said in his Nobel address, "we'er all basically seeking the same things"—when we promote international aid or militarized nation building?

Setting aside the polemical claims by American politicians that they are working to help the middle class—for which, during the Obama administration, there was even a White House Middle Class Task Force headed by the vice president—and surveys that show the vast majority of Americans think they occupy that strata, the very definition of middle class is remarkably fluid even among those social scientists who have studied the subject. A Brazilian economist thus describes the members of this class as "people who are not resigned to a life of poverty, who are prepared to make sacrifices to create a better life for themselves and who have not started with life's material problems solved because they have material assets to make their lives easier."[4] Others argue that middle-class status begins when roughly a third of one's income remains for discretionary spending after basic needs for food and shelter are provided. A number of sociologists distinguish various categories of middle-class existence along dimensions of control of power or the cultural symbols by which their society identifies and orients itself.[5] Thus when we begin to approach the literature on the Middle East we are often faced with vague or conflicting definitions of the very subject of investigation.[6] Perhaps a useful point of entry here are the analyses offered in several recent studies of the middle class in the Middle East, studies that, in rather different ways, are grounded in the belief that the development or lack of development of a middle class is crucial to the political future of the region.

Vali Nasr is dean of the Johns Hopkins School of Advanced International Studies, a member of the State Department's Foreign Affairs Policy Board, and a former advisor to the U.S. senior representative to Afghanistan and Pakistan, Amb. Richard Holbrooke. In his book, *Forces of Fortune: The Rise of the New Muslim Middle Class and What It Will Mean for Our World*, Nasr claims that there does indeed exist a "rising middle class" in the Middle East. Arguing that "the tide has already turned against extremism," Nasr believes the battle is really about access to free markets: "If that battle is won by private-sector business leaders and the rising middle class tied to them, then progress with political rights will follow." Recalling that the Prophet said "the merchant is the beloved of God," he sees pious businessmen as the true supporters of modernity, such that if the Middle East is to become democratic "it will have to be transformed by the capitalist revolution."[7]

Nasr begins by looking at Dubai, which might seem a prime example since it is not dependent on oil revenues and has, though rather unevenly, undergone phenomenal growth. But in 2008–9 the property bubble burst: Foreign workers were heading home at the rate of 5,000 per day, many abandoning cars at the airport. In the years since that Great Recession, Dubai has slowly recovered but it still remains anything but typical: 85–90% of its population is comprised of foreigners who can never receive citizenship, much of its wealth comes from monies funneled to it from abroad, and its combination of playboy haven and uncompleted building projects bespeaks not the formation of a hardworking business class but the development of a precarious brand that cannot easily be replicated elsewhere in the region.[8]

Nasr's example of Iran is more apt. Here, he claims, over half of the population is middle class or above. Moreover, it was this class that he says supported the Islamic revolution but then lost control of it. Following the death of Ayatollah Ruhollah Khomeini in 1989, the governments of Presidents Akbar Ali Hashemi Rafsanjani and Mohammad Khatami encouraged business growth until the Supreme Leader Grand Ayatollah Sayyid Ali Hosseini Khamenei sensed that a rising middle class might also begin demanding changes in society and government. Stalled in their effort to become part of a global business world the Iranian middle class, like those of a number of other countries, eventually allied itself with an authoritarian regime rather than take up an intermediate role between the state and the fundamentalists.

The one success story to which Nasr points would appear to be Turkey. Ataturk, of course, operated under the slogan "For the People, Despite the People," thus not so much exemplifying the natural yearning of a middle class for democracy as the forced elimination of preexisting cultural forms. For all its supposed success Ataturk's secularist model failed elsewhere, says Nasr, because it bred dependence on the state rather than genuine entrepreneurship. That many of the current regime's supporters are pious businessmen is no contradiction. If the business class is allowed greater attachment to global markets, as Nasr says is true of Turkey, it will not be secularism that triumphs but the sort of business-oriented religiosity that characterized the Scottish Enlightenment.[9] Yet the political party most identified with this class in Turkey has, by Nasr's own account, largely fallen into the hands of tycoons. In many respects, then, economic progress and intermittent democratization have run on parallel tracks and their connections do not point in a simple causal direction.

Nasr's faith in the almost ineluctable move from commerce to democracy suffers from its very imprecision. Not only are terms never defined but comparative examples—like Latin America in recent times—are anything but clear-cut. His faith in Hume's assertion that commerce encourages moderation, that the middle class has no interest in extremism, or that it is only dependence on the state that has undermined economic development are cast in a framework that lacks institutional and cultural analysis. With hardly a reference to other Arab countries and absent a fuller social analysis, the result is more akin to that of neoconservative dogma and liberal hopes than a solid argument based on a wide range of Middle Eastern cases.

Francis Fukuyama offers a similarly generalized view of democratic development, one that incorporates an evolutionary view of the sort popular history writers often favor. He characterizes the middle class as composed of those whose occupation and educational level and ownership of housing or goods are significant enough to be threatened by the government, and in the defense of which, particularly if they become the majority, they will develop the democratic values of greater political participation, individual freedom, and toleration of differences.[10] While not specifically analyzing the Middle Eastern countries in detail, his faith in the middle classes as the engine of democratic progress suffuses his work.

> The timing of the spread of democracy in different countries therefore depended on the changing relative positions of the middle class, the working class, landowning elites, and the peasantry. Where the old agrarian order was built around large landowners dependent on servile labor, a peaceful transition to democracy became particularly difficult. But in almost all cases the rise and growth of middle-class groups was critical to the spread of democracy. Democracy in the developed world became secure and stable as industrialization produced middle-class societies, that is, societies in which a significant majority of the population thought of themselves as middle class.[11]

In his review of Fukuyama's book, John Gray, noting the insupportable evolutionism of the author's approach to grand history and describing the work as "a morass of intellectual confusion and category mistakes," notes the fallacy in stressing the inevitable relation of the middle class to democracy:

> Fukuyama believes democracy is the only system of government with a long-term future, a familiar idea emerges: as societies become more prosperous, the growing global middle class will demand more political freedom and governmental accountability. Effectively a restatement of Marx's account of the historical role of the bourgeoisie, it is an idea we have all heard many, many times before. In fact the political record of the middle classes is decidedly mixed. In Europe, throughout much of the 20th century, many middle-class people reacted to economic and political crisis by embracing the enemies of liberal democracy—fascism, communism and ethnic nationalism. Rightly, Fukuyama expresses some concern about the impact on the quality of political life of a middle class that is shrinking rapidly under the effects of globalisation and technological change. But even when the middle class was stronger than it is today, it has rarely acted as *deus ex machina* for democracy.[12]

If Nasr is insufficiently clear about the structures that affect democratic growth and Fukuyama's evolutionism is equally imprecise, Steffen Hertog's *Princes, Brokers, and Bureaucrats: Oil and State in Saudi Arabia* is far more circumstantial.[13] On its face it may not seem to speak to issues of the middle class. Yet it is precisely in such details of political organization that clues to the formation and dependence of such a class may lie. Having worked as a consultant to bureaucracies in Saudi Arabia, Hertog offers a highly detailed and analytically sophisticated view of why certain political and economic reforms that may bear on democratization have succeeded in Arabia and others have not.

Contrary to the usual image of an oil-rich state necessarily resulting in a centralized and bloated bureaucracy of limited institutional design, Hertog argues that the Saudi state is like a hub-and-spoke arrangement in which the center is crucial but coordination is weak. The results are quite varied: Some government offices operate well while others lag in efficiency and innovation. Each unit is really a compact clientele structure in its own right, such that even though the state as a whole may rely on extra-territorial sources of income it is largely fragmented within, each of the bureaucracies forming "statelets within the state." No crosscutting groups materialize within this pattern—neither merchants, nor tribes, nor clerics—each being co-opted to a degree by the patronage and licensing of the state, on the one hand, and the obligations tying each individual to his or her particular patron, on the other. The result is not a stultifying array of hidebound agencies but a heterogeneous assemblage displaying quite variant efficacy and vigor. Hierarchy exists, but given the mini-constellations below them elite control is weak, inactivity is difficult to punish, information is more likely to flow to one's boss than to one's peers, corruption is far less the problem than coordination, and there is little horizontal pressure leading to the emergence of interest groups.

In an environment of such "segmented clientelism" even businessmen find themselves consuming policy rather than lobbying for it, often choosing to move around the bureaucracy through their own connections, at home and abroad, rather than coordinate internal pressures. In what might, then, appear to be a disjointed system, what one actually encounters is a nested set of distinct bodies, each of which may bear the mark of the lassitude or energy of its central figure but none of which reaches across the lines of its own client structure to form impersonal groups pressing for greater political inclusion. Thus where Nasr sees incipient democratic institutions being assembled by historical forces that transcend particular cultures Hertog demonstrates that any such arrangement is utterly contingent and in no way points in any given direction. Indeed, his analysis suggests that economic position within the country's strata is less crucial than the mechanisms of incorporation in a culturally distinctive type of bureaucracy.

Hertog's assessment meshes well with the findings of other scholars. In her *Barriers to Democracy* Amaney Jamal, for instance, shows how the Palestinian government has co-opted those very associations that might constitute the basis for democratic reform.[14] Whether by reinforcing vertically structured patronage networks or through state-sponsored NGOs (which someone has humorously denominated "NoGOs"), the associational life many see as forming the grassroots basis of democratic governance is subverted by the central government. True, the lawyers in Cairo and Pakistan have occasionally stood up as a group against the powers that be, and religious brotherhoods and mosque groups may appear to satisfy Tocqueville's belief that it is in such groupings, "by the reciprocal influence of men on each other," that "feelings and opinions are recruited, the heart is enlarged, and the human mind is developed." But on their own and in the face of state-controlled security and resources, the ability of these associations to counter the daily need to build a durable network of one's own renders them merely the sites for replicating vertical ties. And when an entire sector of the population is cowed or driven out collective formation becomes virtually impossible.

This was certainly the case in Iraq, as indicated by Deborah Amos in her *Eclipse of the Sunnis: Power, Exile, and Upheaval in the Middle East.*[15] For as we are reminded by the author, who reports regularly for National Public Radio, over two million people have been forced from the country as the result of sectarian violence, over 70% of whom were the very professionals vital to a middle class. If there was a surge in Iraq, she quips, it was *out* of Iraq. Were it not for the killings one could laugh at the death lists that included people guilty of eating a kind of bread not used in the Prophet's day, or the forced closure of vegetable stands displaying together (male) cucumbers and (female) tomatoes. The exiles in Syria (who are denied the right to work and are subject to visa renewals every ninety days, many of whom fled again after civil war broke out) and those in Jordan (which started to close its borders after the Amman hotel bombings of 2005) constitute a "middle-class exodus" unprecedented in the Arab world and now find themselves reduced to political impotence and near poverty.

Notwithstanding her lucid and engaging description of their plight, Amos may focus too much on artists and intellectuals who speak English rather than a broad range of cases. She has the journalist's habit of combining angle (the underreported exiles' story), anecdotes (believable because she figures as an eyewitness in most of them), and little-known statistics (15% of the exiles are Christians, in 2009 Iraq was ranked the fourth most corrupt country in the world, and in the same year more Iraqis were still leaving the country than returning). Along the way we learn that Prime Minister Nouri al-Maliki wanted the Syrians to arrest sixty-five Iraqi émigré actors when he visited the country, that housing pressure created by the exiles has made it extremely difficult for middle class Jordanian newlyweds to find apartments, that the UN sanctions that began in 1991 all but impoverished the Iraqi middle class, and that many of the women exiles have descended into the sex trade. And all of this before the military successes of the Sunni fundamentalist "Islamic State" began dividing the country (and obliterating the border to Syria) in 2014. There is, however, no indication why one should believe that, were they able to do so, returning exiles would press for democratic reforms or that their economic position alone would contribute to this impulse.

Amos is no more to be criticized than others for not seeing the twists and turns that have taken place in Iraq and Syria since her book was published. The rise of sectarian groups belies any claim of permanent eclipse, and the claim by the Islamic State leaders, backed by their territorial gains and transnational claims, only shows the fecklessness of any predictions for the region. Whatever else, though, the displaced middle class of Iraq, like that of the mid-economic Syrians, is either irrelevant to the civil conflict or is in no position to press for democratic reforms.

We are left, then, not only with conflicting definitions of the middle class (thus making direct comparisons difficult) but with a questionable claim that, however defined, in any given part of the Middle East such a class actually exists. A number of analysts finesse the issue by simply looking at each country and determining who is in the middle by the standards of developing countries generally. Using this standard the proportion that is in the middle has grown to a little over half of the population of the full range of developing countries in recent years, a goal achieved not by slow gain but in distinct spurts. Thus in places like China or India the surge has been dramatic. Progress in the Middle East, by comparison, has been less impressive. But of equal importance is that even if "middle class" describes an income level it invariably is accompanied by modulations in attitude, outlook, and values so that, as one commenter has put it, the category is "more sociological than logical."[16] Indeed, if we view the category and its connection to political reform together a serious question arises as to whether it even applies to the situation of a number of parts of the Arab world in any useful way.

It may put the matter too strongly but I would suggest that with the possible exceptions of Turkey, Iran, and Lebanon there is no middle class in most of the Middle East, especially among the Arab countries. Previous scholars who have made the same claim have attributed the failure to develop a bourgeois class to such factors as the lack of Islamic legal provisions supporting corporate structures, urban elites who could simply rely on regularly extracting payments from the peasantry, or the absence of a church structure that could be emulated by professional or trade groups.[17] However, my reason for suggesting that no middle class is to be found in most of the Middle East focuses on two ingredients I think are necessary if the idea of a middle class is to be a useful analytic concept, one that is more than an ideal type or taxonomic convenience. The first is that one must have a fair chance of passing one's social status or economic position along to the next generation, and the other is that the class must possess a significant degree of resource independence such that it is not the mere instrument or creation of the state and subject to its arbitrary manipulation. Each of these features requires some elaboration.

If, generally speaking, in the Arab world each person must fabricate a network of personal alliances and if, as the Arabs say, three days after his death, his property dispersed and his alliances dissipated, a man no longer exists, then it is very difficult, short of being very rich or powerful indeed, to pass one's network along to another. Unable to do so those in the middle are particularly vulnerable to rising and, more importantly, falling in the socioeconomic order, and since neither education nor kinship is a clear guarantee against such movement the ability to maintain the features of a class easily slips through one's fingers. Moreover, many of those in the middle in the Arab countries are there at the instigation and sufferance of those controlling government handouts and positions. Without an independent base such a middle class is without resources of its own and as a result lives largely as a handmaiden of those who control the levers of state power. In the absence of these two definitional features it can, therefore, be argued that a true middle class is rare in the Arab world and the Middle East more generally, and that whatever the merits of an argument that democracy will grow out of such a class, the sheer absence of that class vitiates any realistic expectation that democracy will, for this reason, manifest itself anytime soon.

Each of the works that has been discussed here does, however, at least focus our attention of what it might mean to speak of a middle class in the Middle East and, if it is not from this segment of society, whether other groupings might offer some chance for democratic reform. For even if a middle class fails to develop or is not the group from which change can be expected this may not be the only source from which democratic impulses may stem.

Women are another possibility. Women have not only taken their places in many Middle Eastern bureaucracies and limited their birth rate through later marriage and birth control but have contributed to some noteworthy advances in the reform of family law and even property law. Whether it is in microfinance or dress, Quranic interpretation or media exposure, women in the region may gain more control of their finances and their fates in ways that build important changes from the ground up. In that sense it is at least possible that they could substitute for class formation to a limited degree. In the 1920s the Soviets tried to use the Muslim women of central Asia as a kind of "surrogate proletariat."[18] The men, however, reacted sharply, even in some cases violently, against this intrusion into family life. But with far more Arab and Iranian women now in the workplace the situation could have quite different consequences. On the negative side, however, women's presence in an unsegregated public sphere could, once again, constitute a threat to male authority and yield few political dividends for society as a whole.

The causal link between a middle class and democracy thus remains at best unproven. Nasr goes farthest in making the connection: "There is ample evidence that what is true of the rising middle class in the Middle East [and Pakistan] is that given the chance to pursue business growth without stifling government control, a capitalist flourishing will follow, and a thriving middle class will serve as the impetus for moderation and democracy." Moreover, he says (2009, 256), "the West can help this development by encouraging states to loosen their hold on their economies and free their markets. We have to accept that this is the necessary historical process that the Middle East must go through if it is to get to the next stage—the Holy Grail of freedom and prosperity." Fukuyama raises this set of assertions to the level of an almost ineluctable evolutionary scheme which only foolishness could derail. It is the other authors cited, though, who, less bound by ideology, highlight contributing factors that in any given situation may indeed lead to greater representation but from which no universal pattern can be drawn. Their studies remind us that separating institutions from personalities is difficult to come by in the Middle East if it means risking one's carefully constructed network of kin and associates against impersonal bureaucracy, or sacrificing the social pressures of one's own community for the insecurities of the global market.

In understanding the connection of economics to democracy the criteria and definitions we choose may reveal a fuller range of relevant factors, but we can just as easily be led into some form of reductionism. The assertion that insecurity of property has precluded the development of democracy in the Middle East, that the regimes of the area have made people "docile and acquiescent," or that Islam is antithetical to the democratization of religious interpretation are far too one-dimensional to constitute adequate accounts. Similarly the payment of taxes may lead to a vested interest in governmental participation, but this hardly explains why historically burdened lower classes have seldom risen up to demand some form of democracy. And the absence of certain legal tools—corporations, interest-bearing instruments, etc.—may affect exchange, but one cannot say that their relative absence in Islamic law creates autocracy when issues of trust and the interchangeability of obligations are given insufficient attention by analysts. Indeed is it not worth asking whether it is vital to any middle class that they be able to pass their status along to the next generation, something that may be more difficult when security is based on personally fashioned connections rather than transferable property?[19] And when, as noted earlier, an Arab friend quipped that bribery was their form of democracy because it meant you could undercut the commands of a big man by bribing someone lower down to do the opposite thus placing a limitation on power, was he not expressing a vision of democracy that requires some local rather than universal appreciation?

The uprisings of the Arab Spring in 2010–11 cannot be characterized as stemming simply from the middle class. Those who took to the streets of Tunis or Cairo, Benghazi or Manama came from a variety of economic backgrounds and confessional subdivisions. They may all wish in time to have many of the characteristics of people in the middle class of other nations but such factors as the general sense of frustration with corruption, unemployment, and wealth discrepancy played a far more important role than can be attributed to middle-class identity alone.

Barrington Moore's simple proposition "no bourgeois, no democracy" may appeal to free marketers and neocons as much as to liberal ideologues and those struggling out of poverty. But keeping state intrusion out has been enormously difficult. A report by the *Economist* on the developing nations and the middle class claimed that for the first time nearly half of their populations have surged into that category. But the report also pointed out that the middle class is not a homogeneous group, such that the middle classes that have developed as a helpmate to the state may behave very differently than those based on the private sector.[20] Similarly, ignoring the cultural meaning attached by people of the region to concepts of power, representation, and legitimacy in favor of the imagined prerequisites to universal democratization is unlikely to produce useful guidance.[21] What one takes away, then, from these and similar studies is that the course does not run true from economic well-being to political form and that the messy contingencies of local circumstance must be addressed in each Middle Eastern country and beyond if we are to comprehend the means by which a people acquire greater participation in governance and a fairer distribution of its powers.

CHAPTER EIGHT

Trying Terror

Zacarias Moussaoui and His Culture on Trial

In 2008 Judge Leonie M. Brinkema of the Federal District Court for the Eastern District of Virginia gave a talk to the Program in Law and Public Affairs at Princeton University. A couple of years earlier she had presided at the lengthy and fractious trial of Zacarias Moussaoui who was charged with six counts of conspiring to aid the 9/11 attackers. Judge Brinkema's main argument was very straightforward: The federal courts, she said, are perfectly capable of conducting a fair trial of defendants charged with terrorist offenses, such that special federal courts or military tribunals are unnecessary. In the course of her remarks Judge Brinkema said, however, that there were still aspects of Moussaoui's conduct during the trial that she did not understand. Why, she wondered, did he plead guilty when the evidence against him was not really that strong, and why did he keep disrupting the court proceedings with verbal abuse of her and others when, at least intermittently, he seemed to want to avoid the death penalty? She even seemed surprised that he was so forthcoming in naming others who were involved in the 9/11 plot.

In the question-and-answer period that followed I suggested that, based on my experience with North Africans, Moussaoui's actions might be more comprehensible if we consider the context within which, as one who was born and raised in France of Moroccan heritage, he may have been operating. Indeed, I suggested, many of the things he was precluded from saying or doing in court could have been accommodated by the federal rules of evidence and procedure without violating any principles of fundamental fairness. The question, then, is whether the trial of a defendant like Moussaoui, originating from a background different than native-born American defendants and charged with a terrorist-related offense, could have been more accommodating by taking into consideration his cultural background, but without denying the unavoidable distinctiveness of terrorism trials.

This is not a question of Islamic law in any direct sense, but it may be valuable to consider how certain elements of what might be called an Islamic legal ethos may nevertheless have played into Moussaoui's dilemma—how the style of presenting oneself in a strange legal setting and the expectations relating to oaths, evidence, and procedure may become part of the backdrop against which the encounter with a foreign legal system may be cast. To address these issues we have to look more closely at the participants in the trial and the issues that might be raised when culture is brought into the equation.

Trying to understand Moussaoui, however, presents a number of problems. As he was kept isolated and in solitary confinement since his arrest, I was obviously not able to interview him. However, we do have a number of available documents, including his testimony and statements in court, his copious motions to the judge, and his comments about and from the lawyers assigned to him. We also have one book by his brother Abd Samad, a second by his mother, Aïsha el-Wafi, and an account by anthropologist Katherine C. Donahue who attended the trial, as well as a variety of scholarly commentaries, journalistic descriptions, and courtroom artists' renderings. These sources provide a rich picture of Moussaoui, his background, and his attitudes but they do not answer many questions for which there is conflicting testimony. Some of what follows must, therefore, be both speculative and incomplete. My purpose, however, is to raise issues that appeared unresolved to the judge in the case and to any fair reading of the record, and not to claim any definitive interpretation of the man or his actions. Moreover, couched within a book concerning law and the rule of justice as envisioned in many Islamic countries, the case of Zacarias Moussaoui also serves as a window to an alternative perspective on these concerns.

* * *

"I am learning the hard way that every word count [*sic*] in this life."
—Zacarias Moussaoui, July 3, 2002[1]

On 9/11/2001 Zacarias Moussaoui was in jail. He had been arrested three weeks earlier not for anything explicitly related to the attacks that were to take place on that date but, at least nominally, for an immigration violation. It is true that investigators had been alerted by a flight instruction school as to Moussaoui's odd behavior, including paying $19,000 in cash to learn how to fly a 747 jetliner without having previously obtained a pilot's license.[2] It is also true that FBI agents in the Minneapolis office had warned that such a plane could be used as a weapon and, in addition to submitting a long memo that was never read and over seventy warnings to superiors, agents had sought to have Moussaoui's apartment and computer searched for information linking him to terrorist organizations.[3] Indeed, French authorities, who had placed Moussaoui on their watch list in 1999, had communicated to the Bureau their own suspicions about his attachment to such groups. However, FBI officials in Washington failed to pursue the requests emanating from the Minnesota office. When, following the attacks of 9/11, attention was focused on Moussaoui, officials initially claimed that he was the "20th bomber," there having been five terrorists aboard each of the planes that struck the World Trade Towers and the Pentagon but only four on the aircraft that crashed in a field in Pennsylvania. A search of Moussaoui's possessions turned up body armor, a tool with a collapsible knife, and the phone number of the cell in Hamburg, Germany, through which money was funneled to the actual hijackers.

As the only living person in custody who could be linked to the 9/11 attacks, Moussaoui became the central focus of the nation's desire to bring someone to justice.[4]

In many respects Moussaoui was a very likely suspect. Born in 1968 in France of parents who had migrated from Morocco, Zacarias and his family were disrupted by the frequent absence and alleged abuse by his father, the loss of two infant children by his subsequently divorced mother, and the difficult relations Zacarias experienced with his other siblings. He dated a French girl, Karine Bocat, but was told by her parents that he was not welcome in the family. He left France in 1992 to take a business degree in London and except for one brief visit and occasional phone calls did not see his family for another eight years. Instead, he became connected with a radical Islamic preacher at the infamous Finsbury Park mosque in London, and when he did return to see his family he was much changed in appearance and demeanor. Indeed, his mother, on more than one occasion, came to regard him as having been "brainwashed" by the people he encountered once he left France.

More ominously, Moussaoui traveled to several Muslim countries between 1995 and 2001, including Chechnya, Afghanistan, and Pakistan, where he made contact with extremist elements, including Osama bin Laden himself. These connections were, by any reasonable account, somewhat circumscribed: He helped run a guesthouse in Afghanistan for those being trained by bin Laden, but following a trip to Malaysia he was withdrawn from significant involvement in al-Qaeda's main designs because of his inability to follow instructions not to involve himself in the activities of sympathizers in that country.[5] There is testimony to support the prosecution's claim that the organizers of the 9/11 attack intended to have a "second wave" of hijackers fly airplanes into other targets at a later date and in other parts of the United States. Indeed, Khalid Sheikh Muhammad, from his incarceration at Guantánamo, stated that Moussaoui was being considered for just such an attack and was getting flight instruction for that purpose. However, Sheikh Muhammad—acknowledged as the key operative in the 9/11 attacks—insisted in his (highly redacted) statement presented to the court that Moussaoui could not keep his mouth shut and, as a result, was not trusted to have anything whatsoever to do with the actual 9/11 events.[6] Fifteen days after the final verdict in the case was handed down, Osama bin Laden also issued a statement saying that Moussaoui had no involvement in the attacks, claiming that the potential twentieth bomber was a Saudi who died in a firefight in his native country

FIGURE 8.1. Zacarias Moussaoui's mother, Aicha el-Wafi, with a picture of her imprisoned son, December 12, 2001 (AP Photo/ Christophe Ena).

in 2004.[7] Moussaoui's testimony about his own involvement in terrorist plans varied over the course of the years, and his inconstant demeanor was to present the judge presiding at his trial with a number of challenges.

In many respects the frustration that Judge Brinkema experienced throughout the legal process is understandable. Described as a diminutive woman in her early sixties at the time of the trial and, with her hair in a tight bun, looking more like the person who once took a master's degree in library sciences than someone appointed to the federal bench by President Clinton, Judge Brinkema had a well-deserved reputation for running a tight courtroom while maintaining a good sense of humor and unusual rapport with jurors.[8] She had presided over a wide variety of cases and was as well prepared as could be expected for a bench trial involving matters of national security. Prepared or not, she also had to contend with a defendant who saw the legal process, and her role in it, as entirely political. As Moussaoui put it: "I will not entertain the illusion that a U.S. District Judge Leonie Brinkema is an honest broker. Reality tells me that this judge is here as a field general, entrusted with the mission to get this matter over quickly. Every general has a commander in chief, and I know how much the U.S. commander in chief wants me to be over quickly."[9] As a result, Moussaoui made frequent comments and wrote numerous motions in which his language was understandably annoying to the court.

The formal indictment charged Moussaoui with six counts of conspiracy, several of which carried the possibility of a death penalty.[10] He initially refused to plead to the charges, so the judge entered a plea of not guilty on his behalf.[11] He wanted a Muslim attorney but the one he suggested was unacceptable to the court. The attorneys who were appointed for him then sought to plead him insane. Moussaoui not only objected to this tactic but complained loudly and bitterly that the attorneys, who he believed were nothing more than hirelings of the federal government, were not only characterizing him wrongly but were effectively trying to get him killed.[12] After months of wrangling he fired the lawyers and insisted on representing himself. By this time, as he and his attorneys complained, he had been held since his arrest in solitary confinement in a constantly lit cell and without any unmonitored contacts.[13] He even sought to plead guilty, though whether this was to avoid the death penalty, to eliminate his lawyers' attempts to make him appear mentally unbalanced, to demonstrate how connected he was to others in his world, or to highlight his perception of the court's bias is not entirely clear.[14] Uncertain about his legal and mental understanding of what a guilty plea might entail, Judge Brinkema refused Moussaoui's request, at which point he withdrew the plea. Following a mental evaluation, however, the judge ruled that Moussaoui was competent and agreed to his motion to serve as his own lawyer.[15]

Over the course of the next seventeen months Moussaoui filed many handwritten motions (totaling more than 270 over the course of the entire proceeding), some of which Judge Brinkema found so offensive that she sealed the documents and eventually, on November 14, 2003, cited them as a basis for ending the defendant's self-representation altogether.[16] When his motions were rejected Moussaoui frequently made rude and offensive remarks in court. At a hearing on his guilty plea, for example, he repeatedly cursed the judge.[17] Similarly, he said of other religious groups: "For the . . . American Jewish, we will exterminate them. For the Christian, it is different. . . . We have a way to accommodate them if they don't fight us."[18]

Some of Moussaoui's arguments, however, were taken very seriously. In particular, he wanted several al-Qaeda figures being held in custody at Guantánamo to testify on his behalf. The government not only refused to produce the witnesses but, claiming reasons of national security, would not even allow them to respond to questions posed by Moussaoui. Instead, they offered only a limited set of highly edited written answers to questions posed by government interrogators. However, in May 2003 Judge Brinkema ordered that the defendant be given the same access to testimony from the Guantánamo inmates as the government, and when the prosecution refused such access (and the Fourth Circuit Court of Appeals upheld the government's position) she eliminated the death penalty as a possible sentence.[19] The prosecution appealed her decision and on April 22, 2004, once again the Fourth Circuit reversed her ruling, thus reinstating the death penalty.[20] When, exactly a year later, Moussaoui surprised everyone by changing his plea to guilty—a plea the judge now accepted—the trial, with the possibility of death restored, moved to the penalty phase, a process that, following the elaborate selection of a jury, lasted for two months beginning on March 6, 2006.

Before considering possible explanations for Moussaoui's demeanor during the four and a half years the legal process lasted it may be worthwhile to back up for a moment and note some of the ways in which his behavior and appearance were portrayed by those participating in and reporting on the trial. In the courtroom, for example, Moussaoui was always dressed in a green prison jumpsuit—replete with the word "prisoner" written in large letters on his back.[21] During the penalty phase he was forced to wear a stun belt under his jumpsuit so he could be immobilized if he attacked any of the victims' families.[22] He frequently wore a skullcap of the type common to many Muslim men and his beard had become quite full. The journalistic terms and artist renderings used to characterize this appearance, however, were seldom neutral. Indeed, it would not be too much to say that they fit the Western stereotype of what a Muslim fanatic should look like. Thus his beard was described as "unkempt," his demeanor "abrasive," his interruptions a "rant," his quotations about unbelievers from the Quran evidence of his fanaticism, his rejection of his lawyers' efforts as filled with "rancor," and his memos to the judge "angry ramblings." Similarly, courtroom drawings showed him turned away or gesticulating forcefully, suggesting contempt for the overall process. The picture was not that of the young man who had evolved from a smiling youth and recipient of an advanced degree in Britain but of the fearsome terrorist whose dark mien and shaggy appearance was at one with his darker thoughts and designs. In the light of such a portrayal—both by Moussaoui and by the observers—a series of assumptions and contradictions seem to have come into play for the presiding judge.

FIGURE 8.2. Moussaoui before Judge Brinkema (artwork by William J. Hennessy, Jr./Court roomArt.com).

FIGURE 8.3. Moussaoui, graduating with a British business degree, under arrest, and as young man (AFP, FBI-Freebase, Archives Françoise Tallieu).

One of the things that in her Princeton talk Judge Brinkema said mystified her was the final decision by Moussaoui to plead guilty. Recall that initially he refused to enter any plea and that only after many months of contention with the judge and his court-appointed lawyers plus nearly a year and a half representing himself did Moussaoui change his plea to guilty. While his decision took the court and observers by surprise, one possible explanation for his change of plea—as well as his earlier attempts to enter such a plea—appears not to have been considered by the judge or any of the lawyers. The matter can be put quite simply: In Morocco defendants almost always plead guilty in criminal cases. Immediately, one has to qualify and problematize this bare assertion.

At the outset there is the question as to how "Moroccan" Moussaoui really was. Judge Brinkema consistently saw him as French, and certainly having been born and raised in France that seemed a reasonable viewpoint, even though Moussaoui himself rejected such a characterization.[23] But it may also have been a convenient viewpoint for the court to assume: As "French" he was rendered more familiar generally and the court need not consider his unusual cultural background, elements of which might have complicated the case still further.[24] Moreover, as a Frenchman he might seem less able to claim some personal or primordial attachment to the treatment of peoples in the parts of the Muslim world where American actions could be interpreted as provocative at best and colonialist or racist at worst. As a Frenchman he might even be seen as having betrayed the very Enlightenment principles within which he was raised and thus appear less a defender of Islam than a home-bred terrorist whose very presence among us makes his actions all the more threatening if not indeed treasonous. Ironically, treating him as "one of us" was thus more convenient, more damning, and—in important procedural respects—considerably easier to deal with than accommodating one's thinking of him as a complete stranger to our ways. By rendering him more "familiar" than "other" all parties (except Moussaoui himself, of course) could avoid the question of just how Moroccan he was and how that may have affected his plea and his courtroom behavior.

As the trial progressed—and as occasional suggestions in the books by his mother and brother imply—Moussaoui's identity may, however, have been more complex than the judge allowed. We know that he spoke some Arabic. There are instances in the court transcript, for example, where Arabic was used, utterances the court struck from the record.[25] His brother, however, has written that Zacarias, at least growing up, did not know Arabic:

> At home, Aïcha [their mother] never spoke to us in Arabic. So we felt out of place even among North Africans, not knowing their language. When we asked our mother to teach us a few words, she would laugh at our accent and our lousy pronunciation—so we stopped asking. Our sisters, of course, were born in Morocco and went back there almost every year—they spoke Arabic. But when

> Zac [i.e., Zacarias] and I met Moroccan families, they would feel sorry for us. 'Oh, they don't speak Arabic? *Meskeen!* Poor things!' And my mother would respond, 'No they don't, they're right little French boys, those two.'[26]

The brother further notes: "Neither did our mother teach us about Arab ways and customs, or about Muslim culture. . . . Zac and I asked her several times how you prayed and why. She dodged the question. . . . [W]e'd seen our friends going to the mosque with their fathers. So why not us? We felt ridiculous in the company of others."[27] Similarly, Moussaoui's ignorance of religion at that time may have heightened his embarrassment. His brother recalls a particular incident:

> [Once] when Zacarias was reciting alleged verses of the Koran in French, the imam walked in. He listened to my brother for a few seconds, and then asked him, "Can you speak Arabic?" Zacarias answered, "No." "So how do you know that what you are saying is the true meaning of what is said in the Koran? You haven't been able to check it in the book, because it is revealed in Arabic." . . . Zacarias lost his temper. He got to his feet and tried to hit the imam. The young people intervened and threw him out. He walked off hurling insults at them, and calling them *kuffar*—heathens.[28]

However, we know that Moussaoui used Arabic when he was with al-Qaeda elements in the countries from which they operated and he did use some Arabic in court.[29] Such knowledge, like his familiarity with Islam and its rituals, then, probably developed after he left home. But, even if we accept the brother's account, an intriguing issue is how much Moussaoui's cultural background played into his behavior in court. Whatever else, one cannot assume that even within his own family there existed a uniformity of cultural attachments. His mother is said at times to have celebrated Christmas. His brother Abd Samad apparently joined a group of Muslims who were rivals of those with whom Zacarias was affiliated, hence the brother's accounts must not be accepted at face value. Whereas Zacarias became associated with groups practicing the Wahhabi (or Salafi) form of Islam that stems from Saudi Arabia and brooks no intermediaries or ecstatic rituals separating one from Allah, the group to which his brother (and his brother's wife) appear to have been drawn, the Habeche (or Ahbash), is more closely identified with some Sufi sects that are ardently opposed to the Wahhabis. Donahue states: "There is little love lost between the Ahbash and the Wahhabis, or Salafis. Ali Laidi [writing in *Le Nou-*

vel Observateur] reported that Abd Samad Moussaoui was present at a meeting in Montpelier in December, 1999, on the subject of 'Islam in the Republic.' Abu Samad is reported to have told a [non-Habeche] Muslim speaker that he was 'worse than the Jews and the crusaders.' A fight broke out, chairs were thrown, and the police were called in."[30] The existence of rival groups to which the brothers belonged thus underscores both the caution with which one must approach any references to the behavior of one brother by the other and the extent to which such rivalries may have colored Zacarias's views of himself as an Arab and Muslim.

Indeed, we do not really know how much Moussaoui related to the Morocco from which his parents emigrated. He did visit the country several times in his youth (in 1974 and 1977), and his sisters and mother returned more often, but neither in the account by his mother nor that of his brother are we told what if any impact these visits had on him. We do, however, know that in his relationship with his French girlfriend and in several incidents referred to in the accounts of his relatives Moussaoui, like others of his family and friends of North African origins, was, as Donahue notes, "the target of French racism. He and his brother were called 'dirty Arabs.' The nightclub at the bottom of the hill in his middle-class neighbourhood was the site of fights between French youths and those of North African descent."[31] We also know that the children of North Africans raised and living in France commonly find themselves uncomfortable in both Europe and their parents' home country. In Morocco people make fun of those raised abroad because they often cannot speak the local dialect and do not know the local customs; in France and elsewhere in Europe they are frequently regarded as foreigners who are not the social and moral equals of those among whom they are living. Thus in North Africa they are called by a variety of derogatory names while in France they are referred to as *beurs* (a reversal of the word "Arab," occasionally used as a denigratory term). Not surprisingly, then, as a result of their displacement from both sides of the Mediterranean, Moussaoui's generation of Moroccan youth frequently say of themselves that they are "homesick everywhere."

Whereas Moussaoui's lawyers tried to argue that their client's involvement with al-Qaeda was explainable in terms of his dysfunctional family life and mental condition, both the judge and his attorneys downplayed the fact that, whatever his own identity, there was good reason to believe that Moussaoui had long been treated by others not as a Frenchman but as an Arab, while Moroccans saw him as someone who did not know how to be an Arab. He was a man left without a place of his own—a fact to which he himself pointed when, according to his mother, he once said that "in France, we do not have our place" ("En France, nous n'avions pas notre place").[32]

All that said, we still do not know how Moroccan or Arab Moussaoui felt himself to be. However, as one works through the transcripts of the trial there are, as we shall see, clear hints that this identity may very well have affected the style of his testimony and the points he was trying to make. Thus while one cannot say his amalgam of operative cultural concepts bears simple causal connection to events in court the reverberations are suggestive and may help in unpacking the meaning and direction, among his other actions, of his final decision to plead guilty.

There is, it should also be noted, no clear indication that Moussaoui was familiar with Moroccan and Islamic law or procedure, or that this constituted a baseline against which he measured the American process. It is, of course, possible that he was aware—in much the way one absorbs aspects of social and legal style from stories, family accounts, the media, common gossip, etc.—of the way in which legal matters are handled within the culture from which he stemmed.[33] Consider again his eventual guilty plea. To most of those following the trial, as to Judge Brinkema, Moussaoui's guilty plea was rather incomprehensible. Many observers saw it as an act born of ignorance about the legal implications, as evidence that he was seeking to become a martyr, or as yet another instance of his unbalanced mental state.[34] Some of these concerns were understandable, others absurd. As one legal analyst pointed out, Moussaoui entered a guilty plea without "any promise of leniency in exchange for his plea," and that statements in his plea "suggest that Moussaoui [mistakenly] thought he had tricked the prosecution," presumably into going easy on the death penalty claim in return for his telling more about the entire 9/11 event. [35] By comparison, Jonathan Turley, a law professor at George Washington University, expressing a common stereotype, told a CNN interviewer that Moussaoui was a "barking lunatic" who had "done everything short of chewing the carpet in the courtroom" and that by testifying he would be putting his head in a noose.[36] A counterterrorism expert for RAND Corporation said of Moussaoui's rather confusing statements: "If we thought by the end of the day we would find the holy grail as to exactly what the genesis of 9/11 was and what Moussaoui's role in it was, we have been sorely disappointed. This contradiction in his behavior raises more questions than it answers." And the *Washington Post* noted that "it remains uncertain" whether the death penalty trial "will divulge much new information about the plot."[37]

No plea bargain, as we shall see, ever figured in Moussaoui's prosecution so the motivation for his guilty plea cannot be attributed to that factor. And though at times he spoke about his courtroom appearances as "playing" (though probably not in the sense of toying with the system but, as he said, "if I use the word 'playing' . . . for my life") he was earnest about wanting to tell his story. In this regard, then, his guilty plea may make some sense. For, as I have suggested, defendants (career criminals aside) almost always plead guilty in Morocco, a fact to which the judges and lawyers among whom I have worked for decades in that country consistently attest. Why those accused of a crime do so, it is explained, is neither because of pressure from the police or courts nor because they expect better treatment if they so plead. What officials continually point to in this regard is that defendants always assert that they were justified in what they did. Indeed, they want to explain such reasons to the court and know that they will not be cut off from doing so by virtue of a guilty plea. So, for example, the accused may argue that of course he struck the man, and then add a long story about their relationships and connections with others, all of which resulted in a dispute for which the defendant implicitly asks "am I not a man" and draws the conclusion that his actions were perfectly justified. Or, he may readily admit that he took another's cow, but then tell the court about the time the complainant's grandfather took his own grandfather's cow and thus his response was eminently appropriate.[38] By allowing even the defendant who pleads guilty a hearing, the accused feels that he is getting a key ingredient of justice, namely the right to explain himself, to show how connected he is to others (the central feature of being a man in this part of the world), and to demonstrate that justice can only be served by understanding how anyone is placed in a network of obligations the unwarranted disruption of which is indispensable to comprehending his acts and how the court should therefore respond.

Once again, I cannot say that in changing his plea to guilty Moussaoui was prompted by the form of legal culture of the country from which his parents emigrated. But if we now connect his guilty plea to the second element that is integral to such a plea in North Africa our speculation—and a plausible response to Judge Brinkema's mystification—may be taken a step further. For the one thing that repeatedly appears in all of Moussaoui's actions in the course of the trial is that he wanted to tell his story his way—and that the federal rules of evidence and procedure as applied by Judge Brinkema frustrated that desire at every point: "I have not a chance to speak," he repeatedly asserted when, during hearings on motions, he could not tell his story in his own manner.[39] Pleading guilty in a Moroccan procedure would not have precluded the opportunity to explain himself. Indeed, he may very well have known that had the trial taken place in France a guilty plea also does not end the fact-finding portion of the proceedings. Not only is a full hearing necessary to confirm the plea and to hear evidence that bears on the meaning of one's act and the appropriate punishment but French criminal procedure allows the accused to tell his or her story without interruption, unlike the constant interference by counsel on both sides in the American process.[40] Pleading guilty in Judge Brinkema's court may, whatever else was at work, have been a statement of complete frustration for never being able to tell his story in the way that would be true to his view of himself and his actions, but it was also a way to move along to the telling of his story in the penalty phase where mitigation was the crucial legal issue.

Indeed a careful look at Moussaoui's trial shows how constantly the rulings of the court had thwarted Moussaoui's ability to tell that story and why this may help to explain both his decision to change his plea and his disruptive statements in court. During all the months of the guilt determination portion of the trial—which only ended when he changed his plea—Moussaoui did not take the stand nor was he given full license to describe the motivations behind his alleged participation in any terrorist plots. Most of his outbursts were attempts to explain that motivation or to complain about the arguments concerning his sanity being made by his court-appointed attorneys, and on almost every occasion he was ruled out of order. But once the appellate court ruled that the death penalty could again be considered Moussaoui was freer, upon taking the stand, to describe his own thinking. The formal issue before the jury at that point was whether there was anything in the acts to which he now admitted that aggravated or ameliorated the severity of his participation such that the death penalty should be applied, as opposed to a mandatory sentence of life imprisonment without parole. But until he was able to get on the stand his behavior continued to be problematic. Twice he was removed from the courtroom for disruptive outbursts. He objected to the attorneys appointed to represent him in the penalty phase: "I want to be heard. I do not want to be represented by these people. . . . They are not my lawyers. I am al Qaeda. They do not represent me. They are American. . . . This trial is a circus."[41] When barred from the jury selection process he shouted: "You have tried to organize my death for four years."[42] He accused his lawyers of plotting a "trip to the gas chamber . . . These people are not my lawyer (*sic*)," and again, "I am al Qaeda. I am a sworn enemy." When, to the consternation of his lawyers and the strong belief by many (including the judge) that he was making a mistake, he did take the stand he surprised almost everyone by the lucidity, precision, and temperance of his testimony.[43]

What, then, was the story Moussaoui wanted to tell and how might the form of its telling bear on his conduct throughout the trial? As odd as it may seem, an important element of that story may actually have had to do with his willingness to inform on others. From the time of his arrest through to the final verdict Moussaoui was quite willing to name others, living as well as dead, involved in the 9/11 events. On August 17, 2001, when first arrested, Moussaoui disclosed the name of an associate, and as late as his testimony in the penalty phase he identified friends who helped him fake a failure of the French army medical test, including a doctor/friend who could lose his license as a result.[44] We can also see how the guilty plea and informing on others were linked in an earlier colloquy with the judge. In 2002 the judge had refused to allow Moussaoui to plead guilty, questioning his legal and mental ability, but when he renewed the request in April 2005 Judge Brinkema held a hearing on the matter. According to the transcript of their conversation, Moussaoui told the judge that she could not understand why he was making this change because she comes from a different cultural background. He continued: "You are not in charge of my life. You are in charge of my death. . . . You have a lynch mentality. You catch the beast, you have the feather and the tar, you are going to have the party."[45] After referring to himself as a member of al-Qaeda he went on to say:

> I want to enter a plea today of guilty because this will ensure to save my life. . . . It's much more complicated than what you want to make people believe, because even if I plead guilty, I will be able to prove that I have certain knowledge about September 11, and I know exactly who done it. I know which group, who participated, when it was decided. I have many information. . . . But it will ensure me to save my life, because the jury . . . will be able to evaluate how much responsibility I have in this.[46]

The nature of the story Moussaoui apparently wanted to tell, therefore, turns on several factors, the first of which is connected with his willingness to discuss the role of others in the events relating to 9/11.[47] If at no time was the offer of information about others part of a plea bargain, why then was Moussaoui willing to name any co-conspirators? The answer may, once again, lie in an understanding of the culture he said the judge could not comprehend.

Put rather too briefly, for Moroccans—and indeed for Arabs rather generally—what marks one as a man is the formation of a network of people with whom one shares ties of reciprocity.[48] Such networks of dependency must be constructed by each individual. They are not given by kinship and they are neither inheritable nor static: They are constantly bargained out in the course of face-to-face relationships. Indeed, one's network of allies must be shown to exist and to be constantly serviced if one is to be regarded as a person whose actions have consequences in the world, itself measured by the effect on other's sets of relationship. Unlike many cultures in which particular rites of passage mark the transition from one status or role to another, in the Arab world it is by forging a web of allies that one shows arrival at maturity. Marriage is probably the most important act in this respect, since one must call upon a network of supporters to raise the bridewealth payment that makes the marriage, thereby proving that one is indeed connected to the world of negotiated relationships. Showing that such an alliance exists may also be displayed in elaborate wedding celebrations as well as at street demonstrations or funerals for an ally or fallen comrade. Indeed, being involved in a group of "terrorists" may, in many respects, serve as a functional equivalent.[49] Thus Moussaoui's willingness to identify others involved in his actions—indeed, as the above quote indicates, his eagerness to prove such connections—makes sense as a way of establishing that he is a real man, a person of consequence, an individual whose movements affect the networks of others in a world composed by such associations. This is just one of several factors that, when the jury was to hear his claims in mitigation of the death penalty, contributed to the logic of the story he was to tell.

That opportunity took place after the jury had deliberated for six days before unanimously finding that he was eligible for the death penalty. Testimony then commenced to determine the final verdict. The prosecution played tapes from the cockpit recorder of the plane that crashed in Pennsylvania and brought to the stand so many survivors and family members of the 9/11 victims that even Judge Brinkema cautioned the lawyers not to overdo it. Half a dozen family members did testify for the defense in favor of life imprisonment, rather than death. But then even Moussaoui's attorneys tried to portray him as a hanger-on who was "useless," bumbling, and a "knucklehead," in an attempt to characterize him at once as peripheral to the events of 9/11 and too incompetent to have been fully involved in causing so many deaths. Through the use of experts the defense also tried to depict Moussaoui as the victim of dysfunctional upbringing and psychological impairment, his sisters and father being represented as mentally ill and Moussaoui's own references to the judge and lawyers trying to get him killed as evidence of his delusional state. This was, however, at odds with Moussaoui's own testimony when, on two occasions, he took the stand himself.

* * *

"I used to run my own story."—Zacarias Moussaoui[50]

On March 27, 2006, Zacarias Moussaoui finally took the stand to testify on his own behalf. Commenters have mainly noted the substantive admissions that he made during the course of his remarks: that he was a member of al-Qaeda, that he was pleased that they had killed many of the "enemy," and that he had been expecting to participate in a similar attack at a later time.[51] The main thrust of his testimony, as it had been all along, was, therefore, that he was not part of the 9/11 attacks (he had earlier stated, "I ask the government to point out to me a single paragraph where they say I'm guilty of 9/11. . . . [E]veryone know that I'm not 9/11 material"[52]), that it is very important for people to understand that he is telling the truth ("The highest calling is to speak the truth in front of the tyrant"[53]), and that he is not crazy (he had referred to his lawyer as "going around [to the press] and saying Moussaoui is crazy, Moussaoui is crazy. He's crazy to want to defend his life"[54]). It is not, however, primarily these substantive aspects of his testimony on which I want to focus. Rather, I want to note what might be called the cultural emphases that I think were revealed by what he said and how he said it. For purposes of analysis these factors may be divided into three main categories: the narrative, the relational, and the emotional.

Moussaoui's narrative was deeply dependent on his claim that he wanted to tell the truth. Throughout the entire legal process he insisted that was what he wanted to do. On July 25, 2002, he had said: "I want the people to hear what I have to say, what are my responsibility . . . and if 12 people of America find that I have to be put in jail, to be killed for this what I did, but only for what I did, not for what they claim, okay. . . . That's why I want to talk to these 12 people, these 12 American, who are my enemy, but sometimes you can find honest enemy."[55] Similarly, on the last day of his testimony in the penalty phase he repeated, "I know that by testifying truthfully, I will save my life. It is an act of religion."[56] Indeed, at no time in the proceedings was there any claim on the part of the prosecution that Moussaoui lied, though observers on all sides suspected that he exaggerated his actual involvement in 9/11. His statements about telling the truth are revealing. Consider, for example, his assertion about how he knew when others were lying: "Because when two people lie, they look at each other, okay?" Two elements of Arab language and culture may be at work here. First, the tag question is important. Whereas to most male speakers of Western languages such an end question appears to add little, for Arabs it is commonly part of a kind of Socratic dialogue: It requires the listener to validate what the speaker has said, the dialogue being constrained from going forward until the other essentially accepts what the speaker has asserted. Indeed, it is a style that converts a bare utterance into one that can be assessed for its truth-bearing qualities. Moussaoui may have been acting in accord with his Moroccan Arab upbringing by the constant use of this tag question when, in seeking to make them validate his substantive point, he interacted in this fashion with those, including Judge Brinkema, with whom he was contending.

Second, there is the broadly Arab cultural belief that if you look intently at another you can tell if he is lying. T. E. Lawrence called it "the stare," and anyone who has worked intensively in Arab societies has repeatedly experienced it. Even if people do not believe this to be entirely effective two elements about this cultural process come into play: that the person observed is now held to the consequences of one who is, in fact, telling the truth (such that listeners will alter relationships in their own networks accordingly) and that, having made such alterations the speaker risks losing credibility for future associations if others suffer for having trusted to what he said. Indeed, the common pattern is that utterances are regarded as having no truth value until validated by another's reliance on the speaker's believability or by one of several other modes of bringing a bare statement into the realm of the true, including through the offer of a sacrifice or taking an oath. The style may be likened to making a mere statement in the marketplace that something is worth a given sum: Until something more happens (an oath, an action in reliance, etc.) that statement is not, indeed cannot be, assessed for its truth value.[57] The same is especially true for utterances about relationships, thus leaving people free to see what may be possible without implications of lying should no relationship be formed with respect to the utterance. But once one of the forms of validation takes place (and relationships are affected as a result) it matters enormously for one's manhood that it not be seen as a lie since no one will eagerly rely on such a person for his own alliances. In the Arabic idiom, to be a person of consequence is "to have word." For Moussaoui, then, the case can certainly be made that he treated his truthfulness seriously, as when he replied to the prosecutor's question on cross-examination: "Q. Does anything that happens here make a difference? A. Yes, that I should speak the truth."[58]

What, from his perspective, then brings Moussaoui's statements into the realm of the truthful was his use of the oath. On the first day of his penalty phase testimony an intriguing colloquy took place between Moussaoui and the prosecution as to when it is acceptable "to lie." To counsel there is only truth and lying. But to a North African until an oath or its functional equivalent occurs there are really three categories of utterances: those that are not yet assessable for their truth value ("this watch is worth a million dollars") and those that are now susceptible to such characterizations because an oath, reliant act, etc., now make it possible to apply the criteria of truth and lying. Indeed, Moussaoui said that he wanted to take the oath at the end of his testimony because he will then be sure that what he may have said is indeed what he meant to say and that he is now prepared to ratify it.[59] It is rather like putting your signature at the end of a contract or statement, not at the beginning. Indeed, this is the practice in many Islamic and civil law countries (including France), as opposed to the Anglo-American practice of taking the oath at the beginning of one's testimony. Again, for Moussaoui, unvalidated statements grant one the freedom to test whatever the situation may bear, but which must at the end be validated if they are to be counted for their truth value. And he was being scrupulous in wanting to be sure he had stated things correctly before, as it were, he signs off on those statements.[60] By contrast, counsel, who had no idea that an oath or other form of validation is necessary to make a bare utterance testable for its truth completely misunderstood why Moussaoui appeared to be saying that it was okay to lie when for him it was not a question of true or false since no form of validation had yet taken place.

There were other stylistic elements to Moussaoui's way of narrating his story that, because they appear to have been drawn from a cultural tradition with which the participants in his trial were unfamiliar, may add further insight into what it was he had all along been wanting to say. Where others may have regarded some of his usages as indicative of a less than perfect command of English his statements may, as with the notions of truth and lying, have been drawn instead from his cultural mode of relating matters. Thus he frequently answered a question not by saying yes but by saying "I believe so," thus indicating that these statements are validated by a perhaps even religiously based belief and are thus within the realm of statements which, if false, have implications for one's social standing as a reliable witness. He also preferred to use concrete examples, which the lawyers and judge took as inappropriate because they raised the issue of a trial within a trial about the matters claimed. Yet for Moussaoui, as is so common among those growing up in the environs of Arab culture, examples are precisely the way you indicate real world implications. "Can I respond with an example? I find it easier to express myself," he said on the stand: "Can I explain more?"[61] Actual life events—focused on the connections one has negotiated with others—are what define a person, and Moussaoui was intent on the jurors understanding him in the only way he could authentically present himself as a person. Yet the very conception of personhood, as molded by the way the American legal rules permit a witness to fashion such information, did not fit neatly with the criteria by which he would have himself understood by others.

A different sort of example may help make this point. In a number of situations people from East Asian backgrounds may be misunderstood by non-Asian jurors in an American proceeding as stiff, unfeeling, and emotionless, when in fact they are presenting themselves as exercising such self-control that they could not possibly have done the violent deed of which they are accused.[62] Similarly, Moussaoui was being candid in his substantive testimony, which to viewers was taken as self-incriminating and foolish while perhaps missing the cultural cues by which he was validating each of those claims along the way. That he had maintained the integrity of his cultural style is notable: As he said, "So my style is not very elegant style or conventional style, but I'm still alive four year and a half after."[63]

We have already seen some of the ways in which the relational emphasis of Moussaoui's narrative style played out in the proceedings—his willingness to name names in order to show his mature status among his fellow believers, or his personal recitation of religious texts as a way of emphasizing that he should be regarded by others as a reliable witness. Thus it was imperative that he speak for himself if he could not find an acceptable Muslim attorney and those appointed for him wanted him seen as insane. Again, in both Islamic and French proceedings this is the assumed mode. In France, though one possesses the equivalent of a Fifth Amendment right against self-incrimination, that right is almost never exercised because the court has an elaborate dossier with one side of the story and the professional judge would appear to be mistrusted if a defendant did not respond personally to the questions posed by the court. Similarly, in the courts of Islamic countries, though lawyers may certainly be employed, refusal to answer the judge oneself may be taken as a sign of discourtesy or distrust.

Moreover, Moussaoui would appear to be one of those who, like many people appearing in American courts, are more relationally oriented than rule-oriented. Constrained by rules that bar evidence based on hearsay, personal beliefs or feelings, apparent digressions, prior events, or value judgments, witnesses often feel frustrated in relating the facts as they see them. As a result, as Conley and O'Barr (1990, 61) suggest, in many courts "certain categories of litigants are less prone to present legally adequate narratives and accounts." If, as the authors further suggest, people of particular ethnicities or gender are disfavored by the rules in the presentation of information, the proceedings themselves may be hampered to the point of unfairness. Stressing what they call "a broad notion of social interdependence rather than [reliance] on the application of rules," the relationally oriented party may appear to be offering irrelevant testimony. But as Anthony Good points out, "it is not that the perspectives of relationally-oriented litigants are illogical or unstructured, though lawyers tend to view them as such; rather, such reasoning conforms to a logic so different from their own as to be largely imperceptible to those steeped in formal legal analysis. Consequently, the courts 'often fail to understand their cases, regardless of their legal merits, and this frequently results in frustration and alienation.'"[64] Moussaoui's own orientation was clearly more relational than rule-oriented, a factor that may not only have contributed to his behavior in court but to the frustration arising out of a process that could have been more accommodating if the problems had been adequately understood and addressed.

Moussaoui's own emotions also played a significant role in the proceedings. On a number of occasions he made what most people took to be bitter anti-Semitic remarks. Yet when his friend from France, Gilles Cohen, came to court and took the stand in his defense, Moussaoui exited the court with his usual diatribe against America but in Cohen's presence left out the adverse reference to Jews he always added. Perhaps, like most Moroccans, he was distinguishing between social categories and individual persons.[65]

Other cultural styles may have played a significant role as well. It is hardly an exercise in stereotypes to say that people from some cultures express themselves more vociferously than others, that they interrupt more commonly or gesticulate more elaborately or simply fail to sit still. Moussaoui's courtroom behavior was invariably interpreted as disruptive or rude, when it may, at least in part, have been a demonstration of the intensity of his attachment to a given statement, something that is frequently sought in the interaction of Moroccans, for whom the question how strongly one feels about a given issue is extremely important to assessing its implications for ongoing relationships.[66] Just as too much deference to the dominant etiquette of the courtroom may suppress the full expression of matters that are relevant, too little leeway and understanding of the mode of expression of someone from another culture can work against the professed goal of learning all one can before making a final judgment.

It is, of course, impossible to say whether, assuming the factors discussed here are indeed valid, they would or should have made a difference in the outcome of Moussaoui's trial. Indeed, we do not know if the one juror who ultimately voted against the death penalty, thus resulting in the final verdict of life imprisonment, was influenced by how the trial was conducted and not just what evidence was adduced. The factors that have been considered here may, however, not only speak to Judge Brinkema's expressed perplexity about Moussaoui's conduct but, when accompanied by a fuller understanding of the political aspects of the trial, help us understand why, in the years following the trial, even she may have had some second thoughts about the entire process.

* * *

> Q. No remorse?
> A. There is no remorse for justice.
> —Prosecutor questioning Moussaoui[67]

It would be unfair to characterize the Moussaoui trial, as *Time* magazine described the 1925 Scopes evolution trial, as a "fantastic cross between a circus and a holy war."[68] But it would be equally incorrect to ignore the broader context within which the Moussaoui trial took place. While the trial was, of course, preeminently a legal occasion it did not escape Judge Brinkema's notice that there were political aspects of the trial, particularly when she encountered the refusal of the government to supply full disclosure of the testimony of those queried at Guantánamo and the clear implication that the recordings of the detainees' statements exhibited the use of torture. In a speech at American University in 2008, noting that "coerced testimony is inherently unreliable," she went on to say: "The war on terror is an important piece of political leverage. Don't lose sight of the political realities."[69] Those political realities, however, would also have to include the well-known fact that the government prefers to bring terrorism trials in the Eastern District of Virginia not simply because of the experience of courts there in cases involving national security but because so many of those who would be drawn from a jury pool are themselves sympathetic to the nation's security apparatus.[70] Moreover, the Fourth Circuit Court of Appeals is unquestionably one of the most conservative, pro-security establishment appellate courts in the country, their decision to overrule Judge Brinkema's elimination of the death penalty when the prosecution refused to supply more information from Guantánamo inmates—to say nothing of their refusal to reopen the case when even the government admitted that tapes of the interviews had existed and were destroyed—confirming for many the appellate court's proclivities in this area.[71]

But this is not the only sense in which the trial may be seen as politically tinged. At several critical junctures in the trial constitutional protections afforded in normal criminal proceedings were set aside in the name of national security. As one law professor told a National Public Radio interviewer, "there was a great deal of bending of the criminal process to even reach this verdict,"[72] while an editorial writer for the *New York Times* stated more generally: "It's rarely acknowledged that the [9/11] attacks have also led to what's essentially a separate justice system for Muslims. In this system, the principle of due process is twisted and selectively applied, if it is applied at all."[73] Thus, the right to confront witnesses was withheld when Moussaoui was not permitted to quiz Guantánamo detainees or to see various documents the government possessed. He was said to have failed to volunteer information to the FBI in August 2001.[74] But as several commenters have put it: "The government never before has tried to put to death someone whose crime was one of omission, not commission."[75] When, early in the penalty phase, Judge Brinkema learned that an attorney for the Transportation Security Authority, in direct violation of her prior warning, had coached witnesses, the motion for a mistrial was denied even though the judge said it was the most egregious such instance she had ever seen.

Arguably, Moussaoui was also not afforded his Sixth Amendment right to an attorney when the Muslim lawyer he wanted was denied him, Judge Brinkema ruling that "in this type of case where there are national security and classified documents, you don't have totally unrestricted choice even if you have the money available to hire an attorney."[76] Because Moussaoui himself lacked the appropriate clearance, he was not allowed to see any of the classified documents held by the government, and his standby lawyers, who *were* permitted to see them, were barred from revealing even exculpatory information contained in them to Moussaoui, whether he was represented by them or serving as his own counsel.[77] Under the Special Administrative Measure he was, in the name of preventing potential communication with co-conspirators and using his arrest for propaganda purposes, also denied contact with outside sources, including journalists who might have countered the image of him as crazy.

Some of Moussaoui's actions in court were understandably interpreted as extreme, but they were not simply irrational and may have been worthy of greater consideration.[78] For example, he may have been confused when told by the judge that if he pleaded guilty he could not, at the penalty phase, argue that he had no involvement in the events of 9/11. For him there was, it appears, no contradiction between saying he was indeed involved, but not really. At least, he wanted to argue it according to his own logic, and it was not unreasonable for him to bridle at being repeatedly told, even by the lawyers appointed for him, that such an approach was evidence of mental instability. The psychiatrists hired by the government—who never interviewed him—saw in his repeated challenges to the court and his lawyers an indication of delusions, coupled with paranoid schizophrenia, and Moussaoui's own attempts to preclude such psychiatric testimony employed by his lawyers was unsuccessful. And if, for Moussaoui, each attempt to explain himself in his own way was rebuffed, is it truly irrational for him to express outrage at his court-appointed attorneys and to say of his own motions that their goal was to "keep mad, out of control standby herd of blood suckers out of . . . PURE PRO SE LAND"?

Even Judge Brinkema seems to have had some second thoughts about certain aspects of the trial. At a legal forum several years after the verdict she encountered the one juror who held out against the death penalty.[79] He asked if she thought he had done the right thing. As she later put it, he "asked me if I thought they'd got it right, and I said, 'Yeah, I think you did.'"[80] She added that, as concerned that particular juror's vote against the death penalty, he had done "'an extraordinary service to the legal system'" because, as the reporter paraphrased her, "the fallout from the government's failure to turn over evidence would have been horrendous if Moussaoui had actually been sent to death row."[81]

Judge Brinkema may even have regrets about the form of Moussaoui's confinement. In an unrelated case she later ruled that a man convicted of murder and sentenced to death still could not be held in solitary confinement. She described at length the details of what such incarceration is like, something she would have had knowledge about not only from the numerous articles that have appeared in recent years showing that upwards of twenty-five thousand prisoners are held in American prisons in such confinement—sometimes for years and decades—but something about which there was testimony in the Moussaoui case itself.[82] For in the penalty phase a former warden with thirty years' experience testified that people held in close confinement "rot," while other officials have indicated that most prisoners in solitary go mad.[83] And though it was never raised expressly, the question lurking in the background of all terrorism cases tried in an ordinary federal court is "what do we do if the person is found not guilty," a circumstance about which U.S. Attorneys General have consistently avoided comment. Indeed, out of some four hundred terrorism trials that have gone to federal courts the fact that very few have resulted in full acquittal further suggests not that the government always has a perfect case but that judges and juries are reluctant to bear the political implications of releasing back into American society someone who has been so accused.[84]

Does all this suggest that at some level even Judge Brinkema had any regrets about the conduct of the trial or its results? She has always insisted that the trial was fair and that courts like her own can handle cases involving terrorism, and a number of other courts have indeed done so.[85] But in other comments she has indicated that she felt betrayed by the government. She had, after all, specifically asked the government lawyers if there were video or audio tapes of the Guantánamo prisoners' interrogations and was assured there were none. As late as November 3, 2005, the CIA denied any such tapes existed. More than a year after the case ended, however, the prosecutors wrote to the judge to say that such tapes had existed and that they had been destroyed. Indeed, in the fall of 2007 the CIA admitted that they had "erroneously" misled the court, no doubt because the tapes showed harsh interrogation techniques being applied to the prisoners. Additionally, it will be recalled that on March 13, 2006, a week into the penalty phase of the trial, the judge learned that an attorney for the Transportation Safety Authority had coached aviation witnesses in direct violation of her instructions not to contact them, an act that almost resulted in a mistrial and did result in barring those important witnesses from the government's case.[86] "One of the saddest realities I've had to face —in the Moussaoui case in particular—has been the reality that my government didn't always tell me the truth," Brinkema concluded in a 2008 speech at Colby College.[87]

Yet for all these ways of treating constitutional protections differently in a national security case Judge Brinkema has had no hesitation in claiming that federal trial courts are perfectly capable of handling such cases. She bridles at the suggestion that the trial was a "circus" and has stated publicly: "I've reached the conclusion that the system does work."[88] Although at sentencing she praised Moussaoui's lawyers, perhaps it was more for their having to put up with an obstreperous client than because of their talent. At Princeton, however, she specifically said that she did not think they did a very good job and that those who were then carrying his appeal were clearly better. At moments she has also admitted to a certain grudging respect for Moussaoui. Finding him competent to plead guilty, she had said: "Mr. Moussaoui is an extremely intelligent man. He has actually a better understanding of the legal system than some lawyers I've seen in court."[89] She even suggested that approached properly he may have been more forthcoming. "She cited Moussaoui as an example of an individual who likely would have cooperated with the right kind of questioning. 'I'm convinced that if someone sat down and had tea with him and could put up with his ramblings, that they could have gotten some information from him because he couldn't keep his mouth shut,' Brinkema said."[90]

The question thus arises whether, given all of the factors involved, it would have been possible to conduct this proceeding in a way that was at once consistent with the federal rules of evidence and procedure, on the one hand, and, on the other, the need of a culturally distinct individual whose case involved national security concerns to be given the opportunity to relate matters in his own fashion. Some comparisons may be especially helpful in this regard.

The rules of evidence are structured around two connected points: that jurors should not be inappropriately influenced by what is presented to them and that the evidence should meet the courts' criteria of relevance.[91] Toward this twinned goal certain information is excluded, including out of court statements by someone who is not available for cross-examination introduced for the truth of the thing asserted (commonly referred to as hearsay evidence) as well as past acts that are not part of the course of conduct under indictment (lest we have to hold trials within trials as to what really happened in the past). To each of these requirements there have been carved out numerous exceptions—that dying utterances are sufficiently probative of truthfulness to qualify as acceptable hearsay, or that evidence of habitual action constitutes part of a course of conduct leading up to the event being tried. That such rules have developed within a particular historical and cultural context should come as no surprise. But that they may frustrate a richer development of relevant information cannot be ignored. Particularly when dealing with someone from another culture—and especially if the case is heard to the bench rather than a jury (as was true for the Moussaoui trial up to the penalty phase)—the question arises whether a fuller airing of what the defendant regards as relevant might aid understanding both of the nature of the act at issue and the appropriate punishment.

This does not mean that one justifies or excuses an act on the basis of cultural background.[92] Rather, allowing a broader array of evidence the defendant regards as appropriate might help to inform the trier of fact as to the individual's actual motives, itself a feature that can be separated from intent only by the most refined of hair-splitting.[93] The more comprehensive account Moussaoui wished to give of his background and actions could only have better served both his defense and the legal system's need to understand more precisely the nature and meaning of his acts. This may be especially true when the issue is one of conspiracy.

All of the charges against Moussaoui involved allegations of conspiracy. Conspiracy is usually conceptualized in the law as an "inchoate" crime, one in which the forbidden act may range from inciting others by rhetorically asking "who will rid me of this meddlesome priest" (if seen as an act in furtherance of the illegal conduct) to clearer promotion of the ultimate crime. Jurors have a very mixed record, though, when hearing conspiracy, as they are often in disagreement with the prosecution as to what constitutes an act in furtherance of an illegal end, to say nothing of doubting the government's motives in bringing the charges in the first place. During the Vietnam period, for example, when defendants like Father Thomas Berrigan and other draft protesters were arraigned on such charges, juries, recognizing the political nature of the accusations and the hazy line between valid protest and criminal acts, commonly refused to find the parties guilty of the government's conspiracy charges. To determine just how far Moussaoui's actions did indeed further the 9/11 attacks depended on the way his case was presented.

Whatever might be said about the wisdom and skill of his lawyers or that he could have taken the stand in his own behalf in the guilt determination phase of the trial and not waited until the penalty phase, the court itself has a duty to insure that the evidence does indeed fit the charge. Thus, in this case it may not have been enough for the judge to have deferred to counsel for the presentation of evidence. Rather she may be seen as having an affirmative duty to insure that as much evidence as possible about Moussaoui's acts and motives was available to her as the sole decision maker in the guilt-determination phase of the trial. Judge Brinkema kept her sense of order in the court, but she may have achieved greater order, if not greater justice, without usurping the defendant's right to present his own case, had she made a greater effort—through questions from the bench or by allowing jurors to ask questions during in the penalty phase of the trial—with the aim of clarifying just what it was this particular defendant had in fact done or not done.[94]

Even the order of the trial might have been rearranged given Moussaoui's eagerness to testify. He could have been permitted a more expansive opening statement or encouraged not to plead guilty precisely because he would then have the opportunity to take the stand without depending on a lawyer he did not trust, with the judge posing any questions to him. Such flexibility may have calmed him from the outset. After all, if Judge Brinkema thought he was rational, better prepared than many lawyers, and might (as she said) have told the investigators much more if they had simply sat down for a cup of tea with him, would not a more individualized procedure, clarified perhaps in a pre-trial conference, have fulfilled both the needs of fairness and been entirely within the framework of the existing rules of evidence? And was it really not possible to find a Muslim attorney—or if not an attorney, a personal advisor (perhaps even a Moroccan fluent in French)—to serve as a court-appointed aide to someone who was, after all, coming from a very different background? Judge Brinkema even implied at the time of her Princeton presentation, after having some of Moussaoui's cultural orientations pointed out to her, that a sort of cultural translator might have been helpful, an appointment the court could have made if defense counsel did not think to request it. Judges at the local level are often very creative in these ways. A federal judge with a lifetime appointment in so notorious a terrorism trial needs to be equally bold.

One such act of permissible boldness might have related to the physical positioning of the courtroom participants. If Judge Brinkema truly thought Moussaoui might be conducive to greater calm she might have come down from the bench—particularly for hearings on motions—arranged the participants on the same level, with less apparent formality and display of state power, and thus invited a less confrontational style that would still be entirely within the bounds of acceptable proceeding. This has proven effective in a number of other contexts, both in Europe and in the United States, particularly when parties and witnesses are unfamiliar with the form of criminal proceedings involved.[95] If the court is sincere about treating even the foreigner accused of terrorism as innocent until proven guilty, would not this small accommodation have been worth trying? Or would it have appeared too accommodating to someone accused of terrorism and dressed up by the state in a jumpsuit with the word "prisoner" emblazoned on his back for all the world to see?

Courts in other countries also may offer other examples of how the Moussaoui trial might have been conducted differently. One alternative to the style of Moussaoui's trial is suggested by that held in Norway in which Anders Breivik was charged with the deaths of seventy-seven people, sixty-nine of whom were young people attending the Labor Party Youth League meeting on the island of Utøya in July 2011. Breivik testified for more than six days plus a forty-five-minute summation. Not only did he give a clenched-fist salute as he entered the courtroom most days but he was permitted to assert his racist views unchecked. While this was understandably painful for the victims' families the court decided that it was best to let him speak fully since people needed to see and hear his views.[96] He was even permitted to bring his right wing allies to the stand. Most of the trial, however, was taken up with details of the autopsies of the victims and testimony by survivors and family members. Yet as hurtful and incendiary as it was to hear the defendant belittle those he murdered, ultimately the court thought it better to give Breivik a platform for his views than to hide them behind a series of procedural rules. By comparison, Judge Brinkema did not want Moussaoui's trial to appear, as she explicitly said at the sentencing, to be an opportunity for him to make a "political speech," when, perhaps, that would have been precisely the best way to demonstrate what America was faced with in terms of terrorism and precisely what people needed to see about Moussaoui's professed motivation. The question is thus whether Moussaoui's trial might not have served the public better had he, too, been given freer rein from the outset to express himself.

Moussaoui was not from the United States. But the question may well be asked whether we learned all we could have from his trial. Like many trials involving people from other cultures, the Moussaoui case highlights how American courts treat the very idea of culture. For culture in the courts tends to be seen not as a group attribute or as an indelible imprint over which the individual can exercise only limited choice but as an element of one's personal psychology, one of those numerous features—like the choice of wardrobe or food preference—that exists only when incorporated into a person's distinctive identity.[97] No one would argue that Moussaoui's culture made him engage in the acts that brought him under indictment. But ignoring the ways in which the groups from which he stems influenced the ways in which he sought to present himself is equally unwise. As one law professor has put it, "The lawyer must identify and cross the gap between what the client says and what can be said in the language of the law. . . . Failure to translate not only risks a dissatisfied client; it also impoverishes the law."[98] Absent a form of cultural translation one can fairly ask whether Moussaoui received as fair a hearing as may have been possible, and whether the American people learned as much from the trial as they need to in situations that risk cultural misunderstanding.

* * *

> "I had to have some contact with somebody to be aware of what was going on around me. I don't want to, I don't want to die like the silence of the lamb, huh?"
> —Zacarias Moussaoui[99]

Nevertheless, in her final comments at sentencing Judge Brinkema was prepared to silence Zacarias Moussaoui permanently: "In terms of winning and losing, it is quite clear who lost yesterday and who won yesterday." She continued: "You came here to be a martyr and to die in a big bang of glory, but to paraphrase T. S. Eliot, you will die with a whimper." Refusing to allow him a final statement and stopping him from interrupting, she then added: "For the rest of your life you will never get a chance to speak, and that is a fair and appropriate ending." As he left the courtroom, however, Moussaoui said something the court reporter recorded as "inaudible." But a journalist who was nearby reported him saying: "We will come back another day."[100]

Moussaoui has been condemned for life to solitary confinement in the highest security prison in the country, cut off from almost all interaction with others, and Judge Brinkema's final words sum up her frustration after a long trial and the nation's righteous anger at the events of 9/11. Whether those words are fair—indeed, whether the punishment fits the crime or, not for the first time in the law's history, we have created a crime to fit the punishment we wish to inflict—Moussaoui has been largely silenced.[101] But our own claim of having done justice may be no less muted. Determining which form of silence is the greater loss only an honest assessment of what he—and we—have done may have to await a later day of judgment.

EPILOGUE

The Rule of Law or the Rule of Justice?

Justice, it has been said, is only a metaphor. All the theorizing of philosophers and scholars of jurisprudence has not yielded a theory commanding universal acceptance; no simile or analog has finally settled precisely what justice is. But one need not be an unrepentant relativist to acknowledge that the questions logic and philosophy may leave open society and history may have supplied with answers, if only for their particular adherents and their moment in time. This may be because justice is as much felt as comprehended. When an American speaks of having his or her "day in court" and when studies show that such litigants are not simply concerned with winning their case, say, in a small claims or divorce court but with someone attending to their felt sense of injury, we know that somewhere in this larger cultural process may lurk an elusive yet decipherable sense of justice. Indeed, since people often have a more developed sense of injustice than they do of justice it sometimes becomes necessary to approach the culture of the latter through an understanding of the former.[1]

So, too, in the Arab world the concept of justice is absolutely central. But whereas Westerners tend to frame matters in terms of rights, Arabs emphasize a language of justice, whether in assessing a foundational document, the character of a person, or a sense of the age. Unpacking this concept and its place in Arabs' individual and collective sentiments is integral to understanding why, in rounding out this study, it may be necessary to think as much in terms of a rule of justice as of a rule of law.

* * *

Is it possible to specify some of the features that comprise so generalized a concept as justice? Can we do so for a whole people or range of societies that share some things in common? In one sense the attempt must seem both vain and vague. Yet when one watches the occasions in which many Arabs draw immediately on this term and this concept rather than some other—whether it is in the streets of the Arab Spring or in the context of a woman's arguments in court—the very fact of its prevalent usage and its highly situated overtones challenges the outsider to at least grasp some of its repeated elements. The word in Arabic for justice, *'adl*, means "to be straight or balanced," and is more an attribute of a person than a disembodied idea. Justice for many Arabs therefore incorporates several key ingredients: the emphasis on reciprocity, the stress on equivalence rather than equality, and the concentration on persons rather than institutions.[2] Indeed, we have seen each of these characteristics at work in a number of the previous chapters.

Running through these individual features is a crosscutting array of concepts and assumptions that bind the whole together into what might, to borrow Clyde Kluckhohn's elegant phrase, be called a "design for living." Justice, in this generalized Arab sensibility, significantly depends on difference. "If God had willed He would have made you one nation," says the Quran (5:53; 16:95) in several of its most characteristic and striking passages. As people explain it to me, this means that God intended for us to have to investigate one another's customs and personal identities, to seek such knowledge (as the Tradition of the Prophet says) "even unto China" in order to grasp the ways others forge their ties of interdependence and understand how, in turn, you might form a tie with another. The Quran (49:13) also says: "We have created you male and female, and appointed you races and tribes, that you may know one another." As one commenter explains: "Diversity is thus viewed as a challenge to the believer to look at his fellow human being with a discerning and educated eye, rather than with a prejudiced eye that sees stereotypes and outward manifestations of difference."[3] A North African sheep trader once put it to me in these terms: "We say 'It is by the grace of God that contentiousness is put between the buyer and the seller.' Why? Because differences make you pay attention to *who* that other person is and how you could be dealing with him. The market works best when there is diversity and difference—Berbers, Arabs, Jews, Europeans all mixed together."

The importance of difference appears, for example, when people agree that an individual should be punished according to who he is, not simply for the act he committed, since it is not possible to know the nature of the latter without knowing the qualities and associations of the former. For a man is known not only by the company he keeps but how he arranged that company and thus demonstrated how he has applied his God-given reason to create a network of obligation that conjoins them. As one's network becomes more elaborate or intense the consequences of one's actions ramify differently than if one has a very limited or thin set of dependents and allies. Thus one often hears it said—and occasionally sees it displayed even in court decisions—that an educated person should be punished more severely than one who is less educated since his actions have graver repercussions for the networks of others and (rather as most of our parents once said to us) because given our intelligence we (as opposed to that dirty little kid we played with) should have known better.[4] That is why, when people refer to the Tradition in which the Prophet says "God loves those who hide their sins," they do so not out of hypocrisy but because if a person's actions do not become so public as to adversely affect the networks of others the social order upon which all depend will not have been deeply threatened.

Even in humor the point is underscored: "A man hauled another man before [the Prophet's son-in-law] 'Ali and fumed: 'This man claims that he had a wet dream about my mother!' 'Take the accused out into the sun,' ruled 'Ali, 'and execute the punishment (i.e., eighty stripes) . . . on his shadow!'"[5] From this perspective to treat an individual or situation other than as personally embedded in a local set of relationships would be unjust precisely because the emphasis is not on acts alone but on the effects they have on that running imbalance of obligation and recompense, ingratiation and negotiated response, hospitality and delayed reciprocity that can only operate to hold the community of believers together if all ties are kept open for permissible maneuver.

Similarly, the notion that people fall into certain categories but that it would be unfair to treat all those of a given sort as identical is indispensable to the way the concept of justice is commonly explained. Several examples may help in this regard. When I say to Muslim judges that we operate with the principle that similar cases should be decided similarly they always respond that no two cases are the same. I then propose a situation in which the same person commits the same act. They respond, in the sense we might mean by saying that you cannot step in the same stream twice, that those cases are still dissimilar because in the living, ever-changing networks that people create, service, and are defined by the repercussions of a similar act must necessarily imply possible alternative results which it would be unfair, unjust, and simply incomprehensible to ignore. So, Arab judges, both in their formal procedures and in their written and oral comments, repeatedly assert that failure to understand "who" a person is (i.e., their associations, their past interactions) would be to produce a process that is as unwise in the ways of mankind as it would be unjust by any standard of common sense and morality.

A second example concerns a story I was told about an Iraqi judge who was presented with forensic evidence by a Western legal adviser that indisputably pointed to the accused having fired the gun involved in the crime. The adviser was stunned, however, when the judge told him that forensic proof of the act alone was not really very relevant because it told him nothing about the relationship of the two parties, the way the accused had acted in other contexts, and the repercussions for others with whom he is associated, all of which the judge regarded as crucial to understanding the factors that are truly relevant to interpreting the very meaning of the man's act.[6] It is much the same orientation that, as we have seen, may have led Zacarias Moussaoui to be so eager to tell his story in his own way, to be so frustrated when the court said that what he wanted to testify to was irrelevant, and why he consistently marked this shortsighted process as not merely political but, much more importantly in his conceptual repertoire, unjust.

The idea of equivalence may also seem incompatible with the idea of justice to Westerners even though we draw upon it at times ourselves. An example may help. If a believing Catholic woman regards the priesthood as reserved exclusively for men, if an Orthodox Jewish woman has no objection to not being allowed to be called up to the Torah reading or serving as a rabbi, or if a devout Muslim woman is not offended because she cannot lead the prayers, is any of them simply brainwashed or incapable of comprehending that "true" justice must incorporate absolute equality of all acts? But if any of these women believes that what she does in the home is equivalent to what a man does in the place of worship, if to her these seeming incommensurables are equilibrated through a religious division of labor by gender, can one really say that no cognizable sense of justice is at work here? Quite the contrary, Muslims argue, particularly if (as many, though certainly not all of them, would say) one needs to think of people as having baseline category attributes from which, by rearing, background, and biology, they initially take their place in the world. But, they emphasize, these baselines can be superseded by developing one's reasoning capacities to gain control of one's passions and to effectuate a greater contribution to one's dependents and the community at large. To assess another solely on the basis of his or her origins could, therefore, lead to unjust results.

Justice, then, incorporates not some rigid sense of everyone having to be judged by their social origins but their entitlement to being assessed in terms of how they may have overcome or augmented their category beginnings in the course of applying their own intelligence. That factor shows up repeatedly—though by no means for all individuals—when we look at why women may be treated as persons and not simply as category occupants in the family law courts, or why so many women have been able to succeed on the qualifying examinations and move into the workforce and bureaucracies. An interesting example of this conceptual relation of category and personhood is evident in an interview in which Muhammad Morsy, prior to his becoming president of Egypt, was asked whether a Christian could serve in that office.

> "Which Christian?" Morsy responded when I first asked.
> I explained: not a particular Christian, but any Christian.
> "There are no Christians running for president," he said.
> Yes, I know. It's a theoretical question.
> "This is a nonsense question," he said. So I asked him if the [Muslim] Brotherhood had ideological objections to a woman's running for president.
> "Which woman?" he asked.[7]

Morsi may just have been cleverly evading a sensitive issue, but even if that is true the way he did it is still culturally revealing. The main point to be underlined is that a truly just person—indeed anyone who has developed his or her reasoning capacity—looks at the whole person and asks of all individuals not only what their social baseline is but also what they have done beyond it. Category placement is a starting point, while individual person assessment is a process that requires knowledge and experience.[8]

If equivalence is not incompatible with justice—if justice is not in these cultures (and perhaps not necessarily in any philosophical scheme) simply coincident with equality (in the sense of treating all things exactly the same)—then how does one go about establishing equivalencies?[9] To many Westerners equilibrating incommensurables is an open invitation to arbitrariness. The answer I think that most Arabs are comfortable with, however, is that it is the regularity of the *process* of assessment, not the regularity of results that counts. If I try to understand who someone is—by the lights of a culture that stresses embeddedness in a web of social indebtedness and the recognizable modes of its formation—I will be doing justice to that person even if, notwithstanding many similarities, the ultimate treatment differs from one individual or one occasion to another. It is rather like the game we played as children in which you had to start with one word and by changing one or two letters at a time see what result you ended up with. The winner was not judged by simply getting to the end but by the skill and cleverness with which the process of transformations had been employed. In contexts that, to outsiders from the culture, may seem to be identical because of the way these outsiders have defined the situation within their own framework of common sense, results of equal validity may be totally compatible notwithstanding outcomes that are never replicated. In a world perceived as replete with difference—but celebrated for the room to maneuver that such an attribute provides and sanctions—a calculus of equivalence depends on *how* one applies reason to social evaluation, not how one mechanically applies the same outcome to situations whose differences one has failed to grasp. Such application is, crucially, an index of one's knowledge of the world of differences and, as a demonstration of one's ability to negotiate such a world, the reason why others should believe and rely on you. This emphasis may also play a role in the traditional absence of appellate courts in Islam—because cases turn not on uniform endpoints but on the process of assessing particularities—and why, by contrast to Westerners who imagine themselves exquisitely adept at assessing "facts" (tire tracks, fingerprints, DNA), Arabs regard themselves as especially proficient at assessing persons and have developed the conceptual vocabulary to go with it.

If, then, we turn to the role of the state in such an environment some general propositions may also be offered. Several of the preceding chapters have suggested that the state is commonly viewed as incapable of engaging in genuine reciprocity. Indeed, since it is equally common for people in the region to believe that persons cannot be separated from roles one cannot expect institutions to replace the face-to-face personalism seen as indispensable to all relationships.[10] The result is an awkward impasse, one in which each bureaucrat is approached as a person with whom one ought to be able to establish ties of reciprocity but who, relying on money and unwilling to be drawn into every possible obligation, increasingly fails to play the game, so to speak, of building up interpersonal debts that could be converted into multiple and negotiable forms of reciprocation.

Similarly, the state is not consonant with the shari'a, notwithstanding the claims of some that theirs is an Islamic state or their monarch both Commander of the Faithful and ultimate arbiter of the law. As a consequence, the legitimacy of state power and divine law are not combined but diluted. For while state decision-making forums—the divan of an Ottoman ruler, the personal decisions of a contemporary monarch—have a long history of adjudication separable from shari'a precepts and procedures, the inclusion in most present-day instances of the entire legal apparatus within a single ministry of justice undercuts the formal separation of past legal forums. State centralization of the legal system also undermines the use of fatwas from scholars versus the mercy of the ruler, each of which could form a check on the power of the other. For all the efforts of various regimes to combine the legitimacy of the religious and the political, the result has, almost without exception, been a diminution in the connection between the formal structure of the legal system and the popular impulse to distrust the consolidation of power.

It is here, too, that a deeper set of cultural assumptions may come into play. Briefly, these include a host of ways in which ambivalence to power has been pervasive in the practices of different communities in the region. Whether it is the style of political jokes in Egypt or Syria, the earlier ritual inversion of choosing a student to command the Moroccan sultan on one day of the year, the emphasis on addressing even nobles as equals in the Arabian Peninsula, or the often ambiguous approach to living saints in North Africa, a certain ethos appears to inform much of contemporary Arab culture which balks at the exclusion of alternative bases for building power. Throughout much of the region, therefore, there is evidence of a deep sense that too much power should not be in too few hands for too long a period of time. Thus the legitimacy of the "big man" who comes to power through the formation of an elaborate network of obligations may be replaced by a competitor who, by forming a better network, becomes the legitimate holder of power. That is not to say he is liked, only that he holds power legitimately, as would whoever can build a superior network to replace him. In such an environment there may seem to be a total absence of a rule of law, but in fact it is perhaps best to see this as an alternative set of features playing into a different conception of the rule of law, a system, or style, of law in which the constraints of network construction, reciprocity, and legitimization all possess distinctive modes of articulation, enactment, and restraint.

To think in terms of a rule of law model, then, may not always be the most useful way to think about orderliness. In a sense, of course, what reasonable person could oppose the implementation of a rule of law? Would its absence not imply utter lawlessness, a world of Hobbesian force and brutality? But the very idea of "a rule of law" is not unproblematic. Whether one tries to equate it with the rule of reason, the independent judicial review of governmental action, or as an ideal that unites disparate values embodied in a specific set of rules, a number of Western legal scholars have argued that the concept of a rule of law is neither capable of precise characterization nor is it necessarily compatible with democracy insofar as it still requires discretionary interpretation. Indeed, the usual dictionary definition—"a state of order in which events conform to the law"—appears to many a tautology.[11]

A more anthropologically compatible view of the rule of law may be that articulated by Harvard Law Professor Richard H. Fallon (1997) who argues that the very concept is multi-stranded and that to the extent it has real content it arises from the particularities of a culture to which law and the political order give voice and direction. If, as he suggests, the purpose of the rule of law is "to protect against anarchy and establish a scheme of public order, to allow people to plan their affairs with advance knowledge of the legal consequences, and to protect against at least some types of official arbitrariness," and if, moreover, "practices that satisfy Rule-of-Law values in some circumstances may fail to do so in others," then there is much to be said for his conclusion that "a theory of the Rule-of-Law must therefore attend to the diverse contexts in which Rule-of-Law questions arise."[12] He quotes Federal Court of Appeals Judge Richard Posner who further notes that "standards that capture lay intuitions about right behavior (for example, the negligence standard) and that therefore are easy to learn may produce greater legal certainty than a network of precise but technical, non-intuitive rules covering the same ground."[13]

Viewed against this background it may be suggested that while Fallon is right to say that "invocations of the Rule of Law are sufficiently meaningful to deserve attention, but today are too vague and conclusory to dispel lingering puzzlement," we may still be able to triangulate in on the cultural contributors to this notion in particular societies and moments. Thus in the case of the Arab Middle East (again, speaking very generally) we can see that there are indeed constraints on power, that a process based on a cultural idea of person perception takes pride of place over formal substantive rules, that placing people back into workable relationships may be a better way to secure society against chaos than rigid application of formal strictures, and that in each instance—and with considerable local and historical variation—it is possible to discern many related principles that are coincident with a popular sense of when justice is being done.

In this regard Muslim judges and many jurisconsults have always been legal realists; they find no inherent contradiction between the idea of a rule of law and a rule of men in the sense of a person's relationships and attachments to the community not extinguishing individual reason. Moreover they believe that it is unwise to convert justice into a mechanical means of knowing the "uniquely correct decision" that alone would justify any given result. For them, it might be said, a rule of law is both more realistic and more just than a law of rules. But even that is not enough. "Knowledge," Muslims often note, is the second most frequently used term in the Quran after the name of God, and the person who seeks knowledge is not a person whose individual judgment is to be sequestered by rigid propositions but one who may indeed exercise discretion without it necessarily overstepping the bounds of independent reasoning (*ijtihād*). What the nations of the Arab Middle East have not been particularly successful at doing, however, is translating many of these features into so foundational a document as a national constitution.

A written constitution is not, of course, indispensable to national political organization: The British do just fine without one. To some a constitution is indeed vital to the forging of a society-wide consensus; to others it is more a symbol of national distinction—like a national airline or soccer team—than a statement that shapes and accords with the true structure of power. But in the modern period virtually all of the Middle Eastern countries have felt the need for one. The history of Arab constitutionalism is not, however, one of great success. This has been true in practically every country and time period. Reviewing this history, Elizabeth F. Thompson, for example, recites the efforts made by a series of noteworthy individuals over the course of several centuries.[14]

There is Mustafa Ali, the seventeenth-century Ottoman, whose "Circle of Justice," though grounded on a hierarchy of social duties, influenced the nineteenth-century Tanzimat reforms that undercut the very idea of governance by privileged status. When, in 1858, a peasant revolt on Mount Lebanon "went so wrong" it was the claims of equality by the underclass that nevertheless made the extension of the Tanzimat principles imaginable. Later in that century, Ahmed Urabi in Egypt and Nazem al-Islam Kermani in Iran spread the idea of constitutionalism, but like their predecessors found Western support for existing monarchies overpowering.

In the second half of the nineteenth century, deeply influenced by their experience of colonial encounters with France and Britain, a number of Muslims scholars, particularly in Egypt, argued that only a modernization of legal forms coupled with a less centralized distribution of power could allow Muslims the freedom to adapt to modern needs. Jamal ad-Din al-Afghani (1838–1897) could therefore argue that Islamic law should not be bounded by the interpretations of the past alone. Principles of modern science, as grasped through our God-given reason, could provide the guidance and stability that conservatives mistakenly and unnecessarily restrict to the legal and political precepts that took form soon after the death of the Prophet. Muhammad 'Abduh (1849–1905) and Muhammad Rashid Rida (1865–1935), following this path, supplied additional impetus to the argument that legal and governmental forms should move with the times. Nevertheless, constitutions as such did not succeed in embracing modes of organization capable of gaining sustained support and were frequently undermined by authoritarian domination or discarded by opponents frustrated by the colonial, monarchical, or dictatorial regimes that followed one another with considerable regularity.

By the twentieth century, the career of Turkey's "Joan of Arc," Halide Edib (1884–1964), mirrored the failure to bring about Wilsonian ideas of small nation independence. Similarly, Musa Kazim's encounters with David Ben Gurion and the British in Palestine never resulted in converting the claim for self-determination into a concrete governmental structure. Thus by the time Hasan al-Banna organized the Muslim Brotherhood in Egypt, Comrade Fahd revitalized the Communist party in Iraq, and Akram al-Hourani allied with the Ba'ath Party in Syria, the descent into violence had accelerated as autocratic powers sought to crush the movements' popular appeal. Thompson ends with the Arab Spring's Wael Ghonim whose Facebook communications sought to revive his precursors' democratizing efforts, only for the democratically elected government of Muhammad Morsi to be removed by a military coup which, whatever its popular support, followed on the Muslim Brotherhood's failure to reach out to the whole of society and fashion a constitution that would have secured the interests of all Egyptians rather than their own most ardent supporters.

Thus the history of constitutionalism in the region, veering from mimicking Western forms to utter dependence on the whim of those in power, has, for all the talk of creating a document of genuine "authenticity," often been hampered by models and divisions that have seldom resonated with their people's deepest sense of how power is and should be managed. But as vital as a structural model for distributing power is to any constitutional order no such document may achieve broad acceptance entirely on its own. Any nation's political course, even when subject to outside interference, may ultimately depend more on the precedent of its own guiding beliefs and the analogies drawn from its own concept of justice than on outsiders' versions of the past or an untethered list of rights and duties. Regrettably, appropriate precedents and authentic analogies have so far eluded most of those seeking democratic reform in the region.

Scholars, journalists, and politicians attribute the failure of constitutionalism in the Arab world to a variety of factors. To some it is a matter of hostility to the West, misplaced nostalgia for an early Islamic order that was never in fact stable, or gravitation to some "taste for the absolute" that is deeply engrained in the familial, marital, and political life of the region. Thompson (2013, 9) argues that constitutional democracy in the region was, in fact, well on its way to realization around World War I, and she blames its stillbirth on the machinations of Britain and France as well as Woodrow Wilson's failure to overcome the allies' imperial designs. Still others attribute the failure of democracy not to an inherent incompatibility of Islam and democratic constitutionalism but the difficulty of persuading the more conservative members of society that legitimacy can lie in a document other than the Quran and Traditions of the Prophet.

Whatever the merits of these alternative explanations, pessimism about constitutional democracy in the Arab world is understandable. Constitutions are frequently altered to suit the autocratic leader of the moment. King Hassan II changed the constitution of Morocco six times—always by means of a referendum that, not surprisingly, turned up support ranging well over 90%—and his son and heir, Muhammad VI, changed it yet again in response to events during the Arab Spring of 2010–11. Bashar al-Assad, aged thirty-four at the time of his father's death, simply changed the constitution that required Syria's head of state to be at least forty years old, while Abdel Fattah al-Sisi manipulated the election for the presidency by extending the voting period for Egypt's constitutional revisions in order to claim greater support for its alteration. Numerous other regimes have changed their constitutions—whether for the length of time a ruler could serve or as a means of playing musical chairs with the opposition parties—to the point where it became difficult to develop interpretations of the document's provisions before it was again altered. With no viable political arena available other reformers gave up on constitutionalism, at least for the moment, and expressed their claim for justice through domestic violence or terrorist attacks. Thus Abu Iyad's Black September spin-off from Fatah, like Sayyid Qutb's harangues against the corruption of Nasser's Egypt and Western degradation, ended in their being killed, while Ali Shariati saw his belief in a democratic Iran give way to the rule of clerics.

Westerners—especially Americans—have by contrast seen the creation of a constitution as indispensable to the formation of a modern democratic state. The failed attempts at "nation building" by the United States in Iraq and Afghanistan have not only been a result of poor execution and reliance on inappropriate leaders; they have resulted from the assumption that if one simply cleared the field of preexisting political forms and their beneficiaries democracy would, with remarkably little "encouragement," grow naturally.[15] Even in its most seemingly innocuous form the effort may presume a universality that negates any consideration of cultural and historical distinction. Thus when George W. Bush invaded Iraq he assumed that if we simply removed the old regime a democracy not unlike our own would take its place. Once Saddam Hussein was eliminated constitution writers followed in the wake, while in Afghanistan we were assured by some legal scholars that the constitution that was adopted would serve as a model for the entire region.[16]

Characteristically, the constitutions proposed in recent years have included a very large number of provisions, many of which represent issues of concern at the moment of construction, attempts to satisfy all factions, or efforts to preempt later interpretations or amendments. Thus, to choose only the most recent example of a constitution many in the West regard with unusual hope: the Tunisian constitution contains 149 articles, among them the establishment of an Audio-Visual Communication Committee, provision for national support of sports, and a statement in the Preamble (made "an integral part of the Constitution" by Article 145) calling for support of "just liberation movements at the forefront of which is the Palestinian liberation movement."[17] There is ostensible protection of religious diversity. However, as the director of the Human Rights Watch office for Tunisia and Algeria points out, contradictions in Article Six leave open the possibility for quite strict religious views to be enforced under the constitution.[18]

Expecting that a constitution would not address issues of the moment is perhaps unrealistic: Whatever provisions a new U.S. constitutional convention might seek to incorporate one would not, for example, expect the billeting of foreign troops in one's home to be a pressing issue, whereas abortion and gun rights would no doubt garner substantial concern. Yet all of the Middle Eastern constitutions seem to start from the assumption that one must reconcile—or accommodate or defer to—Islam and that much of the structure of governance must flow from this primal concern.[19] One cannot discount the importance of Islam's embodiment in certain institutions—the charitable foundation, the shari'a, and sometimes the monarch as religious head. Nor can one doubt that as a symbol of national solidarity and indeed morality the shari'a occupies for many a crucial place. But Islam lives in the details of its daily application—in the morals of the marketplace, the procedures and assumptions at work in a court of law, and the rituals that fall outside of (and sometimes stand in opposition to) the religious personnel or structures controlled by the central government.[20] That is why it is worth considering that an alternative does exist to the direct application of Islam in the construction of a constitution, a possibility that need not merely render the constitution secular. At least as a thought exercise the alternative to be suggested here may help us to consider the relation of culture to constitutionalism and draw attention to the ways in which a constitution might sufficiently sound in the experience of ordinary people as to garner popular support.

Specifically we might ask whether it is possible to create authentic constitutional forms based on an underlying cultural principle not unlike that which may be said to form part of the basis of the U.S. Constitution. This is in no way to suggest that the American constitution should serve as a model for all. Quite the contrary, the point is that just as the U.S. constitution may, in part, be based on culturally shared ideas that remain largely unexpressed in the final document so, too, other nations might choose to build a constitution from their own version of a cultural base. To see where such a foundation may lie, consider, for example, the role played by the concept of "virtue" in the formation of the American Constitution.[21]

James Madison, like the other Founders, thought that America's relative isolation from the corruption of European regimes gave it a chance to be grounded on "the great republican principle," the proposition

> that the people will have virtue and intelligence to select men of virtue and wisdom. Is there no virtue among us?—If there be not, we are in a wretched situation. No theoretical check—no forms of Government, can render us secure. . . . The institution of delegated power implies that there is a portion of virtue and honor among mankind, which may be a reasonable foundation of confidence. And experience justifies the theory.[22]

"Virtue" was not a vacuous concept for the Founders. Madison and his colleagues infused the idea of virtue with specific content: that people who had control of their own property would be constrained by the opinion of others to seek the law as protection for all; that civic virtue would gain expression through participation in the choice of like-minded persons representing one in the legislature; that the broader and more diverse the nation—indeed, the more complex its tensions—the greater the chance that a balance of contending forces would serve as a counterweight to "the common interest or passion" that would lead a majority to deny others their rights, for "as there is a degree of depravity in mankind which requires a certain degree of circumspection and distrust, so there are other qualities in human nature which justify a certain portion of esteem and confidence."[23]

Thus, to the Founders, if men lived in a political environment in which the principles of nature were afforded the greatest chance of being expressed they could manage their affairs best with a balance of powers that encourages the highest expression of the virtues inherent in social relationships, virtues that would form a hedge against many of the greatest abuses of power no political structure alone can prevent.[24] It is, therefore, possible that, absent the shared belief in government being able to elicit and encourage such virtue, the fabrication of a foundational document embracing a broad range of local and political differences would have been impossible, or at least thought impossible. And if we read a number of specific provisions of that document—as well as those left unenumerated—into our understanding of its success the resultant interpretation does not depend solely on what is on the face of the document but on a set of enfolding cultural propositions that were indispensable to its garnering a sense of authenticity in the first place.

Now if, for the sake of argument, we view the U.S. Constitution as resting to some extent on a shared cultural notion of "virtue," the question may be asked whether there is, perhaps, a functional equivalent present in the Arab countries that could also serve as a basis for the specific propositions incorporated in a formal constitution. Beginning not with the resultant structure of government but with what might be thought of as the scaffolding that is necessary for its construction, we might turn to the assumptions that emerge from a study of Arab cultures, assumptions about the nature of human nature and the proper relations among the members of a common religious and political community. From this foundation we might then ask: What sorts of governmental mechanisms might emerge from or be suited to such cultural values and how might they contribute to the success of a foundational document? In North Africa and the Middle East the basis from which one might start might, therefore, include several of the cultural precepts that can be teased out of the specific situations we have been reviewing. These would include the importance of justice as equivalence, reciprocity and structured personalism, ambivalence to power, and property as collective trust.

Justice as Equivalence. It has been suggested that in much of the Arab world justice means equivalence, not equality in the sense of treating all persons identically. If Madison and his cohort could believe that "the supposition of universal venality in human nature is little less an error in political reasoning than the supposition of universal rectitude"—and draw upon this belief in structuring a government—then arguably one might build on the belief many Arabs exhibit that differences among various categories of persons must not be inconsistent with the way government affects everyday relationships. Because a constitution is neither self-executing nor culturally isolated it may only enshrine stable relationships if grounded on its adherents' views of human nature and how power might realistically be confined.

Justice, then, may for Arabs not have to mean identical treatment but attending to the disparate nature of the category or set of affiliations that characterize each person, an orientation that makes for a very different basis for "democracy" than the self-fashioning Enlightenment-era variety found in the West. To many this may seem as flawed a basis for constitutional protection as the denial of equal rights to women, slaves, and Indians in the original U.S. Constitution. But if one is guaranteed not equality of outcome but equality of attention to one's whole person—particularly one's knowledge and consequential relationships—then provisions in the laws that discriminate against one or another category at the outset have a vital escape clause. So, for example, faced with the situation that Muslim courts frequently grant custody to a better educated and employed mother than a dissolute father who has an overriding statutory right to custody, a more general protection for the process of whole-person evaluation could be the basis for a constitutional right even if agreement cannot be immediately achieved on statutes guaranteeing equality as identical treatment. Provisions that insure full consideration of one's personal attributes, along with foundational guarantees for all categories of persons, may yield specific interpretations over the years that draw together rather than separate groups of persons by dint of the emphasis on vitalizing everyone's opportunities for maturation. Moreover, given the built-in flexibility of Arab concepts of personhood the provisions that may seek to implement broad-scale assessments of the whole person would not be frozen in the meaning given to them at any moment but might possess a dynamic quality that could respond to changes in employment, education, and family organization over the course of time. Such an approach would, moreover, reinforce the common law style of Islamic legal case law and its role as a check on other agencies of government.

Reciprocity and structured personalism. One problem Arab constitutionalists have never solved is how to couple justice as personal embeddedness in a web of malleable obligations with assurance that government will not interfere in one's relationships to the point of distorting or unbalancing the negotiation of such ties. In the history of the Middle East the frustrations occasioned by foreign intrusion and the efforts made by articulate and courageous individuals at constitutional government cannot be underplayed. Nevertheless, many would argue that a valuable accelerant to democratic reform may be the separation of personal affiliations from the institutions of governance. Indeed, if a constitution cannot encourage and enshrine, for example, the separation by a judge or legislator of his or her official powers from personal identity and entanglements then any hope of circumscribing power may fail regardless of constitutional guarantees. In this view the countries of the Middle East did not simply experience an interruption to their independence occasioned by Western interference; they also lacked the urge or breathing space to transform the person situated in a network of obligations into a citizen able to play a variety of discrete roles within a government of limited powers.

But what if one started instead with the view that is so often implicit in Arab culture that the self cannot be fractionated, that people are the concatenation of all their traits and ties and that it is unrealistic—indeed untrue—to maintain that anyone, regardless of office or position, can be expected to act one way in one role and quite another as a matter of personal belief and attachment? Thus when I suggest to judges, for example, that several of our Supreme Court justices have said they personally oppose the death penalty but as judges must nevertheless apply it I am always asked who this man is, who he is connected to, what other events concerning crime have occurred to him or his family, the thrust being that if I knew enough about each man I would see no inconsistency or divisibility in his viewpoint. Can one, then, maintain in a constitutional structure a view of the person as unfractionated and couple it with their view of how it is still possible for power to be divided and balanced?

The answer may lie in the notion that these two cultural postulates are not incompatible. One can simply recognize that an office is not the whole of a person but an aspect of that person and bind an officeholder to the standards of a reliable witness whose full array of attachments must be a part of the transparent public record at all times. Just as Arabs constantly seek information about another's relationships as the basis for establishing an interpersonal tie, so, too, the law could emphasize ways in which all of one's associations must be made part of common knowledge through open qualification, transparent personal and governmental contracts, and greater disclosure of an official's former and current attachments. In addition, following the emphasis in the Quran, the process of engaging in contracts could receive explicit constitutional protection, including methods of weighing the fulfillment of a contract by any of a number of alternative modes of reciprocation. Where local officials have experimented with such openness it has attracted considerable popular support.[25] Again, transferring a cultural propensity into a constitutional protection is not a matter of one-to-one correlation: It is a matter of creating the mechanisms that facilitate the range of relationships commonly accepted while protecting against too much power in too few hands for too long a period of time. This brings us to the next postulate.

Ambivalence to power. Skepticism about the powerful is different from the existence of a number of ways in which such systemic incredulity is actually institutionalized in ritual and social practice. Building cultural ambivalence to power into a constitution can involve a very wide range of mechanisms, from rotation of office to institutionalizing electoral cycles and engaging in redistribution through forms of taxation. Arab nations have tried a broad range of ways to limit power: A few have mandated term limits, election by proportional representation, reservation of a specified number of parliamentary seats for different segments of society, and so on. Power might be significantly devolved to local areas not as a way of deferring to ethnic or confessional differences but as a way of emphasizing the domains in which custom may govern specific issues. There are those who have argued that the Iraqi and Tunisian constitutions, for example, err in allowing any degree of local autonomy, while others assert that its absence in Afghanistan would be a grave error.[26] But electing local governors and councils is more likely to allow the mechanisms of popular limitation on power to be expressed than is seeking hermetically sealed domains of legislative and executive action.

The organization of the legal system is crucial here. Most constitutions claim that Islamic law must be granted substantial deference, or at least that no law be repugnant to it. But more important may be the recognition that Islamic legal systems are not, in fact, similar to civil law systems, in which reference to a set code, organization through a centrally controlled ministry of justice, and advancement based on government decisions is characteristic. Rather, if Islamic law actually operates more like a common law system—emphasizing case by case adjudication, pushing decision making down to the local and bringing cultural concepts in from that base—greater communication among courts may help to legitimize the criteria for insuring each person's right to individual assessment. Removing the law courts from a ministry of justice may actually accord with popular ambivalence to power while further supporting the pride judges and lawyers wish to take in their profession. Encouraging the development of professional associations, which have a long history in the countries of the Middle East, would also assist in the constant battle against corruption.

Juries have been tried in a few Muslim countries. Where they have failed has been revealing. For example, in Morocco I was told by people who had served on juries during their brief tryout that because they could not engage the accused directly with questions and interaction how would it be possible for them to know who this person really is and what the meaning was of his actions? That form of cultural personalism may be drawn upon by using a mixed panel of judges and laymen, all of whom can address the parties directly but whose lay members may bring in local concerns and balance the potential corruption of permanent judges and notaries. By decentralizing the judicial system in a way that is consistent with the style of person assessment in which Islamic law courts and ordinary people approach such matters could, without sounding too Jeffersonian or Tocquevillian a note here, fit with a sense of devolved power and local inclusion in the institutions of governance.

Property as Trust. Public land and resources need to be conceptualized as public assets, not in the sense of those forms of socialism tried in Algeria or Egypt but as capable of distribution to a broad range of individuals, groups, and institutions. Some forms of collective ownership have profound roots in parts of the Arab world. It was the Arabs who, in the development of water law, established the principles of beneficial use and who sought, in the mortmain trusts (*waqf*, *ḥabus*), a vehicle for securing dependents and frustrating the depredations of those in power. Relying on deeper conceptions of the distribution of assets—whether grounded in the concept of revolving patrimony or the concept of the trust—might, then, contribute to support for the constitution as a whole. Some of these property concepts can have as much force within Muslim countries as they might, in our discussion of Israeli-Palestinian ties, have relevance for establishing peaceful relations within and across ethnic, religious, and territorial boundaries in the Middle East.

Finally, the preamble to any constitution might emphasize these shared cultural norms explicitly, rather than recite (as most Middle Eastern constitutions do) vagaries about the nation and its commitments. Succinctly stated and couched in familiar terms, such a preamble could be accessible to all and might set a tone that is all too often lacking in present forms.

* * *

Justice may indeed be only a metaphor. But as one novelist notes: "Just because something is a metaphor doesn't mean it can't be real."[27] Justice and injustice are felt because, like any critical symbol, they are among those condensed concepts that pull into their orbit a wide range of experiences, understandings, relationships, and histories with such force as to define emotions and create reality. Westerners represent justice as blind, so that each case may seem to partake of a general principle, uniqueness being theoretically merged and cancelled in the process. But the Muslim conception, as I understand it, is closer in some ways to the Greek concept of *dike*, in which a dynamic balance of contraries is nevertheless subsumed under a unifying "law." If underneath it all modern Western law, in Martin Jay's phrasing of a point Max Horkheimer and Theodor Adorno once suggested, is "still beholden to a mythic assumption, the fetish of equivalence, the desire for perfect commensurability," Islamic law in its actual practice is not uncomfortable with equivalence as differences that cannot—and should not—be reduced to simple identity.[28] Reasoning may be analogic, but not with the goal of compelling that which is different to be melded into all that is the same. Nor does the Islamic-infused form of case law reasoning seek as its ultimate goal a replicable measure that collapses the temporal difference between past and present into some timeless, religiously sanctioned whole. To the contrary, Islamic law focuses on procedure thereby allowing difference to flourish, settlements to be varied, and the ability to negotiate relationships to be the point of origination for freedom rather than rendering freedom of maneuver a threat to uniform outcome. As a result, the rule of law is more a rule of justice in which a belief in reciprocity can check economic domination and faith in being judged as a whole person is recognized as a right held against all the world.

Justice Rosalie Silberman Abella of the Supreme Court of Canada has said that "Rule of law is a euphemism no one understands" and that instead "we need a Rule of Justice."[29] It is often by their absence, though, that we may at least sense the effects we would have both law and justice entail. The rule of law, vague as it may seem, is indispensable to the reorganization of political and legal culture in the Arab world, but that will not be enough. The question that is usually asked is this: Are there certain preconditions for "democracy" whose development would better serve the people it describes? It is unlikely that such is the case universally, and more likely that local cultural variation may be essential to the development of a sense of inclusion and constancy, especially where the element of religion remains strong. Rather, one might be left with a somewhat different, and even more hopeful, question, namely: Is it possible that what might be of significant assistance in formulating guiding precepts is that vitalizing sense that accompanies a culturally specific rule of justice, and at the end of the day could the linkage that metaphor provides be indispensable to the creation of new realities in the political and social life of the nations of the region?

Notes

Introduction

1. See Bingham 2014. In July 2008, Lord Phillips, Lord Chief Justice of England and Wales, weighed into the fray by agreeing with the archbishop's position. For each of their statements and a series of essays discussing the implications of bringing some elements of Islamic law into common law structures, see Ahdar and Aroney, eds. 2011.

2. See Grunert 2013. Similarly, the lower house of the Idaho legislature initially refused enforcement of an international treaty on child support because it would allow Islamic law to enter the backdoor through judgments by countries that grant the shari'a any applicability. Struyk and Kruesi 2015. For a series of cases attending to Islamic law in U.S. courts, see Shariah in American Courts 2015.

3. Quoted in Graham 2016.

4. "In early 2007, the small town of Hérouxville [Ontario] adopted a document outlining 'Standards for Living' (*normes de vie*) for potential immigrants to the hamlet that provoked charges of insulting Muslims and others. The standards included an inevitably provocative insistence that it was inappropriate 'to . . . kill women by stoning them in public, burning them alive, burning them with acid, circumcising them, etc.' . . . The irony, of course, was that Hérouxville is a tiny crossroads of some 1,300 residents, situated a hundred miles north of Montreal, with exactly one family of immigrants at the time the standards were announced" (Joppke and Torpey 2013, 101–2). See also Emon 2009.

5. This may even be true as compared to the imagined protections of Western law. Thus, American lawyer Rafia Zakaria (2010) tells of the case she handled of a Jordanian woman abused and abandoned by her husband in the United States who would have been accorded no support under Indiana law but who was able to succeed by pleading her Islamic marriage agreement as an enforceable contract, one that had built-in protections for her that American law does not assure. "Her story [Zakaria concludes] exposed to me the superficiality of the logic that, in America

and under American law, justice is a guarantee for women, and that under Islamic law women would perennially be oppressed."

6. See Gesink 2003.

7. Terminiello v. Chicago 1949, 11 (the U.S. Supreme Court is not, said Frankfurter, "a tribunal unbounded by rules. We do not sit like a kadi under a tree dispensing justice according to considerations of individual expediency"). Similarly, Lord Justice Goddard of the English Court of Appeals, writing about a case that could justifiably go either way, said: "The court . . . is really put very much in the position of a Cadi under the palm tree. There are no principles on which he is directed to act. He has to do the best he can in the circumstances, having no rules of law to guide him" (Metropolitan Properties Co. Ltd. v. Purdy, 1940, 188). Pilgram (2012, 777), calling it "legal Orientalism," characterizes this way of approaching Islamic law as one in which "Sharia remains inferior to occidental law because on the one hand, it is too rigid, as it is based on religious principles that cannot be challenged by the individual and are therefore anti-democratic, and on the other hand because it is too unpredictable, as it is not based on a secular positivist notion of law, something Weber called *Kadijustiz*. If played according to its rules, the orientalist game can never be won."

8. Maine 1883, 389.

9. For these and similar examples, see Kadri 2012.

10. Cited in Kadri 2012, 205. The author also notes that while the jurists of various Islamic law schools suggested that homosexuals should be stoned, "there is no account in the hadith collections [of the sayings and actions of the Prophet] or later texts of such a penalty ever actually being applied, however" (Kadri 2012, 97 note).

11. See Drieskens 2008. At the time in 1984 when a woman could demand a divorce if not consulted by her husband upon his taking a second wife, a court in Egypt even awarded the first wife a divorce based on her claim that the husband had married a jinn, whose existence the Quran asserts even though it was acknowledged that science has proved such a marriage impossible. See Edge 1989.

12. See Osanloo 2012a and 2012b. For other instances of victim retribution and mercy in Islamic criminal law, see Dehghan 2015, Erdbrink 2015, and Hubbard 2015.

13. See, e.g., Jennings 1979. For an example of great courage on the part of local judges in early twentieth-century Morocco, see Rosen 2016:29–31.

14. For example, in refusing to recognize the judgment of a Moroccan court the U.S. District Court for the Western District of Texas stated: "There is extensive evidence suggesting that Morocco's judiciary is dominated by the royal family (through no fault of the judiciary, which would prefer to be left to do its job)." Moroccan Foreign Minister Taieb Fassi Fihri (2011) had acknowledged, in response to a question concerning his country's judicial independence: "It's not the reality today. And because some calls [take place] from time to time, from the Justice Department to some judge." See U.S. AID 2010. However, the Fifth Circuit Court

of Appeals reversed the lower court decision in DeJoria, holding: "Based on the evidence in the record, we cannot agree that the Moroccan judicial system lacks sufficient independence such that fair litigation in Morocco is impossible." (DeJoria v. Maghreb Petroleum 2014, 115293.)

15. On Islamic law as a common law system, see Rosen 2000, 38–68. Wael Hallaq (2009, 364–65, 544, 549) says: societies in which Islamic law operated historically were "largely self-governing" because Islamic law was a "non-state, community-based, bottom-up" system that "derived its ethical and moral foundations from . . . the very social order which it came to serve in the first place."

16. Erie 2016. See also Shabana 2010.

17. Rosen 2000, 38–68. Many historians currently make the same argument: see, e.g., Meshal 2014, 41–67; Hallaq 2009; and Jackson 2001. See also Isser 2011 (esp. the chaps. on Afghanistan, Sudan, and Iraq); and Wilson 2015.

18. A typical statement, this one from Sumatra, holds that "all Acehnese people believe *adat* is part of *shariah*" (Bustamam-Ahmad 2009, 34).

Chapter One

1. An intellectual portrait of this man will be found in chap. 2 of Rosen 2016.

2. On the similar difficulties in working with historical legal records, see, e.g., Peirce 1998, 272–73.

3. A 2006 Moroccan study shows that over 71% of women and 75% of men continue to favor the requirement of a marital guardian. Cited in Young 2010, 198.

4. Judges may also now rely to some extent on circumstantial evidence. In doing so judges with whom I have worked have justified their approach by pointing to the Quranic version of the story of Joseph and Potiphar's wife. When the latter tries to seduce Joseph it is one of her own kinsmen who notices that Joseph's garment is torn from in back, rather than in front, thereby supporting Joseph's claim that he was trying to get away from rather than attacking the wife of the captain of Pharaoh's guard. See Goldman 1995.

5. On the use of such go-betweens in Muslim cultures, see Diab 2016. For advice about tactics that can be used in Muslim courts of Nigeria, see Ibrahim 2013.

6. For a time Morocco also tried a series of "community courts," localized small claims courts presided over by an elected official whose jurisdiction did not include matters of marriage and divorce, and which were, in theory, capable of offering quick and cheap resolution of minor disputes. On these courts, see Rosen 2000, 111–32.

7. For examples from various parts of the Muslim world that bear on this issue, see Giunchi 2014.

Chapter Two

1. Originally prepared for the Third International Conference on Islam at the University of Wisconsin, Madison in 2012, this chapter benefited from the helpful comments of the participants, as well as Jessica Carlisle, Abdellah Hammoudi, Livia Holden, Werner Menski, Rachel Newcomb, Claire Nicholas, Euis Nurlaelawati, Arzoo Osanloo, David Powers, Intisar Rabb, Ido Shahar, Nadia Sonneveld, and Erin Stiles—none of whom, of course, is responsible for the arguments made here.

2. For a strongly argued assessment of male violence to women, see Mona El Tahawy 2012. The Bangladesh Bureau of Statistics reports that four out of five married women in that country have been subjected to violence by their husbands. http://www.bbc.co.uk/programmes/p04kxn32 (accessed January 3, 2017). A blanket claim that it is best to approach Islamic family matters by starting from the premise that Muslim women are the subject of oppression is countered by Harvard Divinity School Professor Laila Ahmed (2013, 57–58) who writes: "My overall conclusion then is that it is time now really that we deleted this entire subject of 'the oppression of women in Islam' from our repertoire. It's a subject that is, in reality, no more than a rhetorical device without meaning or content, a device that we've inherited from imperial times. It's time to cast it aside. . . . [T]he way forward is not through the wholesale denigration of 'everything Islamic or through grand assaults on the oppression of women' in Islam, but rather through directly confronting and challenging unjust and cruel laws, customs and behaviours one by one and specifically, wherever they occur." On violence to women, see notes 147 and 148.

3. See, e.g., the candid statement by Mistry (2003, 247): "Existing literature on Muslim women in India is acutely deficient in empirical information on divorce and related issues."

4. See Rosen 2012.

5. Rosen 2007. Another scholar writes: "Works on Islamic legal theory (*uṣūl al-fiqh*) and manuals on Islamic substantive law (*fiqh*) have been the focus of the modern study of Islamic law but they tell us almost nothing about ordinary Muslim men and women. . . . [Q]uestions of women's agency are often obscured. . . . [Wives] understand Islamic law, manipulate it, and act accordingly" (Mathee 2011, 75, 79, 94–95). See also Ali 2003 where he notes that tenth-century C.E. Sunni legal texts demonstrate women's agency. For a historiographic discussion of the study of shari'a courts, see Agmon and Shahar 2008. For a series of essays that, by comparison, do focus on the actual role of the courts in contemporary Muslim family law, see Giunchi 2014.

6. See. e.g., Fawzy 2004.

7. See, e.g., the various reports collected at the website *Women Living under Muslim Laws*.

8. On published opinions, see Shaham 1997. On the problems associated with using certain Ottoman records, see al-Khowli 2005. In many instances cases have

been reported or collected for their individual interest rather than in a fashion that would allow statistical calculations.

9. In Dhaka, Bangladesh 70% of all divorces are initiated by women. http://www.bbc.co.uk/programmes/p04kxn32 (accessed January 3, 2017). In Iran more women brought suit for divorce than did men in 2001; by 2008 twice as many women as men petitioned for divorce (Afary 2009, 363). Since many cases are consensual it is also true that who formally initiates the case may be irrelevant. Thus, while the wife may "win" some or all of the case it may actually be an instance of an agreed-upon action. Even so, operating in the shadow of the law may have had a major effect on the settlement they have negotiated.

10. See, e.g., Peirce 1998.

11. It can, therefore, be misleading to attend only to the manuals of the scholars or the brief records of a case. In the words of one historian, using the example of divorce cases: "It may well be misleading, in fact, to look for exact correspondence with the *sharī'a* categories so carefully explicated in legal manuals, and conversely to rely on legal manuals to interpret the often complex and, to us, opaque cases summarized in the court record. This is in large part because of the messiness of divorce, its complication with other issues. The court record may only be the visible tip of the domestic iceberg, whose indeterminate bulk lies below the surface of the summary record" (Peirce 1998, 285).

12. The term *qadi* (and its many local variants) usually refers to a judge who handles matters of personal status and cases involving documents drawn up by the notaries attached to his court. Nowadays, judges often must be qualified to sit in any chamber (civil, criminal, Islamic personal status) but the title *qadi* is commonly reserved for one who specializes in the handling of personal status matters. The promulgation of national legal codes may be combined with recourse to the legal texts of one or more of the four main schools of Islamic law.

13. A very large number of cases were dropped (68/135, or 50%) while another fifteen (11%) were dismissed by the court. In one case a decisory oath was ordered but the outcome was not recorded. The court heard a total of 410 cases that year, some of which involved property or inheritance, but most of which concerned matters decided under the existing version of the Moroccan *Mudawwana*, or Code of Personal Status. During visits over succeeding years I was given the clear impression by court personnel that similar results were very probable, but since neither the court nor the Ministry of Justice keeps statistics on the relation of gender to outcome—and since I have not engaged in the detailed work such a collection would entail—I cannot vouch for any other years at this level of statistical calculation.

14. Mir-Hosseini 1993a, 113 and 48.

15. Brand (1998, 59) writes: "The woman envisaged in the [personal status code, or] Mudawana [of the 1950s] is a rich woman who does not work outside the home and whose status is guaranteed by reliance on her family. The poor woman

is not really taken into consideration." As Mir-Hosseini's findings and others to be discussed below suggest, this does not accord with the actual outcome of cases.

16. Carlisle 2013. With the introduction of "discord" as a basis for divorce, the number of divorces skyrocketed, 65% of the petitions being brought by women. In 2000, four years before passage of the new law, half of the women did not even know their husbands had divorced them before they received notice from the court, the remainder being equally divided between those who were granted a judicial divorce for abuse or by paying something to the husband. Over 73% of those who succeeded on grounds of abuse nevertheless renounced all or part of the sums owed them or their children. "Plus de divorces en 2007, la faute à la Moudawana?" 2008. A ministry report also indicates that pre-reform types of divorce in Morocco declined by 46% following passage of the new law, while divorces based on new grounds swelled the overall number of divorces by 13% (Shikhani 2010). It may be highly relevant that the rate of women's literacy in Morocco is the lowest (43.9%) of all Middle East countries, including Yemen (46.8%), although literacy and awareness of legal rights may not constitute a simple correlation.

17. Ounnir 2007, 132. Levels of satisfaction with the process were also high: 67% of the litigants (almost equally divided between men and women) felt they were able to freely express themselves to the judge, and 69% deemed the judge to have been fair (129). See also Zeidguy 2007, 238–67, who describes cases from the Rabat court, in almost all of which women win on complaints of failure to support or absence of the husband. On the perceived under-enforcement of the revised code, see Eisenberg 2011. See also Elliott 2015. Whether female judges are more favorably disposed to women and children than male judges is a close question; see El Hajjami 2009.

18. As used here the term "bridewealth" (*mahr*, *sdāq*) refers to the sum of money and/or goods that is transferred by the groom and/or his family to the bride or her marital guardian (*walī*). It is this transfer (often called "dower" in the Western literature), rather than a religious ceremony, that makes the marriage. Customs vary: In some regions the marital guardian may add to the bridewealth and give it to the bride, who retains it in the event of divorce or widowhood; in others the marital guardian may keep it. In most Muslim communities it is possible to pay only a portion of the bridewealth, the remainder being due on demand, at the husband's death, or upon divorce. In many cases a woman may have to forego payment of the remainder in return for her husband divorcing her (*khula'* divorce). The existence of a deferred payment may, however, place a significant constraint on the husband's arbitrary power of divorce: It may also be employed when a woman is marrying up socially if her family wishes to retain further control of the husband's actions. Some communities set the bridewealth amount; for most, however, it is a major subject of negotiation between the bride's representative and the groom's. For the Moroccan practice, see Rosen 1989. The payment may or may not be registered as part of the marriage contract. For the Egyptian practice, see Al-Sharmani

2012, 91–92, 95–96. The dictionary defines "dower" as equivalent to dowry, but since dowry may refer to the portion of a husband's estate that goes to the widow and since some Muslim communities distinguish between the bridewealth and the widow's share, I will generally avoid using "dower." Finally, it should be noted that in many Muslim countries a man may still divorce his wife without going to court; in others modern legislation has limited the power of a man's arbitrary divorce and/or required judicial involvement and registration.

19. Chemais 1996; see also Chemais 1987.

20. Al-Sharmani 2012, 96–97.

21. Al-Sharmani 2012, 98. The author also supplies data on the length of time it took to conclude various proceedings. See also Sonneveld 2012.

22. Al-Sharmani 2013, 45.

23. The remainder of the cases are dropped, dismissed, or reconciled. The figures for men winning *nushuz* cases not only vary among the four courts studied but may, in part, be a function of the fact that plaintiffs of either sex have a greater chance of success than defendants, and/or the willingness of courts to prefer (though they can no longer force) that a woman return to the marital home while the court considers her own suit for divorce, a pattern that is very common in other Muslim countries as well. Note that the term "won" is Al-Sharmani's.

24. Würth 2007, 170.

25. Würth 2007, 174.

26. Antoun 1990, 40.

27. Antoun 1990, 58.

28. Shahar, personal communication. See also Savaya and Cohen 2003, 345–46 (showing a very high proportion of divorced persons blaming family interference for the breakup of the marriage); and Shaham 1997, 181.

29. Hirsch 1998, 127. The terms "win" and "lose" are those used by Hirsch.

30. Hirsch 1998, 128.

31. Hirsch 1998, 129.

32. Gerber 1994, 56.

33. Hallaq 2006, 158, citing Marcus 1989, 111–13. Though he does not indicate their social status, Ergene (2003, 63–65) also finds that in a wide variety of civil cases plaintiffs in seventeenth- to eighteenth-century Ottoman provincial towns won their cases more often than defendants. Thus in one community (Çankırı) plaintiffs prevailed 55% of the time and defendants 28% (N=79; the rest were settled, four cases having an uncertain result), while in another town (Kastamonu) plaintiffs won 43% of the time, defendants 35%, and 21% were settled (N= 572).

34. Tucker 1998, 18. Supporting references are also given to the work of Jennings (1975 and 1993). For a case from Ottoman Palestine in the seventeenth century in which a scholar's opinion (fatwa) strongly favors the woman's position, see Tucker 2005. Another instance of a court in Ottoman Egypt backing the woman's claim is presented in al-Khowli 2005. In her study of the Ottoman provincial capital

of ʻAintab (now Gaziantep) in the mid-sixteenth century, Peirce (1998, 283–84) suggests that many *khulʻa* divorces may have been brought to court not to insure appropriate property distribution but to indicate that it was the wife who was initiating the divorce, it being to her advantage to have proof that "she had obtained that [which] her husband agreed to and that she was now free to remarry." Courts could serve as public acknowledgment or communal mediator: "In different ways, these individuals appealed to the court and its judge to frame their words, to give their words validity by encompassing them in a communal record, or to bound them by setting limits to its consequences" (296). For a revealing instance drawn from marriages between Muslims and non-Muslims, see Kholoussy 2011. By comparison, according to Afary (2009, 40), no statistics are said to be available for divorces in Iran in the nineteenth century. See Tucker 2009.

35. Roberts 2005, 135–41. See also Roberts 2010.

36. Lydon 2001, 38; original italics.

37. Lydon 2010, 148, 156.

38. Stiles 2009, 29 and table 1.5.

39. Welchman 2000, 219.

40. Welchman 2000, 245 and more generally 230–46. It is noteworthy, too, that in the shariʻa court of West Jerusalem, during the years 2001–2005, in only one case of *taʻa* was the ruling in favor of the husband (n = 98). In this single case, the wife consistently refused to attend the hearings or delegate a legal representative, so eventually—and very reluctantly—the qadi had no other recourse but to issue a *taʻa* order. For an interesting case from Sudan in 1940, in which a young woman successfully litigated against the husband's claim of marital disobedience, see Shaheed and Shaheed 2011, 165–66. Fluehr-Lobban (1987, 86) notes that the practice of forcible return to a husband's home was abolished in the Sudan and Egypt in the 1980s.

41. Mitchell 1997, 201–2.

42. Carlisle (2007b, 92, 96, and 99), for example, reports that 90% of divorce requests in the court of Damascus she studied were granted, and since the number of male and female plaintiffs was almost exactly equal one must assume that women "won" much of the time. She also notes that the court was especially prone to grant persistent claims, but that only wives who possessed some financial security from their families were likely to pursue their requests for divorce.

43. Djamour 1966, 147, original italics.

44. Lev 1972, 150. Tanner (1969, 51), writing about the 375,000 matrilineal Muslim Minangkabau living in a district of western Sumatra in 1964, notes: "The Islamic court, then, provides a forum for the grievances of wives . . . Eventually she usually succeeds in obtaining a divorce or annulment."

45. Lindsey and Sumner 2011; see also Sumner and Lindsey 2010. Similar numbers are reported by Nurlaelawati 2013. Of the three cases that Nurlaelawati discusses in detail, all are decided in favor of the women plaintiffs, with no indication

that she chose them because the outcomes were favorable to the wives. Stijn Cornelis van Huis 2015 (263) concludes:

> The Islamic courts are mainly divorce courts, and women approach them mostly in order to petition a divorce. Moreover, the legal analysis of the Islamic courts' judgments demonstrates that Islamic courts in all but very rare cases will grant a divorce, and that they increasingly base their judgments on the concepts of 'no-fault divorce' and 'marriage breakdown', rather than on the statutory legal grounds in the 1974 Marriage Law. The sidelining of the formal divorce grounds are not arbitrary judgments, as their consistent application clearly indicates that they are part of legal doctrine. Although the concepts of no-fault divorce and marriage breakdown are in conflict with statutory norms requiring an at-fault divorce, the outcome of a divorce process at the Islamic courts is very predictable: if reconciliation efforts fail, the courts will grant a divorce. This means that regardless a woman's social position within her local community, clan, or marriage, from a legal perspective she has an equal position in divorce. This means that women living in unhappy marriages who access the Islamic court may do so in order to circumvent traditional, religious or adat-based, patriarchal ideas about marriage and divorce.

46. Vincent-Grosso 2012, 182.

47. Vincent-Grosso 2012, 187.

48. Powers 2006a, 409. See Petry 1998 for the example of a higher-class woman who proves victorious in the fifteenth century.

49. Abdal-Rehim 1996, 105, 111. For Egypt in the sixteenth century, see Jackson 2001.

50. Agmon 1996, 138. See also the case described in Agmon 2003, 208–10.

51. Shaham 1997, 137–38.

52. Shaham 1997, 225–26. On the phenomenon of women as expert witnesses, see Shaham 2011.

53. Starr and Pool 1974, 552, 554. See also Starr 1990, 91.

54. Starr 1989, 507 (for full data see Table 1 at 506). Elsewhere, Starr (1985, 133) gives somewhat different figures: "There has been also a significant increase in the ways women are obtaining results at court by 1966. In 1950, of the 18 women who went to court, 5 or 27.8% obtained divorces, and the same number were denied them. By 1966, 11 out of 20, or 55%, won their suits. When we compare women's versus men's court-sought divorces, we find that in 1950, 26.3% of the women won divorces, while in 1966 42.3% obtained them. In 1950, 14 out of 35 men, or 40%, obtained a divorce; but by 1966 this percentage rises drastically, as 15 out of 20, or 75%, of the men won their suit." Some of the difference may be due to the small

numbers involved and different methods of counting. The author concludes that the changes are due to the fact that "court decisions were more sensitive to the ongoing effects of the legal revolution than the way males or females were perceived and treated by the courts," a conclusion that others have contested. What does appear clear is that women are not failing to win a substantial part of their claims, that whoever brings the case is most likely to prevail, but that given the small numbers and the later move in Turkey back to Islam the author's claim that state law was almost entirely displacing customary law cannot be accepted at face value.

55. Macfarlane 2012, 167. A separate 2009 survey showed women initiated divorce cases 64% of the time. For an example of a Muslim woman's involvement in an American proceeding that concentrated on the contractual aspects of her marriage, see Zakaria 2010. On accommodations reached with Islamic law in some Western countries, see Joppke and Torpey 2013.

56. One British Shari'ah Council official states: "We do recognize that some women are reluctant to give up their dower and in some cases the dowry [wedding gifts], but this is a precarious situation and we have to think of the welfare of all the parties involved. You see if we keep the proceedings dragging on it affects all the parties, including the children, so it's best to sort things out as quickly as possible. In cases where we feel the husband is not at fault, then the applicant must decide if she wants the *khul* and under Islamic law she has every right to do so" (Bano 2012, 219). See also Billaud 2014 and Bowen 2013. The comments by the Archbishop of Canterbury Rowan Williams (2008) concerning the possible inclusion of some Islamic decision making in British law occasioned heated debate: see Bowen 2010. Similar disputes arose when the British lawyers association published rules guiding lawyers in the preparation of Islamic wills. See Bingham 2014. See also Pilgrim 2012.

57. Buttoo 2008 and Corbin 2013. See Büchler 2011 and Fournier 2010.

58. Other family members, including female kin, may also have a stake in the outcome. See, e.g., the case described in Carlisle 2007b.

59. See, e.g., Shatzmiller 2007, 39; Rapoport 2005, 12–22.

60. Rapoport 2005, 17, 24, 76, 94–95; Shatzmiller 2007, 197–98.

61. Thus, in Morocco, for example, the bride's dowry is not registered, the legal fiction being that all household furnishings belong to the wife, a fiction that contributes to the pattern of wives and their mothers frequently pressing the husband for more household purchases to insure the marriage against his divorce or to ameliorate the effects of such an act. See Rosen 1984, 87. Conservative opposition to changes in Moroccan inheritance law must also be seen in the light of the ways parents may insure daughters against formal discrimination. See Al Monitor 2014. Shatzmiller (2007, 88–89) notes that in fifteenth-century Granada extended guardianship was sometimes used by parents to give a daughter time to adjust to the control of her own finances, though at other times extended guardianship could be used against daughters. Overall, Meshal (2014, 213–14) says that for Egypt older patterns were less ossified than those that currently apply.

62. The description of proceedings in Indonesia bear remarkable resemblance to those witnessed in the Middle East: "At Indonesian religious court hearings, the judges, usually the chief judge, begin the session by ascertaining who is who and asking how the litigants are related to each other. The judge's first substantive question is usually the signal for the argument to begin. Although the judge addresses the question to the party petitioning for divorce, each party is eager to tell his or her side of the story and they have no inclination to sit and wait patiently" (Nurlaelawati 2013, 262).

63. Quoted in Christelow 1985, 91.

64. *Divorce Iranian Style* is available at https://freedocumentaries.org/documentary/divorce-iranian-style#watch-film (accessed January 5, 2017); *Divorce Shari'a Style* can be seen at https://vimeo.com/18622831 (accessed January 5, 2017); *Justice at Agadez* is available in French at http://www.dailymotion.com/playlist/x28sdx_mgm_lacoste_justice-a-agadez/1#video=xtqqzo (accessed January 5, 2017); *A Separation* can be downloaded from http://putlocker.is/watch-a-separation-online-free-putlocker.html (accessed January 5, 2017). See also the transcripts of hearings in Hill 1979, 72–101; Peletz 2002; Mir-Hosseini 1993a; Antoun 1990; and Powers 2003. On the making of *Divorce Iranian Style*, see Mir-Hosseini 1999b. By no means are women always successful. Mir-Hosseini's film contains instances of child custody where the woman is given less than full rein in court and a quite contrary image of women in court is rendered in the 1975 Egyptian melodrama *Uridu Halan* ("I Want a Solution"): see Sonneveld 2012, chap. 3; and al-Sharmani 2009.

65. Mir-Hosseini 1993b, 81. On marriage and law as represented in Iranian literature, see Motlagh 2011.

66. Lutfi 1991, 102, 117–18. See also, for Oman, what Wikan (1982, 287 and generally 287–92) calls

> the realistic premises that govern the option of dissolving the marriage. The power to do so lies in the hands of the husband, but the cost of doing so is great, entailing both payments of the *ghayeb* (the deferred dowry) and of a new bride price to establish a new complete household. . . . [I]f she [the wife] is caught up against her will, in a truly unwanted marriage, the threat that an unhappy wife poses to a husband's interests and aspirations is such that the only wise course for him is to acquiesce to a divorce. For these reasons, women are probably correct when they unanimously say, 'It is very easy for a wife to obtain a divorce,' explaining that 'all she has to do is run home to her parents constantly until the husband tires of fetching her back.' This knowledge cannot but contribute to the woman's feeling of confidence and control over her situation.

For postrevolutionary Iran, see Friedl 1994.

67. See, e.g., Wikan (1980, 105–7). Parents may help their daughters by circumventing adverse inheritance rules through the use of gifts or bequests. See *Al-Monitor* 2014.

68. Yong 2010. See also Siddiqui 1995. Afary (2009, 283) notes that in the first years after the Iranian revolution, when women's rights were substantially cut back by the new regime, the divorce rate in Tehran jumped 200%. At present half of all Iranian divorces occur within the first year of marriage: One sociologist reported that a 2005 survey showed that half of Iranian women say they would file for divorce given the opportunity (361–64). It is also of help to Iranian women that Article 1082 of the Civil Code was amended in 1996 to link the *mehrieh* directly to the rate of inflation, so that a woman married for many years was not limited to a sum contracted for long ago and currently worth very little (Afshar 1998, 186). For an example of women's increased awareness of their legal rights, see Abou Ramadan 2006a. The Iranian regime is also concerned that many couples now live together without getting married, sometimes using the ruse of a permissible "temporary" marriage as cover for their cohabitation, a situation that Haleh Esfandiari (2015) regards as evidence of the gap between popular sentiment and official policy.

69. Osanloo 2006, 205 note 29. See also Osanloo 2009 and 2012. On women's knowledge of the law, see also Rabho 2013, 267–68.

70. See, e.g., Wikan 1996, 98–103.

71. Yong 2010.

72. I witnessed a number of instances in Morocco in which a woman would go to jail rather than obey a decision that went against her, and then use the "shame" people attributed to her being jailed to pressure the husband to relinquish his claim. For a description of how this played out in a sixteenth-century provincial capital of southeastern Anatolia, see Peirce 2003, 203–8. On women having to tolerate physical abuse in such situations, see Inhorn 1996, 120–21. Men, too, may risk imprisonment when they claim a God-given right to arbitrary divorce even though state law requires permission from the court. See, e.g., Layish 1975, 140–41, 187–90. On women calling for police assistance with domestic disputes—or committing suicide—in late nineteenth-century Iran, see Afary 2009, 31–39. In Pakistan a woman may claim that because the husband "hates" her she cannot stay "within the bounds of Allah" and thus failure to grant her relief would put her in a position of committing *zina*, i.e., engaging in sexual intercourse when the marriage is no longer valid (Werner Menski, personal communication).

73. See, for the Malaysian example, Hassan and Cederroth 1997. On conciliation in the Egyptian family courts, see Bernard-Maugiron and Dupret 2008; and Al-Sharmani 2013.

74. Shehada 2009, 32–33.

75. On judicial discretion, see Chemais (1996, 71–72), who states that in roughly half of the cases involving a divorce claim based on harm the case was sufficiently clear-cut that the Egyptian judge did not have to exercise any discretion. For a case

that turns on the concept of harm, see Powers 2006a, 9–15. Layish (1991) gives the example of Libyan judges who stretched the concept of *khul'a* so a women who could not afford to repay her dower could remarry and use the new bridewealth to pay off the former debt, even though the shari'a clearly requires a full divorce before remarriage, custom, as Layish (1988) indicates, playing a significant role in this process. Such an approach provided an "equitable" solution that was said to render the woman's life more humane. A similar approach is reported for Gaza, where a judge told the researcher who pointed out that his decision in a case was contrary to the law in that the judge did not allow the woman the right to marry without her father, who worked in Israel, appearing in court: "The law is blind, we are not. . . . [W]e cannot, as a court, turn a blind eye to the consequences of our decisions." In this case, he said, "What would be the father's response? Some fathers have limited minds. They might kill their daughters or at least force them to divorce their husbands. Our society is full of such fathers" (Shehada 2009, 36). For judicial discretion in the Druze situation, see Layish 1977. In one study of a Tunisian court's treatment of cases involving a wife's abandonment of the marital home (*nushuz*) judges told the ethnographer that they always look for the reasons a wife has left: "A notary may also be brought to the marital home to certify the wife's absence. As one judge told me, however, he would only accept a divorce case based on *nushuz* if the wife told him herself that she had left home for no reason, *even if a notary's report had witnessed her absence*. This approach is a reaction to the potential for abuse in the production of this type of evidence" (Vincent-Grosso 2012, 190; emphasis added). However, while discretion may allow flexibility, in the Tunisian case and no doubt elsewhere, "this degree of interpretation, this uncertainty, is a breeding ground for anxiety, shared among litigants, and sometimes also by the judge" (Vincent-Grosso 2012, 195). For additional forms of judicial discretion see the case described in Carlisle 2008. See also the cases reported in Carlisle 2007a. For similar instances see Behar (2004, 556), where the author concludes: "The shari'a was paramount in personal law, and few compromises were possible in civil litigation. But the shari'a predominated only to the extent that the *kadi*s were given the opportunity to judge. There was no accommodation of custom or of local practice if they frequently violated the law. Nevertheless, pragmatic local adjustments in violation of the shari'a did indeed exist, even in matters where the shari'a was supposed to rule unchallenged. Therefore, studies privileging exclusively shari'a court records may be skewing the accurate appraisal of some aspects of social life in the Muslim Middle East."

The judges' own conservatism may also lead them to exercise their discretion to disfavor statutory liberalization: see Bernard-Maugiron and Dupret 2008, and their citation to Arabic sources at n. 40. On the debate over codification versus discretion, compare the proponents of the former as a check on the whim of the qadi with the statement of the judge of a Shi'i court in Bahrain who argues that a unified law of personal status risks that "'cases will not be given their full due by examining the considerations that vary from one case to another. The existence of a written law binds the *sharʿī* judge, resulting in wrongs to men and women alike'" (Quoted in Welchman 2007, 22). Further discussions of judicial discretion in the application of the revised Moroccan code will also be found in Mouaqit 2007 and Zeidguy 2007. For Tunisia, see Voorhoeve 2012a.

Discretion may also involve choosing from among, or combining, local customary law and/or elements of several different schools (*madhhab*) of Islamic law, rather than adhering strictly to the dominant one in a given jurisdiction. See, e.g., Fadel (1997, 56–57), where judges in fourteenth- to fifteenth-century Granada followed the requisite guidance of the main textual source, Khalil's *Mukhtasar*, only about half of the time. Belonging to a madhhab "did not mean one accepted a mere body of rules; instead, it contained within it as well a series of concepts and principles that allowed for the revision of old doctrine as well as the creation of new" (76). See Solanki 2011. See also Jennings 1979.

76. Rabho 2012, 126. On delay and costs in proceedings see, e.g., Al-Sharmani 2012, 89–91, 96–99.

77. Again, it must be emphasized that an indeterminate number of cases may involve consensual divorce (*k̲hulʿa*). Rapoport (2005, 69), for example, indicates that such cases during the Ottoman period he studied were always initiated by the wife.

78. Al-Sharmani 2013, 41 (on cases not necessarily being about what has been claimed).

79. Considerable judicial discretion, as well as local custom and perceptions of class expectations, may figure in a wife's claim for divorce based on harm (*ḍarar*). See, e.g., Sonbol 1996, 282–85.

80. An excellent discussion of this factor in the Moroccan instance is related by Boukaissi 2007.

81. Würth 2007, 177.

82. Layish 1975, 248, 162. In other reported instances, however, the court helps the woman retain custody by threatening the husband (and quite likely his present wife) with actually having to take care of children he does not really want. See, e.g., the Palestinian case in which the deputy qadi coaches the wife in a divorce case to agree that the husband should have all of the children, the children in turn being instructed to act dreadfully in the house of the father and his new wife—"especially your youngest monster. . . . Once they are there, they should be noisy, break plates, play football indoors and switch the TV on and off all the time. In other words they have to drive the wife crazy. Your children will be returned the next day." Actually, they were returned within an hour (Shehada, 2009, 36). The "best interests of the child" is a standard found in various forms in Islamic legal tradition and incorporated in the statutes and practices of the courts of a number of countries (including Morocco, the Emirates, and Qatar), sometimes as a right of the custodian, sometimes as a right of the child, and sometimes by court decision

in clear departure from the more traditional code. See, e.g., Fluehr-Lobban 1982; Hutterer 2014 (including a lecture on this topic by the researcher featured in Hutterer's article, Nadjma Yassari, of St. Anthony's College, Oxford).

83. Mir-Hosseini 1993a, 82. However, on finding 'harm' as a basis for allowing a woman to obtain a divorce in postrevolutionary Iran, see Mir-Hosseini 2007. In an update of that article Mir-Hosseini notes that the Ayatollah Khomeini had indicated at one point that a husband's refusal to grant his wife a divorce was itself proof of hardship in the marriage, thus warranting a judicial divorce. The author is quick to note, however, that this approach has not been adopted in Iran and that "an examination of court cases clearly shows that what lies at the root of many marital disputes that make their way to the courts is the problem of the unequal construction of gender relations in family law—something the Islamic Republic, for ideological reasons, has so far been unable to address" (Mir-Hosseini 2012, 80–81). For an example of a woman who would not bargain away her property rights in order to secure child custody, see Osanloo 2006. See also Sonbol 2003, 174–75. For modern Egypt, see the studies by Al-Sharmani 2012, and other studies cited in Hasso 2011, 150–51. See also the examples for Syria in Carlisle 2007a, and for Egypt in Al-Sharmani 2013, 49. Yet, as Zilfi (1997, 295) argues from the eighteenth-century Ottoman records: "Hul [*khul'a*] attenuated the social system's singleminded tilt toward male expediencies in the taking on and discarding of sexual partners. It gave legal sanction to the right of women to 'bargain with patriarchy,' in Deniz Kandiyoti's insightful phrase, by legitimating their will to disown an unwanted mate." See also Marcus 1989, 205–6.

84. See Bernard-Maugiron and Dupret 2008. Judges may, however, use their discretion to regard a case as one of harm and thereby increase the share of resources a woman may be awarded. See Naveh 2002. Such cases may also require more time and expense, which can work against the woman's interest or persistence.

85. "These women's decision making process of filing for *khul* was not simply determined by the problems of their marriages. It is also shaped by the underlying message that was being indirectly but clearly conveyed to the women by state welfare policies and community development programs of NGOs. The message was: as a legally divorced and single mother with children, these women had much better chance of accessing the meager but still much needed services of the state and the civil society" (Al-Sharmani 2012, 93 n. 5). Because women may still have to file a separate suit to gain their post-divorce rights, because enforcement of awards in their favor are often lax, and because of the realities of marriage relationships, the practice of *khul* in Egypt "is merely functioning as a mitigating alternative to the problems of fault-based divorces on the one hand, and the contradictions of the legal narrative of marriage and marital roles, on the other hand" (Al-Sharmani 2012, 103). For the similar circumstances of women in Gaza, who often cannot afford the cost of a *khul'a* divorce, see Othman 2015. In Mauretania, by contrast, a woman relinquishes her furnishings and any outstanding bridewealth as a sign of

her autonomy and dignity, as well as the honor of her family (Fortier 2012, 162–64). It is unclear whether judges commonly place greater obstacles in the way of fault-based claims for divorce (*taṭliq*) by women or pressure them to forgo other benefits to which they may be entitled, but some researchers have suggested that this may be the case.

86. Carlisle 2013. Nadia Sonneveld, in a personal communication, also notes: "According to my data, women in shiqaq cases are no longer entitled to the mut'a compensation [payment] but they do not pay an additional sum of money [to the husband to gain the divorce]." For a description of a conciliation proceeding conducted by the judge in a Tangier court, see Ounnir 2007, 128 ff. In a questionnaire Ounnir administered to 46 men and 56 women of diverse levels of education, employment, age, and knowledge of the revised code—all of whom were litigants in the courts of several Moroccan cities—84% said they had tried some form of outside mediation first: of these, 65% went to family members, 26% to friends of the family, and 9% to neighbors. (116). Nearly half (48%) saw a lawyer before a first hearing in court. (121); 64% said they had benefited from the conciliation, while 37% thought it useless. (126). Notably, of 185 cases of *shiqāq* (discord) heard by the Tangier court, in only six cases did the requisite conciliation result in the couple dropping their suit and agreeing to remain together. (128). A woman usually has a right, too, to demand a new place of residence away from her husband's kin and "among righteous people" (*bin qaumen saliḥin*) who could serve as witnesses in any subsequent dispute. Neighbors may, however, be reluctant to testify in court: Though such participation appears more common in Morocco, it has been reported that in Tunisia "two or more witnesses may prepare a written statement in the court or in front of a notary. The Judge was aware, however, that it is difficult to find witnesses in personal status cases, and it was extremely rare to find this kind of evidence in the case files. . . . Whilst I knew that some neighbours in the [urban] area I studied would sometimes intervene to help resolve marital disputes, people seemed far more reluctant to become involved with a court case or issues involving the police. This form of evidence, therefore, was rarely forthcoming" (Vincent-Grosso 2012, 180). For an example of a woman seeking help through mediation in Morocco, see Susan S. Davis 1983, 96–98. For descriptions of mediation sessions in Syria, see Carlisle 2007c, van Eijk 2012, and van Eijk 2016. See also Al-Sharmani 2009, 96, where she notes that one of the mediator experts in each Egyptian case must be a woman. See Drieskens 2006. On women as mediators and the classical background of mediation in family law, see Zahraa and Hak 2006, 20–21.

87. See, e.g., Layish (1975, 135–36), where, in his study of a number of Muslim courts in Israel in the period 1948–70, three-quarters (N=1359/1807) of the registered divorces involved a woman renouncing something owed her or in which she compensated her husband for his agreement to divorce her, when the alternative might have been a judicially sanctioned arbitrary divorce by the husband. On a woman's limited choice, see Al-Sharmani 2013, 50.

88. Oded Zinger (2014, 117–19) suggests this is also true for the Jewish court proceedings of the Geniza period. S. D. Goitein also cites instances in which Jewish women in the same period were not only outspoken but threatened to take their cases to Muslim courts if not given satisfaction in the Jewish proceeding. On the styles used by both men and women to conduce the judge's approbation, see Shehada (2009, 38), particularly his statement that "Women for their part are granted protection so long as they appear to be victimized" (Shehada 2009, 39). See also Hirsch 1998.

89. See Rosen 2000, 153–75; and Rosen 2008, 60–72.

90. See Hill 1979, 92; Rugh 1984, 180; Fluehr-Lobban 1987, 151–52 ("Bringing a case involving divorce to the court must be viewed as a last act of desperation on the part of the woman"); and Fluehr-Lobban 2012, 235–46 (where the author finds increased rate of divorce and added bases for women claiming divorce since her earlier study).

91. On go-betweens, see Huxley 1978. See also Reiter 1997, 214–20. The informal, non-binding, and frequently quite general opinion (fatwa) of a learned expert in Islamic law may also serve to direct a result. Thus, "Saudi families very often forego a binding judgment and submit internal disputes to the fatwa of a religious figure whom all members respect" (Vogel 1996, 267). Judges may effectively suspend a formal session to talk like a mediator, as in the Lebanese example described by Clarke 2012, 112–13: "Shaykh C let them wrangle on: 'Now we are talking outside of the court,' he told them, 'like human beings [*hakī insānī*].' . . . This is Shaykh C's standard tactic: to open the discussion 'outside the court' (*khārij al-mahkama*) to try to find a solution. . . . If the dry language of the session then fails to satisfy, Shaykh C may drop out of it again: 'Okay, before we were speaking in the language of the court session. Now I'll speak normally [*tabī'ī*], that is, 'like a brother' rather than a judge."

92. Tucker 1998, 182. On judges in the Ottoman period in Cairo as guarantors of women's rights, see also Meshal 2014, 148–55.

93. Little 2006, 84.

94. Al-Qattan 1999, 436.

95. Tucker 1998, 184. On the best interests of the child in custody cases, see also Tucker 1998, 145 and 182; and Tucker 1997. See also Shaham 1997, 188–91; Rugh 1984, 178; and Abou Ramadan 2002. On the distinctive period of childhood in Muslim social thought and practice, see Giladi 1992, and Meriwether 1999.

96. Gerber 1999, 96. Muhammad al-Zurqani (1645–1710), for example, has often been quoted by other Islamic scholars for his assertion that "a woman is poor by nature" because her relative dependency places her in greater need. Ironically, the portrayal of women as inherently less capable of decision making may lead courts to be more forthcoming in attending to their needs. Thus, the Muslim Brotherhood, after the fall of Hosni Mubarak, might have been expected to foster legal concern for women's welfare but instead grew more conservative in the name of women's supposed biological incapacity. See El-Naggar 2012.

97. Shehada 2009, 36. However, Shehada (39) adds: "The judge's familiarity with the community norms direct him to find solutions that do not depart from the prevailing morality of the community. This further implies that flexibility might be stretched or tightened in accordance with judges' embeddedness in, and responsiveness to, the norms of their community. Their adherence to the notion of "protecting the weak" is not informed by a desire to compensate for gender asymmetry or hierarchies based on age. Like all members of society, they are influenced by the dominant gender discourse, and they act in such a way that their "protective" solution neither disturbs the community's norms nor questions the gender asymmetry and age hierarchy inherent in law and social practice."

98. Agmon 2006.

99. Shehada 2009, 32–33. Similarly, Islamic courts are often sensitive to the situation of women whose illnesses may lead their husbands to divorce them and attempt to avoid support or repaying a dower. "In recent generations . . . [a wife who is ill, say, with epilepsy] has a better chance of receiving a larger portion of the dower, especially if her marriage is consummated. On the other hand, a man has to prove, if this is his intention, that his wife was disabled before their marriage, hence she deceived him regarding her state of health" (Rispler-Chaim 1996, 105).

100. See Rosen 2000. In other instances the resort to courts may be associated with weakening kin relationships such that the emphasis falls on the specific roles of the couple and the court as a place for the dissolution, rather than the collective re-negotiation, of broader social group ties. See, e.g., Würth 1995.

101. Thus, Al-Sharmani (2012, 103) says of modern Egypt: "In particular, it is poor women who find *khul* to be a vital and beneficial option, notwithstanding the price that they pay for taking this legal course. This suggests that there is need for future and large scale studies that will investigate the scope and the ways in which *khul* is becoming poor women's pathway of not only accessing divorce but also gendered citizenship rights such as welfare."

102. Aspects of legitimacy may turn on both procedure and substantive rules. On the problem of "illegitimate" children, see Bargach 2005. On the presumption of marital consummation favoring women in Tunisia, see Messaoudi 1979. On the classical background to judicial reasoning in a variety of instances, see Zysow 2013.

103. Mir-Hosseini 2002, 140. See also Mir-Hosseini 1999a. Precisely why the judge makes this assumption is, however, not indicated. Some commenters on the Iranian situation have been more negative: "This author, in all the years that she has spent in the Family Courts, has not once seen a man's request for divorce to have been finally rejected except where there has been administrative problems such as his inability to prove that the marriage has been consummated etc." (Mir-Hossein 2002, 140; quoting a Persian language article from 1995 by Mehrangiz Kaar in Afshar 1998, 178). See also the use of presumptions and procedures favoring women in Abou-Ramadan 2006b, 63–66; and the development of presumptions

about the best interests of the child, which deeply affect women's concerns, in custody situations in Abou Ramadan 2002, 606–7 and 627–35.

104. Voorhoeve 2012b, 174.

105. Shaham 1999, 481. See also the cases described in Al-Sharmani 2013, 41–44.

106. See Agmon 1996, 138–39. See also the examples at Agmon 2006, and Rosen 1989, 32–35.

107. Islamic Family Law (Federal Territory) Act [Malaysia], 1984, as quoted in Anwar 2008, 275–76. Some Malay states subsequently passed contrary legislation.

108. Tucker 1998, 145. See also Meriwether 1996.

109. See Mir-Hosseini 2008, 223–34. Mir-Hosseini 1996. For another Iranian example, see Goodwin 2003, 113. See also Zulficar 2008, 245–46. On pre- and post-Ottoman marriage contract stipulations, see Sonbol 2005. For a case from Andalusian Spain that emphasizes the role of contractual stipulations and the advice of court notaries, see Zomeño 2002. For examples of early Muslim women and the conditions some had placed in their marital contracts limiting the husband's ability to take another wife or deny his present wife a divorce, see Shaheed and Shaheed 2011, xxvi–xxvii, and 4–6; for examples from the fourteenth to fifteenth centuries in Egypt, Syria, and Turkey, see pp. 41–47. For similar contractual conditions in Ottoman Cairo, see Meshal 2014, 159–66. A marriage contract stipulation that enables a woman to demand a divorce is quite common in Bangladesh, where it is referred to as *talaq-e-tafwi* (Werner Menski, personal communication). Indeed, according to a BBC broadcast of January 3, 2017, officials in Dhaka have significantly curtailed a man's right to arbitrary divorce. Under Islamic law a husband would have to give his wife the right to divorce him. But, says human rights lawyer Nini Boushami, "the column in the marriage certificate [specifying this grant] was always left blank. Now it is mandatory to fill it in, making it easier for women to choose what they want." http://www.bbc.co.uk/programmes/p04kxn32 (accessed January 3, 2017).

110. A wife might, in some Muslim countries, also be placed in the house of a reliable witness during the course of a dispute (or for the three months following a divorce, during which any pregnancy on her part would be attributable to the husband); alternatively the reliable person might be placed in the party's own home to witness events. Called at different periods and places the *dar thiqa*, *dar joued*, and *dar 'adel*, this arrangement may be prescribed by local custom (see Layish 1995), judicial practice, or contemporary code (e.g., Morocco, where, as Mir-Hosseini 1993a and Dwyer 1977 also note, it was still very much in use during the period of my own initial fieldwork in the 1960s). See also Fierro 2006, 335–43. In some instances the woman could be ordered to the *dar* by her husband or when a woman was refusing to marry the choice of her family, thus transforming "a preventive institution to a repressive one" (266). Without, therefore, denying that at times it served as a check on them, this institution, in fact, often benefited women

and their claims. "It is far from being a prison. To the contrary, the institution as it actually functioned, was a sort of juridical guarantee in favor of the woman, inasmuch as in most cases she was the victim of excess and violence on the part of her husband" (266). Placement was usually at the discretion of the qadi (though some traditions allowed the husband the first option of designating the house of one of his female relatives), but the use of this institution was often requested by the wife. While marital differences were the common basis for using this institution, it might also be relied upon in highly unusual situations: In at least one case, when a wife claimed that her husband was having an illicit relation with his own mother, it was the latter two who were sent to the *dar thiqa* for observation (266).

111. This may occur within the context of a court proceeding or as a result of a state-sponsored alternative dispute resolution mechanism, such as the appointment of arbitrators. See Holden 2012. See also the case of a woman who wins a divorce described in Dupret 2006.

112. See, e.g., Saheb 2003, 245. Qadis, in my experience, are often concerned to see how strongly people feel about the matters at issue—or how upset they are with each other—and thus turn litigants loose for a time to argue with each other in court before deciding how best to handle the relationship. See also, in this respect, Billaud 2014. The absence of discretionary power may, by contrast, lead a judge to feel hemmed in by the law. A Taliban judge in Dahane-Ghori, Afghanistan, could thus tell an interviewer in the autumn of 2011 about such an instance:

> A man had pronounced his wife divorced three times on a single occasion, which is enough to prove that the divorce had happened, but then he wanted to patch up with her. According to Islamic laws when you say the word "divorce" three times, divorce happens. But he did not want to leave her anyway. The case was brought before me. "According to Sharia, if someone divorce his wife and then want to keep her again as his wife, the woman will have to marry another man and then get the divorce from him before living as a wife with the first husband," I told them. I handed over divorce letter to them and both, the man and his wife, left the court. Though according to the rules and Sharia I had done a right job, as a human being this really left me shocked but I had to stand by Sharia laws (Giustozzi, Franco, and Baczko 2012, 26). See also Ahmed 2015.

113. Starr 1992, 168 and 165.

114. Agrama 2012, 170.

115. Carlisle, 2007a.

116. See Rosen 1984, 1989, and 2000.

117. See, e.g., Sonneveld 2016, 16, 22, 27, 31, 34, and 36. On the use of a judge's discretion to contravene even a clear legal requirement that benefits a woman, see

Sonneveld 2016, 27–29, 32–33. On women's employment in the public sector, see *Morocco World News* 2014.

118. Whether the judge must accept the recommendation of the arbitrators he has appointed is a matter of some discussion. In the Maliki school of Islamic law the judge was traditionally bound by their findings, for example, on whether there was "harm" (*darar*) to one of the parties, while retaining the right to appoint such arbitrators in the first place if he thought the litigants had indeed reached a point of "quarrel and difference" (*nizāʿ wa-shiqāq*). In other instances, the arbitrators' conclusions were treated as recommendations to the court which could set them aside in the interests of "justice." See, e.g., Abou Ramadan 2002.

119. See Bernard-Maugiron and Dupret 2008, 63–64. See also Al-Sharmani 2009. Conciliation may, however, stimulate discussions between the parties that are not easily achieved in the absence of the court initiative. See Sonneveld 2010. In both Egypt and Tunisia, however, women commonly feel the marriage is already in jeopardy when conciliation takes place and that it may exacerbate the situation by shaming the husband publicly. In Malaysia "the Islamic intermediaries do not attend to the real issues in a dispute, namely power relations, control of the family's economic resources, and incompatibility of character," focusing instead on the moral expectations of spouses (Hassan and Cederroth 1997, 233–37). Concerning the Turkish decision to end pre-trial mediation: "The drop in male-initiated divorce cases [in the 1960s] coincides with the directive to abandon pre-trial mediation in 1963, a change that may have discouraged divorce claims by males who were using the courts to threaten and punish their wives rather than because they were intent on divorce" (Starr 1989, 505). On required conciliation in Iran see Osanloo 2006, 207 n. 63. In Syria, the court appoints two mediators in each case, both of whom are lawyers (Carlisle 2007b).

120. Agrama 2012, 159, original italics.

121. Hassan and Cederroth 1997, 191. For a comparison of parts of Malaysia and Indonesia, see Bustaman-Ahmad 2009. See Mir-Hosseini 1993a, 178–82, on judicial discretion in the award of child custody. See also Shaham 1997, 42, 231–32, on the flexible approach of Egyptian qadis to the concept of legal privacy.

122. Davis 1998, 12.

123. See, e.g., Shaham 1997, 93, 96–97, 138, 224, 230–32; Arabi 2001; Layish 1991; Rosen 2000, 85–98; Sonbol 2003, 255. See, too, for the Chinese region studied by Erie 2016 ("custom is an integral part of how they practice Islam, influencing, for example, practices of worship and the regulation of property, marriage, and inheritance. Chinese customs may either enhance certain rules of Islamic law or transform them"). Codification or the eclectic application of diverse schools of Islamic law may even out local customs or further legitimize differences, while in other countries increasing legal pluralism may find greater political acceptance. See, e.g., Menski 2012.

124. Hasso 2011, 168.

125. Hasso 2011, 173. See also Kholoussy 2010.

126. Welchman 2007, 335–46; see also Afshar 1998, 105–8. Judicial resistance to state-mandated change often remains very significant. For the Moroccan case, see Newcomb 2009, 105–28, and Perkins 2004.

127. In Tunisia, for example, husbands whose wives claimed "moral" or "material" harm in 1982 found themselves having to pay three times more in compensation than was required of them for the same causes in 1962. The authors of the study in which this is reported are not sure, however, whether legislation and practice that favors increased payments by husbands might not have the undesirable effect of perpetuating the unequal position of women ("Ne continue-t-on pas à infantiliser la femme en la sur-protégeant ainsi?") (Hermassi and Hmed 1983, 80). This study contains a wealth of data about the socioeconomic and procedural aspects of divorce but no data on case outcomes.

128. See, e.g., Massell 1974.

129. Bowen 2007, 191–92.

130. Rugh 1984, 273–74.

131. It is true that on May 26, 2012, the lower house of Egypt's Islamist-led parliament approved a law that extended certain medical benefits to female-headed households. "Parliament's Greatest Achievement Supports Rights of Female-Headed Households" 2012. But there is disagreement as to how much the Islamists and the 2011 revolution actually contributed to or detracted from women's legal enhancement: *Compare* Sonneveld and Lindbekk 2015 ("the Egyptian revolution of 25 January 2011 opened space in the public debate for a new group of political actors that had a personal interest in seeking to strengthen the rights of fathers and mothers in the case of divorce") *with* Tadros 2014 ("The Salafis acquiesced to the introduction of the same set of women's rights in the Egyptian constitution that they had vehemently opposed only a year earlier. The decision was evidently one of political manoeuvring in order to secure that they did not alienate themselves from the centres of power. This was a classic case of de-privileging ideological creed in favour of political survival").

132. See the discussion of recent studies of Egypt in Hasso 2011, 149–51. On the complex implications of delay in Egyptian courts, see Hegel-Cantarella 2012. Judges may, of course, be more conservative than the statutes and endeavor to avoid their implementation. Writing about Iran in 1996, the daughter of President Akbar Hashemi Rafsanjani, Faezeh Hashemi, said, upon her election to parliament: "Right now according to the existing laws women's rights are ignored by the courts. Even the implementation of marriage contract stipulations is subject to the court's decisions" (quoted in Afshar 1998, 195). Similar difficulties have been reported for many other countries, including Morocco, where, notwithstanding changes in the Code of Personal Status in 2004, judges not infrequently fail to apply the law, find exceptions, or are lax in enforcement (Rachel Newcomb, personal communication). There is also little hard data about corruption in the courts,

though anecdotal evidence would suggest that gender is not the key factor even when judicial results are so affected.

133. See the cases described in Moustafa 2013.

134. Gerber 1980, 231. Women may also be creditors to their husbands, thus further bolstering their property rights: See Guechi 2005.

135. Doumani 2003, 173 and 183. Citing examples from biographical dictionaries of eleventh- to fifteenth-century Egypt and Syria, Shaheed and Shaheed (2011, 40–41) state:

> We also know that women had access to legal courts and the liberty to pursue an education, and also that women asserted their rights in a multitude of ways: in contracting and dissolving marriages, travelling short and long distances, or taking charge of their economic affairs. Strategies for claiming their rights included representations in court and approaching notables for intervention, as well as sometimes taking matters into their own hands. . . . Contrary to popular perceptions, women were active in many spheres of life. Records show women had access to, and control over, economic resources: they participated in trade and commerce and held property in their own names. . . . Indeed Ottoman *waqf* [pious foundation] records show that women accounted for almost 40% of all endowments.

136. Bowen 2003, 87.

137. Shatzmiller 1995, 255. See also Shatzmiller 2007, 1: "Ninety-five per cent of the documents refer to a female either transacting family and business deals in some capacity or exercising one or several of her legal entitlements to property." For numerous examples of women transacting business and engaging in the public marketplace, see Pennell 1987. See, for the Palestinian situation, Moors 1995.

138. In Iran, for example, the average age of women marrying for the first time was 19.7 years in 1976 and twenty-four in 2007, by which time 78% of all women marrying were over the age of twenty (Afary 2009, 360). Iran is also threatening women that they must have babies and not use contraceptives or risk not being allowed to hold jobs (Amnesty International 2014). So-called white marriages, in which couples, for reasons both economic and social, simply live together are now quite common in Iran. See Esfandiari 2015 and Nasseri 2015. On the Iranian government's warning to unmarried public workers to find a spouse within a year or risk losing their jobs, see Anonymous 2015. Studies also indicate that women have been the heads of households in many parts of the Muslim Middle East at rates approaching 15% for quite a long time, a factor that may also affect their pursuit of legal cases and their success rate. See, e.g., Okawara 2003; Fay 2003; Rapoport 2005, 38–44; and Geertz, Geertz, and Rosen 1979, 494–500. Traditionalists have defeated attempts to equalize inheritance law in Morocco even though,

as proponents of change have pointed out, the extended family—in which women are cared for by the men—has been replaced by the nuclear family and in 20% of all instances women are the financial mainstay of their families (*Al-Monitor* 2014).

139. On Jordan, see Sonbol 2003; on Algeria, "Algeria: 20 Years Is Enough" (n.d.); on Gaza, Jalal 2016 (allowing men to use grounds of verbal abuse by wife to avoid payments to her upon divorce). Birth rates have also declined by one-third to one-half in most of the Muslim world in the past generation: see Eberstadt and Shah 2011. An exception is Egypt, where the government hopes to reduce the number of children a woman gives birth to from 3.5 to 2.4 by 2030 (Rohan 2015). On Turkey, see "Women's Rights, Turkish Style" 2004. *Hurriyet Daily News* (2015) reports a recent decision from the Constitutional Court removing penalties for conducting a religious marriage without first conducting a wedding before a state official, thus opening the way for possible child marriages and polygamy. On Afghanistan, see Barr 2013. On the willingness of liberals to compromise women's interests even on the issue of divorce on demand in Egypt, see El Naggar 2012. In many additional situations women are the primary breadwinners, particularly when husbands are ill or unemployed: see Rabho 2012.

140. For example, women now occupy almost 40% of the positions in the Moroccan bureaucracy, including 17% of the highest positions. *Morocco World News* 2014.

141. On Bahrain's plan, see Zahra 2014. On the experiences of an Afghan woman judge, see Basel and Hollywood 2005–6. For Syria, see Cardinal 2010; for the Kurdish Rajava region, "Syria's Trailblazing Kurdish Region" 2016. For Pakistan, see Mehdi 2012. For Palestine, see Hadid 2015. On Saudi Arabia, see Carrington 2013. See also Bauer 2010, Abdelkader 2014, Nurlaelawati and Salim 2013, Sonneveld 2016, and several essays on women judges in Baderin 2014. Documentary films that deal with the training of Muslim women judges and law specialists include *Lady Judges of Pakistan* and *Class of 2006: Morocco's Female Religious Leaders*. Among the refugees from the Western Sahara committees of women have been set up to counsel and resolve marital disputes. See Fiddian-Qasmieh 2014, Isser 2011, Sonneveld and Lindbekk 2017, and Wilson 2015.

142. Hammami 2004, 141–42. On the price women in Gaza may have to pay to free themselves through a *khul'a* divorce, see Othman 2015. In a survey of 304 women and 295 men in Morocco, half of the men (and less than 20% of the women) opposed the legally prescribed division of marital property instituted by the 2004 reforms (M'chichi 2007, 69).

143. Souaiaia 2008, 107. For an example of a case from fifteenth-century Morocco in which officials had to contend with the uncertainties and fairness of applying Islamic inheritance law as opposed to Berber customary law, see Powers 2006b.

144. Statistics, where available, vary: In the Emirates four out of ten marriages fail (Elass 2009); in Saudi Arabia, 62% of marriages are ending in divorce while in Malaysia the divorce rate doubled between 2002 and 2009 (WikiIslam 2014). See

also "Omanis Stay Married, Less Divorces than Neighbor Gulf States" 2014, and Cammack and Heaton 2011. In North America about one in three Muslim marriages ends in divorce (Ghayyur 2010).

145. Shaham 1997, 234. Shaheed and Shaheed (2011, xxxi), however, remind us that "over the centuries, many men in Muslim contexts have called for better gender relations and justice; countless men have been key supporters and facilitators of women's assertions of self. The notion that all men in Muslim societies are misogynistic is as much a myth as the notion that all women are silent victims." Reference is then made to the statement by Ibn Rushd (Averroës) in the twelfth century: "In these [our] states, however, the ability of women is not known, because they are merely used for procreation. They are therefore placed at the service of their husbands and relegated to the business of procreation, child-rearing and breastfeeding. But this denies them their [other] activities [b]ecause women in these states are considered unfit for any of the human virtues" (ibid.).

146. Moreover, if it does prove true that women are "winning" with considerably greater frequency than Western popular and scholarly opinion have assumed, it may be necessary for students of Islamic law to rethink the relation of the texts to the practices of the courts, inasmuch as many of the classic sources appear to be far more restrictive in their views of women's nature and legal situation than are the actual court decisions. Bridging the gulf between textual studies and on-the-ground studies of legal practice does not have to imply that the one is "more true" than the other even when the two may seem to operate in separable spheres.

147. See, e.g., Newcomb 2009, 79–92. See also Sonbol 2003, 174:

> It is no exaggeration to describe the usual experience that women get out of *shari'a* courts today as traumatic. The breakdown of the marriage is usually blamed on her, except in situations in which the husband's reputation is unredeemable. . . . Lacking financial resources, even the cost of transportation to and from court becomes difficult. Lawyer Manal Shamut, an experienced shari'a court lawyer, described these difficulties and how unwilling judges are to expedite cases so that wives do not have to struggle to come to court, leaving daily jobs and losing wages, and paying for transportation they can ill afford. Ratib al-Zahir, who is a practicing *shari'a* court lawyer and was previously a judge in *shari'a* courts of Jordan, confirmed Shamut's assessment of the difficulties faced by women who come to *shari'a* courts, as did a leading male lawyer-activist who censured Jordan's judges for making the situation even harder on both women and men than it need be.

148. Sexual harassment, frequently in public, is even more extensive: One survey reports that 95% of the women in Cairo have been subject to such acts (HarassMap 2014). In 2016 Algeria passed a law punishing domestic violence and sexual

harassment. Officials, however, noted that, owing to women's reluctance, the 7,500 cases reported in 2015 probably represent only 20% of the actual offenses. Associated Press 2016. Similarly, few cases are reported in Jordan: See Husseini 2016. So-called seasonal marriages, traditionally aimed at permitting temporary marriage in order to avoid prostitution among long-term travelers, have been the subject of recent legislation in Egypt, which requires a deposit of money to a bank account for the woman, but is seen by many as a form of licensed prostitution, particularly for Gulf states' tourists. See Farid 2016. See also Haeri 2002.

149. See Cody 2012. The actual figures for 2009 were 33,253 and 41,098 for 2010. Some Islamists have argued in favor of marriage for girls as young as nine. See "Plus de 41.000 mineures mariées en 2010 au Maroc" 2011. See also the statistics from several local courts in Ounnir 2007, 108–10. On female suicide, see, e.g., Hauslohner 2010, Campbell and Guiao 2004, and Arango 2012. For statistics on domestic violence in Muslim countries, and the attitudes of both men and women toward wife-beating, see WikiIslam 2016. On Islam, domestic violence, and the traditional sources, see Chaudhry 2014. Morocco has changed its law that allowed rapists to avoid jail by marrying their victims (Bakhadda 2014).

150. McCoy 2014. On cases where abused women strike back, see Rubin 2014. On the very low numbers of "honor killings" by Muslims living in Germany, see Oberwitter and Kasselt 2014; and Kasselt 2010.

151. For example, in Indonesia,

> while the state bureaucracy now applies a uniform body of Islamic divorce rules, those rules have only a limited purchase with ordinary Muslims. The law requires that all divorces receive judicial approval, but only about half of all divorces are processed through the courts. . . . Despite the widespread evasion of statutory divorce requirements, the significance of the government's accomplishments should not be underestimated. . . . [C]hanges to the law that require reasons for divorce and grant increased rights to wives are undoubtedly changing popular attitudes, and new ideas about marriage and divorce are an important element in the complex of factors that are driving divorce rates down (Cammack, Donovan, and Heaton 2007, 126–27).

Chapter Three

1. See, e.g., Merry 1988, Olgiati 1997, Tamanaha 1993, and Vanderlinden 1989. For an application to Islamic law, see Shahar 2008.

2. See, e.g., Dupret et al. 1999 and Just 2001.

3. The reference here is to my own experience: Once word got around that I was studying the courts people occasionally asked me for advice or sought to have

me draw up documents similar to those rendered by notaries or clerks of the court. Sometimes these requests came from people who were trying to keep their affairs private; at other times they were trying to avoid having to give "presents" to court personnel they thought might otherwise not expedite their interests.

4. See Adam 1949–50 and Agoumy 1997. For Saudi Arabia, see Bukhari 1982. See also Ababsa et al. 2012.

5. On the north side of the city, starting in 1945, a settlement called Kaf el Mal developed, while around the same time the larger area to the west of the city, Sidi Hamed Tadli, also developed spontaneously. These areas contrast, say, to the municipal sponsored settlement of Slaoui, which was constructed after the disastrous flood of 1950 but has always been recognized by the administration. For a description and pictures of these settlements, see Benhalima 1987, 230–32.

6. A high court judge recently suggested to me as alternative phrasings, *al 'aqd shari'at al muta'aqidin* or *annas 'inda shaurutihim*, which are less strongly framed. Both phrases imply that the parties, being tied together and having fixed the mutual conditions of their agreement, are thus linked to the shari'a and its purpose of adhering to one's contracts. The phrasing I have employed is, however, one I have heard repeatedly from both ordinary citizens and court personnel.

7. On the concept of social benefit (*maṣlaḥa*) generally, see Sattam 2015.

8. See Rosen 2000, 85–98. The context of the Berber Dahir is discussed in Halstead 1967.

9. The emphasis on who says a thing also applies in the religious domain (where a chain of credible persons legitimizes, say, the certification of Quranic learning), and in the law (where a fatwa's import depends on the purveyor's capacity to build a network of people who believe his word to count). See Rosen 2002, 56–72.

10. Customary practices may, of course, be adopted as part of the formal system of state-supported law. For an important example of the conceptualization of custom as Islamic law, see Layish 2008.

11. For an interesting historical example that may very well have contemporary analogues, see Tamdoğan 2008.

12. For a general account of the relation of law and culture, with examples from Islamic law, see Rosen 2006.

13. To the best of my knowledge Geertz never wrote up this idea, but it certainly appeared in his conversations and in his fieldnotes, which are now archived at the University of Chicago's Regenstein Library, along with my own fieldnotes. Personally, I came to the view that there was no systematic displacement of a *qaid*'s authority but that what we were seeing was an instance of the more general pattern of seeking big men as mediators in many situations. Geertz, perhaps having come to the same conclusion, may not have published his first thoughts about a shadow *qaid* system for similar reasons.

14. At the annual Cherry Festival held in the city of Sefrou, which draws tribesmen from throughout the rural hinterland, Qaid Said's tent would always be larger

than that of the local *qaid*. Many thought of it as his political party's tent as well as his own central receiving tent. When, at the 1967 Cherry Festival, a sing-off (what anthropologists often call a "song duel") occurred between two disputing groups as a way of airing, and hopefully settling, their differences, the participants did not, however, congregate in front of Said's tent but at the tent of the local *qaid*, everyone understanding that Said did not, at least in this instance, want to seem to be visibly displacing the local official in his own town.

15. See Rosen 1984.

16. See Foblets 1996.

17. A number of lawyers and legal scholars in Holland have told me that this practice is so common as to be the norm among their Moroccan female clients who originate from the Rif Mountains in Morocco.

18. I am indebted to Alex Wamboldt for bringing this example to my attention. As people nowadays frequently move from their original locales, mimicking state law forms may, of course, be taking the functional place of local custom.

19. The term "shari'a" may be used by people to refer to a particular body of rules and orientations or as a generalized term for law. Moreover, individuals may, at times, be in a position to choose between courts that have overlapping jurisdiction but different procedural or evidentiary rules. For an example of a religious man who took his party wall case not to the local qadi's court but to one operating under state statutes because he had the proofs necessary to win in the latter court that he lacked in the former, see chap. 1 and, more fully, Rosen 1989, 29–30.

20. See Mnookin and Kornhauser 1979.

21. Absent more information one should not assume that the legal systems of even jihadist regimes are necessarily unpopular or unfair. As one observer writes: "In conurbations where there has been no policing and no judiciary owing to the collapse of central government, these courts are largely popular; citizens can bring cases directly to the courts, which are able to process cases quickly and, in most cases, reasonably. Justice is said to be impartial, with ISIS soldiers subject to the same punishments as civilians" (Ruthven 2015).

22. See Rosen 2008, 23–38.

23. On the jinn in this regard, see Ben Jelloun 1996, 15–16, 23–25, and 56, Shah 2006, Maarouf 2007, and Spadola 2009.

24. This may also be thought of as a form of the power of weakness, a situation in which a relatively weak party may nevertheless choose which among competing powerful figures to depend upon. In a situation of legal pluralism the state may be only one among several possible "patrons." Going to other forums may also be a vehicle for protesting various state policies. See Scott 1985.

25. It is also not uncommon nowadays for some people in the marketplace to prefer to deal with a merchant who wears a beard and Islamic garb on the assumption that he may be more honest than those whose appearance does not advertise their Islamist proclivities. However, everyone also knows that there are merchants

who dress in this fashion precisely in order to lure customers when, in fact, they are neither religious nor honest.

26. The Islamic Courts Union of Somalia may have been such an example: A coalition of numerous groups, it constituted itself as a political force opposed to the Transitional Federal Government, in part, by instituting its own non-state courts of Islamic law. The courts operated from 1991–2006, when they were disbanded. See Santoro 1999.

27. One should never make too much of party affiliation in Morocco, particularly in Sefrou which elected one of the first municipal socialist governments and has a long history of getting attention from the capital by such protest votes. The recent mayor referred to here was previously an employee of the Ministry of Tourism in Fez, wears elegant tropical suits and a Fidel Castro–style cap, plays golf, subsequently failed to be elected to Parliament from Sefrou, and though popular and much admired for his practice of transparency nevertheless chose not to seek reelection.

28. In other parts of Morocco, particularly in zones they wished to develop with industry, the government began tearing down thousands of squatter buildings in the aftermath of the Arab Spring uprisings elsewhere. See Pelham 2012.

Chapter Four

1. There were occasions when a Jew did serve as a silent partner with a Muslim. The record denominated "El Meftah" (Title No. T1153, Sefrou Medina, Taksebt 234), for example, involves just such a relation between a Jew named Amram ben Yaakob ben Youssef ben Aich with no less a figure than the pasha of Sefrou Muhammad ben Allal Cheradi (elsewhere called Lamuri) in 1916. Lamuri was, however, a rather corrupt character: See Rosen 2015, 75, 287–88. The more common Muslim-Jewish partnership is represented by the land record Title No. T5393, "Mebrouka 13," Derb el-Miter, Sefrou, where, as of 1946–48, half of the property in question was owned by a Muslim and the remainder divided among five (later, through inheritance, ten) Jews. The Moroccan examples are particularly telling since, it should be recalled, a quarter of all the Jews in the Middle East, including Turkey, lived in Morocco in 1948. Sefrou itself was for a very long time half-Jewish.

2. This example is found at *Mukhtalifa Notebook* No. 38 (1939).

3. Dossier 65/76, Case No. 396, Notebook 4 B (Sefrou, Morocco 1965).

4. See also Zafrani 1980.

5. Milliot 1920b, 92ff. (Succession Al-Hadj At-Thiyyib v. Tobias Lévy, Appeal no. 63, order of September 25, 1916).

6. Milliot 1920b, 88–92 ('Allâl ben Al-Hadj Al-Mawsâwi et sa femme v. l'Israëlite 'Azzâr ben Ya'qoûb, Appeal No. 104, May 22, 1917).

7. Milliot 1920a, 354–62 (Appeal no. 116, order of January 20, 1918).

8. See Marglin 2013. See also Marglin 2014, 210–15.

9. See, e.g., the Malaysian situation described in Saad 2010.

10. Marglin 2013, 83 and 134. Jews would often have to present a group of twelve Muslim witnesses (the same number required of Muslims) to establish the facts in a case, but their own oaths could also be taken on occasion. Marglin 2013, 80. See also the citations at Marglin 2013, 82 n. 48.

11. Marglin 2013, 134.

12. Marglin 2013, 142–43. A distinction needs to be drawn between the Islamic law courts, which were not supposed to accept Jewish evidence, and the forums of the state acting in its political role, where such rules did not apply and where Jewish documents, evidence, and rabbinical expertise could more easily be considered, possibly as a form of customary practice.

13. This may explain why, in one case cited, two Jews came to the Muslim court to act as mediator in a case involving a Muslim and a Jew. Marglin 2013, 94.

14. Goulven 1921, 15 n. 1. See also Marcus 1989, 104.

15. The sharing of saints in North Africa is very common. Indeed, it is said that in rare instances a Jewish saint would be stolen and reburied in a Muslim graveyard—or even that a living Jewish saint would be killed and taken to one of their cemeteries—in order for the Muslims to use him in their own ritual oath takings.

16. Marglin 2013, 69.

17. Marglin 2013, 69.

18. Marglin 2013, 77. On the similar situation in Egypt, see Shaham 1995.

19. Marglin 2013, 109.

20. Marglin 2013, 32. For a not dissimilar pattern in the historical interaction of Christian and Muslim systems, see Apellániz 2016.

21. Hacker 1994, 165–66; and Jennings 1978. See also the sources cited at Shaham 1995, 113 n. 1. For more recent examples of forum shopping by Muslims in Israel/Palestine, see Shahar 2015.

22. See, e.g., the case described by Marglin 2014, and the works cited therein at 208 n. 9.

23. Simonsohn 2011, 175–204. Apparently sales and loan agreements drawn by Muslim notaries were acceptable to some Jewish courts but gifts were not, the distinction ostensibly being that the former ratify relationships already established while gift transfers need to be carefully monitored because they may affect the distribution of assets among a number of Jews and hence the overall peace of the entire community.

24. Simonsohn 2011, 196.

25. It was as true of Jewish as of Muslim judges that there was considerable discretion, the credibility of a judge depending in no small part on his personal reputation and connections. On the personalism of Jewish judges in the Geniza period, see Zinger 2014, 234–44; on the common use of multiple forums, see Zinger 2014, 201–76.

26. See, e.g., Goitein 1973, 253. Goitein does say: "Christian and Jewish merchants used to settle their disputes and other legal affairs before their communal courts. . . . Any non-Muslim could apply to a Muslim, that is, government, court . . . but this was resented. . . . All in all, the organization of law in Medieval Islam markedly enhanced the cohesiveness of the non-Muslim communities and the communal attachment of the merchants" (Goitein 1973, 11).

27. Goitein 1967, 204

28. Goitein 1967, 251–52.

29. Goitein 1971, 365.

30. Goitein 1971, 367–68.

31. Goitein 1971, 331.

32. Goitein 1967, 259–60.

33. Goitein 1971, 395–96.

34. Goitein 1971, 402.

35. Goitein 1971, 402.

36. Goitein 1978, 83 and 330–32.

37. Cohen 1984, xi. Cohen continues (223, and generally 110–39):

> As the court protected the rights of weak elements of society in accordance with the provisions of the Shari'a, so the Jews brought to the Muslim court all those matters over which their own religious court had no authority. But the kadi was more than a last resource for them. There were many disputes between Jew and Jew, criminal and civil cases, and even issues involving personal relations that the Jews brought to the kadi rather than the dayyān [rabbi] for adjudication. Men learned in the laws of Judaism tried to limit the kinds of issues Jews were permitted to bring before the Muslim judge. Rabbi David Ben Zimra, the Radbaz, for example, stated that bills of divorcement were not to be brought to the Gentiles, nor were Jews to take an oath before them. But as we learn from the Responsa literature, even this limitation was breached during his own lifetime. Essentially an unlimited variety of issues was brought to the Muslim court by Jews, and neither their language nor their religion seems to have been a barrier between them and the judge.

Indeed, Cohen concludes (1984, 224): "The entire supervisory mechanism governing implementation of the [Muslim] religious law was often slanted in favor of the Jews, thereby counterbalancing pressures exerted by local society, the ruler, and his soldiers."

38. Al-Qattan 1999, 430. Similarly, Meshal (2014, 220) notes that in the days following the fall of Hosni Mubarak, Egyptian Coptic Christians, whose church severely limits divorce, demonstrated alongside Muslim students from the mosque-university

Al Azhar "for right of access to the shari'a courts, something that would allow them to obtain a Muslim divorce, as in the past, without converting to Islam, currently the only means available to thousands of Christians."

39. Al-Qattan 1999, 436.

40. Al-Qattan 1999, 438.

41. Al-Qattan 1999, 438. Interestingly, a contemporary Pew survey shows that only 29% of Moroccans think that Islamic law should be applied to non-Muslims (Pew Research 2013).

42. Al-Qattan 1999, 440.

43. Shaham 1995, 114–15.

44. Wagner 2007, 210. See also Wagner 2014.

45. Boum 2013, 35.

46. Boum 2013, 39.

47. Tribes, says Lowie, "sample alternate social forms" from other tribes (quoted in Boon 1982, 102).

48. For example, in Morocco Jews were often metal workers, in part because this also let them work as plumbers, in which capacity they could enter a Muslim's home, see their women and beyond the guestroom, and yet be unlikely to turn such knowledge to the advantage a fellow Muslim seeking assistance in some reciprocal venture might covet. For a number of examples of the psychological relationship with resident Jews in Morocco, see Rosen 1984 and 2015.

49. For example, the Hanafi writer of the sixteenth century, Ibrahim al-Halabi, characteristically states: "Sale is concluded by offer and acceptance expressed by two verbs of the past tense, such as 'I have sold' and 'I have bought.' . . . If the seller says: 'Take the thing for such and such' and the buyer answers: 'I have taken,' or 'I have consented' the sale is valid." Similarly, the Ottoman Civil Code (*Majalla*, Article 175), says that "a sale is called a sale through conduct of the parties," thus focusing on the consequences for the parties' networks that have already been set in train. For these and similar provisions, see Liebesny 1975, 210–11.

50. See Libson 2003.

51. See generally the articles on *mushāraka* (partnership) in *Arab Law Quarterly* 1999. See also Hassan 2017.

52. On these concepts, see Sattam 2015.

53. Udovitch 1970, 128. Moreover, the famous legal scholar "Ibn Qayyim al-Jawziyya [1292–1350] wrote that the Prophet had a partnership with the Jews of Khaybar in the medina" (Boum 2013, 48).

54. On the concept of trust in these cultures, see Rosen 2000, 133–50.

55. Even American courts often cited this story in justification of Fifth Amendment compensation for the taking of another's property for a public purpose. See cases cited at Failinger 2012, 23 n. 130.

56. Such examples tend, however, to be government-to-government arrangements, as at the Kaesong Industrial Complex where North Korea supplied cheap

labor and South Korea paid the workers' salaries directly to a government that is greatly in need of hard currency. Kaesong, however, was shut down by the South Koreans early in 2016 in retaliation for the North's nuclear testing. See Sang-Hun 2016. Kaesong and similar examples are quite different, however, from what is suggested here.

57. See, e.g., the Israeli-based organization *Ta'ayush, Arab-Jewish Partnership*, whose web address is www.taayush.org (accessed January 5, 2017).

58. See Grossman 2003–4. On Muslim property law generally, see Schacht 1964, chap. 19, "Property". For a broad overview of property rights and their relation to concepts of justice, see Harris 1996.

59. Cover 1987, 65.

60. Cover 1987, 66.

61. Cover 1987, 71.

62. Cover 1987, 73.

63. Indeed, Prime Minister Netanyahu has proposed building a fence around the entire country: "In our neighborhood, we need to protect ourselves from wild beasts. At the end of the day as I see it, there will be a fence like this one surrounding Israel in its entirety. We will surround the entire state of Israel with a fence, a barrier" (Beaumont 2016).

64. For a collection of Banksy's graffiti on the Israel separation wall, see https://images.search.yahoo.com/yhs/search;_ylt=A0LEVvAmCKdYJioASWknnIlQ;_ylu=X3oDMTByMjB0aG5zBGNvbG8DYmYxBHBvcwMxBHZ0aWQDBHNlYwNzYw—?p=Banksy+Israel+Wall+Images&fr=yhs-mozilla-003&hspart=mozilla&hsimp=yhs-003 (accessed February 17, 2017).

65. The more conventional approach is well represented by Ari Shavit (2014, 30) when he proposes that "first, Israel will freeze all settlement activity beyond the separation barrier. Then Israel will initiate limited pullouts from designated areas in the West Bank. The Palestinians will commit to turning every piece of liberated land into a development zone in which massive building projects (resembling those in the new Palestinian city of Rawabi) will take center stage." Such "final status" solutions go far beyond my modest proposal but, characteristically, lack specificity or much greater hope for adoption. On the literary representations of Palestinian-Israeli cooperation and intersubjectivity, see Hochberg 2007.

66. See in this regard Bennett 2014.

67. A wide range of customary contracts can be found in the region: see, e.g., for Bedouin practices that may be suggestive, Stewart 2003.

68. "During the 1980s and '90s, tens of thousands of Palestinians from the West Bank and Gaza Strip worked in Israel. They learned Hebrew and built relations with their Israeli employers. . . . In turn, Israelis would venture on weekends into the West Bank, where they would get their cars fixed, shop for vegetables and snack on plates of unparalleled hummus. They attended weddings of their Palestinian employees and their children. Some Israelis and Palestinians even went into

business together" (Bronner 2014). Israel issued 116,000 permits for Palestinians to work in the country at the time of the first Intifada in the early 1990s; that number had dropped by 90% by the time of the second Intifada in 2000. At the time of the first Intifada, 40% of Gazans also worked in Israel; that number is now zero.

69. Bravmann 1962, 39.

70. Leviticus 23:22. Deuteronomy 24:19 also speaks of leaving the overlooked sheaf for "the foreigner, the fatherless, and the widow."

71. Pullan 2013, 24–27.

Chapter Five

1. Recounted in Helmke 2007, 54–55.

2. See, e.g., this phrasing in Rose-Ackerman 1999, 91. The same definition is used by the Asia Foundation and the World Bank. Similarly, Transparency International defines corruption as "the abuse of entrusted power for private gain." In their corruption index Arab countries rate poorly. Transparency International 2015. See also Transparency International 2016 for detailed country reports.

3. To the extent that various surveys profess to be based on people's own perceptions of corruption rather than a strictly universalized definition they nevertheless may miss the distinct meanings attached to "corruption" by different cultural groups. Similarly, asking the same question over many years does not necessarily get at the issue of whether that question holds different implications over the course of time.

4. See Rosen 2000, 187–99.

5. Gellner's way of putting the matter, though not one I agree with fully, is phrased thus: "The Hobbesian problem arises from the assumption that anarchy, absence of enforcement, leads to distrust and social disintegration. We are all familiar with the deductive model which sustains and re-enforces that argument, but there is a certain amount of interesting empirical evidence which points the other way. The paradox is: it is precisely anarchy which engenders trust or, if you want to use another name, which engenders social cohesion. It is effective government which destroys trust" (Gellner 1988, 143). For my own take on the matter, see Rosen 2000, 133–50.

6. Ben Jelloun 1995.

7. See Cunningham and Sarayrah 1993.

8. Faisal 2011.

9. "Corruption in Afghanistan, Bribery as Reported by the Victims" 2010, 22. See also "Corruption in Afghanistan: Patterns and Trends" 2012; and De Lauri 2011.

10. Perhaps even criminals feel an analogous pull. As a novelist once had a character say: "He was too dishonest to be a good crook. Crooks are honest men.

They have to be. When you think of the deals they do with each other, then they daren't put anything in writing. You couldn't run an underworld for five minutes with the cheating that goes on in big business: breaking contracts, sub-standard goods, fighting law suits" (Lyall 1971).

11. Goodwin 2009.

12. For a fascinating historical overview of these and related issues, see Noonan 1984. For Islam generally, see Rosenthal 1964. For an intriguing comparison of American anti-corruption legislation and the thinking of scholars in Central Asia in the medieval period, see Johansen 2002. On eradicating corruption, see Rotberg 2017.

13. On the desire of young lawyers to take pride in their profession in the face of corrupt legal officials, see Rosen 2002, 3–20. In 2012 and again in 2014 judges in Morocco took to the streets of the capital to emphasize their desire to be a truly independent branch of government. See Associated Press 2012a, Associated Press 2012b, Abdennebi 2014.

14. My own views have been elaborated in Rosen 2000, 153–75; and Rosen 2008, 60–72.

Chapter Six

1. The Wannous quote comes from Rodenbeck 2011.

2. Rodenbeck 2011.

3. Quoted in Friedman 2011b. See Keefe 2015. On the payment of petty bribes, see *Morocco World News* 2015.

4. For a description of the "Battle of the Camel," when Mubarak on February 2, 2011 sent thugs to attack the protesters in Tahrir Square, see Cambanis 2015, 56–57.

5. In Egypt, there is even a practice of holding fake wedding festivities as a way of raising money that is then distributed on a rotational basis for actual weddings, a further example of establishing adulthood through reciprocity and alliance formation. Feteha 2015.

6. At various times and in parts of the Arab world, communities or status groups have sought to fix the bridewealth as constant for all marriages, but the practice has almost invariably succumbed to competition. For an earlier example from Saudi Arabia, see Serjeant 1962; for a current attempt to set the bridewealth in the country at about $13,000 for a virgin and $5,300 for a widow or divorcee (and to discourage the high cost of renting a wedding venue), see Habtor 2015. Attempts have even been made to cap the number of wedding guests in Afghanistan to lower the cost of marriage. Goldstein 2015. On the costs of marriage, see Hasso 2010, 65–70, Singerman 2008, Salem 2011, and, on women's contributions to the costs of marriage, Sieverding 2012, 72–91.

7. See Anonymous 2014. ("The illusory right to housing still haunts millions of young people in Egypt, particularly among the poor.")

8. Bohn 2013. Bohn quotes University of Toronto sociology professor Rania Salem, who notes that housing has been a particular frustration for the unmarried in the wake of the failed Arab Spring: " 'The post-uprising moment was a hopeful one, with a lot of potential for young people who saw their marital trajectories tied up in the country's political and economic circumstances. They were hopeful that public housing and other services would be reformed, which would help them in the marriage project. But there's much less hope for improved circumstances today.' "

9. Esfandiari 2015; Anonymous 2015.

10. For Morocco, see Perkins 2004, 103 n. 16. For Egypt, see *Ahram Online* 2014.

11. Krajeski 2011. See Kholoussy 2010 and Aal 2010.

12. The Arabic reads *irḥal ʿāwiz atgawwiz*. For other banners see Zack 2012. On the crucial role of humor in the events surrounding Tahrir Square, see also Colla 2013, Helmy and Frerichs 2013, and Sussman 2011. On Arab political humor generally, see Kishtainy 1985. Humor may also arise from misperception. As a new professor at Brown University, Kamal Abdel-Malek recalled his confusion when he saw a group of joggers running in the streets: " 'I just assumed they were running from the police,' he said. 'In Egypt, this was the only time you would see people running like this' " (quoted in A. Shah 2011).

13. For an extension of this argument, see Rosen 2008, 39–46. The self-immolation of other men, imitating the act of Tunisian Muhammad Bouazizi, may also couple with the sense of frustration that stems from the inability to create such networks. A number of women also burned themselves around this same time.

14. Zimmer 2011 and Friedman 2011a. Cohen 2016, too, continues the myth by mistakenly referring to the Arab Spring in Egypt as a time of "Twitter-empowered Arab youth ascendant." Similarly, Juan Cole (2014) overemphasizes the role of social media in the Arab Spring: See my review of his book, Rosen 2014. See also El Rashidi 2011 on the shutdown and avoidance of social media.

15. Among those making this point are Abul-Magd 2012, 566–67 ("The whole event was then mistakenly called a Facebook and Twitter revolution to celebrate the Westernized side of it, but none of those who were posting to Facebook or tweeting were severely injured or died in the protests [which] were neither a peaceful nor a middle-class youth action of occupation or revolution . . ."); Levinson and Coker 2011 ("On Jan. 25, the first day of protests, the . . . demonstrators weren't, as the popular narrative has held, educated youth who learned about protests on the Internet."); Rangwala 2011 ("Initial results from a large-scale polling project [taken in eighteen Arab countries through 2011] suggest that revolution is powered by issues more complex than phone-wielding twenty-somethings."); Gregory 2013 ("Many commentators on events in Egypt have insisted on the power of digital social media, and especially Facebook, Twitter and YouTube, to activate and

co-ordinate political opposition to the Mubarak regime. But conventional means of communication also played a crucial role, and the presence of large crowds gathered together in public spaces was vital to the immediate gains made in what was a remarkably heterogeneous revolution. . . . Helga Tawill-Souri argues (I think convincingly) that 'the primary channels of mobilization were not mass mediated or high-tech at all' but relied on means like 'face-to-face meetings, graffiti, posters and landline calls.' One survey found that nearly 50 percent of people in its sample first heard about the demonstrations in Tahrir through face-to-face communication, 28 percent via Facebook and 13 percent via their mobile phone."), citing Tawil-Souri 2012, 92; and Tufekei and Wilson 2012.

16. See Hebblethwaite 2011. *Time* magazine even named El Général one of the most important people of the year (Walt 2011). However, he was, it should also be noted, a Muslim fundamentalist who publicly supported shari'a law over civil statutory law (Cole 2014, 129 and 177).

17. Indeed, Ghannim subsequently indicated that the social media were more divisive than unifying. See Friedman 2016; and Ghannim's TED Talk at https://www.ted.com/talks/wael_ghonim_let_s_design_social_media_that_drives_real_change (accessed January 5, 2017). Ahmed Salah, another activist involved in Tahrir Square and subsequently tortured and driven out of the country, also stresses that the social media, which were carefully monitored by the police, proved "a poor recruiting tool" and criticizes those who have "swung too far toward a misleading obsession with tech-savvy activists who bring down dictators with a tweet" (J. Zack 2016). See Salah 2016.

18. Quoted in Salah 2016. Support for many of the points raised here can be found in the writings of witnesses and commenters on the events. Among the most useful are Amar 2013, Bishara 2013, Khatib and Lust 2014, Schielke 2015, and Steavenson 2015.

19. See, e.g., the photos of *Time* magazine at http://content.time.com/time/photogallery/0,29307,2046351_2233426,000.html (accessed January 5, 2017). See also the film *The Square* produced by Netflix. A young physician-activist told one anthropologist: "Of course, my parents tried to prevent us from going [to Tahrir Square], but my sister and I told them, 'We are no better than the martyrs who lost their lives, and this is our country and our future!' Not only did they not stop us, they later joined us there" (Hamdy 2012, 45). Clearly not everyone was an unattached youth. An army colonel confronted the crowd in Tahrir and tried to tell them to go home: " 'Do any of you here have children?!' 'My children are home,' came back a voice, 'but I am here for their sake' " (Cambanis 2015, 15).

20. Rangwala 2011. On the development of youth attitudes in various Arab countries, see Tessler 2002, Hoffman and Jamal 2012, and the ASDA'A Burson-Marsteller Arab Youth Survey 2014.

21. The role of soccer and the politics of Egyptian life are carefully followed by Dorsey 2016.

22. Levinson and Coker 2011. Reviewing Shenker 2015, a writer for the *Economist* noted: "To many in the West, the hip, young liberals who made up a portion of the protesters in Tahrir are the embodiment of Egypt's uprising. But it was seasoned labourers in obscure cities who struck the first blows against authoritarian rule" (Anonymous 2016). See also Bar'el 2017.

23. Similarly, Thomas L. Friedman writes: "I often reflect on interviews I did with Egyptian women at an all-female voting station in the poorest neighborhood in Cairo in the 2012 election that brought a Muslim Brotherhood leader to the presidency. Almost all of them had voted for the Muslim Brotherhood candidate, Mohamed Morsi. But when I asked why, not a single one cited religion. Instead they said that Morsi would bring jobs, security, sidewalks, better living conditions and an end to corruption—in short, better governance. Morsi was eventually toppled for bringing none of these, not because he was impious" (Friedman 2014).

24. See the poll figures at Rogers 2011.

25. See Beaumont 2011. Bouazizi's real first name was Tarek: "At some point in the internet discussion, he became confused with a Facebook user named Mohamed Bouazizi, and so that is how he came to be known" (Cole 2014, 128). One could argue that calling him Muhammad not only associated him with Islam and the Prophet but, as an added element of legitimacy in the narrative, rendered him a kind of Tunisian/Muslim Everyman, Muhammad being the most common name in Muslim countries.

26. Wright 2015.

27. Subsequently, many Tunisians were critical of Bouazizi and of his family's notoriety (Rozen 2014). There had been numerous protests in various Muslim countries in the period leading up to the Arab Spring but they were mostly political protests lacking the personal elements of Bouazizi's situation. See, e.g., Cole 2014, 121 and 126; on the demonstrations by fifteen thousand to twenty thousand Sahraouis in October–November 2010, see Wilson 2013.

28. Cole 2014, 26.

29. Steavenson 2015, 31.

30. Greer 2011.

31. Lally 2011. Given that nearly all women in Cairo report being sexually harassed under "normal" circumstances, the respect shown women in the Square is all the more evidence that protestors treated it like private space. Masr 2014.

32. From a lecture by Rasha Salti at the Marrakech Biennale, February 29, 2012, cited in W. J. T. Mitchell 2012, 898–99.

33. Rodenbeck 2011. Once a year there is a "sweeping of the tomb" of the granddaughter of the Prophet Muhammad in Cairo, a ritual that elides with the cleaning of Tahrir Square as non-public space. Cambanis (2015, 57) writes: "Garbage brigades picked up litter, while street kids distributed donated sandwiches and cookies. The ass-grabbing, sexual harassment, and rape that were everyday

hazards for women in downtown Cairo subsided to almost zero. . . . The youth in the square welcomed anyone who entered with requisite humility."

34. Lally 2011.

35. "The formation of such [neighborhood] groups marked the first time in their lives that many Egyptians met their neighbors living in adjacent apartment buildings. It was certainly the first time that many identified so completely with fellow Egyptians across class barriers. . . . The neighborhood mosque's muezzin spoke through loudspeakers each time a suspicious van entered the neighborhood, sometimes jam-packed with would-be looters" (Hamdy 2012, 45).

36. Similarly, in January 2011: "Although working-class youth from the poor quarters were the most numerous participants in the ongoing urban demonstrations, a realization had set in among many Tunisians that what had begun as a jobs protest would falter if it did not go all the way" (Cole 2014, 137). Even climate change may have played a role, as drought and general water shortages have plagued a number of the countries in which the Arab Spring took place. See Werrell et al. 2013. On the history, often displaced, of protests in the Arab world, see Burke 1986.

37. Geertz 1971; Berque 1958.

38. Gellner 1981, 194–206.

39. Indeed, it was by "reverse engineering" Saddam Hussein's network that the Iraqi dictator was tracked down. See C. Wilson 2010.

40. On Islamic concepts of justice, see Rosen 2000, 153–75; and Rosen 2008, 60–72.

41. "The Arab millennials . . . forever changed their societies"; "This generation of New Arabs has . . . forever changed the world" (Cole 2014, ix and 287).

42. World Bank 2014; Gall 2015.

43. Hauslohner 2013. Another eyewitness wrote afterward: "I must have crossed Tahrir Square dozens of times in the first few weeks of my last visit, and I found it chilling to see only faint signs of the protests remaining, like the charred surface of the National Party's headquarters, which had been lit afire, or the national statues quickly dulling again after having been scrubbed clean by young activists in their triumphal gesture to reclaim the square after Mubarak's resignation" (Hamdy 2012, 43–44).

44. Michelet 1967 [1847].

Chapter Seven

1. Aristotle 1932, no. 73, pp. 327, 129, 331. See especially book IV.11 of the *Politics*. See Sinclair 1951; 224–31, and Glassman 1995.

2. For example, Soner Cagaptay 2013, director of the Turkish Research Program at the Washington Institute for Near East Policy, has written "that modernization

theory—the idea that economic development leads to more democracy—is in the process of being proved right in Turkey. Indeed, as countries become middle class, they tend to become irreversibly diverse and democratic, developing the bedrock for democratic governance, including consensual politics and respect for individual and minority rights."

3. Ober 2010 and Ober 2014.

4. "Burgeoning Bourgeosie" 2009.

5. See Coser 1968.

6. Several passages in the following discussion, reprinted by agreement, are drawn from an earlier review article published as Rosen 2011b.

7. As for the role of religion, Nasr states (2009, 144): "The lesson the West must take away from Iran's fate is that it matters less that the middle class is secular than that it is the right sort of middle class, one rooted in commerce and therefore focused on economic growth and on the loosening of state control, so that it will see past the false promise of radicals to protect its interests in robust, capitalist prosperity."

8. See Ali 2010.

9. Nasr (2009, 261) also states: "Over time the profit motive will be our strongest ally; it will lead the growing middle class to push increasingly for business-friendly economic reform and the reliable rule of law, as well as the opening up of their economies to trade with the world. They will push with increasing clout for good government, just as the business communities in India and China have forced the hands of their governments in instituting wide-ranging reforms and opening up the global economy." He concludes by quoting favorably a Western-educated and very successful Pakistani businessman, who tells him: "Grow the economy; the rest will sort itself out" (263).

10. Fukuyama 2014, 441.

11. See Fukuyama 2014, 414–18. Excerpts quoted here are from the book's advertisement on Amazon.com.

12. Gray 2014 states: "Slipping insensibly from arguments about the ethical standards by which governments are to be judged to speculative claims about the moving forces of modern history, Fukuyama blurs facts, values and theories into a dense neo-Hegelian fog. Liberal democracy may be in some sense universally desirable, as he maintains. That does not mean it will always be popular, still less that it is the normal destination of modern development."

13. Hertog 2011.

14. Jamal 2007.

15. Amos 2011.

16. Quoted in "Burgeoning Bourgeoisie" 2009.

17. See Ruthven 2006, 169–70.

18. Massell 1974.

19. See Kuran 2012.

20. "Burgeoning Bourgeoisie" 2009.

21. For a typical political science approach that ignores cultural context, see Diamond 2014.

Chapter Eight

1. Trial 7/3/02, Docket No. 272, quoted in Donahue 2007, 36.

2. Moussaoui previously attended a flight school in Norman, Oklahoma, paying $5,000 in advance, but even after three months and fifty-seven hours of flight instruction (when twenty should have sufficed) he left without taking a license. Following the trial, Clarence Prevost, a flight instructor at the Minnesota school who alerted authorities, received the $5 million reward offered by the government for information concerning the 9/11 attacks ("Colleagues Question $5M Moussaoui Reward" 2008).

3. The repeated warnings by the FBI local office in Minneapolis occurred between August 11 and September 10, 2001.

4. One former CIA official told Seymour Hersch (2002): " 'They cast a wide net and the guy [Moussaoui] happened to be a little fish who got caught up in it. They know it now. And nobody will back off,' " thus recalling Proudhon's quip that laws are "fishing nets in the hands of the government." A former federal public defender, worried that this may be a case of "Goliath on one side and a slingless David on the other," also told Hersch: " 'It appears that Moussaoui is not competent to represent himself, because he doesn't seem to understand the fundamentals of the charges against him, but I am starting to feel that the rest of us are crazier. . . . For all our expertise and professionalism, we may let this man talk himself to death to soothe our sense of vulnerability.' "

5. Even in Chechnya Moussaoui was rejected by fighters he met there. One of the lawyers appointed for him told Seymour Hersch (2002): " 'They sent Moussaoui packing. Who wants him around? He brought nothing to the table. He's trouble.' "

6. "Sheikh Mohammed also said that Moussaoui's self-confidence led him to talk too much" (U.S. District Court Eastern District of Virginia 2006a, 48, exhibit 941). See also United States v. Moussaoui 2006a. Additional documents relating to the Moussaoui trial can be found at *FindLaw Legal News*. A number of documents for 2002–2006 were placed online by Cryptome, but when funding ran out they no longer collected documents. See United States v. Moussaoui 2006b; and U.S. District Court, Eastern District of Virginia 2001–2006.

7. "He [Moussaoui] had no connection at all with Sept. 11 . . . Since Zacarias Moussaoui was still learning to fly, he wasn't No. 20 in the group, as your government has claimed. It knows this well" ("Bin Laden Purportedly Says Moussaoui Had Nothing to Do with Sept. 11" 2006). On the identity of the 20th bomber, see "Le 20è homme du 11/09" 2006.

8. Dwyer 2006a.

9. Reporters often characterized Moussaoui's comments in the harshest of terms: thus Moussaoui "viciously insulted" the judge with the quoted remark (Emerson and Garterstein-Ross 2005).

10. Ultimately, Moussaoui was charged with a variety of conspiracies, including "Conspiracy to Commit Acts of Terrorism Transcending National Boundaries, Aircraft Piracy, Destroy Aircraft, Use Weapons of Mass Destruction, Murder United States Employees, and Destroy Property." The first four carry the death penalty. Interestingly, the government never offered Moussaoui a plea bargain, something investigative journalist Seymour Hersch (2002), who was not the only one who thought the case against Moussaoui was weak, could not understand: "Moussaoui was certainly connected to Al Qaeda, but his real value to the United States may have been as a witness and not as a stand-in for the dead hijackers." U.S. Attorney General John Ashcroft would have had to agree to waive the death penalty in any such plea bargain. Much later (February 6, 2006), when the jury was preparing to hear evidence in the penalty phase, Moussaoui and the FBI failed to reach an agreement that could have spared him the possibility of the death penalty. The government's proffer at that time contained the following clause: "4. You are not to use your offer to cooperate with the United States as a mitigating factor during the penalty phase of this case" (U.S. District Court, Eastern District of Virginia, 2006c).

11. In fact, the indictment was modified three times. Judge Brinkema entered not guilty pleas for him in January 2002, in June 2002 (when he tried to plead 'no contest'), and again in July 2002 when he tried to plead guilty.

12. It is not clear from the record whether Moussaoui knew how rarely an insanity defense succeeds in an American court, notwithstanding media images to the contrary. If so, his assertions that the lawyers ostensibly working on his behalf were going to get him killed was far from irrational.

13. "[Moussaoui] wanted a chance to speak for himself. The Special Administrative Measures (SAM) under which he was confined meant that he could not make statements from the detention center. No reporters could interview him. Communication with the world outside the detention center was impossible. The courtroom was the one place where he could speak. Representing himself would allow him to say what he wanted to say" (Donahue 2007, 36).

14. See, e.g., U.S. District Court, Eastern District of Virginia, 2001–2006, trial transcript, July 18, 2002. At a number of junctures in the trial commenters and Moussaoui's own lawyers suggested that by pleading guilty he was trying to martyr himself, but given his frequent statements about wishing to live and that it would be a violation of Islam for him to seek death in a non-combative context this is not a plausible interpretation. As we shall see, what he really appears to have wanted was to tell the true story of his involvement as he saw it.

15. Hersch (2002) reports that while the assessment of psychiatrist Dr. Raymond Patterson is sealed, the judge was told that Moussaoui's memoranda were

"well-researched" and that "he attributed much of Moussaoui's seemingly strange behavior to the 'subculture' to which he belonged."

16. U.S. District Court, Eastern District of Virginia, 2001–2006, transcripts from September 6–19, 2003. In her ruling the judge referred to Moussaoui's motions as "irrelevant, inflammatory, and insulting rhetoric . . . containing threats, racial slurs, calls to action . . . or other irrelevant and inappropriate information" (quoted in Hersch 2002, citing the hearing of August 16, 2003).

17. "THE DEFENDANT: I'm leaving. I'm taking my papers. That's all I do. God curse you and America. THE COURT: Now, we have some business to take care of. THE DEFENDANT: Yes, Take care of my death. THE COURT: The first one is I have received a fax from [his mother] Mrs. Moussaoui. THE DEFENDANT: God curse you. (Defendant taken from courtroom.) THE COURT: And I want to reflect the defendant continued to shout 'curse you' as he left the courtroom" (U.S. District Court, Eastern District of Virginia, 2001–2006, trial transcript of February 14, 2006, p. 8, lines 12–17).

18. U.S. District Court, Eastern District of Virginia, 2001–2006, Trial transcript, April 13, 2006, p. 3,661, lines 8–11.

19. The order eliminating the death penalty was issued on October 2, 2003 (United States v. Moussaoui 2003a). On June 3, 2003, the Fourth Circuit had refused to allow Moussaoui to conduct live video depositions with Guantánamo detainee Ramzi bin al-Shibh, who reputedly sent Moussaoui money from Germany, while the German (like the French) authorities refused to forward evidence of such a contact because of their opposition to the death penalty: Seeking to depose an enemy combatant, the court held, is not the same as requesting discovery of classified documents. (United States v. Moussaoui 2003b). On October 21, 2003, the Fourth Circuit refused to allow Moussaoui to represent himself on the appeal of Brinkema's order to the prosecution to allow him to interview the Guantánamo detainees.

20. United States v. Moussaoui 2004. An appeal of the Fourth Circuit decision to the U.S. Supreme Court failed on March 21, 2005.

21. In Estelle v. Williams 1976, the Supreme Court held that a prisoner has a right to be dressed in civilian clothes, but if he knowingly waives this right he has not been denied due process. Justices Brennan and Marshall dissented, arguing that such dress always makes the accused appear less than innocent. It is not indicated in the record whether Moussaoui waived his right not to appear in a prison jumpsuit with the word "prisoner" emblazoned on his back. In this regard one is reminded of Maimonides comment: "If one of the parties to a suit is well clad and the other ill clad, the judge should say to the former, 'either dress him like yourself before the trial is held or dress like him, then the trial will take place'" (*Laws of Sanhedrin*. c. 21, quoted in Cover 1987, 72). On the question whether a defendant should be closer to the jury, see Shepard 2006.

22. Lewis 2006a.

23. After he had been warned that if he were not silent he would be barred from the courtroom during the selection of jurors for the penalty phase, Moussaoui, who had been insisting that the lawyers appointed for him were working for his death sentence, told the judge: "I understood the letter that you sent me which threatened me to kick me out of the court if I don't become silent for my, my organized death. I understand fully (Arabic spoken.) So I'm going to respond to your question because I have a more technical point to—today. I stand here as a French citizen. I want to make clear that I am not French and have no relation. I'm a sworn enemy of France. So I want to make this in the record that I'm not French, okay? I tell you I am a Muslim, and I have nothing to do with a nation of homosexual Crusaders. And I am not a frog" (United States. v. Moussaoui. 2002–2006, court docket item No. 1564, March 7, 2006). On another occasion, referring to his not wanting to be conscripted into the French army, he also said, "I'm not French" (U.S. District Court, Eastern District of Virginia, 2001–2006, Trial transcript, p. 3,682). Donahue (2007, 54), too, misleadingly refers to "Zacarias, who was of the West." Moussaoui also called himself by several Arabic names, including Shaqil and Abu Khalid al-Sahrawi (after what he said was his father's tribe in Morocco), names that are included in the headnote of various court documents as a/k/a names. See U.S. District Court, Eastern District of Virginia, 2001–2006, Trial transcript, March 27, 2006, pp. 2,308–9.

24. When culture is taken into account in American criminal proceedings it is commonly seen as an aspect of the individual rather than as something that inheres in a collectivity, and being amalgamated in our conceptual system with psychological composition is thus rendered largely relevant to personality and intent as opposed to social identity and group cohesion. Thus, as one wit put it, the insanity defense is our cultural defense. Indeed, we usually deprive assassins of their political point by simply characterizing them as crazy, the tactic Moussaoui's lawyers, to the last, seemed to think would simultaneously save his life and fulfill the expectation of the political/cultural system of which they were a part that he was more madman than political actor. See Rosen 2017.

25. For example, at File Moussaoui 32706, testimony of March 27, 2006, p. 527: "A. Again, I said bayat is—can I say in Arabic? Q. (Arabic spoken). Mr. Karas: Your Honor, objection. We can't do this in Arabic. The Court: Yes, we're not going to do it in Arabic. Anything in Arabic is stricken from this record."

26. Moussaoui 2003, 49.

27. Moussaoui 2003, 49.

28. Moussaoui 2003, 114.

29. U.S. District Court, Eastern District of Virginia, 2001–2006. Trial transcript at p. 2388: "Their Arabic is not good—like my Arabic."

30. Donahue 2008, 18.

31. Donahue 2008, 18. In November 2005 young men of North African heritage rioted first in some of the suburbs of Paris and then in a number of other French

cities, triggering the declaration of a state of emergency by the prime minister and focusing attention on the economic situation and alleged police racism to which these youth were subject.

32. el-Wafi 2006, 163.

33. See U.S. District Court, Eastern District of Virginia, 2001–2006. Trial transcript, February 20, 2006. See also U.S. District Court, Eastern District of Virginia, 2001–2006, Trial transcript, March 27, 2006, pp. 2,383–84.

34. Moussaoui sought to plead guilty on April 22, 2005: See his signed admission of guilt and the statement by Attorney General Gonzalez following acceptance of the plea at Denniston 2005. Judge Brinkema was extremely careful to make sure Moussaoui understood the effects of a guilty plea, including what he would not be able to claim during the penalty phase, and there is every indication he understood these cautions very clearly. The idea that he was seeking to martyr himself is rebutted by John Rosenthal (2007). Indeed, Moussaoui himself rebutted the notion when he testified: "If I wanted to, to have the death penalty, I will not have aborted my first guilty plea. I have plenty of occasion to have the death penalty on me, and for the last four years I have been fighting alone" (U.S. District Court, Eastern District of Virginia, 2001–2006, Trial transcript, April 13, 2006, p. 3620, lines 10–13). In pleadings filed after the trial ended—when Moussaoui sought to withdraw his guilty plea because one juror blocked the death penalty and he hoped a new jury would follow that lead and reach a different verdict altogether—Moussaoui indicated that he pled guilty because he feared his lawyers would not allow him to testify and that the only way he could do so would be if the government called him as a witness.

35. Dorf 2005.

36. Quoted in Donahue 2007, 79–80, from an interview of March 27, 2006.

37. Markon 2005.

38. Anthropologists have encountered the same truthfulness and guilty pleas in a number of societies, including some colonized by Western countries. Thus E. E. Evans-Pritchard (1940, 171–72) writes of the Sudan that people brought before government tribunals "have no need to [lie], since they are only anxious to justify the damage they have caused by showing that it is retaliation for damage the plaintiff has inflicted earlier."

39. See, e.g., U.S. District Court, Eastern District of Virginia, 2005. p. 31, April 22.

40. "Witnesses are not interrupted in the course of their statement . . ." French Code of Criminal Procedure, article 331 (2015). As Freed (1957, 749) notes: "Each witness is allowed to tell what he knows of the case in his own way . . . without interruption." When asked why he hated America Moussaoui said, "It is going to be long . . . I tell you because you don't cut me." To which the lawyer responds, "I am not cutting you off" (U.S. District Court, Eastern District of Virginia, 2001–2006. Trial transcript, p. 3,657).

41. U.S. District Court, Eastern District of Virginia, 2001–2006.Trial transcript, p. 3,657. February 20, 2006.

42. "THE DEFENDANT: I will testify. I will take the stand and tell the truth.

THE COURT: For the third time, Mr. Moussaoui—

THE DEFENDANT: Everybody know now that I will testify of the entire truth that I know.

THE COURT: Mr. Moussaoui, you have been asked by the Court before not to speak. This is not your opportunity. Now, would you please sit down?

THE DEFENDANT: For four years, I have no opportunity to oppose.

THE COURT: I will ask the marshals to remove Mr. Moussaoui from the court yet again.

THE DEFENDANT: This is pure tyranny. I will take the stand—

THE COURT: Mr. Moussaoui—

THE DEFENDANT: —and I will testify of the entire truth. Nobody can not say now that they don't know that I want to testify. I will take the stand, and I will say the truth that I know. And this defense is a fraud. This is not my defense. It is an entire fraud. They are lying from top to end" (U.S. District Court, Eastern District of Virginia, 2001–2006.Trial transcript, February 6, 2006; also at J. Rosenthal 2007, 1).

43. "Mr. Moussaoui, who has been truculent through proceedings in the past three years and whose outbursts have drawn rebukes from the judge, spoke calmly with a heavy French accent, leaning forward in the witness chair, sometimes casually holding out an empty cup for a marshal to fill with water" (Lewis 2006b).

44. U.S. District Court, Eastern District of Virginia, 2001–2006. Trial transcript, March 27, 2006, pp. 2,346ff., where Moussaoui identifies the people he talked to or met in Afghanistan and other places; on his doctor/friend see Trial transcript, p. 3,684.

45. Abramson 2005.

46. U.S. District Court, Eastern District of Virginia, 2001–2006. Trial transcript, July 18, 2002, pp. 26–27, lines 1–13. On several occasions Moussaoui also indicated that he thought President George W. Bush would exchange him for a prisoner held by al-Qaeda, a belief that may also have played into his desire to plead guilty and not be executed. Had this been a primary consideration, though, it is unclear why he would not have urged the government to engage in any plea bargaining.

47. U.S. District Court, Eastern District of Virginia, 2001–2006, Trial transcript, July 18, 2002, p. 9, lines 20–25. At p. 10, line 1: "The conspiracy that I was involved, it's an ongoing conspiracy who have started since around 1995 and it still carries on until this day of this finding of this indictment and my pure plea. So I have specific allegation, substantiate with proof, of course, regarding the existence until today of a group of people who are intend—who intend to commit terrorist act."

48. For an elaboration of this analysis, see Rosen 1984.

49. See the chap. entitled "Why Do Arab Terrorists Kill Themselves?," in Rosen 2008, 39–46.

50. U.S. District Court, Eastern District of Virginia, 2001–2006. Trial transcript, p. 2,345.

51. Moussaoui repeatedly stated that, given U.S. attacks on Palestinian and other Muslim civilians, he had no regrets about the 9/11 acts. "Q. Do you have regret for the victim's families . . . A. Not whatsoever. . . . I find it disgusting that some people will come here to share their grief in order to obtain the death of someone else . . . We want to inflict pain on your country, We wanted— I'm glad they have received pain, I'm glad their family are suffering pain, and I wish there would be more pain because I already can forecast, after tomorrow, next week, the week after, the children of Palestine will be in pain" (U.S. District Court, Eastern District of Virginia, 2001–2006. Trial transcript, April 13, 2006, p. 3,664, lines 3–5, 9–10, 23–25; and p. 3,665, lines 1–3).

52. U.S. District Court, Eastern District of Virginia 2005, 28–30 and 31. Moussaoui also testified that he was not an important figure—"intermediate" is the way he phrased it (U.S District Court, Eastern District of Virginia, 2001–2006. March 27, 2006, Trial transcript , p. 2344). He also said, "I was not a big shot, no." 2,345.

53. Trial transcript, 3,678.

54. See Donahue (2007, 56), citing the transcript of trial testimony of April 22, 2005 at p. 32, lines 16–21. On April 18 a defense-appointed psychologist testified that Moussaoui exhibited classic symptoms of schizophrenia, testimony that was sharply contested by the prosecution (Lewis 2006c).

55. United States v. Moussaoui 2002–2006. Trial transcript, July 25, 2002, p. 12, lines 7–11. Judge Brinkema acknowledged that Moussaoui always wanted to testify (U.S. District Court, Eastern District of Virginia, 2001–2006. Trial transcript, March 27, 2006, p. 2,303).

56. Trial transcript, April 13, 2006, p. 3,673.

57. See Rosen 1984, 120–33.

58. U.S. District Court, Eastern District of Virginia, 2001–2006. Trial transcript, March 27, 2006, p. 2,407. Moussaoui acknowledges that there are three occasions when it is permissible for a Muslim to lie: When making peace between two Muslims, when trying to reconcile a husband and wife, and during jihad (March 27, 2006, p. 2,330).

59. "Q. Is it okay for you to lie? A. Yes, it is. Q. Including in this proceeding, correct? It is okay for you to lie in this proceeding? A. If you ask me when you mean this proceeding, you mean now, right now? Q. The question is as part of your testimony, is it—in this court, is it okay for you to lie? A. Apart from my testimony that I'm doing now, you just say that. Q. No, as part—in relation to your testimony, as part of your testimony, is it okay for you to lie? A. I don't understand your question. Can I say something? Q. When I ask a question. Do you recognize the legal authority of this court? A. You know perfectly I do not recognize anything. Q. That's a 'no,' correct? A. Indeed, I recognize, the only thing I recognize, it is before leaving the stand, I will take an Islamic oath. . . . We in Islam, we don't

make an oath to tell the truth. We first make the statement and say that we have say the true, because otherwise you might deviate during your testimony from the true, you might get carried away or maybe Satan twist your mind. So when I will have testified, I will be able to think about what I have said, and then say, okay. . . . And then you will be certain that I have stated the truth" (Trial transcript, pp. 2,383–84).

60. Trial transcript, March 27, 2006, pp. 2,382ff.

61. Trial transcript, April 13, 2006, p. 3,614; and March 27, 2006, p. 2,336, respectively.

62. Describing a Japanese-American on trial, novelist David Gutterson (1995, 154–55) wrote: "His father taught him: the greater the composure, the more revealed one was, the truth of one's inner life was manifest . . . [t]he face of a war veteran who had forever sacrificed his tranquility in order that they might have theirs. He had . . . not allowed the jurors to read in his face the palpitations of his heart." Similarly, comedian Jon Stewart profoundly misunderstood the demeanor of Secretary of Veteran Affairs Rick Shenseki's testimony before Congress when he said, apropos the Japanese-American Secretary's comment concerning possible falsification of records, that he was "mad as hell"—"Your 'mad as hell' face looks a lot like your 'Oh, we're out of orange juice' face" (Shear and Weisman 2014).

63. U.S. District Court, Eastern District of Virginia, 2001–2006. Trial transcript, April 13, 1006, p. 3,670.

64. Good 2007, 21–22 (the internal quote is from Conley and O'Barr, 1990).

65. This point is discussed in Rosen 1984, 165–79.

66. See Rosen 1989, 6–12. On Muslim judges turning parties loose to argue with one another in open court, in an attempt on the judge's part to gauge the intensity of their attachments, see chap. 1 above.

67. U.S. District Court, Eastern District of Virginia, 2001–2006. Trial transcript, April 13, 2006, p. 3,691, lines 8–9.

68. "Education: The Great Trial" 1925.

69. Barakat 2008b.

70. See Peters 2013.

71. In more recent years Judge Brinkema has been less prone to side with the government in security cases. For example, she quashed a subpoena that would have required an author to reveal his source in a matter relating to Iran's development of nuclear power (Savage 2011). Whether the distrust she expressed of government actions in the Moussaoui case affected this decision is not indicated.

72. Lithwick 2006. A broader criticism has been raised by retired Supreme Court Justice John Paul Stevens (2014) who wants to abolish the death penalty by constitutional amendment in part because he says that the way the Court has construed the rules of evidence and procedure favor the prosecution and thus make the imposition of the death penalty easier than it should be.

73. Rosenthal 2012.

74. A CNN legal analyst noted that Moussaoui's guilty plea "makes little sense." "Moussaoui may have actually had a chance to be proven not guilty because of the many thorny legal issues his case raises (two suspected members of the al-Qaeda Hamburg cell have been found not guilty in German courts because they have not been allowed access to testimony from al-Qaeda prisoners who might exonerate them), and Moussaoui so far has been denied access to those same prisoners" (Dorf 2005).

75. Lindner 2006. Dahlia Lithwick (2006), legal analyst for *Slate* said: "But again, as recently as last week, Brinkema was telling the prosecutors that she had real problems with their constitutional theory here, with their criminal theory. And that, to quote her, 'I don't know of a case where the failure to act is a basis for the death penalty.' And the allegation that Moussaoui had some duty to come forward and tell the FBI everything he knew about the plots is just not a sound theory on which to kill someone."

76. United States v. Moussaoui 2008, 30. See U.S. District Court, Eastern District of Virginia, 2001–2006. Trial transcript, April 22, 2005, p. 30, lines 5–12. The hearing of April 22 has a full account by Moussaoui of his relationships with his attorneys, Judge Brinkema having given him an expansive opportunity to tell his version of this story, particularly his desire for a Muslim attorney.

77. This was one of the reasons they urged him not to plead guilty, though they could not reveal to him this basis for their recommendation. Trial transcript, p. 17.

78. "You won't even organize a hearing to hear my very rational reason why I oppose these people to be my lawyer" (Trial transcript, March 27, 2006, p. 5, lines 21–23).

79. The holdout juror was, however, never identified to his fellow jurors at the time of their deliberations, all balloting being anonymous. Dwyer 2006b.

80. Barakat 2008a. For other comments by one of the jurors, see Markon and Dwyer 2006. While teaching at the National Judicial College, I learned that a number of state court trial judges actually meet with the whole jury panel after they have rendered their verdict. Jurors, I was told, are not asking whether the judge agrees with their verdict but whether their decision seemed to the judge to be within the realm of the acceptable. They need a sense of closure, several judges said.

81. Interestingly in 2015 Brinkema gave former CIA agent Jeffrey Sterling a far lighter sentence than expected for sharing classified material with a *New York Times* reporter, indicating in her ruling that the federal guidelines for sentencing in such cases were set too high (Maass 2015).

82. In Wilkinson v. Austin (2005), with Justice Kennedy writing the unanimous opinion, the U.S. Supreme Court held that while an inmate has a liberty interest under the Due Process Clause of the Fourteenth Amendment not to be automatically confined to a maximum security prison, Ohio's procedures for determining

which prisoners should be placed there did not show that such incarceration would be excessive, did not interfere with the inmate's potential appeals, and did further a legitimate penal goal. However, in the Virginia case before her (Prieto v. Clarke 2013), Judge Brinkema ruled that these criteria were not met:

> Plaintiff's conditions of confinement on death row are undeniably extreme. He must remain alone in his cell for nearly 23 hours per day. The lights never go out in his cell, although they are scaled back during the overnight hours. Plaintiff is allowed just five hours of outdoor recreation per week, and that time is spent in another cell at best slightly larger than his living quarters. He otherwise has no ability to catch a glimpse of the sky because the window in his cell is a window in name only. Nor can he pass the time in the company of other inmates; plaintiff is deprived of most forms of human contact. His only real break from the monotony owes to a television and compact disc player in his cell and limited interactions with prison officials. Such dehumanizing conditions are eerily reminiscent of those at the maximum-security prison in *Wilkinson*. . . . The Court likewise finds it significant that plaintiff has already spent five years in this placement, and there is no end in sight. Plaintiff has not even begun federal post-conviction proceedings, which are likely to play out over the course of several years and further delay the carrying out of his sentence. For all practical purposes, his placement "is for an indefinite period of time."
>
> The crucial fact in such a case, she said, is "the overwhelming fact of isolation—plaintiff is left alone in a small cell for nearly every hour of every day" (Moshenberg 2014).

What Judge Brinkema did not add is that the "eerily reminiscent" conditions to which she refers are precisely those to which she condemned Zacarias Moussaoui. Justice Kennedy, who wrote the Wilkinson opinion, later testified before Congress that solitary confinement "literally drives men mad" (New York Times Editorial Board 2015). Then, in a concurring opinion in a death penalty case (Davis v. Ayala 2015), Kennedy sharply criticized solitary confinement generally. Prieto was executed before his case could be heard by the U.S. Supreme Court.

83. James E. Aiken, a former warden, thus testified:

> A. What the mission is here is incapacitation. What we're talking about here is incapacitation.
>
> Q. When you say incapacitation, can you give the jury a picture of what he is going to be looking at?
>
> A. He is going to be looking at four walls, a toilet, a sink, a slab of concrete with a mattress on it and a stool made out of

concrete. He is going to be allowed to see sunshine, based on his behavior. And he is going to stay that way. It is going to be constant.

. . .

Q. Now, if I read you correctly, Mr. Moussaoui is not going to have an opportunity to sit and talk with staff while he is locked up?

A. Well, he can talk. There will be interactions, but nobody is there to make friends with him. He is going to be checked for his psychological well-being, his medical well-being. He is going to be checked to ensure that he remains stable. And that's in quotations, because he will deteriorate. He will deteriorate. And he would eventually come to a realization. Time takes a toll on all of us, especially in a high-security, high-pressure situation like that. Something that he doesn't even know yet. But I have been in this business well over 30 years and I have seen them rot, they rot" (U.S. District Court, Eastern District of Virginia, 2001–2006. Trial transcript, April 13, 2006, pp. 3,559–61).

Atul Gawande (2009) writes:

> In 1995, a federal court reviewing California's first supermax admitted that the conditions "hover on the edge of what is humanly tolerable for those with normal resilience." But it did not rule them to be unconstitutionally cruel or unusual, except in cases of mental illness. The prison's supermax conditions, the court stated, did not pose 'a sufficiently high risk to all inmates of incurring a serious mental illness.' In other words, there could be no legal objection to its routine use, given that the isolation didn't make *everyone* crazy. The ruling seemed to fit the public mood. By the end of the nineteen-nineties, some sixty supermax institutions had opened across the country. And new solitary-confinement units were established within nearly all of our ordinary maximum-security prisons. The number of prisoners in these facilities has since risen to extraordinary levels. America now holds at least twenty-five thousand inmates in isolation in supermax prisons. An additional fifty to eighty thousand are kept in restrictive segregation units, many of them in isolation, too, although the government does not release these figures. . . . It is unclear how many prisoners in solitary confinement become psychotic. Stuart Grassian, a Boston psychiatrist, has interviewed more than two hundred prisoners in solitary confinement. In one in-depth study, prepared for a legal challenge of prisoner-isolation practices, he concluded that about a third developed acute psychosis with hallucinations.

See also Binelli 2015; Dayan 2011, chap. 3; Will 2011; Ravindran 2014; Rideau 2013 (psychological effects described by man held in solitary for twelve years); and U.S. Department of Justice 2016.

Solitary confinement in American prisons has a curious history. In 1831, as part of his study of American prisons, Alexis de Tocqueville visited the Eastern State Penitentiary in Philadelphia. The Quakers, who had opened the prison two years earlier, believed that long-term solitary confinement was an ideal form of religious penitence (whence the term *penitentiary*) and would hasten prisoners' rehabilitation and reintegration into society. They saw it not as extreme punishment but as a progressive idea, far preferable to the giant holding pens typical of the age, where mutilations and violence among prisoners were common, and spiritual betterment all but unthinkable.

Tocqueville was favorably impressed. "Can there be a combination more powerful for reformation," he wrote, "than that of a prison which hands over the prisoner to all the trials of solitude, leads him through reflection to remorse, through religion to hope, and makes him industrious by the burden of idleness?"

Ten years later, Dickens paid his own visit to Eastern State, and came away with a rather different opinion. Solitary confinement, he found, inflicted unimaginable torment on the minds of those subjected to it. Far from leading prisoners to enlightenment, it ruined their concentration and haunted them with hideous visions. They fell into deep despair, losing track of time and of themselves. "I hold this slow and daily tampering with the mysteries of the brain, to be immeasurably worse than any torture of the body," he wrote in his *American Notes for General Circulation*: "Because its ghastly signs and tokens are not so palpable to the eye and sense of touch as scars upon the flesh; because its wounds are not upon the surface, and it extorts few cries that human ears can hear. . . . It wears the mind into a morbid state, which renders it unfit for the rough contact and busy action of the world" (Gumbel 2013).

84. A study by the Center on National Security at Fordham Law School of 391 terrorism cases found that 91% ended in conviction (Finn 2012). Most of the accused never went to trial but took plea deals. According to the New York University Center on Law and Security's Terrorism Trial Report Card (2011), 87% of terrorism indictments result in conviction (N=431), sentences being 8.5 times longer than for comparable non-terrorism crimes.

85. When U.S. Attorney General Eric H. Holder, Jr. sought to hold trials of some of the Guantánamo prisoners in New York, however, Congress passed legislation barring the use of such a venue. National Defense Authorization Act for Fiscal Year 2012, H.R. 1540 (112th Congress).

86. Judge Brinkema said of the attorney's actions that she had "never seen such an egregious violation of court's rules on witnesses," though she did praise the prosecution for bringing the matter to her attention and she did permit substitute aviation experts to testify.

87. Barakat 2008a. On July 29, 2011, Judge Brinkema also ruled against the government in the case of a *New York Times* reporter who refused to reveal his source for a story involving an unauthorized disclosure of information by a CIA agent (Savage 2011). The Fourth Circuit Court of Appeals overruled her decision on July 19, 2013, and the U.S. Supreme Court refused to hear the case.

88. Savage 2011. A former public defender told Seymour Hersch (2002) that the way the case was being conducted augured well for proponents of holding such cases before military rather than civilian courts, describing Judge Brinkema's courtroom in 2002 as "just a meltdown presided over by an incurious Judge who wants to get it moving"—a criticism which, when uttered by Moussaoui himself, was taken as an indication of his delusional state. For the argument that defendants like Moussaoui should be tried in special military tribunals, see the article by former deputy assistant attorney general (criminal division) and chief counsel for the Senate Select Committee on Intelligence Victoria Toensing 2010.

89. U.S. District Court, Eastern District of Virginia, 2005, April 22, p. 23.

90. Barakat 2008b.

91. The rules of evidence remain the same whether, as in this instance, the case is being tried to the bench or to a jury. It is as if, in their historical development, the rules assume the possibility of a jury, notwithstanding the fact that, particularly given plea bargaining, only a small fraction of criminal cases continues to be heard by a jury.

92. See my discussion of the cultural defense plea in Rosen 2017, chap. 1.

93. See Hessick 2006.

94. At Princeton Judge Brinkema said that she allows jurors to ask questions in civil cases, and though she would not be barred from allowing such questioning in criminal matters she does not permit it because it actually bolsters the prosecution's case insofar as jurors faced with an assertion by the prosecution then tend to think the defendant should be able to refute it when there is neither a legal nor always a logical way for him to prove a negative. She also told the organizer that if there should be a new trial she would recommend that someone familiar with Moussaoui's cultural background be put in touch with his new lawyers.

95. On rearranging the court in the Netherlands for trials of Turkish defendants, see Rossum 1996, 295–96.

96. The proceedings were not broadcast, but a purloined tape of Moussaoui's summation was put online. See Borchgrevink 2013.

97. See Rosen 2017.

98. Cunningham 1989, 2,491 and 2,493. Another scholar notes "that there are important practical lessons that attorneys should attend to. For example, we may begin to see that regardless of content, the form of one legal story may give it significantly more credibility than another story whose form fails to trigger any of the applicable tropes, narrative genres, and familiar storylines that are in our minds" (Sherwin 1994, 78).

99. U.S. District Court, Eastern District of Virginia, 2001–2006, Trial transcript, April 13, 2006, p. 3,629, lines 8–9.

100. Another report stated: "Moussaoui tried to get in the last word as he was led from the courtroom for the last time. 'I will be free, and my liberation will be proof that we are the soldiers of God, and you are the army of Satan. I will see you before the end of George W. Bush. Before his end, I will be out,' he said. Lisa Beilke, whose husband, Max, died in the Pentagon attack, replied, 'In your dreams'" (Hirschkorn 2006).

101. However, in October 2014 lawyers for survivors of the 9/11 attack interviewed Moussaoui for two days in his supermax prison where he asserted that members of Saudi Arabia's royal family were donors to the terrorist network in the late 1990s and that he had himself discussed with a member of the Saudi Embassy a plan to shoot down Air Force One with a Stinger missile. Lengthy solitary confinement does not seem to have driven Moussaoui insane: One of the attorneys participating in the deposition said, "My impression was that he was of completely sound mind—focused and thoughtful" (Shane 2015).

Epilogue

1. See Shklar 1992 and Greenhouse 1989.

2. Many of these points have been elaborated in Rosen 2000, 153–75; and Rosen 2008, 60–72.

3. Freamon 2005, chap. 2, p. 31. The contrast is thus quite sharp to that of "amoral familism" as described by Banfield 1958.

4. On varying the punishment depending on one's status, see, e.g., Liebesny 1975, 229.

5. Quoted in Maghen 2008, 331.

6. See Shakes 2015, 38, 61–62, and table 2 at p. 80 (74.6% of legal personnel surveyed disagree that forensic evidence is an important characteristic of Iraqi culture, whereas over 82% say that oral testimony is). See also Warnock 2010.

7. Goldberg 2011, 50.

8. The issue of person perception is more fully explored in Rosen 1984.

9. Indeed, some scholars believe the very concept of equality is highly problematic. See Westen 1982, Greenawalt 1983, and Westen 1983.

10. A telling example is supplied by what happened after the death of King Hassan II of Morocco in July 1999. People were lined up all over the country at post offices sending greetings to the new king. But they were sending their messages "return receipt requested" as a way of trying to establish a relationship to the new monarch in the nearest thing to a face-to-face manner.

11. For critiques of the rule of law approach, particularly in the cultures of the Middle East, see Carothers 1998 and 2010, and Esmaeli 2011.

12. Fallon 1997, 42–43.

13. Posner 1993, 48, quoted at Fallon 1997, 49–50.

14. Thompson 2013. For an overview of constitutionalism in Muslim countries, see Grote and Röder 2012.

15. See Rosen 2011a.

16. Feldman 2003. "Many Muslims, if freed to make their own democratic choices, will choose Islam over secularism. A case in point is the newly released draft of the Afghan constitution, which enshrines Islamic values even as it guarantees basic liberties." Feldman describes himself in the article as "a senior adviser for constitutional law to the Coalition Provisional Authority in Iraq." See also Feldman and Martinez 2006.

17. A translation of the constitution will be found at Tunisian Republic 2014. On the praise of foreign leaders, including France's Premier Hollande and President Obama, as well as the release of International Monetary Fund support following the constitution's adoption on January 26, 2014, see Foreign Leaders Hail Tunisian Constitution 2014.

18. Guellali 2014.

19. See Parolin 2013.

20. For example, in my analysis of Clifford Geertz's study of the marketplace in Sefrou, Morocco I suggest that, far from having never fully addressed religion's role in the social life of the society, it was in his study of the bazaar that Geertz positioned his study of Moroccan Islam. See Rosen 2010a.

21. See Withington 1991, Sinopoli 1992, Pangle 1990 and 2007, Signer 2015, Wood 1998, and Yarbrough 1998.

22. Quoted in Bailyn 2003, 34 and 124. Signer (2015, 272–73) recounts the remarks of Madison during the debate on ratification of the new constitution before the Virginia delegation in June 1788:

> He began by conceding that many gentlemen supposed the new Congress would do "every mischief they possible can." While he admitted that he did not expect the "most exalted integrity and sublime virtue" from the men in the new federal government, he proudly declared his faith notwithstanding in "this great republican principle": that the people would have "virtue and intelligence to select men of virtue and wisdom." He then pulled back the veil on the hidden cynicism in [Patrick] Henry's "self-love" doctrine. "Is there no virtue among us?" he demanded. Without virtue, he said, "We are in a wretched situation." No "theoretical checks" could save the country. Without "virtue in the people," even liberty itself was a "chimerical idea."

Notwithstanding their sharp differences, both the Federalists and the Anti-Federalists shared a conception of virtue and contested their viewpoints in no small part through this cultural category (see Pangle 1990 and 2007).

23. James Madison, in Hamilton, Madison, and Jay 1948 [1787–88], No. 55, p. 286. Benjamin Franklin, who said that "only a virtuous people are capable of freedom," gives, in his autobiography, a specific list of the features that comprise virtue. Similarly, John Adams wrote: "Virtuous principles eschew prejudice and discrimination, confirming that 'all men are created equal.' Virtue encompasses characteristics of goodwill, patience, tolerance, kindness, respect, humility, gratitude, courage, honor, industry, honesty, chastity and fidelity" (Adams 1854, 9: 229). Each of these concepts would, in turn, require unpacking.

24. "It was society that Jefferson and Paine always celebrated. Society, wrote Paine in the opening paragraph of *Common Sense*, 'promotes our happiness *positively* by uniting our affections.' Government acted only '*negatively* by restraining our vices.' To Jefferson and Paine government was a plunderer. All the evils in society—inequalities, privileges, social distinctions, monopolies, even excessive wealth and property—came from connections to government. This is why Jefferson and his followers believed that the government that governed least was best" (Wood 2014). See also Smith 1997.

25. Recall, in this regard, the description in chap. 5 of the mayor of Sefrou, Morocco, who garnered great popularity and support for his efforts at running a highly transparent administration.

26. See for Iraq, Makiya 2005 (arguing against allowing regional autonomy, which will serve "the interest of every popular demagogue").

27. Pratchett 2013.

28. Jay 1999, 25–26, referring to Horkheimer and Adorno 2007.

29. Harlan Lecture, Princeton University, March 3, 2011.

Bibliography

Aal, Ghada Abdel. 2010. *I Want to Get Married!* Austin: University of Texas Center for Middle East Studies.

Ababsa, Myriam, Baudouin Dupret, and Eric Denis, eds. 2012. *Popular Housing and Urban Land Tenure in the Middle East: Case Studies from Egypt, Syria, Jordan, Lebanon, and Turkey.* Cairo: American University in Cairo Press.

Abdal-Rehim, Abdal-Rehim Abdal-Rahman. 1996. "The Family and Gender Laws in Egypt during the Ottoman Period." In *Women, the Family, and Divorce Laws in Islamic History*, edited by Amira El Azhary Sonbol, 96–111. Syracuse, NY: Syracuse University Press.

Abdelkader, Engy. 2014. "To Judge or Not to Judge: A Comparative Analysis of Islam Jurisprudential Approaches to Female Judges in the Muslim World (Indonesia, Egypt and Iran)." *Fordham International Law Journal* 37: 310–72.

Abdennebi, Zakia. 2014. "Morocco Bans Judges' Protest, Riot Police Close Streets in Capital." *Reuters*, February 8. http://www.reuters.com/article/us-morocco-justice-protest-idUSBREA170IE20140208 (accessed January 6, 2017).

Abou Ramadan, Moussa. 2002. "The Transition from Tradition to Reform: The *Shari'a* Appeals Court Rulings on Child Custody (1992–2001)." *Fordham International Law Journal* 26, no. 3: 595–655.

———. 2003. "Judicial Activism of the Shari'ah Appeals Court in Israel (1994–2001): Rise and Crisis." *Fordham International Law Journal* 27: 254–98.

———. 2006a. "Divorce Reform in the Sharī'a Court of Appeals in Israel (1992–2003)." *Islamic Law and Society* 13, no. 2: 242–74.

———. 2006b. "Islamic Legal Reform: Sharī'a Court of Appeals and Maintenance for Muslim Wives in Israel." *Hawwa* 4, no. 1: 29–75.

Abramson, Larry. 2005. "Transcript Details Moussaoui's Talk with Judge." April 28. www.npr.org/templates/story/story.php?storyId=4622789 (accessed January 6, 2017).

Abul-Magd, Zeinab. 2012. "Occupying Tahrir Square: The Myths and the Realities of the Egyptian Revolution." *South Atlantic Quarterly* 111, no. 3: 565–72.

Adam, André. 1949–50. "Le 'Bidonville' de Ben M'sik à Casablanca." *Annales de l'Institut d'Études Orientales* 8: 61–198.

Adams, Charles Francis, ed. 1854. *The Works of John Adams, Second President of the United States*. Boston: Little, Brown, and Co.

Afary, Janet. 2009. *Sexual Politics in Modern Iran*. Cambridge: Cambridge University Press.

Afshar, Haleh. 1998. *Islam and Feminisms*. London: Macmillan.

Agmon, Iris. 1996. "Muslim Women in Court According to the *Sijil* of Late Ottoman Jaffa and Haifa." In *Women, the Family, and Divorce Laws in Islamic History*, edited by Amira El Azhary Sonbol, 126–40. Syracuse, NY: Syracuse University Press.

———. 2003. "Text, Court, and Family in Late-Nineteenth-Century Palestine." In *Family History in the Middle East*, edited by Beshara Doumani, 201–28. Albany: State University of New York Press.

———. 2006. *Family and Court: Legal Culture and Modernity in Late Ottoman Palestine.* Syracuse, NY: Syracuse University Press.

Agmon, Iris, and Ido Shahar. 2008. "Shifting Perspectives in the Study of Shari'a Courts: Methodologies and Paradigms." *Islamic Law and Society* 15, no. 1: 1–19.

Agoumy, Taoufik. 1997. "The Eradication of the Shantytowns in Morocco." *DOMES: Digest of Middle East Studies* 6, no. 1: 24–32.

Agrama, Hussein Ali. 2012. *Questioning Secularism: Islam, Sovereignty, and the Rule of Law in Modern Egypt.* Chicago: University of Chicago Press.

Ahdar, Rex, and Nicholas Aroney. 2011. *Shari'a in the West*. Oxford: Oxford University Press.

Ahmed, Azam. 2015. "Taliban Justice Gains Favor as Official Afghan Courts Fail." *New York Times*, January 31.

Ahmed, Laila. 2013. "The Perceived Oppression of Muslim Women Is Used to Justify Islamophobia." In *Islamophobia*, edited by Dedria Bryfonski, 54–58. New York: Greenhaven Press/Gale Cengage.

Ahram Online. 2014. "Almost a Fifth of Egyptian Households Are Headed by Women." English.ahram.org.eg/NewsContent/3/12/101284/Business/Economy/Almost-a-fifth-of-Egyptian-households-are-headed-b.aspx (accessed January 6, 2017).

"Algeria: 20 Years Is Enough." n.d. http://www.wluml.org/sites/wluml.org/files/Family%20code%20in%20Algeria%20-%20comment%20piece.pdf (accessed January 6, 2017).

Ali, Kecia. 2003. "Progressive Muslims and Islamic Jurisprudence: The Necessity for Critical Engagement with Marriage and Divorce Law." In *Progressive Muslims: On Justice, Gender, and Pluralism*, edited by Omid Safi, 161–82. Oxford: Oneworld.

Ali, Syed. 2010. *Dubai: Gilded Cage*. New Haven, CT: Yale University Press.

al-Khowli, Ramadan. 2005. "Observations on the Use of *Shari'a* Court Records as a Source of Social History." In *Beyond the Exotic: Women's Histories in Islamic Societies*, edited by Amira el-Azhary Sonbol, 139–51. Syracuse, NY: Syracuse University Press.

Al Monitor. 2014. "Morocco's Inheritance Dilemma." February 9. http://www.almonitor.com/pulse/culture/2014/02/morocco-debate-inheritance-law-women.html (accessed January 6, 2017).

Al-Qattan, Najwa. 1997. "The Fullness of Affection: Mothering in the Islamic Law of Ottoman Syria and Palestine." In *Women in the Ottoman Empire*, edited by Madeline C. Zilfi, 232–52. Leiden: Brill.

———. 1999. "*Dhimmīs* in the Muslim Court: Legal Autonomy and Religious Discrimination." *International Journal of Middle East Studies* 31: 429–44.

Al-Sharmani, Mulki. 2009. "Egyptian Family Courts: A Pathway of Women's Empowerment?" *Hawwa* 7, no. 2: 89–110.

———. 2012. "Egyptian *Khul*: Legal Reform, Courtroom Practices, and Realities of Women." In *Interpreting Divorce Laws in Islam*, edited by Rubya Mehdi, Werner Menski, and Jørgen S. Nielsen, 85–104. Copenhagen: DJØF.

———. 2013. "*Qiwāma* in Egyptian Family Laws: 'Wifely Obedience' between Legal Texts, Courtroom Practices and Realities of Marriages." In *Gender and Equality in Muslim Family Law*, edited by Ziba Mir-Hosseini et al., 37–55. London: I. B. Tauris.

Amar, Paul. 2013. *Dispatches from the Arab Spring: Understanding the New Middle East.* Minneapolis: University of Minnesota Press.

Amnesty International. 2014. "Proposed Laws Reduce Iranian Women to 'Baby Making Machines' in Misguided Attempts to Boost Population." March 11. http://www.amnestyusa.org/news/press-releases/proposed-laws-reduce-iranian-women-to-%E2%80%98baby-making-machines-in-misguided-attempts-to-boost-populatio (accessed January 6, 2017).

Amos, Deborah. 2011. *Eclipse of the Sunnis: Power, Exile, and Upheaval in the Middle East.* Washington, DC: Public Affairs.

Anonymous. 2014. "Egypt's Housing Crisis Makes Marriage a Luxury." *Al-Monitor*, August 4. http://www.al-monitor.com/pulse/culture/2014/08/httpalhayatcomarticles3828731.html# (accessed January 6, 2017).

Anonymous. 2015. "The No. 1 Mullahs Dating Agency." *Economist*, February 7.

Anonymous. 2016. "Reading Piketty on the Nile." *Economist*, February 6, p. 76.

Antoun, Richard T. 1990. "Litigant Strategies in an Islamic Court in Jordan." In *Law and Islam in the Middle East*, edited by Daisy Hilse Dwyer, 35–60. New York: Bergin & Garvey.

Anwar, Zainah. 2008. "Advocacy for Reform in Islamic Family Law: The Experience of Sisters in Islam." In *The Islamic Marriage Contract: Case Studies in Islamic Family Law*, edited by Asifa Quraishi and Frank E. Vogel, 275–84. Cambridge, MA: Islamic Legal Studies Program, Harvard Law School.

Apellániz, Francisco 2016. "Judging the Franks: Proof, Justice, and Diversity in Late Medieval Alexandria and Damascus." *Comparative Studies in Society and History* 58, no. 2: 350–75.

Arab Law Quarterly. 1999. *Arab Law Quarterly* 14, no. 3: 191–301.

Arabi, Oussama. 2001. "The Itinerary of a *Fatwā*: Ambulant Marriage (*al-Zawāj al-Misyār*), or Grass Roots Law-Making in Saudi Arabia of the 1990s." In *Studies in Modern Islamic Law and Jurisprudence*, 147–67. The Hague: Kluwer Law International.

Arango, Tim. 2012. "Where Arranged Marriages Are Customary, Suicides Grow More Common." *New York Times*, June 6.

Archbishop of Canterbury. 2008. "Archbishop's Lecture: Civil and Religious Law in England: A Religious Perspective." February 7. http://rowanwilliams.archbishop ofcanterbury.org/articles.php/1137/archbishops-lecture-civil-and-religious-law -in-england-a-religious-perspective (accessed January 6, 2017).

Aristotle. 1932. *Politics*. Trans. by H. Rackham. Cambridge, MA: Harvard University Press Loeb Classical Library.

ASDA'A Burson-Marsteller Arab Youth Survey 2014. 2014. http://burson-mars teller.eu/innovation-insights/arab-youth-survey/ (accessed January 6, 2017).

Associated Press. 2012a. "Morocco's Judges Demand Greater Independence." *Al Arabiya News*, May 15. http://english.alarabiya.net/articles/2012/05/15/214343.html (accessed January 6, 2017).

———. 2012b. "Judges in Morocco Lead Sit-In Calling for Autonomous Judiciary." *New York Times*, October 6.

———. 2016. "New Law in Algeria Punishes Violence against Women." February 2. http://www.cbsnews.com/news/new-law-in-algeria-punishes-violence-against -women/ (accessed January 6, 2017).

Atwan, Abdel Bari. 2015. *Islamic State: The Digital Caliphate*. London: Saqi.

Baderin, Mashood A. 2014. *Islamic Law in Practice*. London: Routledge.

Bailyn, Bernard. 2003. *To Begin the World Anew: The Genius and Ambiguities of the American Founders*. New York: Alfred A. Knopf.

Bakhadda, Fadoua. 2014. "How NGOs Helped Change Moroccan Law on Rapists Marrying Their Victims." *Guardian* (London), February 7.

Banfield, Edward C. 1958. *The Moral Basis of a Backward Society*. Glencoe, IL: Free Press.

Bano, Samia. 2012. *Muslim Women and Shari'ah Councils*. London: Palgrave Macmillan.

Barakat, Matthew. 2008a. "Judge to Moussaoui Jury: You Got It Right." *USA Today*, July 23. http://usatoday30.USAToday.com/news/nation/2008-07-23-356 2612326_x.htm (accessed January 6, 2017).

———. 2008b. "Moussaoui Judge: Terror Trials Work." *USA Today*, February 1. http://usatoday30.usatoday.com/news/nation/2008-02-01-88957434_x.htm (accessed January 6, 2017).

Bar'el, Zvi. 2017. "Tahrir Square, from Place to Space: The Geography of Resistance." *Middle East Journal* 71, no. 1: 9–22.

Bargach, Jamila. 2005. "An Ambiguous Discourse of Rights: The 2004 Family Law Reform in Morocco." *Hawwa* 3, no. 2: 245–66.

Barr, Heather. 2013. "In Afghanistan, Women Betrayed." *New York Times*, December 10.

Basel, Marzia, and Dana Michael Hollywood. 2005–2006. "Under a Cruel Sun: My Life as a Female Judge and Underground Educator under the Soviets, the Taliban, and the Americans." *William and Mary Journal of Women and the Law* 12: 205–38.

Bauer, Karen. 2010. "Debates on Women's Status as Judges and Witnesses in Post-formative Islamic Law." *Journal of the American Oriental Society* 130, no. 1: 1–21.

Beaumont, Peter. 2011. "Mohammed Bouazizi: The Dutiful Son Whose Death Changed Tunisia's Fate." *Guardian* (London), January 20.

———. 2016. "Netanyahu Plans Fence around Israel to Protect It from 'Wild Beasts'." *The Guardian* (London), February 10.

Behar, Cem. 2004. "Neighborhood Nuptials: Islamic Personal Law and Local Customs: Marriage Records in a *Mahalle* of Traditional Istanbul (1864–1907)." *International Journal of Middle East Studies* 36: 537–59.

Belkeziz, Abdelilah. 2012. "Morocco and Democratic Transition: A Reading of the Constitutional Amendments; Their Context and Results." *Contemporary Arab Affairs* 5, no. 1: 27–53.

Benhalima, Hassan. 1987. *Petites villes traditionnelles et mutations socio-economiques au Maroc: Le cas de Sefrou*. Rabat, Morocco: Publications de la faculté des lettres et des sciences humaines de Rabat, Université Mohammed V.

Ben Jelloun, Tahar. 1995. *Corruption*. New York: New Press.

Bennett, Naftali. 2014. "For Israel, Two-State Is No Solution." *New York Times*, November 5.

Bernard-Maugiron, Nathalie, and Baudoin Dupret. 2008. "Breaking Up the Family: Divorce in Egyptian Law and Practice." *Hawwa* 6, no. 1: 52–74.

Berque, Jacques 1958. *Al-Yousi*. Paris: Mouton & Co.

Billaud, Julie. 2014. "Ethics and Affects in British Sharia Councils: 'A Simple Way of Getting to Paradise'." In *Islam and Public Controversy in Europe*, edited by Nilüfer Göle, 159–72. Farnham, Surrey, UK: Ashgate.

Binelli, Mark. 2015. "Inside America's Toughest Federal Prison." *New York Times*, March 26.

Bingham, John. 2014. "Islamic Law Is Adopted by British Legal Chiefs." *The Telegraph*, March 22. http://www.telegraph.co.uk/news/religion/10716844/Islamic-law-is-adopted-by-British-legal-chiefs.html (accessed January 6, 2017).

"Bin Laden Purportedly Says Moussaoui Had Nothing to Do with Sept. 11." 2006. *USA Today*, May 23.

Bishara, Marwan 2013. *The Invisible Arab: The Promise and Peril of the Arab Revolutions.* New York: Nation Books.

Bohn, Lauren. 2013. "Egypt's Marriage Crisis: Sons and Daughters Too Broke to Be Married, Waiting for Adulthood." *NBC News*, December 8. http://www.nbcnews.com/news/other/egypts-marriage-crisis-sons-daughters-too-broke-be-married-waiting-f2D11711756 (accessed January 6, 2017).

Boon, James A. 1982. *Other Tribes, Other Scribes.* New York: Cambridge University Press.

Borchgrevink, Aage. 2013. *A Norwegian Tragedy: Anders Behring Breivik and the Massacre at Utøya.* Cambridge: Polity.

Boukaissi, Fatima Zohra. 2007. "Du déroulement des audience à la justice de la famille près les tribunaux de la première instance de Rabat." In *Le code de la famille: Perceptions et practique judiciaire*, edited by Malika Benradi et al., 189–216. Fez: Friedrich Ebert Stiftung.

Boum, Aomar. 2013. *Memories of Absence: How Muslims Remember Jews in Morocco.* Stanford, CA: Stanford University Press.

Bowen, John R. 2003. *Islam, Law and Equality in Indonesia.* Cambridge: Cambridge University Press.

———. 2007. "Fairness and Law in an Indonesian Court." In *Islamic Law in Indonesia*, edited by R. Michael Feener and Mark E. Cammack, 170–92. Cambridge, MA: Islamic Legal Studies Program, Harvard Law School.

———. 2010. "How Could English Courts Recognize Shariah?" *St. Thomas Law Journal* 7, no. 3: 411–35.

———. 2013. "Sanctity and Shariah: Two Islamic Modes of Resolving Disputes in Today's England." In *Religion in Disputes: Persuasiveness of Religious Normativity in Disputing Processes*, edited by Franz von Benda-Beckmann et al., 129–45. London: Palgrave Macmillan.

Brand, Laurie A. 1998. *Women, the State, and Political Liberalization: Middle Eastern and North African Experiences.* New York: Columbia University Press.

Bravmann, Meir M. 1962. "'The Surplus of Property': An Early Arab Social Concept." *Der Islam* 38: 28–50.

Bronner, Ethan. 2014. "For Israelis and Palestinians, Separation Is Dehumanizing." *New York Times*, July 11.

BTI Transformation Index 2016. http://www.bti-project.org/en/index/overview/ (accessed January 6, 2017).

Büchler, Andrea. 2011. *Islamic Law in Europe: Legal Pluralism and Its Limits in European Family Law.* Farnham, Surrey, UK: Ashgate.

Bukhari, M. Saleem. 1982. "Squatting and the Use of Islamic Law." *Habitat International* 6, nos. 5–6: 555–63.

"Burgeoning Bourgeosie." 2009. *Economist*, February 12.

Burke, Edmund III. 1986. "Understanding Arab Protest Movements." *Maghreb Review* 11, no. 1: 27–32.

Bustamam-Ahmad, Kamaruzzaman. 2009. *Islamic Law in Southeast Asia: A Study of Its Application in Kelantan and Aceh*. Chiang Mai, Thailand: Silkworm Books.

Buttoo, Sanjay. 2008. "Some Imams 'Biased against Women.'" *BBC News*, December 15.

Cagaptay, Soner. 2013. "The Middle Class Strikes Back." *New York Times*, June 5.

Cambanis, Thanassis. 2015. *Once upon a Revolution: An Egyptian Story*, New York: Simon & Schuster.

Cammack, Mark E., Helen Donovan, and Tim B. Heaton. 2007. "Islamic Divorce Law and Practice in Indonesia." In *Islamic Law in Contemporary Indonesia*, edited by R. Michael Feener and Mark E. Cammack, 99–127. Cambridge, MA: Islamic Legal Studies Program, Harvard Law School.

Cammack, Mark E., and Tim B. Heaton. 2011. "Explaining the Recent Upturn in Divorce in Indonesia: Developmental Idealism and the Effect of Political Change." *Asian Journal of Social Science* 39, no. 6: 776–96.

Campbell, Elizabeth A., and Isabella Z. Guiao. 2004. "Muslim Culture and Female Self-Immolation." *Health Care for Women International* 29, no. 5: 782–93.

Cardinal, Monique C. 2010. "Why Aren't Women Sharīʿa Court Judges? The Case of Syria." *Islamic Law and Society* 17:185–214.

Carlisle, Jessica. 2007a. "'*Asbab L'Il-Darb Ktir Basita*': The Legality of Claims of Violence during Judicial Divorce Cases in Damascus." *Hawwa* 5, nos. 2–3: 239–61.

———. 2007b. "Mother Love: A Forced Divorce in Damascus." *Anthropology of the Middle East* 2, no. 1: 89–102.

———. 2007c. "Raconter des Histoires: L'arbitrage des Demandes de Divorce Judiciaire à Damas." In *La Syrie au présent*, 661–70, edited by Baudouin Dupret et al. Paris: Sindbad.

———. 2008. "From Behind the Door: A Damascus Court Copes with an Alleged Out of Court Marriage." In *Les métamorphoses du marriage au Moyen-Orient*, edited by Barbara Drieskens, 59–74. Beirut: Institut français du Proche-Orient.

———. 2013. "Moroccan Divorce Law, Family Court Judges and Spouses' Claims: Who Pays the Cost When the Marriage Is Over?" In *Feminist Activism, Women's Rights and Legal Reform*, edited by Mulki Al-Sharmani, 151–76. London: Zed.

Carothers, Thomas. 1998. "The Rule of Law Revival." *Foreign Affairs* (March/April): 95–106.

Carrington, Daisy. 2013. "Meet Saudi Arabia's First Female Lawyer." *CNN News*, May 9. http://www.cnn.com/2013/05/09/business/saudi-arabia-first-female-lawyer/ (accessed January 6, 2017).

Chaudhry, Ayesha S. 2014. *Domestic Violence and the Islamic Tradition*. Oxford: Oxford University Press.

Chemais, Amina. 1987. "Le divorce de la femme en droit musulman: Le cas de l'Égypte." Doctorat d'état diss., Université de droit, d'économie et des sciences sociales de Paris (Paris II).

———. 1996. "Obstacles to Divorce for Muslim Women in Egypt." In *Shifting Boundaries in Marriage and Divorce in Muslim Communities*, edited by Homa Hoodfar, Special Dossier 1: 52–74. Grabels, France: Women Living under Muslim Laws.

Christelow, Allan. 1985. *Muslim Law Courts and the French Colonial State in Algeria*. Princeton, NJ: Princeton University Press.

Clarke, Morgan. 2012. "The Judge as Tragic Hero: Judicial Ethics in Lebanon's Shari'a Courts." *American Ethnologist* 39, no. 1: 106–21.

Cody, Edward. 2012. "New Arab Order: In Morocco, Uproar over Marriage Law Tests Islamist Government." *Washington Post*, April 15.

Cohen, Amnon. 1984. *Jewish Life under Islam: Jerusalem in the Sixteenth Century*. Cambridge, MA: Harvard University Press.

Cohen, Roger. 2016. "The Arab Withering." *New York Times*, May 12.

Cole, Juan. 2014. *The New Arabs: How the Millennial Generation Is Changing the Middle East*. New York: Simon & Schuster.

Colla, Elliott. 2013. "In Praise of Insult: Slogan Genres, Slogan Repertoires and Innovation." *Review of Middle Eastern Studies* 47, no. 1: 37–48.

"Colleagues Question $5M Moussaoui Reward." 2008. *USA Today*, January 25. http://usatoday30.usatoday.com/news/nation/2008-01-25-moussaoui-reward_N.htm (accessed January 6, 2017).

Conley, John M., and William M. O'Barr. 1990. *Rules versus Relationships: The Ethnography of Legal Discourse*. Chicago: University of Chicago Press.

Corbin, Jane. 2013. "Are Sharia Councils Failing Vulnerable Women?" *BBC News*, April 6.

"Corruption in Afghanistan, Bribery as Reported by the Victims." 2010. United Nations Office on Drugs and Crime. January. http://www.unodc.org/documents/data-and-analysis/Afghanistan/Afghanistan-corruption-survey2010-Eng.pdf (accessed January 6, 2017).

"Corruption in Afghanistan: Patterns and Trends." 2012. United Nations Office on Drugs and Crime. http://www.unodc.org/documents/frontpage/Corruption_in_Afghanistan_FINAL.pdf (accessed January 6, 2017).

Coser, Lewis A. 1968. "Class." In *Dictionary of the History of Ideas*, edited by Philip P. Weiner, 441–49. New York: Charles Scribner's Sons.

Coulson, Noel. 1964. *A History of Islamic Law*. Edinburgh: Edinburgh University Press.

Cover, Robert M. 1987. "Obligation: A Jewish Jurisprudence of the Social Order." *Journal of Law and Religion* 5, no. 1: 65–74.

Crone, Patricia. 2003. *Pre-Industrial Societies*. London: Oneworld.

Cunningham, Clark D. 1989. "A Tale of Two Clients: Thinking about Law as Language." *Michigan Law Review* 87, no. 8: 2459–94.

Cunningham, Robert B., and Yasin K. Sarayrah. 1993. *Wasta: The Hidden Force in Middle Eastern Society*. Westport, CT: Praeger.

Davis, John. 1998. Introduction to *Legal Documents on Libyan Tribal Society in Process of Sedentarization* by Aharon Layish. Wiesbaden, Germany: Harrassowitz Verlag.

Davis, Susan S. 1983. *Patience and Power: Women's Lives in a Moroccan Village*. Cambridge, MA: Schenkman.

Davis v. Ayala. 2015. 135 S. Ct. 2187.

Dayan, Colin. 2011. *The Law Is a White Dog: How Legal Rituals Make and Unmake Persons*, chapter 3. Princeton, NJ: Princeton University Press.

Dehghan, Saeed Kamali. 2015. "Amineh Bahrami: Was I Right to Pardon the Man Who Blinded Me with Acid?" *The Guardian* (London), April 26.

DeJoria v. Maghreb Petroleum. 2014. 38 F.Supp.3d 805 (W.D. TX), reversed, 804 F.3d 373 (5th Cir. 2015).

De Lauri, Antonio. 2011. "Afghanistan: Corruption and Injustice in the Judicial System." *Journal of Law and Social Research* 2, no. 1: 45–60.

Denniston, Lyle. 2005. "Moussaoui Pleads Guilty, Plea Accepted." SCOTUSblog (Supreme Court of the United States Blog). April 22. http://www.scotusblog.com/2005/04/moussaoui-pleads-guilty-plea-accepted/ (accessed January 6, 2017).

Diab, Rasha. 2016. *Shades of Sulh: The Rhetorics of Arab-Islamic Reconciliation*. Pittsburgh, PA: University of Pittsburgh Press.

Diamond, Larry. 2014. "Postscript: From Activism to Democracy." In *Taking to the Streets: The Transformation of Arab Activism*, edited by Lina Khatib and Ellen Lust, 322–34. Baltimore: Johns Hopkins University Press.

Djamour, Judith. 1966. *The Muslim Matrimonial Court in Singapore*. London: Athlone.

Donahue, Katherine C. 2007. *Slaves of Allah: Zacarias Moussaoui vs. the USA*. London: Pluto Press.

———. 2008. "The Religious Trajectories of the Moussaoui Family." *International Institute for the Study of Islam in the Modern World (ISIM)*, no. 21: 18–19.

Dorf, Michael C. 2005. "Why Zacarias Moussaoui's Guilty Plea Likely Won't Spare His Life." *Special to CNN*, April 28. www.cnn.com/2005/LAW/04/28/dorf.moussaoui/ (accessed January 6, 2017).

Dorsey, James M. 2016. *The Turbulent World of Middle East Soccer*. http://mideastsoccer.blogspot.com/ (accessed January 6, 2017).

Doumani, Beshara. 2003. "Adjudicating Family: The Islamic Court and Disputes between Kin in Greater Syria, 1700–1860." In *Family History in the Middle* East, edited by Beshara Doumani, 173–200. Albany: State University of New York Press.

"Drama on Tahrir Square." 2011. *Time*, February 3. http://content.time.com/time/photogallery/0,29307,2046351_2233426,00.html (accessed January 6, 2017).

Drieskens, Barbara. 2006. " 'A Cairene Way of Reconciling.' " *Islamic Law and Society* 13, no. 1: 99–122.

———. 2008. *Living with Djinns: Understanding and Dealing with the Invisible in Cairo*. London: Saqi.

Dupret, Baudouin. 2006. "The Practice of Judging: The Egyptian Judiciary at Work in a Personal Status Case." In *Dispensing Justice in Islam*, edited by Muhammad Khalid Masud, Rudolph Peters, and David S. Powers, 143–68. Leiden: Brill.

Dupret, Baudoin, Maurits Berger, and Laila al-Zwaini. 1999. *Legal Pluralism in the Arab World*. Alphen aan den Rijn, Netherlands: Kluwer International.

Dwyer, Daisy Hilse. 1977. "Bridging the Gap between the Sexes in Moroccan Legal Practice." In *Sexual Stratification: A Cross-cultural View*, edited by Alice Schlegel, 41–66. New York: Columbia University Press.

Dwyer, Timothy. 2006a. "A Firm Grip on the Gavel." *Washington Post*, March 17.

———. 2006b. "One Juror between Terrorist and Death." *Washington Post*, May 12.

Eberstadt, Nicholas, and Apoorva Shah. 2011. "Fertility Decline in the Muslim World: A Veritable Sea-Change, Still Curiously Unnoticed." *American Enterprise Institute, Working Paper Series on Development Policy*, no. 7, December.

Edge, Ian. 1989. "Egyptian Family Law: The Tale of the *Jinn*." *International and Comparative Law Quarterly* 38, no. 3: 682–85.

"Education: The Great Trial." 1925. *Time*, July 20.

Eisenberg, Ann M. 2011. "Law on the Books vs. Law in Action: Under-Enforcement of Morocco's Reformed 2004 Family Law, the *Moudawana*." *Cornell International Law Journal* 44: 693–728.

Elass, Rasha. 2009. "Islamic Family Expert Says High Divorce Rates Are a Disaster for Emirati Society." *National*, June 6.

El Hajjami, Aïcha. 2009. *Le code de la famille à l'épreuve de la pratique judiciaire*. Marrakesh, Morocco: El Watanya.

Elliott, Katja Žvan. 2015. *Modernizing Patriarchy: The Politics of Women's Rights in Morocco*. Austin: University of Texas Press.

El Menyawi, Hassan. 2012. "The Gift of Ambiguity: State Giving beyond the Either/or of Secularism and Religion in Islamic Divorce Law." In *Islam, Law and Identity*, edited by Marinos Diamantides and Adam Gearey, 89–112. Abingdon, UK: Routledge.

El-Naggar, Mona. 2012. "Family Life according to the Brotherhood." *New York Times*, September 4.

El Rashidi, Yasmine. 2011. "'Tomorrow to Tahrir, Again.'" *New York Review of Books*, January 30.

El Tahawy, Mona. 2012. "Why Do They Hate Us?" *Foreign Policy* 193: 64–70.

el-Wafi, Aïcha. 2006. *Mon fils perdu*. Paris: Plon.

Emerson, Steven, and Daveed Garterstein-Ross. 2005. "In the Interest of Justice." *Washington Times*, January 8.

Emon, Anver M. 2009. "Islamic Law and the Canadian Mosaic: Politics, Jurisprudence, and Multicultural Accommodation," *Canadian Bar Review* 87, no. 2: 391–425.

Erdbrink, Thomas. 2015. "An Eye for an Eye," *New York Times*, April 22.

Ergene, Boğaç A. 2003. *Local Court, Provincial Society and Justice in the Ottoman Empire: Legal Practice and Dispute Resolution in Çankırı and Kastamonu (1652–1744)*. Leiden: Brill.

Erie, Matthew. 2016. *China and Islam: The State, Sharia, and Muslim Minorities*. Cambridge: Cambridge University Press.

Esfandiari, Haleh. 2015. "Iran Hard-Liners' Newest Obsession: Cohabitation." *Wall Street Journal*, April 29.

Esmaeili, Hossein. 2011. "The Nature and Development of Law in Islam and the Rule of Law Challenge in the Middle East and the Muslim World." *Connecticut Journal of International Law* 26, no. 2: 329–66.

Estelle v. Williams. 1976. 425 US 501 (1976).

Evans-Pritchard, E. E. 1940. *The Nuer*. Oxford: Oxford University Press.

Fadel, Mohammad. 1997. "Rules, Judicial Discretion, and the Rule of Law in Naṣrid Grenada." In *Islamic Law: Theory and Practice*, edited by R. Gleave and E. Kermeli, 49–86. London: I. B. Tauris.

Failinger, Marie A. 2012. "Islam in the Mind of American Courts: 1800 to 1960." *Boston College Journal of Law and Social Justice* 32, nos. 1–2: 1–29.

Faisal, Abdulla A. 2011. "Favoritism (Wasta): An Exploratory Study of University Students." *Digital Archive for Journal of King Saud University*, May 9. http://digital.library.ksu.edu.sa/paper2193.html (accessed July 10, 2015).

Fallon, Richard H. 1997. "'The Rule of Law' as a Concept in Constitutional Discourse." *Columbia Law Review* 97, no. 1: 1–56.

Farid, Sonia. 2016. "Does Egypt's New Tourist Marriage Law Really 'Protect Women'?" *Al Arabiya*, January 18. http://english.alarabiya.net/en/perspective/analysis/2016/01/18/Does-Egypt-s-new-tourist-marriage-law-really-protect-women-.html (accessed January 6, 2017).

Fawzy, Essem. 2004. "Muslim Personal Status in Egypt." In *Women's Rights and Islamic Family Law*, edited by Lynn Welchman, 15–94. London: Zed.

Fay, Mary Ann. 2003. "From Warrior-Grandees to Domesticated Bourgeoisie: The Transformation of the Elite Egyptian Household into a Western-Style Nuclear Family." In *Family History in the Middle East*, edited by Beshara Doumani, 77–97. Albany: State University of New York Press.

Feldman, Noah. 2003. "A New Democracy, Enshrined in Faith." *New York Times*, November 13, p. A31.

Feldman, Noah, and Roman Martinez. 2006. "Constitutional Politics and Text in the New Iraq: An Experiment in Islamic Democracy." *Fordham Law Review* 75, no. 2: 883–920.

Feteha, Ahmed. 2015. "Welcome to Egypt's Fake Weddings: Get High, Leave Lots of Cash." *Bloomberg News*, June 23.

Fiddian-Qasmieh, Elena. 2014. *The Ideal Refugees: Islam, Gender, and the Sahrawi Politics of Survival*. Syracuse, NY: Syracuse University Press.

Fierro, Maribel. 2006. "Ill-Treated Women Seeking Divorce: The Qur'anic Two Arbiters and Judicial Practice among the Malikis in Al-Andalus and North Africa." In *Dispensing Justice in Muslim Courts*, edited by M. Khalid Masud, R. Peters, and D. S. Powers, 323–47. Leiden: Brill.

Fihri, Taieb Fassi. 2011. *Embracing Reform: A Message from King Mohammed VI of Morocco*. Washington, DC: Brookings Institution.

Finn, Peter. 2012. "Documents Provide Rare Insight into FBI's Terrorism Stings." *Washington Post*, April 13.

Fluehr-Lobban, Carolyn. 1982. "Issues in the *Sharīa* Child Custody Law of the Sudan." *Northeast African Studies* 4, no. 2: 1–9.

———. 1987. *Islamic Law and Society in the Sudan*. London: Frank Cass.

———. 2012. *Shari'a and Islamism in Sudan: Conflict, Law and Social Transformation*. London: I. B. Tauris.

Foblets, Marie-Claire, ed. 1996. *Famille-Islam-Europe: Le droit confronte au changement*. Paris: L'Harmattan.

"Foreign Leaders Hail Tunisian Constitution." 2014. *Al-Jazeera*, February 7.

Fortier, Corinne. 2012. "The Right to Divorce for Women (*khul'*) in Islam: Comparative Practices in Mauretania and Egypt." In *Interpreting Divorce Laws in Islam*, edited by Rubya Mehdi et al., 155–75. Copenhagen: DJØF.

Fournier, Pascale. 2010. *Muslim Marriage in Western Courts*. Farnham, Surrey, UK: Ashgate.

Freamon, Bernard K. 2005. "Piety, Tribalism and Slavery." SJD diss., Columbia University School of Law.

Freed, Doris Jonas. 1957. "Aspects of French Criminal Procedure." *Louisiana Law Review* 17: 730–55.

French Code of Criminal Procedure. 2015. http://www.wipo.int/wipolex/en/details.jsp?id=14295 (accessed January 6, 2017).

Friedl, Erika. 1994. "Sources of Female Power in Iran." In *In the Eye of the Storm: Women in Post-Revolutionary Iran*, edited by Mahnaz Afkhami and Erika Friedl, 151–67. London: I. B. Tauris.

Friedman, Thomas L. 2011a. "Advice for China." *New York Times*, June 4.

———. 2011b. "Pharaoh without a Mummy." *New York Times*, February 15.

———. 2014. "Flying Blind in Iraq and Syria." *New York Times*, December 16.

———. 2016. "Social Media: Destroyer or Creator?" *New York Times*, February 3.

Fukuyama, Francis. 2014. *Political Order and Political Decay: From the Industrial Revolution to the Globalization of Democracy*. New York: Farrar, Straus and Giroux.

Gall, Carlotta. 2015. "Widespread Graft Expanded after Tunisian Revolt, Study Says." *New York Times*, June 25.

Gawande, Atul. 2009. "Hellhole." *New Yorker*, March 30.

Geertz, Clifford. 1971. *Islam Observed*. Chicago: University of Chicago Press.

Geertz, Clifford, Hildred Geertz, and Lawrence Rosen. 1979. *Meaning and Order in Moroccan Society*. New York: Cambridge University Press.

Gellner, Ernest. 1981. *Muslim Society*. Cambridge: Cambridge University Press.

———. 1988. "Trust, Cohesion, and the Social Order." In *Trust: Making and Breaking Cooperative Relations*, edited by Diego Gambetta, 142–57. London: Basil Blackwell.

Gerber, Haim. 1980. "Social and Economic Position of Women in an Ottoman City, Bursa, 1600–1700." *International Journal of Middle East Studies* 12: 231–44.

———. 1994. *State, Society and Law in Islam*. Albany: State University of New York Press.

———. 1999. *Islamic Law and Culture, 1600–1840*. Leiden: Brill.

Gesink, Indira Falk. 2003. "'Chaos on the Earth': Subjective Truths versus Communal Unity in Islamic Law and the Rise of Militant Islam." *American Historical Review* 108, no. 3: 710–33.

Ghannam, Jeffrey. 2011. "In the Middle East, This Is Not a Facebook Revolution." *Washington Post*, February 18.

Ghayyur, Taha. 2010. "Divorce in the Muslim Community: 2010 Survey Analysis." SoundVision.com. July 22. http://www.soundvision.com/article/divorce-in-the-muslim-community-2010-survey-analysis (accessed January 6, 2017).

Giladi, Avner. 1992. *Children of Islam: Concepts of Childhood in Medieval Muslim Society*. London: Macmillan.

Giunchi, Elisa, ed. 2014. *Adjudicating Family Law in Muslim Courts*, London: Routledge.

Giustozzi, Antonio, Claudio Franco, and Adam Baczko. 2012. *Shadow Justice: How the Taliban Run Their Judiciary*. Kabul: Integrity Watch Afghanistan. http://www.baag.org.uk/sites/www.baag.org.uk/files/resources/attachments/Integrity%20Watch%20Shadow%20Justice%20Dec.%202012.pdf (accessed January 6, 2017).

Glassman, Ronald M. 1995. *The Middle Class and Democracy in Socio-Historical Perspective*. Leiden: Brill.

Goitein, S. D. 1967. *A Mediterranean Society*. Volume 1, *Economic Foundations*. Berkeley: University of California Press.

———. 1971. *A Mediterranean Society*. Volume 2, *The Community*. Berkeley: University of California Press.

———. 1973. *Letters of Medieval Jewish Traders*. Princeton, NJ: Princeton University Press.

———. 1978. *A Mediterranean Society*. Volume 3, *The Family*. Berkeley: University of California Press.

———. 1983. *A Mediterranean Society*. Volume 4, *Daily Life*. Berkeley: University of California Press.

Goldberg, Jeffrey. 2011. "Danger: Falling Tyrants." *The Atlantic*, June, pp. 46–54.

Goldman, Shalom. 1995. *The Wiles of Women/The Wiles of Men: Joseph and Potiphar's Wife in Ancient Near Eastern Jewish and Islamic Folklore*. Albany: State University of New York Press.

Goldstein, Joseph. 2015. "At Afghan Weddings, His Side, Her Side and 600 Strangers." *New York Times*, April 18.

Good, Anthony. 2007. *Anthropology and Expertise in the Asylum Courts*. Abingdon, UK: Routledge-Cavendish.

Goodwin, Jan. 2003. *Price of Honor*, rev. ed. New York: Plume.

Goodwin, Joseph Kearns. 2009. "Afghanistan's Other Front." *New York Times*, September 16.

Goulven, J. 1921. *Traité d'économie et de législation marocaines*. Paris: Librairie des sciences économiques et sociales.

Graham, David A. 2016. "Gingrich's Outrageous Call to Deport All Practicing U. S. Muslims," *The Atlantic*, July 15.

Gray, John. 2014. "Review of Francis Fukuyama, Political Order and Political Decay." *Literary Review* (September).

Greenawalt, Kent. 1983. "How Empty Is the Idea of Equality?" *Columbia Law Review* 83, no. 5: 1167–85.

Greenhouse, Carol J. 1989. *Praying for Justice: Faith, Order and Community in an American Town.* Ithaca, NY: Cornell University Press.

Greer, Launa. 2011. "AUC's Ibrahim Covers Role of Young Egyptians in Talk." *Daily Princetonian*, April 27, p. 2.

Gregory, Derek. 2013. "Tahrir: Politics, Publics and Performances of Space." *Middle East Critique* 22, no. 3: 235–46.

Grossman, Andrew. 2003–2004. " 'Islamic Land': Group Rights, National Identity and Law." *UCLA Journal of Islamic and Near Eastern Law* 3: 53–89.

Grote, Rainer, and Tilmann J. Röder. 2012. *Constitutionalism in Islamic Countries*. Oxford: Oxford University Press.

Grunert, Jeremy. 2013. "How Do You Solve a Problem like Sharia? *Awad v. Ziriax* and the Question of Sharia Law in America." *Pepperdine Law Review* 40, no. 3: 695–734.

Guechi, Fatima Zohra. 2005. "*Mahkama* Records as a Source for Women's History." In *Beyond the Exotic: Women's Histories in Islamic* Societies, edited by Amira El-Azhary Sonbol, 152–61. Syracuse, NY: Syracuse University Press.

Guellali, Amna. 2014. "The Problem with Tunisia's New Constitution." *Human Rights Watch*, February 3. http://www.hrw.org/news/2014/02/03/problem-tunisia-s-new-constitution (accessed January 6, 2017).

Gumbel, Andrew. 2013. "The Scorched Earth Solution: Solitary Confinement in America." *Los Angeles Review of Books*, October 6. https://lareviewofbooks.org/article/the-scorched-earth-solution-solitary-confinement-in-america/ (accessed January 6, 2017).

Gutterson, David. 1995. *Snow Falling on Cedars*. New York: Vintage.

Habtor, Abdulhadi. 2015. "Dowry Rates Fixed to Contain Spinsterhood." *Arab News*, August 19. http://www.arabnews.com/saudi-arabia/news/793606 (accessed January 6, 2017).

Hacker, Joseph. 1994. "Jewish Autonomy in the Ottoman Empire, Its Scope and Limits: Jewish Courts from the Sixteenth to the Eighteenth Centuries." In *The Jews of the Ottoman Empire*, edited by Avigdor Levy, 153–202. Princeton, NJ: Darwin Press.

Hadid, Diaa. 2015. "Palestinian Woman Is First to Oversee Muslim Wedding Vows." *International New York Times*, September 22.

Haeri, Shahla. 2002. *Law of Desire: Temporary Marriage in Shi'i Iran*. Syracuse, NY: Syracuse University Press.

Hafez, Sherine. 2012. "No Longer a Bargain? Women, Masculinity, and the Egyptian Uprising." *American Ethnolog*ist 39, no. 1: 37–42.

Hallaq, Wael. 2006. "What Is Shari'a?" In *Yearbook of Islamic and Middle Eastern Law*. Volume 12, *2005–2006*, edited by Eugene Cotran, Martin Lau, and Victor Kattan, 151–80. London: Centre of Islamic and Middle Eastern Law, SOAS.

_____. 2009. *Shari'a: Theory, Practice, Transformation*. Cambridge: Cambridge University Press.

Halstead, John P. 1967. *Rebirth of a Nation: The Origins and Rise of Moroccan Nationalism, 1912–1944*. Cambridge, MA: Harvard Middle East Monograph Series.

Hamdy, Sherine F. 2012. "Strength and Vulnerability after Egypt's Arab Spring Uprisings." *American Ethnologist* 39, no. 1: 43–48.

Hamilton, Alexander, James Madison, and John Jay. 1948 [1787–1788]. *The Federalist, or The New Constitution*. New York: E. P. Dutton & Co.

Hammami, Rema. 2004. "Attitudes towards Legal Reform of Personal Status in Palestine." In *Women's Rights and Islamic Family Law*, edited by Lynn Welchman, 126–43. London: Zed.

HarassMap. 2014. *Towards a Safer City: Sexual Harassment in Greater Cairo*. Cairo: HarassMap.

Harris, J. W. 1996. *Property and Justice*. Oxford: Oxford University Press.

Hassan, Hussein. 2017. *Contracts in Islam Law*. London: I. B. Tauris.

Hassan, Sharifah Zaleha Syed, and Sven Cederroth. 1997. *Managing Marital Disputes in Malaysia*. Richmond, UK: Curzon.

Hasso, Frances S. 2010. *Consuming Desires: Family Crisis and the State in the Middle East.* Stanford, CA: Stanford University Press.

Hauslohner, Abigail. 2010. "Afghanistan: When Women Set Themselves on Fire." *Time*, July 7.

———. 2013. "Tahrir Largely Empty Once Again." *Washington Post*, July 4.

Hebblethwaite, Cordelia. 2011. "Is Hip Hop Driving the Arab Spring?" *BBC News Middle East*, January 24. http://www.bbc.com/news/world-middle-east-14146243 (accessed January 6, 2017).

Hegel-Cantarella, Christine. 2012. "Waiting to Win: Family Disputes, Court Reform, and the Ethnography of Delay." In *Family Law in Islam*, edited by Maaike Voorhoeve, 111–46. London: I. B. Tauris.

Helmke, Matthew. 2007. *Humor and Moroccan Culture*. Self-published.

Helmy, Mohamed M., and Sabine Frerichs. 2013. "Stripping the Boss: The Powerful Role of Humor in the Egyptian Revolution 2011." *Integrative Psychological & Behavioral Science* 47, no. 4: 450–81.

Hermassi, Abdelbaki, and A. Marie Hmed. 1983. *Le Divorce dans la Region de Tunis*. Tunis: U.N.F.T. Alliance des Femmes de Carrière Juridique.

Hersch, Seymour. 2002. "The Twentieth Man." *New Yorker*, September 30, p. 56.

Hertog, Steffen. 2011. *Princes, Brokers, and Bureaucrats: Oil and State in Saudi Arabia*. Ithaca, NY: Cornell University Press.

Hessick, Carissa Byrne. 2006. "Motive's Role in Criminal Punishment." *Southern California Law Review* 80: 89–149.

Hill, Enid. 1979. *Mahkama! Studies in the Egyptian Legal System*. London: Ithaca Press.

Hirsch, Susan F. 1998. *Pronouncing and Preserving: Gender and the Discourse of Disputing in an African Islamic Court*. Chicago: University of Chicago Press.

Hirschkorn, Phil. 2006. "Moussaoui Curses America but Judge Gets Final Word." CNN.com. May 4. www.cnn.com/2006/LAW/05/04/moussaoui.verdict/ (accessed January 6, 2017).

Hochberg, Gil Z. 2007. *In Spite of Partition: Jews, Arabs, and the Limits of Separatist Imagination*. Princeton, NJ: Princeton University Press.

Hoffman, Michael, and Amaney Jamal. 2012. "The Youth and the Arab Spring: Cohort Differences and Similarities." *Middle East Law and Governance* 4: 168–88.

Holden, Livia. 2012. "2nd Background Paper: India Team, Andromaque." June 30. http://womenproperty.hypotheses.org/ (accessed May 23, 2016).

Horkheimer, Max, and Theodore W. Adorno. 2007. *Dialectic of Enlightenment*. Translated by Edmund Jephcott. Stanford, CA: Stanford University Press.

Hubbard, Ben. 2015. "Saudi Justice, Harsh But Able to Spare the Sword." *New York Times*, March 22.

Hurriyet Daily News. 2015. "The Creepy Decision of the Constitutional Court." June 6.

Husseini, Rana. 2016. "Tragic: One in Three Jordanian Women Experience Violence, Only Three Percent Would Report It." *Albawaba*, February 29. http://www.albawaba.com/editorchoice/tragic-one-three-jordanian-women-experience-violence-only-three-percent-would-report-it (accessed January 6, 2017).

Hutterer, Michaela. 2014. "God's Law on the Path to Modernity." *Max Planck Research* (March): 24–29.

Huxley, Frederick Charles. 1978. *Wasita in a Lebanese Context; Social Exchange among Villagers and Outsiders*. Ann Arbor: Museum of Anthropology, University of Michigan.

Ibrahim, Hauwa. 2013. *Practicing Shariah Law: Seven Strategies for Achieving Justice in Shariah Courts*. Chicago: American Bar Association.

Inhorn, Marcia C. 1996. *Infertility and Patriarchy: The Cultural Politics of Gender and Family Life in Egypt.* Philadelphia: University of Pennsylvania Press.

Isser, Deborah H., ed. 2011. *Customary Justice and the Rule of Law in War-Torn Societies.* Washington, DC: United States Institute of Peace Press.

Jackson, Sherman A. 2001. "*Kramer versus Kramer* in a Tenth/Sixteenth Century Egyptian Court: Post-Formative Jurisprudence between Exigency and Law." *Islamic Law and Society* 8, no. 1: 27–51.

Jalal, Rasha Abou. 2016. "How This New Divorce Law Further Marginalizes Gaza's Women." *Al-Monitor*, March 15. http://www.al-monitor.com/pulse/originals/2016/03/gaza-husbands-file-divorce-abuse-by-women.html#ixzz46HanGLzr (accessed January 6, 2017).

Jamal, Amaney A. 2007. *Barriers to Democracy: The Other Side of Social Capital in Palestine and the Arab World.* Princeton, NJ: Princeton University Press, 2007.

Jay, Martin. 1999. "Must Justice Be Blind? The Challenge of Images to the Law." In *Law and the Image*, edited by Costas Douzinas and Lynda Nead, 19–35. Chicago: University of Chicago Press, 1999.

Jennings, Ronald C. 1975. "Women in Early 17th Century Ottoman Judicial Records: The *Sharia* Court of Anatolian Kayseri." *Journal of the Economic and Social History of the Orient* 18: 53–114.

———. 1978. "Zimmis (Non-Muslims) in Early 17th Century Ottoman Judicial Records: The Sharia Court of Anatolian Kayseri." *Journal of the Economic and Social History of the Orient* 21, no. 3: 225–93.

———. 1979. "Limitations of the Judicial Powers of the Kadi in 17th c. Ottoman Kayseri." *Studia Islamica* 50: 151–84.

———. 1993. "Divorce in the Ottoman *Sharia* Court of Cyprus, 1580–1640." *Studia Islamica* 78: 155–67.

Johansen, Baber. 2002. "Le corruption: Un délit contre l'ordre social, *Les qāḍī-s de Bukhārā.*" *Annales Histoire, Sciences Sociales* 57, no. 6: 1561–89.

Joppke, Christian, and John Torpey. 2013. *Legal Integration of Islam: A Transatlantic Comparison.* Cambridge, MA: Harvard University Press.

Just, Peter. 2001. *Duo Donggo Justice: Conflict and Morality in Indonesia.* Lanham, MD: Rowman and Littlefield.

Kadri, Sadakat. 2012. *Heaven on Earth: A Journey through Shari'a Law.* New York: Farrar, Strauss and Giroux.

Kasselt, Julia. 2010. "Honour Killings in Germany, 1996–2005." Max Planck Institut. https://www.mpicc.de/en/forschung/forschungsarbeit/kriminologie/ehrenmorde.html (accessed January 6, 2017).

Keefe, Patrick Radden. 2015. "Corruption and Revolt." *New Yorker*, January 19, pp. 30–36.

Khatib, Lina, and Ellen Lust, eds. 2014. *Taking to the Streets: The Transformation of Arab Activism.* Baltimore: Johns Hopkins University Press.

Kholoussy, Hanan. 2010. *For Better, for Worse: The Marriage Crisis that Made Modern Egypt.* Stanford, CA: Stanford University Press.

———. 2011. "Interfaith Unions and Non-Muslim Wives in Early Twentieth Century Alexandrian Islamic Courts." In *Untold Histories of the Middle East: Recovering Voices from the 19th and 20th Centuries*, edited by Amy Singer, Christoph K. Neumann, and Selçuk Akşin Somel, 54–70. Abingdon, UK: Routledge.

Kishtainy, Khaled. 1985. *Arab Political Humor*. London: Quartet.

Kraidy, Marwan M. 2016. *The Naked Blogger of Cairo: Creative Insurgency in the Arab World.* Cambridge, MA: Harvard University Press.

Krajeski, Jenna. 2011. "Love and Revolution." *New Yorker*, February 14.

Kuran, Timur. 2012. *The Long Divergence: How Islamic Law Held Back the Middle East.* Princeton, NJ: Princeton University Press.

Lally, Kathy. 2011. "Egypt Women Stand for Equality in the Square." *Washington Post*, February 18.

Larguèche, Dalenda. 1996. "Confined, Battered, and Repudiated Women in Tunis since the Eighteenth Century." In *Women, the Family, and Divorce Laws in Islamic History*, edited by Amina El Azhary Sonbol, 259–76. Syracuse, NY: Syracuse University Press.

Layish, Aharon. 1975. *Women and Islamic Law in a Non-Muslim State*. New York: John Wiley & Sons.

———. 1977. "Compensation to the Divorced Woman in the Israeli Druze Family." *Israel Law Review* 12, no. 3: 330–43.

———. 1988. "Customary *Khul'* as Reflected in the *Sijil* of the Libyan *Sharī'a* Courts." *Bulletin of the School of Oriental and African Studies* 51, no. 3: 428–39.

———. 1991. *Divorce in the Libyan Family*. New York: New York University Press.

———. 1995. "*Dār 'adl*: Symbiosis of Custom and *Sharī'a* in a Tribal Society in Process of Sedentarization." *Jerusalem Studies in Arabic and Islam* 19: 198–213.

———. 2008. "Islamization of Custom as Reflected in Awards of Tribal Arbitrators in the Judean Desert." *Jerusalem Studies in Arabic and Islam* 35: 285–334.

"Le 20è homme du 11/09." 2006. *Le Nouvel Observateur*, June 13.

Lev, Daniel S. 1972. *Islamic Courts in Indonesia*. Berkeley: University of California Press.

Levinson, Charles, and Margaret Coker. 2011. "The Secret Rally That Sparked an Uprising." *Wall Street Journal*, February 11.

Lewis, Neil A. 2006a. "Logic Turns Upside-Down during Moussaoui Trial." *New York Times,* April 17.

———. 2006b. "Moussaoui Now Ties Himself to 9/11 Plot." *New York Times*, March 26.

———. 2006c. "Witness Says Moussaoui Exhibited Mental Illness." *New York Times*, April 19.

Libson, Gideon. 2003. *Jewish and Islamic Law: A Comparative Study of Custom during the Gaonic Period.* Cambridge, MA: Harvard University Press.

Liebesny, Herbert J. 1975. *The Law of the Near and Middle East*. Albany: State University of New York Press.

Lindner, Douglas O. 2006. "The Trial of Zacarias Moussaoui: An Account." http://law2.umkc.edu/faculty/projects/ftrials/moussaoui/zmaccount.html (accessed January 6, 2017).

Lindsey, Tim, and Cate Sumner. 2011. "Indonesia: Islamic Courts as Governance Institutions." *East Asia Forum*, July 9.

Lithwick, Dahlia. 2006. "State's Jurisprudence: A Mistrial for Moussaoui?" *NPR*, March 14. http://www.npr.org/templates/story/story.php?storyId=5279297 (accessed January 6, 2017).

Little, Donald P. 2006. "A Fourteenth-Century Jerusalem Court Record of a Divorce Hearing." In *Mamluks and Ottomans*, edited by David J. Wasserstein and Ami Ayalon, 67–85. London: Routledge.

Lutfi, Huda. 1991. "Manners and Customs of Fourteenth-Century Cairene Women: Female Authority versus Male Shar'i Order in Muslim Prescriptive Treatises." In *Women in Middle Eastern History*, edited by Nikki R. Keddie and Beth Baron, 99–121. New Haven, CT: Yale University Press.

Lyall, Gavin. 1971. *The Most Dangerous Game*. London: Pan Books.

Lydon, Ghislaine. 2001. "Thus Ruled the Qadi of Ndar: Civil Litigation in a Colonial Muslim Tribunal, 1880s–1920s." *The 7th Stanford-Berkeley Law and Colonialism Symposium, Muslim Family Law and Colonialism in Africa*, May 11–12.

———. 2010. "Obtaining Freedom at the Muslims' Tribunal: Colonial Kadijustiz and Women's Divorce Litigation in Ndar (Senegal)." In *Muslim Family Law in Sub-Saharan Africa*, edited by Shamil Jeppie, Ebrahim Moosa, and Richard Roberts, 135–57. Amsterdam: Amsterdam University Press.

Maarouf, Mohammed. 2007. *Jinn Eviction as a Discourse of Power: A Multidisciplinary Approach to Moroccan Magical Beliefs and Practices*. Leiden: Brill.

Maass, Peter. 2015. "CIA's Jeffrey Sterling Sentenced to 42 Months for Leaking to New York Times Journalist." *The Intercept*, May 11. Firstlook.org/theintercept/2015/05/11/sterling-sentenced-for-cia-leak-to-nyt/ (accessed January 6, 2017).

Macfarlane, Julie. 2012. *Islamic Divorce in North America*. Oxford: Oxford University Press.

Maghen, Ze'ev. 2008. "The Merry Men of Medina: Comedy and Humanity in the Early Days of Islam." *Der Islam* 83: 277–340.

Maine, Henry S. 1883. *Dissertations on Early Law and Custom*. London: John Murray.

Makiya, Kanan. 2005. "Present at the Disintegration." *New York Times*, December 11, p. WK13.

Marcus, Abraham. 1989. *The Middle East on the Eve of Modernity: Aleppo in the Eighteenth Century*. New York: Columbia University Press.

Marglin, Jessica. 2013. "In the Courts of the Nations: Jews, Muslims, and Legal Pluralism in Nineteenth-Century Morocco." PhD diss., Department of Near East Studies, Princeton University.

———. 2014. "Jews in *Shari'a* Courts: A Family Dispute from the Cairo Geniza." In *Jews, Christians and Muslims in Medieval and Early Modern Times*, edited by Arnold E. Franklin et al., 207–25. Leiden: Brill.

———. 2016. *Across Legal Lines: Jews and Muslims in Modern Morocco.* New Haven, CT: Yale University Press.

Markon, Jerry. 2005. "Moussaoui Pleads Guilty in Terror Plot." *Washington Post*, April 23.

Markon, Jerry, and Timothy Dwyer. 2006. "Some Saw Moussaoui as Bit Player, Juror Says." *Washington Post*, May 5.

Marranci, Gabriele, ed. 2014. *Islam in Practice*. London: Routledge.

Marx, Karl, and Freidrich Engels. 2012 [1848]. *The Communist Manifesto*. Edited by Jeffrey C. Issac. New Haven, CT: Yale University Press.

Masr, Mada. 2014. "95% of Cairo Women Have Been Sexually Harasses, Says Survey." *Mada Masr*, December 11. http://www.madamasr.com/news/95-cairo-women-have-been-sexually-harassed-says-survey (accessed January 6, 2017).

Massell, Gregory. 1974. *The Surrogate Proletariat: Moslem Women and Revolutionary Strategies in Soviet Central Asia, 1919–1929*. Princeton, NJ: Princeton University Press.

Mathee, Mohamed Shaid. 2011. "Women's Agency in Muslim Marriage: *Fatwā*s from Timbuktu." *Journal for Islamic Studies* 31: 75–95.

McCoy, Terence. 2014. "In Pakistan, 1,000 Women Die in 'Honor Killings': Why Is This Happening?" *Washington Post*, May 28.

M'chichi, Houria Alami. 2007. "Changement social et perceptions du nouveau code de la famille." In *Le code de la famille: Perceptions et practique judiciaire*, edited by M. Benradi et al., 27–88. Fez: Friedrich Ebert Stiftung.

Mehdi, Rubya (coordinator). 2012. "Female Judges in Southern Punjab, Pakistan" and "Lady Lawyers in Pakistan." *Journal of Law and Social Research* (Pakistan), no. 3 (2012): 113–47.

Menski, Werner. 2012. "The Uniform Civil Code Debate in Indian Law: New Developments and Changing Agenda." In *The Many Faces of India: Law and Politics of the Subcontinent*, edited by Malcolm MacLaren, 136–82. New Delhi: Sanskriti.

Meriwether, Margaret L. 1996. "The Rights of Children and the Responsibilities of Women: Women as *Wasi*s in Ottoman Aleppo, 1770–1840." In *Women, the Family, and Divorce Laws in Islamic History*, edited by Amira El Azhary Sonbol, 219–35. Syracuse, NY: Syracuse University Press.

———. 1999. *The Kin Who Count: Family and Society in Ottoman Aleppo, 1770–1840.* Austin: University of Texas Press.

Merry, Sally. 1988. "Legal Pluralism." *Law and Society Review* 1988: 869–96.

Meshal, Reem A. 2014. *Sharia and the Making of the Modern Egyptian: Islamic Law and Custom in the Courts of Ottoman Cairo*. Cairo: American University in Cairo Press.

Messaoudi, Slaheddine. 1979. *La consommation du marriage en droit tunisien.* Memoire Presente du Diplome d'Études Superieures de Droit Privé, Université de Tunis.

Metropolitan Properties Co. Ltd. v. Purdy. 1940. 2 *All England Reports* 188.

Michelet, Jules. 1967 [1847]. *History of the French Revolution.* Chicago: University of Chicago Press.

Milliot. Louis. 1920a. *Recueil de Jurisprudence Chérifienne*, vol. 1. Paris: Ernest Leroux.

———. 1920b. *Recueil de Jurisprudence Chérifienne*, vol. 2. Paris: Ernest Leroux.

Mir-Hosseini, Ziba. 1993a. *Marriage on Trial: A Study of Islamic Family Law*. London: I. B. Tauris.

———. 1993b. "Women, Marriage and the Law in Post-Revolutionary Iran." In *Women in the Middle East*, edited by Haleh Afshar, 59–84. London: Macmillan.

———. 1996. "The Delegated Right to Divorce in Law and in Practice in Iran and Morocco." In *Talaq-i-Tafwid: The Woman's Contractual Access to Divorce: An Information Kit*, edited by L. Carroll and H. Kapoor, 121–33. Grabels, France: Women Living under Muslim Laws.

———. 1999a. *Islam and Gender: The Religious Debate in Contemporary Islam.* Princeton, NJ: Princeton University Press.

———. 1999b. "Making Divorce Iranian Style." *ISIM Newsletter* 2: 17.

———. 2002. "Tamkin: Stories from a Family Court in Iran." In *Everyday Life in the Muslim Middle East*, edited by Donna Lee Bowen and Evelyn Early, 136–50. Bloomington: Indiana University Press, 2nd ed.

———. 2007. "When a Woman's Hurt Becomes an Injury: Hardship as Grounds for Divorces in Iran." *Hawwa* 5, no. 1: 111–26.

———. 2008. "A Woman's Right to Terminate the Marriage Contract: The Case of Iran." In *The Islamic Marriage Contract: Case Studies in Islamic Family Law*, edited by Asifa Quraishi and Frank E. Vogel, 215–30. Cambridge, MA: Islamic Legal Studies Program, Harvard Law School.

———. 2012. "The Politics of Divorce Laws in Iran: Ideology versus Practice." In *Interpreting Divorce Laws in Islam*, edited by Rubya Mehdi, Werner Menski, and Jørgen S. Nielsen, 65–83. Copenhagen: DJØF.

Mistry, Malika B. 2003. "Muslim Women and Divorce: Two Case Studies." In *Divorce and Remarriage among Muslims in India*, edited by Imtiaz Ahmad, 247–62. New Delhi: Manohar.

Mitchell, Ruth. 1997. "Family Law in Algeria before and after the 1404/1984 Family Code." In *Islamic Law: Theory and Practice*, edited by R. Gleave and E. Kermeli, 193–204. London: I. B. Tauris.

Mitchell, W. J. T. 2012. "Report from Morocco." *Critical Inquiry* 38, no. 4: 892–901.

Mnookin, Robert N., and Lewis Kornhauser. 1979. "Bargaining in the Shadow of the Law." *Yale Law Journal* 88, no. 5: 950–97.

Moors, Annelies. 1995. *Women, Property, and Islam: Palestinian Experiences, 1920–1990*. Cambridge: Cambridge University Press.

Morocco World News. 2014. "Women Represent 39.40% of Public Servants in Morocco." November 18. http://www.moroccoworldnews.com/2014/11/144392/women-represent-39–40-of-publicservants-in-morocco/ (accessed January 6, 2017).

———. 2015. "70% of Moroccans Were Forced to Pay Bribes to Access Public Services." April 30. http://www.moroccoworldnews.com/2015/04/157370/70-moroccans-forced-pay-bribes-accesspublic-services/ (accessed January 6, 2017).

Moshenberg, Dan. 2014. "Judge Leonie Brinkema and the Overwhelming Fact of Isolation." *Women In and Beyond the Global*. January 12. http://www.womeninandbeyond.org/?p=6710 (accessed January 6, 2017).

Motlagh, Amy 2011. *Burying the Beloved: Marriage, Realism, and Reform in Modern Iran*. Stanford, CA: Stanford University Press.

Mouaqit, Mohamed. 2007. "Disposition culturelle/axiologique du juge et interpretation du nouveau code de la famille." In *Le code de la famille: Perceptions et practique judiciaire*, edited by M. Benradi et al., 141–88. Fez: Friedrich Ebert Stiftung.

Moussaoui, Abd Samad. 2003. *Zacarias, My Brother: The Making of a Terrorist*. New York: Seven Stories Press.

Moustafa, Tamir. 2013. "Liberal Rights versus Islamic Law? The Construction of a Binary in Malaysian Politics." *Law and Society Review* 47, no. 4: 771–802.

Nasr, Vali. 2009. *Forces of Fortune: The Rise of the New Muslim Middle Class and What It Will Mean for Our World*. New York: Free Press.

Nasseri, Ladane. 2015. "Iran Bans Women's Magazine for Backing Unmarried Households." *Bloomberg News*, April 27. http://www.bloomberg.com/news/articles/2015–04–27/iran-bans-women-s-magazine-for-promoting-cohabitation (accessed January 6, 2017).

Naveh, Immanuel. 2002. "The Tort of Injury and Dissolution of Marriage at a Wife's Initiative in Egyptian Maḥkamat al-Naqḍ Rulings." *Islamic Law and Society* 9, no. 1: 16–41.

Newcomb, Rachel. 2009. *Women of Fes*. Philadelphia: University of Pennsylvania Press.

———. 2012. "Justice for Everyone? Implementation of Morocco's 2004 *Mudawana* Reforms." In *Interpreting Divorce Law in Islam*, edited by Rubya Mehdi, Werner Menski, and Jørgan S. Nielsen, 105–28. Copenhagen: DJØF.

New York Times Editorial Board. 2015. "Justice Kennedy's Plea to Congress." *New York Times*, April 4.

New York University Center on Law and Security. 2011. "Terrorism Trial Report Card." http://www.lawandsecurity.org/Portals/0/Documents/TTRC%20Ten%20Year%20Issue.pdf (accessed January 6, 2017).

Noonan, John T. 1984. Jr. *Bribes*. New York: Macmillan.

Nurlaelawati, Euis. 2013. "Muslim Women in Indonesian Religious Courts: Reform, Strategies, and Pronouncement of Divorce." *Islamic Law and Society* 20, no. 3: 242–71.

Nurlaelawati, Euis, and A. Salim. 2013. "Gendering the Islamic Judiciary: Female Judges in the Religious Courts of Indonesia." *Al-Jami'ah* 51, no. 2: 247–78.

Ober, Josiah. 2010. "Wealthy Hellas." *Transactions of the American Philological Association* 140: 241–86.

———. 2014. *The Rise and Fall of Classical Greece*. Princeton, NJ: Princeton University Press.

Oberwittler, Dietrich, and Julia Kasselt. 2014. "Honor Killings." In *The Oxford Handbook on Gender, Sex, and Crime*, edited by R. Gartner and B. McCarthy. 652–70. Oxford: Oxford University Press.

Okawara, Tomoki. 2003. "Size and Structure of Damascus Households in the Late Ottoman Period as Compared with Istanbul Households." In *Family History in the Middle East*, edited by Beshara Doumani, 51–75. Albany: State University of New York Press.

Olgiati, Vittorio. 1997. "Le pluralism juridique comme lute pour le droit." *Canadian Journal of Law and Society* 12, no. 2: 47–74.

"Omanis Stay Married, Less Divorces than Neighbor Gulf States." 2014. *Albawaba.com*, February 11.

Osanloo, Arzoo. 2006. "Islamico-Civil 'Rights Talk': Women, Subjectivity, and Law in Iranian Family Court." *American Ethnologist* 33, no. 2: 191–209.

———. 2009. *The Politics of Women's Rights in Iran*. Princeton, NJ: Princeton University Press.

______. 2012a. "'The Measure of Mercy': Islamic Justice, Sovereign Power, and Human Rights in Iran." *Cultural Anthropology* 21, no. 4: 570–602.

———. 2012b. "When Blood Has Spilled: Gender, Honor, and Compensation in Iranian Criminal Sanctioning." *POLAR: Political and Legal Anthropology Review* 35, no. 2: 308–26.

———. 2014. "Les pratiques sociales et léales du pardon dans le système judiciare iranien." In *Justice, Religion, Réconciliation,* edited by Yazid Ben Hounet, Sandrine Lefranc, and Deborah Puccio-Den, 83–94. Paris: Editions L'Harmattan.

———. Unpublished manuscript. "Humanity and Forgiveness in Islamic Criminal Sanctioning in Iran."

Othman, Mohammed. 2015. "Divorce in Gaza Comes at Steep Price." *Al-Monitor*, April 13. http://www.al-monitor.com/pulse/originals/2015/04/gaza-divorce-sharia-courts-khul-wealthy-women.html# (accessed January 6, 2017).

Ounnir, Abdellah. 2007. "Les justicibles dans le circuit judiciaire relative au contentieux de loi famille." In *Le code de la famille: Perceptions et practique judiciaire*, edited by Malika Benradi et al., 89–139. Fez: Friedrich Ebert Stiftung.

Pangle, Thomas L. 1990. *The Spirit of Modern Republicanism: The Moral Vision of American Founders and the Philosophy of Locke*. Chicago: University of Chicago Press.

———. 2007. *Great Debates: Advocates and Opponents of the American Constitution*. The Great Courses (The Teaching Company), CD recording.

"Parliament's Greatest Achievement Supports Rights of Female-Headed Households." 2012. May 28. http://www.ikhwanweb.com/article.php?id=30028 (accessed January 6, 2017).

Parolin, G. P. 2013. "Religion and Sources of Law: *Sharīʿah* in Constitutions." In *Law, Religion, Constitution*, edited by Cristiana Cianitto et al., 89–104. Aldershot, UK: Ashgate.

Peirce, Leslie. 1998. "'She Is Trouble—I Will Divorce Her': Orality, Honor, and Representation in the Ottoman Court of 'Aintab." In *Women in the Medieval Islamic World*, edited by Gavin R. G. Hambly, 269–300. New York: St. Martin's Press.

———. 2003. *Morality Tales: Law and Gender in the Ottoman Court of Aintab.* Berkeley: University of California Press

Peletz, Michael. 2002. *Islamic Modern: Religious Courts and Cultural Politics in Malaysia.* Princeton, NJ: Princeton University Press.

Pelham, Nicolas. 2012. "How Morocco Dodged the Arab Spring." *New York Review of Books*, July 5.

Pennell, C. R. 1987. "Women and Resistance to Colonialism in Morocco: The Rif 1916–1926." *Journal of African History* 28: 107–18.

Perkins, Elisa. 2004. "The 2004 *Mudawwana* Reforms and the Problem of Moroccan Masculinity." *Al-Raida* 21, nos. 104–5: 99–104. http://iwsawassets.lau.edu.lb/alraida/alraida-104–5.pdf (accessed January 6, 2017).

Peters, John O. 2013. *From Marshall to Moussaoui: Federal Justice in the Eastern District of Virginia.* Petersburg, VA: Dietz Press.

Petry, Carl F. 1998. "Conjugal Rights versus Class Prerogatives: A Divorce Case in Mamluk Cairo." In *Women in the Medieval Islamic World*, edited by Gavin R. G. Hambly, 227–40. New York: St. Martin's Press.

Pew Research, Religion and Public Life Project 2013. "Beliefs about Sharia." April 30. http://www.pewforum.org/2013/04/30/the-worlds-muslims-religion-politics-society-beliefs-about-sharia/ (accessed January 6, 2017).

Pilgrim, Lisa. 2012. "British-Muslim Family Law and Citizenship." *Open Democracy*, November 8.

"Plus de divorces en 2007, la faute à la Moudawana?" 2008. Bladi.net. October 14. http://www.bladi.net/divorces-moudawana-maroc.html (accessed January 6, 2017).

"Plus de 41.000 mineures mariées en 2010 au Maroc." 2011. Bladi.net. May 18. http://www.bladi.net/maroc-mineures-mariees.html (accessed May 20, 2016).

Pocock, J. G. A. 2003. *The Machiavellian Moment: Florentine Political Thought and the Atlantic Republican Tradition.* Princeton, NJ: Princeton University Press.

Posner, Richard A. 1993. *The Problems of Jurisprudence.* Cambridge, MA: Harvard University Press.

Powers, David S. 2003. "Women and Divorce in the Islamic West: Three Cases." *Hawwa* 1: 29–45.

———. 2006a. "Four Cases Relating to Women and Divorce in Al-Andalus and the Maghrib, 1100–1500." In *Dispensing Justice in Muslim Courts*, edited by M. Khalid Masud, R. Peters, and D. S. Powers, 383–410. Leiden: Brill.

———. 2006b. "Law and Custom in the Maghrib, 1475–1500: On the Disinheritance of Women." In *Law, Custom, and Statute in the Muslim World*, edited by Ron Shaham, 17–40. Leiden: Brill.

Pratchett, Terry. 2013. *Reaper Man*. New York: Harper.

Prieto v. Clarke. 2013. U.S. Dist. LEXIS 161783 (E.D. VA, November 12), reversed 780 F. 3d 245 (4th Cir. 2015), cert. denied 136 S. Ct. 319 (2015).

Pullan, Wendy. 2013. "Spatial Discontinuities: Conflict Infrastructures in Contested Cities." In *Locating Urban Conflicts: Ethnicity, Nationalism and the Everyday*, edited by Wendy Pullan and Britt Baillie, 17–36. London: Palgrave Macmillan.

Quraishi, Asifa and Frank E. Vogel, eds. 2008. *The Islamic Marriage Contract: Case Studies in Islamic Family Law*. Cambridge, MA: Islamic Legal Studies Program, Harvard Law School.

Rabho, Laila Abed. 2012. "Problems No Longer Solved over a Cup of Coffee: Arab Women Take their Complaints to the West Jerusalem Muslim Court." *Hawwa* 10, nos. 1–2: 113–26.

———. 2013. "From Victimhood to Empowerment: Muslim Women's Narratives in the Shari'a Courts of Jerusalem and Taibe." *Contemporary Islam* 7: 267–81.

Rangwala, Glen. 2011. "Debate: The Arab Spring Is Not about Twitter." *Cambridge Alumni Magazine*, Michaelmas Term: 40–41.

Rapoport, Yossef. 2005. *Marriage, Money and Divorce in Medieval Islamic Society*. Cambridge: Cambridge University Press.

Ravindran, Shruti. 2014. "Twilight in the Box." *Aeon*, February 27. http://aeon.co/magazine/living-together/what-solitary-confinement-does-to-the-brain (accessed January 6, 2017).

Reiter, Yitzhak. 1997. "*Qāḍī*s and the Implementation of Islamic Law in Present Day Israel." In *Islamic Law: Theory and Practice*, edited by R. Gleave and E. Kermeli, 205–31. London: I. B. Tauris.

Rezaei, Hassan. 2006. "Searching for the Origins of Gender Violence in the Sharia Discourse." In *Conflicts and Conflict Resolution in Middle Eastern Societies: Between Tradition and Modernity*, edited by Hans-Jörg Albrecht et al., 335–46. Berlin: Duncker & Humblot.

Rideau, Wilbert. 2013. "When Prisoners Protest." *New York Times*, July 16.

Rispler-Chaim, Vardit. 1996. "Islamic Law of Marriage and Divorce and the Disabled Person: The Case of the Epileptic Wife." *Die Welt des Islams* 36, no. 1: 90–106.

Roberts, Richard. 2005. *Litigants and Households: African Disputes and Colonial Courts in the French Soudan, 1895–1912*. Portsmouth, NH: Heinemann.

———. 2010. "Custom and Muslim Family Law in the Native Courts of the French Soudan, 1905–1912." In *Muslim Family Law in Sub-Saharan Africa*, edited by Shamil Jeppie, Ebrahim Moosa, and Richard Roberts, 85–108. Amsterdam: Amsterdam University Press.

Rodenbeck, Max. 2011. " 'Volcano of Rage.' " *New York Review of Books*, March 24.

Rogers, Joel Faulkner. 2011. "Arab Spring Update." *YouGov-Cambridge* (August). http://today.yougov.com/news/2011/08/31/arab-spring-update/ (accessed May 20, 2016).

Rohan, Brian. 2015. "Overpopulated Egypt Seeks to Reduce Fertility Rate by 2030." *ABC News*, June 9.

Rose-Ackerman, Susan. 1999. *Corruption and Government: Causes, Consequences, and Reform*. Cambridge: Cambridge University Press.

Rosen, Lawrence. 1984. *Bargaining For Reality: The Construction of Social Relations in a Muslim Community*. Chicago: University of Chicago Press.

———. 1989. *The Anthropology of Justice: Law as Culture in Islamic Society*. Cambridge: Cambridge University Press.

———. 2000. *The Justice of Islam*. Oxford: Oxford University Press.

———. 2002. *The Culture of Islam*. Chicago: University of Chicago Press.

———. 2003. "Comparative Law and Anthropology." In *Cambridge Companion to Comparative Law*, edited by Mauro Bussani and Ugo Mattei, 73–87. Cambridge: Cambridge University Press.

———. 2006. *Law as Culture: An Invitation*. Princeton, NJ: Princeton University Press.

———. 2007. "Orientalism Revisited: Edward Said's Unfinished Critique." *Boston Review* 32, no. 1: 31–32.

———. 2008. *Varieties of Muslim Experience*. Chicago: University of Chicago Press.

———. 2010a. "Observing *Islam Observed*: The Family Resemblance and the Pun." *Journal of North African Studies* 14, no. 3: 491–502.

———. 2010b. "Understanding Corruption." *American Interest* 5, no. 4 (March/April): 78–82.

———. 2011a. "Anthropological Assumptions and the Afghan War." *Anthropological Quarterly* 84, no. 2: 535–58.

———. 2011b. "Will the Middle Class Save the Middle East?" *Contemporary Islam* 5, no. 2: 185–90.

———. 2012. "Comparative Law and Anthropology." In *Cambridge Companion to Comparative Law*, edited by Mauro Bussani and Ugo Mattei, 73–87. Cambridge: Cambridge University Press.

———. 2014. "Review of Juan Cole, The New Arabs: How the Millennial Generation Is Changing the Middle East." *The Guardian* (London), August 14.

———. 2016. *Two Arabs, a Berber, and a Jew: Moroccan Lives Entangled*. Chicago: University of Chicago Press.

———. 2018. *The Judgment of Culture: Cultural Assumptions in American Law*. London: Routledge.

Rosenthal, Andrew. 2012. "Liberty and Justice for non-Muslims." *New York Times*, March 30.

Rosenthal, Franz. 1964. "Gifts and Bribes: The Muslim View." *Proceedings of the American Philosophical Society* 108, no. 2: 135–44.

Rosenthal, John. 2007. "Doing Justice to Zacarias Moussaoui." *Policy Review, Hoover Digest*, no. 146 (December 1).

Rossum, Wibo Van. 1996. "Showing Respect: The Appearance of a Turkish Defendant in a Dutch Courtroom." *International Journal for the Semiotics of Law* 9, no. 27: 287–303.

Rotberg, Robert I. 2017. *The Corruption Cure: How Citizens and Leaders Can Combat Graft*. Princeton, NJ: Princeton University Press.

Rozen, Joel. 2014. "Civics Lesson: Ambivalence, Contestation, and Curricular Change in Tunisia." *Ethnos: Journal of Anthropology* 80, no. 5: 605–29.

Rubin, Alissa J. 2014. "Rebelling against Abuse, Afghan Women See Signs of Change." *New York Times*, May 27.

Rugh, Andrea B. 1984. *Family in Contemporary Egypt*. Syracuse, NY: Syracuse University Press.

Ruthven, Malise. 2006. *Islam in the World*, 3rd ed. (Oxford: Oxford University Press.

———. 2015. "Inside the Islamic State (review of Abdel Bari Atwan, *Islamic State: The Digital Caliphate*). *New York Review of Books*, July 9.

Saad, Zulfakar Ramlee. 2010. "The Status of Non-Muslims for Giving Evidence in the Islamic Judicial System: Past and Present." *Journal of Islamic Law Review* 6: 175–85.

Saheb, Shaikh Abdul Azeez. 2003. "*Chowdu* (Divorce): A Study of Divorce among the Rajamundry Muslims of Andhra Pradesh." In *Divorce and Remarriage among Muslims in India*, edited by Imtiaz Ahmad, 231–46. New Delhi: Manohar.

Salah, Ahmed (with Alex Mayyasi). 2016. *You Are Under Arrest for Masterminding the Egyptian Revolution: A Memoire*. Charlotte, NC: Spark Publications.

Salem, Rania. 2011. "Economies of Courtship: Matrimonial Transactions and the Construction of Gender and Class Inequalities in Egypt." Unpublished PhD diss., Princeton University.

Sang-Hun, Choe. 2016. "North Korea to Freeze South's Assets at Kaesong Industrial Park." *New York Times*, February 11.

Santoro, Lara. 1999. "Islamic Clerics Combat Lawlessness in Somalia." *Christian Science Monitor*, July 13.

Sattam, Abdul Aziz bin. 2015. *Sharia and the Concept of Benefit: The Use and Function of Maslaha in Islamic Jurisprudence*. London: I. B. Tauris.

Savage, Charlie. 2011. "Judge Agrees to Limit Writer's Testimony." *New York Times*, July 29.

Savaya, Rivka, and Orna Cohen. 2003. "Divorce among Moslem Arabs Living in Israel: Comparison of Reasons Before and After the Actualization of Marriage." *Journal of Family Issues* 24, no. 3: 338–51.

Schacht, Joseph. 1964. *An Introduction to Islamic Law*. Oxford: Clarendon.

Schielke, Samuli. 2015. *Egypt in the Future Tense: Hope, Frustration, and Ambivalence before and after 2011*. Bloomington: Indiana University Press.

Scott, James C. 1985. *Weapons of the Weak: Everyday Forms of Peasant Resistance.* New Haven, CT: Yale University Press.

Serjeant, R. B. 1962. "Recent Marriage Legislation from al-Mukallā, with Notes on Marriage Customs." *Bulletin of the School of Oriental and African Studies* 15: 472–98.

Shabana, Ayman. 2010. *Custom in Islamic Law and Theory*. London: Palgrave Macmillan.

Shadid, Anthony. 2011. "In One Slice of the New Egypt, Few Are Focusing on Religion." *New York Times*, February 15.

Shah, Angela. 2011. "Travel Anthology Looks at Arab Views of U.S." *New York Times*, April 21.

Shah, Tahir. 2006. *The Caliph's House: A Year in Casablanca*. New York: Bantam.

Shaham, Ron. 1995. "Jews and the Sharīʿa Courts in Modern Egypt." *Studia Islamica* 82, no. 2: 113–36.

———. 1997. *Family and the Courts in Modern Egypt: A Study Based on Decisions by the Shariʿa Courts 1900–1955*. Leiden: Brill.

———. 1999. "State, Feminists and Islamists: The Debate over Stipulations in Marriage Contracts in Egypt." *Bulletin of the School of Oriental and African Studies* 62, no. 3: 462–83.

———. 2011. *The Expert Witness in Islamic Courts: Medicine and Crafts in the Service of Law.* Chicago: University of Chicago Press.

Shahar, Ido. 2008. "Legal Pluralism and the Study of Shariʿa Courts." *Islamic Law and Society* 15, no. 1: 112–41.

———. 2015. *Legal Pluralism in the Holy City: Competing Courts, Forum Shopping, and Institutional Dynamics in Jerusalem.* London: Routledge.

Shaheed, Farida, and Aisha Lee Shaheed. 2011. *Great Ancestors: Women Claiming Rights in Muslim Contexts*. Karachi: Oxford University Press.

Shakes, David L. 2015. "Legal Anthropology on the Battlefield: Cultural Competence in U.S. Rule of Law Programs in Iraq." MA thesis in Judicial Studies, University of Nevada, Reno.

Shane, Scott. 2011. "In Islamic Law, Gingrich Sees Mortal Threat." *New York Times*, December 21.

———. 2015. "Moussaoui Calls Saudi Princes Patrons of Al Qaeda." *New York Times*, February 3.

"Shariah in American Courts: The Expanding Incursion of Islamic Law in the U.S. Legal System." 2015. Center for Security Policy. January 5. http://www.centerforsecuritypolicy.org/2015/01/05/shariah-in-american-courts-the-expanding-incursion-of-islamic-law-in-the-u-s-legal-system/ (accessed January 6, 2017).

"Sharia Law." *Newsmax*, May 18. http://newsmax.com/PrintTemplate.aspx/?nodeid=645360 (accessed January 6, 2017).

Shatzmiller, Maya. 1995. "Women and Property Rights in Al-Andalus and the Maghrib: Social Patterns and Legal Discourse." *Islamic Law and Society* 2, no. 3: 219–57.

———. 2007. *Her Day in Court: Women's Property Rights in Fifteenth-Century Granada*. Cambridge, MA: Islamic Legal Studies Program, Harvard Law School.

Shavit, Ari. 2014. "Plan for Peace." *New Republic*, May 12, pp. 28–30

Shear, Michael D., and Jonathan Weisman. 2014. "V.A. Accusations Aggravate Woes of White House." *New York Times*, May 20.

Shehada, Nahda. 2009. "Flexibility versus Rigidity in the Practice of Islamic Family Law." *POLAR: Political and Legal Anthropology Review* 32, no. 1: 28–46.

Shenker, Jack. 2015. *The Egyptians: A Radical Story*, London: Allen Lane.

Shepard, Steven. 2006. "Should the Criminal Defendant Be Assigned a Seat in Court?" *Yale Law Journal* 115: 2203–10.

Sherwin, Richard K. 1994. "Law Frames: Historical Truth and Narrative Necessity in a Criminal Court." *Stanford Law Review* 47: 39–83.

Shikhani, Ammar. 2010. "Divorce Rates in Morocco Plunge 46%." *Global Arab Network*, October 12.

Shklar, Judith N. 1992. *The Faces of Injustice*. New Haven, CT: Yale University Press.

Siddiqui, Mona. 1995. "*Mahr*: Legal Obligation or Rightful Demand?" *Journal of Islamic Studies* 6, no. 1: 14–24.

Sieverding, Maia. 2012. "Gender and Generational Change in Egypt." Unpublished PhD diss., University of California, Berkeley. http://digitalassets.lib.berkeley.edu/etd/ucb/text/Sieverding_berkeley_0028E_12932.pdf (accessed January 6, 2017).

Signer, Michael. 2015. *Becoming Madison*. New York: PublicAffairs.

Simonsohn, Uriel I. 2011. *A Common Justice: The Legal Allegiances of Christians and Jews under Early Islam*. Philadelphia: University of Pennsylvania Press.

Sinclair, T. A. 1951. *A History of Greek Political Thought*. London: Routledge & Kegan Paul.

Singerman, Diane. 2008. "Marriage and Divorce in Egypt: Financial Costs and Political Struggles." In *Métamorphoses du Marriage au Moyen-Orient*, edited by Barbara Drieskens, 75–96. Beirut: Presses de L'ifpo.

Sinopoli, Richard C. 1992. *The Foundations of American Citizenship: Liberalism, the Constitution, and Civic Virtue*. Oxford: Oxford University Press.

Smith, Rogers. 1997. *Civic Ideals*. New Haven, CT: Yale University Press.

Solanki, Gopika. 2011. *Adjudication in Religious Family Law: Cultural Accommodation, Legal Pluralism, and Gender Equality in India*. New York: Cambridge University Press.

Sonbol, Amira El-Azhary. 1996. "Law and Gender Violence in Ottoman and Modern Egypt." In *Women, The Family, and Divorce Laws in Islamic History*, edited by Amira El-Azhary Sonbol, 277–89. Syracuse, NY: Syracuse University Press.

———. 2003. *Women of Jordan: Islam, Labor, and the Law*. Syracuse, NY: Syracuse University Press.

———. 2005. "History of Marriage Contracts in Egypt." *Hawwa* 3, no. 2: 159–96.

Sonneveld, Nadia. 2010. "*Khul'* Divorce in Egypt: How Family Courts Are Providing a 'Dialogue' between Husband and Wife." *Anthropology of the Middle East* 5, no. 2: 100–120.

———. 2012. *Khul' Divorce in Egypt: Public Debates, Judicial Practices, and Everyday Life.* Amsterdam: Amsterdam University Press.

———. 2016. "Seeking Portia and the Duke: Male and Female Judges Dispensing Justice in Paternity Cases in Morocco." Unpublished manuscript.

Sonneveld, Nadia, and Monica Lindbekk. 2015. "A Revolution in Muslim Family Law? Egypt's Pre- and Post-Revolutionary Period (2011–2013) Compared." *New Middle Eastern Studies* 5: 1–19.

———. 2017. *Women Judges in the Muslim World: A Comparative Study of Discourse and Practice*. Leiden: Brill.

Souaiaia, Ahmed E. 2008. *Contesting Justice*. Albany: State University of New York Press.

Spadola, Emilio. 2009. "Writing Cures: Religious and Communicative Authority in Late Modern Morocco." *Journal of North African Studies* 14, no. 2: 155–68.

Starr, June. 1985. "Folk Law in Official Courts of Turkey." In *People's Law and State Law: The Bellagio Papers*, edited by Anthony Allott and Gordon R. Woodman, 123–41. Dordrecht, Netherlands: Foris.

———. 1989. "The Role of Turkish Secular Law in Changing the Lives of Rural Muslim Women, 1950–1970." *Law and Society Review* 23, no. 3: 497–523.

———. 1990. "Islam and the Struggle over State Law in Turkey." In *Law and Islam in the Middle East*, edited by Daisy Hilse Dwyer, 77–98. New York: Bergin & Garvey.

———. 1992. *Law as Metaphor: From Islamic Courts to the Palace of Justice*. Albany: State University of New York Press.

Starr, June, and Jonathan Pool. 1974. "The Impact of a Legal Revolution in Rural Turkey." *Law and Society Review* 8: 533–60.

Steavenson, Wendell. 2015. *Circling the Square: Stories from the Egyptian Revolution*. New York: Ecco.

Stevens, John Paul. 2014. *Six Amendments: How and Why We Should Change the Constitution.* Boston: Little Brown.

Stewart, Frank H. 2003. "The Contract with Surety in Bedouin Customary Law." *UCLA Journal of Islamic and Near Eastern Law* 2, no. 2: 163–280.

Stewart, Matthew. 2014. *Nature's God: The Heretical Origins of the American Republic.* New York: Norton.

Stiles, Erin. 2009. *An Islamic Court in Context: An Ethnographic Study of Judicial Reasoning.* London: Palgrave Macmillan.

Struyk, Ryan, and Kimberlee Kruesi. 2015. "Idaho Legislators Pass Bill that Was Nixed Over Sharia Law." *US News & World Report*, May 18.

Sumner, Cate, and Tim Lindsey. 2010. *Courting Reform: Indonesia's Islamic Courts and Justice for the Poor*. New South Wales, Australia: Lowy Institute.

Sussman, Anna Louie. 2011. "Laugh, O Revolution: Humor in the Egyptian Uprising." *The Atlantic*, February 23.

"Syria's Trailblazing Kurdish Women." 2016. *BBC World Service*. http://www.bbc.co.uk/programmes/p03kpv2y (accessed January 6, 2017).

Tadros, Mariz. 2014. "The Politics of Mobilizing for Gender Justice in Egypt from Mubarak to Morsi and Beyond." *Institute of Development Studies Working Papers* (April): 442.

Tamanaha, Brian. 1993. "The Folly of the 'Social Scientific' Concept of Legal Pluralism." *Journal of Law and Society* 20, no. 2: 192–217.

Tamdoğan, Işık. 2008. "*Sulh* and the 18th Century Ottoman Courts of Üsküdar and Adana." *Islamic Law and Society* 15, no. 1: 55–83.

Tanner, Nancy 1969. "Disputing and Dispute Settlement amon the Minangkabau of Indonesia," *Indonesia* 8 (October): 21–67.

Tawil-Souri, Helga. 2012. "It's Still about the Power of Place." *Middle East Journal of Culture and Communication* 5: 86–95.

Terminiello v. Chicago. 1949. 337 U. S. 1.

Tessler, Mark. 2002. "Islam and Democracy in the Middle East: The Impact of Religious Orientations on Attitudes toward Democracy in Four Arab Countries." *Comparative Politics* 34, no. 3: 337–50.

Thompson, Elizabeth F. 2013. *Justice Interrupted: The Struggle for Constitutional Government in the Middle East.* Cambridge, MA: Harvard University Press.

Toensing, Victoria. 2010. "The Case for Military Tribunals." *Weekly Standard*, February 1.

Transparency International. 2015. "Corruption Perceptions Index." http://www.transparency.org/cpi2015/ (accessed January 6, 2017).

Transparency International. 2016. "Country Reports." https://www.transparency.org/country/ (accessed January 6, 2017).

Tucker, Judith. 1997. "The Fullness of Affection: Mothering in the Islamic Law of Ottoman. Syria and Palestine." In *Women in the Ottoman Empire: Middle Eastern Women in the Early Modern Era*, edited by Madeline C. Zilfi, 232–52. Leiden: Brill.

———. 1998. *In the House of the Law: Gender and Islamic Law in Ottoman Syria and Palestine.* Berkeley: University of California Press.

———. 2005. " 'And God Knows Best': The *Fatwa* as a Source for the History of Gender in the Arab World." In *Beyond the Exotic: Women's Histories in Islamic Societies*, edited by Amira el-Azhary Sonbol, 165–79. Syracuse, NY: Syracuse University Press.

———. 2009. "Women: Islamic Law." In *Oxford Encyclopedia of Legal History*, vol. 6, edited by Stanley N. Katz, 125–30. Oxford: Oxford University Press, 2009.

Tufekei, Z., and C. Wilson. 2012. "Social Media and the Decision to Participate in Political Protest: Observations from Tahrir Square." *Journal of Communication* 62: 363–79.

Tunisian Republic. 2014. *Constitution*. Trans. by Jasmine Foundation. January 26. http://www.jasminefoundation.org/doc/unofficial_english_translation_of_tunisian_constitution_final_ed.pdf (accessed January 6, 2017).

Udovitch, Abraham L. 1970. *Partnership and Profit in Medieval Islam*. Princeton, NJ: Princeton University Press.

United Nations Office on Drugs and Crime. 2010. "Corruption in Afghanistan, Bribery as Reported by the Victims." January 19. http://www.unodc.org/unodc/en/frontpage/2010/January/corruption-widespread-in-afghanistan-unodc-survey-says.html (accessed January 6, 2017).

United States Congress. 2012. *National Defense Authorization Act for Fiscal Year 2012*. H.R. 1540 (112th Congress).

United States. v. Moussaoui. 2003a. 282 F. Supp. 2d 480 (E.D. VA 2003).

———. 2003b. 333 F. 3d 509 (4th Cir. 2003).

———. 2004. 382 F.3d 453 (4th Cir. 2004).

———. 2006a. Substitution for the Testimony of Khalid Sheikh Mohammed. http://news.bbc.co.uk/2/shared/bsp/hi/pdfs/06_04_06_testimony.pdf (accessed January 6, 2017).

———. 2006b. Trial Transcript. Cryptome. http://cryptome.org/usa-v-zm-dt2.htm (accessed January 6, 2017).

———. 2008. Brief of Appellant, Record No. 06–4494. U.S. Court of Appeals, 4th Circuit, January 17.

U.S. AID, *Morocco Rule of Law Assessment, Final Report 2010*. September. http://pdf.usaid.gov/pdf_docs/Pnadt305.pdf (accessed January 6, 2017).

U.S. Department of Justice. 2016. *Report and Recommendations Concerning the Use of Restrictive Housing [in the Federal Bureau of Prisons], Final Report*, January. https://www.justice.gov/dag/file/815551/download (accessed January 6, 2017).

U.S. Department of Justice, United States Attorney, Eastern District of Virginia. 2006. Government Exhibit GX00023, 01–455-A, Letter to Zacarias Moussaoui, February 2. (Same as U.S. District Court, Eastern District of Virginia. 2006c.)

U.S. District Court, Eastern District of Virginia. 2001–2006. USA v. Moussaoui Trial Documents. https://archive.org/details/USAVZacariasMoussaouiTrialDocs (accessed January 6, 2017).

———. 2005. Transcript of Plea Hearing, Defendant's Exhibit 954, April 22.

———. 2006a. Substitution for the Testimony of Khalid Sheikh Mohammed Exhibit # 941 Defense Trial Exhibits, p. 48. www.vaed.uscourts.gov/notablecases/moussaoui/exhibits/defense.html (accessed January 6, 2017).

———. 2006b. Trial Transcript. Cryptome. http://cryptome.org/usa-v-zm-dt2.htm (accessed January 6, 2017); and http://cryptome.org/usa-v-zm-cd.htm (accessed January 6, 2017).

———. 2006c. Trial Exhibits, Prosecution. February 2. http://www.vaed.uscourts.gov/notablecases/moussaoui/exhibits/prosecution/GX00023.pdf (accessed January 6, 2017).

Vanderlinden, Jacques. 1989. "Return to Legal Pluralism: Twenty Years Later." *Journal of Legal Pluralism and Unofficial Law* 28: 149–57.

van Eijk, Esther. 2012. "Divorce Practices in Muslim and Christian Courts in Syria." In *Family Law in Islam*, edited by Maaiki Voorhoeve, 147–70. London: I. B. Tauris.

———. 2016. *Family Law in Syria: Patriarchy, Pluralism, and Personal Status Codes*. London: I. B. Tauris.

van Huis, Stijn Cornelis. 2015. "Islamic Courts and Women's Divorce Rights in Indonesia: The Cases of Cianjur and Bulukumba." PhD diss., University of Leiden.

Vincent-Grosso, Sarah. 2012. "*Maktub*: An Ethnography of Evidence in a Tunisian Divorce Court." In *Family Law in Islam*, edited by Maaike Voorhoeve, 171–98. London: I. B. Tauris.

Vogel, Frank E. 1996. "The Complementarity of *Iftā'* and *Qaḍā'*: Three Saudi Fatwas on Divorce." In *Islamic Legal Interpretation: Muftis and Their Fatwas*, edited by M. Khalid Masud, Brinkly Messick, and David Powers, 262–69. Cambridge, MA: Harvard University Press.

Voorhoeve, Maaike. 2012a. "Judicial Discretion in Tunisian Personal Status Law." In *Family Law in Islam*, edited by Maaike Voorhoeve, 198–229. London: I. B. Tauris.

———. 2012b. "Judicial Practice at the Court of First Instance Tunis: The Case for Divorce for Harm on the Grounds of Domestic Violence." *Hawwa* 10: 151–78.

Wagner, Mark S. 2007. "Jewish Mysticism on Trial in a Muslim Court: A *Fatwa* on the *Zohar*; Yemen 1914." *Die Welt des Islams* 47, no. 2: 207–31.

———. 2014. *Jews and Islamic Law in Early 20th-Century Yemen*. Bloomington: Indiana University Press.

Walt, Vivienne. 2011. "El Général and the Rap Anthem of the Mideast Revolution." *Time*, February 15.

Warnock, D. 2010. "The Iraqi Criminal Justice System: An Introduction." *Denver Journal of International Law and Policy* 39: 1–53.

Welchman, Lynn. 2000. *Beyond the Code: Muslim Family Law and the Shari'a Judiciary in the Palestinian West Bank*. The Hague: Kluwer Law International.

———. 2007. *Women and Muslim Family Laws in Arab States*. Amsterdam: University of Amsterdam Press.

Werrell, Caitlin E., Francesco Femia, and Anne-Marie Slaughter. 2013. *The Arab Spring and Climate Change*. Center for American Progress, February 28. https://www.americanprogress.org/issues/security/report/2013/02/28/54579/the-arab-spring-and-climate-change/ (accessed January 6, 2017).

Westen, Peter. 1982. "The Empty Idea of Equality." *Harvard Law Review* 95, no. 3: 537–96.

———. 1983. "To Lure the Tarantula from Its Hole: A Response." *Columbia Law Review* 83, no. 5: 1186–208.

Wikan, Unni. 1980. *Life among the Poor in Cairo*. London: Tavistock.

———. 1982. *Behind the Veil in Arabia: Women in Oman*. Baltimore: Johns Hopkins University Press.

———. 1996. *Tomorrow, God Willing: Self-Made Destinies in Cairo*. Chicago: University of Chicago Press.

WikiIslam. 2014. "Muslim Statistics (Marriage)." July 31. http://wikiislam.net/wiki/Muslim_Statistics_-_Marriage (accessed January 6, 2017).

———. 2016. "Wife Beating in Islam." December 17. http://wikiislam.net/wiki/Wife_Beating_in_Islam#Statistics_on_Domestic_Violence_in_the_Muslim_world (accessed January 6, 2017).

Wilkinson v. Austin. 2005. 545 U.S. 209 (2005).

Will, George F. 2011. "When Solitude Is Torture." *Washington Post*, February 20.

Wilson, Alice. 2013. "On the Margins of the Arab Spring." *Social Analysis* 57, no. 2: 81–98.

———. 2015. "Rethinking Custom in Western Sahara's Quest for Statehood." *PoLAR: Journal of the Association for Political and Legal Anthropology* 38, no. 1: 72–90.

Wilson, Chris. 2010. "Searching for Saddam." *Slate*, February. http://www.slate.com/articles/news_and_politics/searching_for_saddam/2010/02/searching_for_saddam_5.html (accessed January 6, 2017).

Withington, Ann Fairfax. 1991. *Toward a More Perfect Union: Virtue and the Formation of American Republics*. Oxford: Oxford University Press.

Wood, Gordon S. 1998. *The Creation of the American Republic 1776–1787*. Chapel Hill, NC: University of North Carolina Press.

———. 2014. "A Different Idea of Our Declaration. Review of Danielle Allen, Our Declaration: A Reading of the Declaration of Independence in Defense of Equality." *New York Review of Books*, August 14.

Women Living under Muslim Laws. www.wluml.org (accessed January 6, 2017).

"Women's Rights, Turkish Style." 2004. *New York Times*, September 12.

World Bank. 2014. *The Unfinished Revolution: Bringing Opportunity, Good Jobs and Greater Wealth to All Tunisians*. Washington, DC: World Bank.

Wright, Robin. 2015. "How the Arab Spring Became the Arab Cataclysm." *New Yorker*, December 15.

Würth, Anna. 1995. "A Sana'a Court: The Family and the Ability to Negotiate." *Islamic Law and Society* 3, no. 2: 320–40.

———. 2007. "The Normativity of the Factual: On the Everyday Construction of Shari'a in a Yemeni Family Court." In *Shari'a: Islamic Law in the Contemporary Context*, edited by Abbas Amanat and Frank Griffel, 165–77. Stanford, CA: Stanford University Press.

Yarbrough, Jean M. 1998. *American Virtues: Thomas Jefferson on the Character of a Free People*. Kansas City: University Press of Kansas.

Yong, William. 2010. "Iran's Divorce Rate Stirs Fears of Society in Crisis." *New York Times*, December 6.

Young, Amy Elizabeth. 2010. "Irreconcilable Differences? *Shari'ah* Human Rights, and Family Code Reform in Contemporary Morocco." In *Mirrors of Justice: Law and Power in the Post-Cold War Era*, edited by Kamari Maxine Clarke and Mark Goodale, 191–207. Cambridge: Cambridge University Press.

Zack, Jessica. 2016. "Arab Spring Leader Building New Life in S.F." *San Francisco Chronicle*, April 23, p. 1.

Zack, Liesbeth. 2012. "'Leave, I Want to Have a Shower!' The Use of Humour on the Signs and Banners Seen during the Demonstrations in Tahrir Square." In *Between West and East: Festschrift for Wim Honselaar*, edited by R. Genis et al., 711–29. Amsterdam: Uitgeverij Pegasus.

Zafrani, Haim. 1980. "Les rélations judéo-musulmanes dans la literature juridique." In his *Les rélations entre juifs et musulmans en Afrique du Nord, XIX-XXè siècles*, 32–48. Paris: Editions CNRS.

Zahra, Noor. 2014. "Women to Make Up 5p pc of New Judges." *Gulf Daily News*, October 28. http://www.gulf-daily-news.com/NewsDetails.aspx?storyid=388691 (accessed January 6, 2017).

Zahraa, Mahdi, and Nora A. Hak. 2006. "*Taḥkīm* (Arbitration) in Islamic Law within the Context of Family Disputes." *Arab Law Quarterly* 20, no. 1: 2–42.

Zakaria, Rafia. 2010. "Muslim Grrrls." *Guernica*, September. https://www.guernicamag.com/features/zakaria_9_15_10/ (accessed January 6, 2017).

Zeidguy, Rabha. 2007. "Analyse de la jurisprudence." In *Le code de la famille: Perceptions et practique judiciaire*, edited by Malika Benradi et al., 217–71. Fez: Friedrich Ebert Stiftung.

Zilfi, Madeline C. 1997. "'We Don't Get Along': Women and *Hul* in the Eighteenth Century." In *Women in the Ottoman Empire*, edited by Madeline C. Zilfi, 264–96. Leiden: Brill.

Zimmer, Ben. 2011. "How the War of Words Was Won." *New York Times*, February 13, p. WK4.

Zinger, Oded. 2014. "Women, Gender and Law: Marital Disputes According to Documents from the Cairo Geniza" Unpublished PhD diss., Princeton University, Department of Near East Studies.

Zomeño, Amalia. 2002. "Abandoned Wives and Their Possibilities for Divorce in al-Andalus: The Evidence of the *Wathā'iq* Works." In *Writing the Feminine: Women in Arab Sources*, edited by Manuela Marin and Randi Deguiljem, 111–26. London: I. B. Tauris.

Zulficar, Mona. 2008. "The Islamic Marriage Contract in Egypt." In *The Islamic Marriage Contract: Case Studies in Islamic Family Law*, edited by Asifa Quraishi and Frank E. Vogel, 231–74. Cambridge, MA: Islamic Legal Studies Program, Harvard Law School.

Zysow, Aron. 2013. *The Economy of Certainty: An Introduction to the Typology of Islamic Legal Theory*. Atlanta: Lockwood Press.

Index